Grameen Bank Multiple Services in Bangladesh

KAZI ABDUR ROUF

iUniverse

GRAMEEN BANK MULTIPLE SERVICES IN BANGLADESH

iUniverse books may be ordered through booksellers or by contacting:

iUniverse
1663 Liberty Drive
Bloomington, IN 47403
www.iuniverse.com
1-800-Authors (1-800-288-4677)

ISBN: 978-1-5320-5997-1 (sc)
ISBN: 978-1-5320-5998-8 (e)

Print information available on the last page.

iUniverse rev. date: 10/15/2018

Dedicated to
My late Grand father Basuruddin Sarker, late my
mother Nurjahan Begum and my uncle
Late Quazi Abdul Gaffur

Preface

Grameen Bank is world famous for its group-based micro-credit services in Bangladesh. It is a leading micro finance organization in the world although there are now many different micro credit models are funcitioning in the world even in Bangladesh. However, it serves many other services in Bangladesh like campaigning for dowryless marriages, teen age marriages, child education, adult education, planting trees, keep family size small, and build sanitary latrines and networking among borrowers etc. It is also provides housing services, safe drinking water tube well loans to its borrowers in Bangladesh. However, few people know about these Grameen credit plus program and services in Bangladesh because maximum Grameen Bank study conducted on GB micro-credit delivery system and its impact on micro borrowers in Bangladesh. Many studies show micro finance institutions (MFIs) have huge impact on micro-borrowers to increase their (micro-borrowers) earnings, reduce their poverty, regeneration their economics, creates self-employment and revitalizing local living economics in different countries. However, there are huge debates on micro credit impact among MFIs' micro borrowers in the world.

I had been working in Grameen Bank Bangladesh and many other MFIs in different countries for more than three decades. I myself was involved in many GB credit plus programs in Bangladesh. Therefore, it is important to inform readers about Grameen Bank multi-dimentional services that it hase been functioning in Bangladesh since its ineption

1976. My working experience and my academia drives my interest to research on Grameen Bank micro-credit multiple services and look at its impact to its borrowers from different perspectives.

The results of my research analyses are presented in different papers of this book in a way that offers answers to many questions raised about micro-credit effectiveness of Grameen Bank in Bangladesh. This book brings together my synthesized research results. My different research papers published in different international journals. This book is an attempt and outcomes to provide the readers hardcopies of my post-doc fourteen research papers in one place in the book.

The papers in this book describe how Grameen Bank (GB) women borrowers and other MFIs' borrowers have handled their micro-credit borrowing, their savings and how MFIs could serve better to micro-borrowers for their social, political and economic empowerment within their community. Each paper also contains how MFIs could serve better integrated financial services (socio-economic services for the micro-borrowers) to disadvantaged women that can lead to better provision of integrated micro credit services to them. I approach the papers of this book as a researcher looking for solutions to empower micro-borrowers' socio-economic development.

The book thanks to Muhammad Yunus for his advises to publish my papers in a book form. My thank to Professor Roger Hensall, President, Noble International University, Bishajit Ganguly, Professor Abedin Kusno, Director, York Center for Asian Research (YCAR) and my mentor Professor Ellie Perkins, Faculty of Enviromental Studies, York University for their constant support and encouragement to conduct research on Grameen social business services in Bangladesh and how to reframe the research and to refine my analysis. I acknowledge with thanks for encouraging me given by my wife, Sabina Mozammel, for publishing the book.

Kazi Abdur Rouf

Contents

Group-based micro-borrowers social space development policies in Bangladesh- A case study Grameen Bank Sixteen Decisions

Abstract

This policy brief looks at Grameen Bank micro credit sixteen decisions policies to (1) examine the degree to which women borrowers of the Grameen Bank are empowered to participate in familial decision-making around the management of income and expenditures, such as food, children's education, dowry and teenage marriages; and (2) to examine women borrowers' engagement in community activities, such as the degree of freedom women are granted to visit public places like schools, local councils, banks and markets. This policy brief research is based of previous Grameen Bank micro credit research done by the author, which found 98 per cent of GB women borrower participants are engaging in community organizations after receiving micro credit and 94 per cent do not face problems with this community engagement. In the 2009 UpZilla (Municipal Sub-district) local government election, out of 481 seats, 114 female chairs (25 per cent of the total) were elected from the GB women borrowers and their families. These results show Grameen Bank policies have resulted in the increased participation of women in their families and communities, but also shows a movement towards greater progress towards development.

Key Words: Grameen Bank, GB Sixteen Decisions, Green Social Business, Community Organizations, Community Development, Dowry Marriages, Patriarchy, Leadership, and **Women Empowerment**

Acronyms: Grameen Bank (GB), Japan Bank for International Cooperation (JBIC), Ontario Institute of Studies in Education (OISE), Small and Medium Enterprise development (SME), Union Parishad (UP), United Nations Development Program (UNDP) and United Nations High Commissions for Refugee (UNHCR).

1.0. Introduction

This policy brief research attempts to understand whether the Grameen Bank (GB) Sixteen Decisions are sufficient to enhance GB women borrowers' development as well as emancipate them from the dominance of their male partners in their familial and community life, addressing patriarchal chauvinism. Under this umbrella objective, the policy research explores GB Sixteen Decisions policies, barriers GB borrowers experience in their family and community, and the leadership of GB women borrowers and their ability to transfer their leadership skills to other public spaces. The study finds that support is needed for GB women borrowers to take part in decisions that pertain to the family and the community.

Bangladesh is a patriarchal, religious, and village-dominated country. It is one of the world's most densely populated countries with 160 million people, 49 per cent of whom live below the national poverty line and suffer from human rights abuses (The Hunger Project 2010 Bangladesh). It is impacted by the worldwide problem of the feminization of poverty, which is one of the world's most pressing problems. For example, 67% of the world's women live below the poverty line (Bornstein and Davis 2010). In Bangladesh, women's male partners treat them as secondary members of the family meaning they have a limited voice, choice and decision-making power within the family, and even less in the community where males are considered the primary members (Belal 2008; and Jahan 1995).

This policy brief suggests, in spite of economic advances, GB women borrowers are still limited by patriarchal social structures in their family and community (Goetz, 2004). Microcredit institutions (MFIs) are not looking at these oppressive situations that affect women's self-esteem. These issues need more exploration; hence, this policy brief will observe where research is limited to demonstrate if this holds true or not. Grameen Bank is group-based micro credit that is provided to poor women in Bangladesh. Grameen Bank and its sixteen decisions policies aim to empower its women borrowers, improve the well-being of the poor, and to empower them in society, both economically and socially. In addition, its GB sixteen decisions policies, mentioned below, and their implementation by GB women borrowers are driving forces for their leadership development through borrowers' participations in the neighborhood. This policy srudy focuses on to GB group members (five poor women form a group) and centres micro borrowers (5-10 groups' members form a center in their neighborhoods) and their ability to understand the Sixteen Decisions and to follow them. The study reflects that GB should directly include gender equality development agenda in its Sixteen Decisions to address the issue of women's equality, which is urgent for women's empowerment in Bangladesh. This could help, as a result, women borrowers' decision making participation in their families and communities while solving their family poverty issues. Their participation in decision making practices will drive them to improve their overall family wellbeing and liberate them from male exploitations.

The Grameen meeting centre is a place where 30-40 women clients gather and repay their loans, discuss their family problems, exchange business information, and other concerns. GB meeting centres are seen as a catalyst for networking among clients. This group system helps clients to interact freely amongst each other, receive and repay loans, and address broader social concerns. By this process, all members of the Centre have an opportunity to take leadership roles. This helps to enhance leadership qualities within and externally of the family. Borrowers are able to continue their interactions with each other beyond their groups and contribute to their community. However, it is not clear that GB Sixteen Decisions policies and their implementation enable the GB women borrowers' to use their leadership skills outside GB community activities.

2.0. Grameen Bank Sixteen Decisions

The GB Sixteen Decisions are a combination of various socio-civic, economic and environmental messages. Central to the GB approach has been to raise the civic consciousness of women through some of the Sixteen Decisions. The following are the Grameen Bank Sixteen Decisions:

1. We shall follow and advance the four principles of the Grameen Bank - discipline, unity, courage and hard work - in all walks of our lives.
2. We shall bring prosperity to our families.
3. We shall not live in dilapidated houses. We shall repair our houses and work towards constructing new houses.
4. We shall grow vegetables all year round. We shall eat plenty of them and sell the surplus.
5. During the plantation seasons, we shall plant as many seedlings as possible.
6. We shall plan to keep our families small. We shall minimize our expenditures. We shall look after our health.
7. We shall educate our children and ensure that they can earn to pay for their education.
8. We shall always keep our children and the environment clean.
9. We shall build and use pit-latrines.
10. We shall drink water from tube wells. If it is not available, we shall boil water or use alum or water purifying agent table.

11. We shall not take any dowry at our sons' weddings; neither shall we give any dowry at our daughters' wedding. We shall keep our centre free from the curse of dowry. We shall not practice child marriage.
12. We shall not inflict any injustice on anyone; neither shall we allow anyone to do so.
13. We shall collectively undertake bigger investments for higher incomes.
14. We shall always be ready to help each other. If anyone is in difficulty, we shall all help him or her.
15. If we come to know of any breach of discipline in any centre, we shall all go there and help restore discipline.
16. We shall take part in all social activities collectively.

GB realizes that various socio-economic and environmental development messages need to be given to GB borrowers in addition to their loan transactions with the Bank. In 1984, GB center leaders in the Jaydevpur National Women Borrowers Workshop created Sixteen Decisions that borrowers agree to uphold these decisions before they receive any loan from Grameen Bank. GB always encourages borrowers to follow these Sixteen Decisions after receiving their loan, borrowers must do so voluntarily. All decisions are designed and stated in a simple way, few of them have direct tangible messages to create awareness among borrowers about socio-civic, economical and environmental issues. In the 1980s, and 1990s, different campaign strategies were developed to raise awareness and to encourage borrowers to follow the Sixteen Decisions including workshops and special meetings.

GB has been distributed the Sixteen Decisions' flyers to each center and asked borrowers to discuss them in groups in the weekly center meetings and during their leisure time. GB also printed flipcharts on the Sixteen Decisions and distributed them to the GB branches since 1984. Workshop facilitators and GB officials discussed in detail the "themes and benefits of the Sixteen Decisions". Currently, the Sixteen

Decisions are printed on the backside of the passbooks given to all borrowers, and the passbooks stay at the borrowers' homes so that they can read and think about them. If they need clarification on any of the decisions, borrowers can discuss them at the bank. Although GB changed its loan policies, financial products, documentation system, and the monitoring of the credit performance of the borrowers in 2000, the Sixteen Decisions have remained the same as when they were composed in 1984.

These Sixteen Decisions are the focal point of GB's efforts to improve the socio-economic plight of women, their families, and develop community space. These decisions promote anti-dowry and anti-teenage marriages campaigns, environmentalism, and women's collectivity development in their community. Although the GB's main function is to provide microcredit to poor women in Bangladesh, the intensive social interactions that develop between GB employees and clients through loan transactions also have the potential to transform the lives of these women and their families. Recently, however, the Grameen Bank Sixteen Decisions Campaign strategies have shrunk because of the Bank's efforts to promote profit generation; in turn, hampering these micro-borrowers social space development in Bangladesh.

3.0. Policy Critique

Below is the analysis of the Grameen Bank Sixteen Decisions policies, their gaps and policy suggestions that could help the effective empowerment of GB women borrowers'.

Through utilizing GB loans, 8.5 million rural-poor borrowers in 83,967 villages in Bangladesh (GB Monthly Report June 2010) increased their income, created assets for their families, and reduced the poverty cycle in Bangladesh (Ahmed & Hakim 2004; Chu 2007; Counts 2008; Gibons 1995; Khandker 1998; Yunus 1994). A repayment rate of 97 per cent has been sustained since 1979. Moreover, 58 per cent of GB women borrowers have crossed the poverty line: people are able to afford/ fulfill their basic needs food (three meals a day), clothing, shelter, send their children to school, use mosquito nets, and are able to buy medicine etc.. Kofi Anan (2005), the former UN Secretary General, says that microcredit has proved its value in many countries as a weapon against poverty and hunger. He also comments that microcredit has made progress in achieving the Millennium Development Goals (MDGs), by working towards eliminating poverty and promoting gender equality and women's empowerment (United Nations 2000a; Grameen Dialouge 2005).

These figures and statements demonstrate GB services have made a positive impact on reducing poverty to its borrowers and promoting a space for women in their communities. However, this policy brief, as a result of research, points to concerns about women empowerment in the community.

First, although Grameen Bank Sixteen Decisions policies support the empowerment of women borrowers socially and economically, in practice, concerns still exist regarding Grameen Bank women borrowers' social space development (dowry free marriage, teen age marriage, loan control, women's participation in community activities) in Bangladesh.

For example, dowry demand is a conditional materials demand on girls' before their marriages. If a dowry demand is not met by the girls' parents, their husbands torture them mentally and physically. Another social problem is the marriage of teenage girls (teenage marriages characterized as occuring without physical and mental maturity). These dominant patriarchal values and practices, defined as the rule of men in the family and in the community, over women, or the subordination of women, hampers women's empowerment in Bangladesh. This is a significant worry and it affects half of all women of Bangladesh, (Bangladesh Profile 2010). Although there have been many success stories of the emancipation of women through

Grameen bank microcredit, Isserles cautions that many women are still dominated by their husbands and do not enjoy the benefits of their financial gains or loan investments. In many cases, their husbands use the loans to their own businesses without consulting them (Isserles, 2003). Moreover, Robin Isserles in her study mentions (2003) that 57 per cent of women saw a rise of verbal aggression after they received loans for their households. In rural Bangladesh, where all GB women live, 67 per cent of women experience domestic violence. In 70 per cent of the cases, husbands were held responsible for the violence (Hossain, 2006).

However, the Sixteen Decisions are silent on gender discrimination and male aggression towards women and thus limits the effectiveness of the Sixteen Decisions ability to empower women. Hence, many researchers (Amin, Becker, & Bayes 1998; Goetz 2001; Mahmud 2004; and Mayoux 2002) have argued that the GB must develop additional strategies to raise awareness of gender inequality and the injustice of male domestic violence, while mobilizing women to protest various social ills that afflict women. For this reason, it is essential for women borrowers to understand the barriers- causes and effects of social space development. By doing so, it will be easier for women to address issues such as lack of empowerment and leadership development in the family and in community spaces.

GB women borrowers' understanding and adherence to the GB's by-laws and Sixteen Decisions is very important. These GB policies can help to remove barriers in empowering women against male domination in family and community in rural Bangladesh. Grameen Bank field workers could organize special meetings with GB women borrowers and with their male partners together in their centers and discus about the negative effects of male domination over women. Moreover, group members need to maintain solidarity amongst themselves, attend weekly center meetings regularly, exchange business information, help each other by discussing and sharing ideas on conflict resolutions, community problems and family problems, and be aware of and protest against abusive situations. Moreover, they should repeatedly read the Sixteen Decisions policies and developed strategies to apply these policies to their own customized situations.

Second development barriers exist for GB women borrowers in their family and community space development too. Statistics from 1997 to 2003 indicate that dowry-related violence in the family is increasing day-by-day in Bangladesh (Ain O Salish Kendro 2000). Dowry is one of the most strongly entrenched patriarchal traditions in Bangladesh. If dowry demands are not fulfilled by the bride's family, then dowry demand problems start, like physical violence, rape, murder and desertion by the husband/husband's family. The GB's Sixteen Decisions do speak against dowry, but not forcefully enough. The GB maintains that gender development is an evolutionary process that takes place through women's economic development, as provided through the microcredit program. However, gender/equity development education for men and women is essential to learning how to make decisions together through consensual processes (Abendroth 2007). Hence, there needs to be a greater emphasis on consensual decision-making between women and men, something that the GB could do by involving its borrowers in special meetings for both men and women. GB could include gender equity education in its Sixteen Decisions.

Third, the research is also about GB women borrowers gaining transferrable leadership skills in community spaces. The research demonstrates key findings on how to achieve this better and demonstrates the importance of empowering women. The method used by the researcher was face-to-face interviews on a random sample of sixty two GB women borrows in Bangladesh and collected relevant secondary data from GB in March 2010-July 2010. The research finds that many GB women borrowers participated in the Union Parishad (UP) local council elections in 1997 and 2003. GB women borrowers' local council election participation shows that they have voted more and their participation in at the local government and community levels have increased from the 1997 to 2009 election. For example, among GB members, there were 57 UP female chairpersons elected from GB women borrowers in 1997 and this figure increased to 81 in the 2003 UP election, which means GB women borrowers local public space development is increasing. Moreover, for UP councilor's positions, 3,325 GB women members were elected in 1997 and 4,116 in 2003. In the 2009 UpZilla (municipal sub-district) election, out of the 481 seats, 114 female chairs (25 per cent of the total) were elected from the GB women borrowers (Grameen Bank 2009). In addition, the number of women borrowers serving as local councilors has increased from 1,572 in 1997 to 1,950 in 2003. This data indicates that the number of women borrowers acting in formal leadership roles is increasing (Grameen Bank 2009) and could be interpreted as meaning that the GB groups, centre management and leadership development processes have empowered GB members to participate more actively in their communities. This could also be evidence that GB woman borrowers' liberation at the community level has succeeded. Although this is an example of GB women borrowers' formal leadership in the community is increasing, it also shows a movement towards greater progress of inclusion of women in public spaces in Bangladesh. The trend could be accelerated if GB directly encouraged and campaigned for women borrowers' participations in community activities and encouraged them to be involved in formal leadership activities.

Fourth, support is needed for GB women borrowers to take part in decisions that pertain to their family and community. The research conducted on the topic that looks at the 7th decision of GB, on the promotion of adult education and child education, and the 11th decision, which mentions women borrowers should be against of dowry demand indicates that all participants know how to sign their name, which is significant in Bangladesh where most rural women do not know how sign their names, read and write (Belal 2008). Regarding borrowers' education, the data shows that the 33 per cent of women who attended centre schooling were illiterate before joining the GB. The research conducted on this topic finds participants have a strong voice in their family for their children's education and they were very aware about dowry and teenage marriage issues. However, in relation to teenage marriage, the study results indicate that often marriages takes place for economic reasons as it is easier for parents to find educated and well-to-do husbands for younger girls. Moreover, young women are often the victims of dowry, eve-teasing and harassment. In addition, parents fear their daughters would be sexually assaulted or kidnapped. Therefore, teenage marriage is viewed as a form of protection in rural Bangladesh.

GB officials explained the negative effects of dowry and teenage marriage and the benefits of topics as diverse as using sanitary latrines and women's unity. Participants arranged dowry-less marriages in the workshop and received encouragement from the workshop facilitators for doing so. However, women borrowers alone cannot challenge the patriarchal norms and cannot completely free from dowry abuse and teen age marriages problems. Therefore, social problems like dowry and teenage marriages still persist, even with improvements in some areas due to GB micro credit. For example, 25 per cent of participants reported that their male partners made dowry demand decisions without consulting them. However, 82 per cent indicated that they manage the GB loans that they received. Helal Uddin, Grameen Bank branch manager and a participant of the study mentions:

> *Grameen Bank gives loans to its women borrowers. They do their businesses in collaborations with their husbands and their family members. GB encourages to its borrowers for anti-dowry marriages and anti-teen age marriages. However, loan control, dowry demand and teen age marriage by the women borrowers is still progressing.*

These statistics confirm that GB women borrowers are becoming more empowered as they can control their loans and are aware about dowry problems. The researcher hopes the policy emphasis in regards to dowry, teen age marriage, and loan control by the women borrowers will help women to address these issues.

Fifth, the research for this policy brief looked at whether these women micro borrowers are empowered to engage in their communities. In order to understand GB women borrowers' community space empowerment, the research looked at GB 15th and 16th decisions (15th decision: GB borrowers participate in the community activities and events, and 16th decision: women borrowers themselves solve their social problems). Regarding their public space empowerment, findings indicated that the vast majority of women are engaging in community organizations and do not face problems engaging in these activities. It is also indicated that 96 per cent communicate with their neighbors more than once a month and that 56 per cent did not know their neighbors before joining GB. Almost all of them had connections with other NGOs like Annesha, Destiny Life Insurance Company, Nutrition projects, Village Arbitration Committee, Grameen Shikha, and many others. This indicates that GB women borrowers social ties among them have strengthen and their community space development have increased.

4.0. Policy Suggestions

All of these findings and analysis demonstrate some gains for GB women borrowers in their family and community spaces as they have participated in local elections and village development committees. This suggests that this policy is a success. However, raising male awareness by rural elites to rural males about women's civic participation in the communities is also crucial. Although women are progressing, the system of patriarchy has been around for centuries. In that regard, if GB mounted a strong public campaign against dowry, dowry violence and teenage marriage, it would enhance the likelihood help combat these social ills. Such a strategy would follow from Gender Development theory (Mies, 1998; and Miles 1996) which believes gender inequality should be addressed directly rather than through the indirect approach that the GB uses.

This policy brief research suggests a consciousness-raising process is needed to investigate the interplay between the family and community spheres and identify cultural and customary obstacles to the full participation of women in decision-making. The results of studying such a process could provide a basis for overcoming these obstacles and facilitating the inclusion of women in decision-making. An important component of the GB program in achieving this is the education of the second generation of Grameen Bankl borrowers. The GB has encouraged the second generation or children of borrowers of Grameen Bank for higher education by providing them with education loans. Moreover, GB sister organization Grameen Shakti (Renewable Energy) has a vocational training program where GB second generations can receive vocational skills development training to develop their human capitals and social capitals. These programs are working to empower GB second generations to ensure long lasting effects of GB policies. Grameen Shikka Newsletter (2009) mentions that GB second generation youth have the skills to lobby for their own rights and are capable of taking action for the rights of marginalized women. Hopefully, through collective actions (GB borrowers, GB, and other community organizations in Bangladesh) these women borrowers and second generations could fill gender equality gap.

The study conducted on this topic also indicates that the majority of GB's borrowers are aware of dowry-less marriage, teenage marriage, and the related domestic abuse. However, a study conducted by the Japan Bank for International Cooperation (JBIC) has found that the practice of dowry is expanding across Bangladesh (JBIC 2006). The Bangladesh government has enacted legislation against dowry-related violence called the Dowry Prohibition Act, 1980; however, this act needs to be enforced as it is still embedded in the culture of Bangladesh. The government, especially the Ministry of Women and Children's Affairs and the Women's Council, should be proactive in enforcing the dowry act at the grassroots level. This policy brief suggests the GB and other NGOs in Bangladesh could launch a massive campaign and lobby the government to enforce the act more quickly. Therefore, a separate activism strategy needs to be developed to address these issues. Although GB's Sixteen Decisions have included economic issues and other social issues, none directly discuss gender equality and this omission inhibits the family and community development of GB borrowers. Given the influence of the GB, perhaps a revision of the Sixteen Decisions as well as inclusion of the gender equality agenda is needed.

Although the Grameen Bank has been working with its micro-borrowers for their economic development and leadership development, the bank is not directly engaging in promoting gender equality. Even though the research for this policy brief suggests that the GB's program has had an impact upon the family and community development of women borrowers', the research also suggests that this positive impact could be enhanced through adapting the Sixteen Decisions to address gender development and patriarchal issues more directly. Moreover, it is necessary that GB women borrowers create strong ties among themselves and collectively lobby and fight against dowry and teen marriages, and against all forms of women discrimination, violence and abuses.

Overall, the findings of this research indicate progress of public space development awareness of GB women borrowers; however, to shift continuing social problems (unethical dowry demands, dowry related violence and forced teen age marriages etc.), this policy brief suggests these women need the support of agencies to facilitate the expression of their opinions/desires/voices and to protest against unethical dowry demands, teen age marriages abuse and male domination over women. Moreover, this policy brief suggests government law enforcement is necessary for accelerating their collective actions and to protest against dowry and teen age marriages. In addition to theses, dowry related customary laws in Bangladesh need to be reviewed and streamline them towards gender equality. In Bangladesh, research indicated agencies like Grameen Bank, Bangladesh Rural Advancement Committee (BRAC), Women for Women, and Ain-Shalishi Kendra should come forward to mobilize these marginalized rural women and to strengthen these grassroots marginalized women's liberation movement against dowry demands, teen age marriages and violence against women. Moreover, this policy brief suggests that these agencies could extend their cooperation and support for enforcement of anti-dowry laws and anti-teen age marriages laws in rural areas in Bangladesh.

5.0. Conclusion

The GB has been instrumental in providing income generating opportunities to women and for their overall empowerment through the extension of collateral-free banking to rural poor women in Bangladesh (Ahamed & Hakim 2008; Mahmud 2004; and Todd 1996). The research conducted on this topic finds that women's dependency on male family members is being reduced and there is an emerging pattern of more equitable relationships in their households and in the society. The GB women borrowers are also emerging as a social force to fight prejudices and obstacles to economic and social progress in Bangladesh. The present study on this topic shows that women's participation in the GB results in their increased participation in their families and communities. However, this policy brief concludes that GB Sixteen Decisions policies should change to improve gender equality to ensure women's access to productive resources, to break down patriarchal dominance in the family and in the community and to alter economic and institutional arrangements to promote more choices for women.

6.0. References

Abendroth, H. G. (2007). Matriarchal society and the gift paradigm: Motherliness as an ethical principle. In Genevieve Vaughan (Ed.), *Women and the gift economy* (pp. 99-107). Toronto: Inanna Publications

Ahmed, S., & Hakim, M. (Eds.). (2004) *Attacking poverty with microcredit.* Dhaka: The University Press Limited and Palli Karma-Sahayak Foundation

Ain O Salish, Kendro. (2000). *Human rights in Bangladesh: 1999.* Dhaka: Shahitya Prokash.

Amin, R. Becker, S., & Bayes A. (1998). NGO promotes micro-credit programmes and women's empowerment in rural Bangladesh: Quantitative and qualitative evidence. *The Journal of Developing Areas, Winter,* pp. 221-36

Bangladesh Demographics. (2010). *Demographics of Bangladesh.* Retrieved from http://en.wikipedia.org/wiki/Demographics_of_Bangladesh#Age

Belal, A. R. (2008). *Corporate social responsibility reporting in developing countries: A case of Bangladesh.* Farnham, U.K.: Ashgate Publishing Ltd.

Bornstein, D. and Davis, S. (2010) Social entrepreneurship: what everyone needs to know: New York: Oxford University Press

Chu, M. (2007). Commercial returns at the base of the pyramid: Innovations. In B. Aghion & J. Morduch (Eds.), *The economics of microfinance* (pp. 115-146). Cambridge: MIT Press

Goetz, A. M. (2001). Women development workers: Implementing rural credit programs in Bangladesh. *World Development, 24* (1), 45-63. Retrieved from http://180-scholarsportal:info.ezpnxy.library.yorku.ca/pdf

Grameen Bank. (2009). *Grameen Sixteen Decisions.* Retrieved from http://www.grameen-info.org

Grameen Bank. (2010a). *Monthly statement.* Retrieved from http://www.ethicalmarkets.com/2010/08/15/grameen-bank-monthly-update-june-2010/

Grameen Bank. (2010b). *At a glance.* Retrieved from http://www.grameen-info.org/index.php?option=com_content&task=view&id=26&Ite=mid=175

Hossain, S. R. (2006). Women's Rights. In *Hunan rights in Bangladesh* (Eds.) In H. Hossain & S. Hossain (pp. 139-153). Dhaka: Ain-0-Salish Kendra (ASK)

Isserles, R. G. (2003). Microcredit: The rhetoric of empowerment, the reality of development as usual, *Women's Studies Quarterly*, Vol. 3(4), pp. 38-57.

Jahan, R. (1995). *The elusive agenda: Mainstreaming women in development.* Dhaka: The University Press Ltd

Japan Bank for International Cooperation (JBIC). (2006). *Ex-post monitoring survey of the rural development credit* (Grameen Bank) project-summary report on preliminary findings. Dhaka: Japan Bank for International Cooperation

Khandker, S. R. (1998). Micro-credit program evaluation; a critical review. *IDS Bulletin*, Vol. 29(4), pp. 11-20.

Kofi, A. (2005). Message from *Message from UN Secretary General. Grameen Dialogue #60*. Dhaka: Grameen Trust.

Mahmud, S. (2004). Microcredit and women's empowerment in Bangladesh. In S. Ahmed & S. Hakim (Eds.), *Attacking poverty with microcredit* (pp. 148-153). Dhaka: The University Press Limited

Mayoux, L. (2009). *Sustainable learning for women's empowerment: Ways forward in microfinance.* Herndon: Stylus Publishing

Mies, M. (1998). *Patriarchy & accumulation on a world scale: Women in the international division of labor.* London: Zed Books Ltd.

Moser, C. (1993). *Gender planning and development: Theory, practice and training.* New York: Routledge

Quadir, F. (2003). How is "civil" society? Authoritarian state partisan civil society and the struggle for democratic development in Bangladesh. *Canadian Journal of*

Development Studies, Vol. 21(3), pp. 425-438.

Rahman. A. (1999). Micro-credit Initiatives for equal and sustainable development: Who pays?

World Development, Vol. 27(1), pp. 67-82

Rouf, K. A. (2012). The Impact of the Grameen Bank upon the Patriarchal Family and Community Relations of Women Borrowers in Bangladesh, T-Space, University of Toronto

Rouf, K. A. (2008). *Green microcredit for environmental development.* Unpublished Master's Thesis. Toronto: York University

The Hunger Project 2010 Bangladesh (2010). *Bangladesh*. Retrieved from http://www.thp.org/where_we_work/south_asia/bangladesh dated June 28, 2012.

The Hunger Project (2010). Reducing Child Marriage and Domestic Violence: Bangladesh Retrieved from http://www.thp.org/where_we_work/south_asia/bangladesh/overview?gclid=COGRttLG_qUCFcbsKgodqUrLnw dated February 20, 2011.

The Ministry of Women and Child Affairs. (2007). *Gender equality in the NSAPR*. Dhaka: Policy Leadership and Advocacy for Gender Equality (PLAGE-11).

Todd, H. (1996). *Women at the centre: Grameen Bank borrowers after one decade*. Dhaka: The University Press Limited

United Nations. (2000a). *United Nations millennium declaration document* A/Res/55/2. New York

Yunus, M. (1994). *Banking on the poor*. Dhaka: Mahatab Offset Printers

Yunus, M. (2010a). *Grameen dialogue 2010* #72: Bangladesh: Grameen Trust.

Yunus, M. (2010b). *Building social business: A new kind of capitalism that serves humanity's most pressing needs*. New York: Public Affairs

Zeller, M. (2004). *Review of poverty assessment tools*. Report submitted to IRIS and USAID as part of the Developing Poverty Assessment Tools Project. Retrieved from http://www.povertytools.org.

While poverty is a global problem resulting from global issues, its definition and solution can only be found locally

Abstract

There is a debate on whether there should be a global definition of poverty that applies to all countries. Many people ask questions why we not have a more universal approach to address poverty. Is it too pragmatic to think that a universal approach is needed to address global poverty? However, my working experiences in different countries show external agencies universal definition of poverty and poverty prescriptions for social and economic development are not effective to local living socio-economic development rather contextually designed good governance programs suite for local development and to address the issue of poverty. For example, Grameen Bank micro-finance, Grameen America USA, Desjadin Credit Union Canada, Mondragon Spain, Natural Agriculture Thailand, Participatory Budget Brazil, BRAC non-formal education and BIKASH in Bangladesh, and SWEA of Indian women cooperatives are well known local initiatives to address the issue of local poverty and unemployment. Therefore, the article emphasis that while poverty is a global problem resulting from global issues, its solution can only be found locally and therefore the nature of poverty must be defined locally.

Key Words: Capitalism; Globalization; Multinational Corporations (MNCs); Poverty; and Structural Adjustment Policy.

1.0. Introduction

Poverty is a threat to human survival and development. Thomas Allen (2002) says, "It is a part of global crisis" (p-16). It is not an isolated social catastrophe rather, it is socially constructed (Rouf, 2015). It is a process of social exclusion of the poor, and is a product of uneven development across and within the state. Capitalism and globalization of the free market economy make poverty global and the third world is more impoverished. Polani says (1957), "This big transformation is self-destruction" (p-4). According to Professor John O'Neil (2007) of York University, capitalism is the production of wealth and poverty. It is advantageous to wealthy nations, but developing countries have less wealth and significant social problems that are not encouraging to resource creation. As a result, the world has become an increasingly unequal place-the gap between the haves and have-nots has widened. For example, over fifty five countries are now poorer than they were ten years ago. Life expectancy has fallen in over thirty countries (Bibby & Shaw, 2005). Martin Wolf (2004) says, "It is the net result of massive growth in inequality" (p.139). There is no turning point from this process unless there is an alternative development strategy for the world. Hence, this paper argues that while poverty is a global problem resulting from global issues, its solution can only be found locally and therefore, the nature of poverty must be defined locally.

2.0. Paper focused on fulfillment of basic needs of bottom people

The paper attempts to demonstrate that the way we define poverty has a direct relationship with how we propose to eliminate it. For the author, poverty is depriving poor people of access to local public resources to achieve anything beyond fulfilling their basic needs in both developing countries and developed countries. This leads to suffering from malnutrition, ill heath, lower life expectancy, infant mortality, unemployment and injustice to poor people in society. One of the major problems among the poorer communities is increased violence because of poverty. Therefore, poverty is one of the most important issues to be examined in development studies.

3.0. Objectives of the paper

Poverty eradication is targeted as the number one Millennium Development Goal (MDG) by United Nations (UN) in the 21st Century. However, one of the first questions is: who is included in the definition of poverty and who is excluded? If we define one person as living in poverty and in need of assistance based on an absolute definition (poor people suffer from basic necessities of life like food, shelter, clothing, education and heath), then are we are excluding their neighbors because they have an extra change of clothing? Therefore, the objective of paper is to discern roots of causes of poverty and find alternative local tools that can assist local people to get out of sufferings of poverty misery.

4.0. Definitions of poverty

Poverty means the state of being extreme poor. Poverty is the condition of having little or no money, goods, or means of support; condition of being poor (Dictionary.com). Poverty is general scarcity of one who lacks a certain amount of material possessions or money. It is a multifaceted concept, which includes social, economic, and political elements. There are two types of poverty: Absolute or acute poverty or restitution and relative poverty. Absolute poverty or destitution refers to the lack of means necessary to meet basic needs such as food, clothing and shelter. Absolute poverty is considered to be about the same independent of location. Relative poverty occurs when people in a country do not enjoy a certain minimum level of living standards as compared to the rest of the population and so would vary from country to country, sometimes within the same country

Most international social agencies spend considerable effort creating rules and deciding who qualifies for support and who does not. This is a complex process, and no matter how sophisticated the rules, the rules cannot account for each unique situation (Hick, 2004). Families have different numbers of family members, some face chronic illness, some are limited in their ability to work, some live in remote depressed areas of the country, some have little or no education, some have the spirit to escape poverty, and other are just worn out. Features of poverty problem are different. Therefore, poverty solution needs to be addressed by identifying the particular elements of poverty for particular segment of the local people as well as finding out what local resources available for them and what process can engage them that can enhanced them their participations in the community to be social actors and economic actors, politically active and accelerate their socio-economic benefits to fulfill their basic needs.

Poverty usually measured in terms on income and therefore, fiscal economists decide how could provide assistance and select who gets assistance from the state based on specific data (e.g., income, money in the bank, assets). However, maximum marginalized people do not have such statistics in the developing countries. Therefore maximum poor people are excluded from the state acute poverty accounting, but usually state fiscal policy and poverty measures are based on relative poverty. This relative poverty is measured against standards that make sense within each country. However, this sometimes presents a challenge when evaluating the situation of remotest marginalized poor, tribes, immigrants and refugees (Hick, 2004, p. 123).

The World Bank is using an updated international poverty line of $1.90 a day, which incorporates new information on differences in the cost of living across countries. The new line preserves the real purchasing power of the previous line (of $1.25 a day in 2005 prices)

in developing countries. Using this new line (as well as new country-level data on living standards), the World Bank projects that extreme poverty in South Asia would fall to 13.5 percent in 2015, compared to 18.8 percent in 2012.

5.0. Sequence of the paper discussion

I am first going to discuss what it means to examine poverty from a universal and local perspective. Secondly, I discuss poverty measures suggested by different institutions and scholars, and the effects of globalization on poverty. Lastly, the paper looks at the poverty definition and discusses how poverty could be addressed in the local context.

6.0. Poverty as seen by Scholars

Poverty has a long history and it is present everywhere in the world. Poverty is often directly related to exploitation of one group of people by a more aggressive or wealthier group of people. For instance, for 200 years, India's wealth has been transferred to the UK by British colonization. The plantation economy and slavery systems have been introduced in Central and Latin America by the Europeans (Korten, 1995a). That economic process put the colonized Central Americans and Latinos into the state of poverty. Although there are huge resources available in these regions, they are suffering from local resource utilization. Because the resources are in the hands colonizers and they control local resources. Currently the plantation economy is in the multinational corporations' hands.

In early Britain, *English Poor Laws* were promoted as a way to address widespread poverty in England and to stop the commoners from begging. The laws classified the poor as being either worthy or unworthy of relief. The worthy ones are children, along with the aged, sick or disabled (Hick, 2004, pp. 34-35).

Less than 1% economic growth was in Indo-Pak subcontinent during and before British period rule. British had stolen and exploited Indian resources during their ruling period in India. There were no development projects like education, healthcare, land development, food security, flood protection, infrastructure development, peasants' wellbeing services etc. during British period. Rather they introduced and imposed land tax to peasants and collect land tax from Indian peasants and sent this money to London. There were several famines occurred during the British period. Many people died from starvation and disease. Although Indo-Pak-Bengal subcontinent free from British rule in 1947 and initiated many development projects, maximum of these projects' ideas are from West. Very few initiatives can be found that are appropriate and locally suited. However, in the Twenty First century these countries government and NGOs are active to reduce the poverty. According to World Bank South East Asia remains the world's fastest-growing region although capital inflows declined, inflation has been on the rise, and remittances from oil-exporting countries started to weaken. Economic growth in Banglsdesh rose to 6.9 percent in 2015, up from 6.7 percent in 2014, and is projected to slightly lower at 6.7 percent in 2016. It will accelerate to 6.8 percent in 2017 and 7.1 percent in 2018.

7.0. Poverty Debate

There is a debate on whether there should be a global definition of poverty that applies to all countries. Why do we not have a more universal approach to address poverty? Is it too pragmatic to think that a universal approach is needed to address global poverty? Although the depth of poverty (poverty gap measurement of how much additional income would be required to raise an individual or household out of poverty) varies from region to region, country to country, poverty exists all over the world.

Poverty is the direct result of global forces and actions by the various global actors (Sen, 1981). The rich and poor can be found between countries and within a country because the world is connected through globalization. Globalization is closely associated with poverty because it creates great inequality between rich and poor, as well as international conflicts and environmental degradation (Ibid, 1981). Companies now operate globally, so it is becoming more difficult to limit their activities as they move from country looking for cheap resources and exploiting cheap labor. Poverty is not just a local problem; it has global connections. So how can a 'one-world view' ever justify the gross social differences that exist in our integrated global system? However, many experts believe poverty solutions should be global.

In a capitalist society, poverty relates to those who live 'outside' the consumer society. They are blamed for not fitting in, but really they are victims of unemployment, falling wages, downsizing, and a growing sense of insecurity. Poverty victims are suffering from powerlessness due to a lack of formal and informal representations from them. Therefore they are freedom from 'elite' dominations and deprivations. So it is a societal problem, not a matter of individual failures. It is an outcome of the value system of global international capitalism. It is made worse through baldly reputed poverty brokers: IMF, World Bank, World Trade Organization (WTO) and multinational corporations (MNCs). Although these organizations talk a lot about poverty, they are not reducing absolute poverty. Rather, they are the institutions which help induce misery and famine all over the world (Dickson, 1997)). They prescribe poverty solutions as external actors of the impoverished society. Therefore Jeffry Sacks (2005) finds that the rich world dominates third world countries by employing Ph.D. economists in international institutions like the International Monetary Fund (IMF) and the World Bank.

However, it is a wrong strategy of the World Bank and IMF because rich countries' economic development policies, strategies and paths are different from those of developing countries. Hence it is appropriate to let the developing countries themselves identify their own resource strengths, resource gaps, and resource needs, and possible solutions for their own socioeconomic development. The international organizations (IMF, World Bank and World Trade Organization) exist to regulate the global economy under the sponsorship and direction of the U.S. (Thomas & Allen. 2002: p-204). Their efforts often result in damage to the local economy, and to other local social and environmental institutions. Their mandate and ideology may be to support countries' economies, but through lack of understanding of the local culture and short-term as opposed to long-term projects, they usually hinder marginalized people's development rather than help.

The economic theory of western world "aid' can be traced to assist develop the UDCs and to assist poor to eradicate their poverty situation. W. Rostow renowned theory five stages of development emphasis on the 'aid' from DCs to UDCs for UDCs ('take-off to self-sustaining growth) development. In the view DCs 'aid has an important role to play for UDCs to attain a self-sustaining process of economic development. Aid donors use three general approaches to help promote democracy; direct support; indirect support, by, for instance, encouraging economic 'development'; and pressure to encourage policy reform, including the threat of use of sanctions (Ahmad, 2001). Many international agencies and many DCs provided huge 'aid' to many UDCs; however, the result is not so promising that dependency theory asserts. Rather aid has resulted opposite to self-sustaining and made them 'aid dependency' to DCs. Maximum 'aid' money has gone to elites pockets instead to assist poor to overcome their poverty. Gunner Middle studied 'aid' results to UDCs and comments 'aid has no paid'. Opponents of 'aid' conclude that 'aid' actually increases poverty, and causes widespread environmental degradation and increase socio-economic divide in society. Although 'aid' has undoubtedly helped improve living standard among recipients, its contribution to poverty alleviation has fallen short of expectations (Ahmad, 2001). The impact of 'aid' on poverty reduction raises even more serious questions. Because maximum money has gone to elites' pockets instead run projects for the poor. According to UNDP data, only 10 percent of 'aid' is channeled towards the basic needs of the UCDs. 'Aid remain biased in favor the unban middle classes to the detriment of the poorest of the poor. Hence many scholars suggest for reviewing all 'aid' to UDCs, with a view to reallocating unless a special case can be made based on the 'aid's poverty-reducing effects. Muhammad Yunus thinks instead of providing handouts to poor, it effective gives them micro-credit for running small business.

Recently, the pressures of debt payments, debt crisis, and structural adjustment policies have made less developed countries (LDCs) vulnerable to these institutions. As a result, poor people tend to experience more poverty, malnutrition, and health problems, and they are at a higher risk for substance abuse and violence. This is because developed countries impose their own policies on LDCs in the name of democracy, aid, technical support and development. Capitalism and globalization processes focus entirely on economic growth at the cost of human dignity. Although neo-liberalism and capitalism are two global forces where some scholars argue in their works towards solving poverty, capitalism widens the wealth gap and leaves a large group marginalized in severe poverty with no effective means of improving their situation. The capitalist system dominates and controls the local market and continually threatens the local economy.

Trade liberalization, export oriented markets, globalization and the structural adjustment policy (SAP) of IMF all have some negative effects on poverty. Although all of them are working under liberal democracy, they create inequality and unemployment in societies. Since the 1980s, the market forces have gained headway (Thomas 2000a, p-40). SAP through IMF intervention has led to rapid increases in prices which contributed to a recession in the Latin American countries in the 1980s and in Bangladesh in 1990s. Although the SAP of IMF attempts to solve poverty and improve economies, in practice, it is opposite.

Every country has its own 'Economic Master Plan' and 'Five Year Plan' following Western orthodox economics. These plans are political and serve as eye wash to the public. In addition to this, geopolitics, globalization, misrule of the rich countries (particularly US and Britain) leads the poor countries to poverty and to be dependent on them. Hence Kazi Rouf (2014) believes poor countries should challenge the prescriptions of Western donors and develop UDCs own economics in considering local context and situation.

From the above discussion, we see that poverty is a global systemic issue that is a by-product of the global capitalist system. Therefore, poverty should be defined internationally because it is a global problem caused by global systems. How can local governments hope to deal with poverty which results from global forces well beyond their control?

In practice, global capitalism is an example of a failed universalistic attempt at solving poverty. In almost every case, capitalist institutions fail to take into account the local contextual conditions, preferring to impose a set of conditions which are seen as suitable to every situation. This has largely failed, and has only resulted in increases in poverty, particularly in countries already subjected to SAPs. Therefore, an anti-SAP movement is needed against globalization's hegemonic policies.

If we define poverty without defining it at a local level and conceptualize it as a global problem, we are then denying that poverty is in fact a local issue. Are global solutions not simply a continuation of the oppressor pushing their ideas on the oppressed? Therefore, for the sake of practicality, "poverty must be defined in relation to its local conditions which can promote *people centered development* and contribute to human wellbeing" (Korten 1995b, pp.178-9). The face of poverty is extremely different in each country. In Canada, for example, poverty counts those whose annual income is below $19,256 annually (National Council of Welfare 2002), while in Bangladesh it means living off less than $1 a day. So each country defines its own low-income cut-off (LICO) in relation to its individual situation. Some people think welfare and free health care will address poverty. Canada has social assistance program for the the needy for a certain period. However, Muhammed Yunus (2013), founder of the Grameen Bank, does not believe in handouts. Rather, he prefers self-reliant strategies like micro-credit program for poor people where they utilize their credit and own skills to meet their needs.

8.0. Grameen Bank, a local initiative to address poverty in Bangladesh

Political heritage, various religious and cultural beliefs have an effect on how a country addresses poverty issues. Therefore, local definitions are more meaningful since they take into account the local conditions. Universal definitions fail to capture local conditions and local reference points. In Bangladesh, the hardcore poor are defined as those who are landless and 'wealth less'. The Grameen Bank defines the poor as those who have household total assets amounting to less than $250. The urban poor are those who live in slums and are fully dependent on temporary manual daily labor. In Canada, the poor are those who spend 56.2% or more of their household income (either paid income or government assistance) on basic necessities and therefore, they are 'in need' (National Council of Welfare, 1999a; Chappell, 2001: p.182). Here in Canada, the social safety net is fairly well developed for dealing with poverty. However, in Bangladesh the poor live by on their own resources and must survive on their own efforts. There is no state supported safety net there. Thus, both the poverty definition and its solutions are different in these two countries. Hence Peter Penz (1998) criticizes 'income poverty' and suggests poverty should be seen from people's capacity to purchase/afford their basic needs.

Multinational corporations (MNCs) are expanding their socio-economic power over the state through trade agreements, but there are no international bodies which can make and enforce laws. Thus, it is up to the local governments to create and enforce laws which limit global companies and the actions of the local economy and ensure a reduction in poverty. Although NGO initiatives are incapable of dealing with the root of the problem and are only band-aid solutions, they work locally for poverty because the solutions can only be found and implemented locally. Gramen Bank and other MFIs in Bangladesh are providing micro-credit and other services that assist poor people to engage in small business and run social businesses within their community and earn income and develop their social space in their neighborhoods.

9.0. Poverty different measures

United Nations Development Program (UNDP) explains poverty in more relative terms, but it also has different criteria for explaining poverty depending on whether we're talking about developing countries or more industrialized nations. UNDP uses the Human Development Index (HDI) and Human Poverty Index (HPI) for poverty management (Thomas, 2000, p. 16). This is a composite measure which includes different indicators from local perspectives. A lack of health care, education, and social involvement, along with inadequate environmental quality, can also be referred to as poverty. Thus, it is multi-dimensional. Although human development (HDI) developed by UN is widely used now, there is no separate UN agency solely dedicated to poverty eradication. World Bank thinks vibrant urbanization and private sector development can support faster job creation. Investments in quality education, healthcare, and social protection can lead to better jobs.

Now development has both positive and negative effects on society. It could either decrease or increase human wellbeing because dominant business elites are greedy for profit, and they exercise control over people through the market economy. Development ethics really don't exist (Gasper, 2004, p.1). They decide what areas of wealth increase and in what ways.

The designs of wealth creation and distribution affect the whole world. Power decides what resources go to which third world country with what conditions. It is even determined in UN voting, IMF voting and G-8 meetings, G-20 meetings. These voting decisions affect the third world because the first world has forced their ideas onto the third world countries. However, those ideas do not fit appropriately into the third world poverty reduction strategies. For example, first world ideas of GNP calculation ignore female/domestic labor. Their work is not included in the GNP calculation, rather devaluing their efforts. Therefore, a universal poverty definition and universal solution policy cannot cover all the different pockets of poverty within a different society.

Moreover, multinational corporations (MNCs), the source of a lot of 'working poverty' do not generally focus on local conditions. Their owners and operators are located in far away rich countries. MNCs are care only about profits and their business. Local poverty and the environment is not one of their concerns. To address the issue of poverty, there are different opinions/ approaches developed by different institutions and experts discuss below.

10.0. Approaches to Poverty Analysis

A number of ideas have been proposed for measuring the rate of poverty. Here are three approaches to poverty analysis: (1) the Poverty Line Approach focuses on economic measures for meeting basic needs, but it says less about the depth of poverty (poverty gap); (2) The Capabilities Approach explores endowments and entitlements of functioning achievements; and (3) Participatory Poverty Assessment (PPA) explores the cause and effect of poverty in a specific context. The PPA looks at the experience of poverty from the poor people's perspective. It is a bottom-up evaluation where the poor give input, and it encourages active participation in finding comprehensive policies to address poverty. Participatory budget of town house meeting in Argentina and Brazil are an example of PPA approach to prepare and to develop budgets and projects for the public especially for the disadvantaged people in Argentina and Brazil. In Bangladesh, some municipalities already started public town house meeting; many local citizens' male and female (young, adults and seniors) are participating in these town house public meetings and provide their voices and opinions in the meetings. Citizens' participation in the town house meetings assists municipalities tailoring their plan and budgets to the local needs. Toronto Community Housing (TCH) has introduced the participatory budget analysis meetings for the tenants of the TCH in Toronto. The TCH participatory budget analysis meeting provides opportunity to talents of TCH to be involved in budget analysis that enhanced marginalized TCH tenants benefits in Canada.

Now the paper is going to discuss how poverty is viewed by economists as the lack of money, income or capital resources to provide for oneself and one's family. The poverty line, the GNP and LICO are a few of the major elements used to measure poverty from an economic perspective. The poverty line identifies poverty as the limitation in earnings and purchasing power. LICO is used in Canada to measure absolute poverty (acute poverty) and relative poverty.

The *poverty line approach* separates the poor from the rich (cut-off point) and focuses on (a) the national per capita income at the micro level, and (b) the per capita household income. It defines daily income to be the minimum level necessary for survival of household members. About one-quarter of the world's population lives on less than $1 per day and over half lives on $1 per day and are suffering from absolute poverty (Daley-Harris, 2002). The highest poverty region in the world is South Asia (44%). 841 million people worldwide are malnourished and 885 million adults worldwide are illiterate (World Bank Report 2000). Within these huge numbers of poor, women are the most affected (67%) and children are the worst victims (Hick, 2004, p. 147). Poverty also exists in developed countries (11%) for people that have less than $14.40 per day of income. In Canada, 3.3 million people (14.4%) live below the poverty line (Chappell, 2001).

Although GNP per capita and GDP are used as tools to measure poverty at the macro level, they are not appropriate to measure poverty because they are based on the average GNP income of a state. The advantages of the poverty line approach are that it provides empirical data which enables the planners to map the extent of poverty. However, macro level economics and statistics cannot measure local conditions especially when it comes to health and quality of life.

Free trade and global investments do not decrease the gap between rich countries and the poor. In 1960, the gap between developed countries (DCs) and under developed countries (UDCs) average income was only 20 times, while in 1990 the ratio had increased to 55 times (Hick, 2000. p-147). Therefore, Jeffry Sacks (2005) and Peter Penz (1997) say that neo-liberal democratic capitalism is increasing income poverty unequally. Hence global inequality among individuals has increased the poverty gap.

Conversely, the poor world is suffering not only from income shortages, but other concerns such as unequal access to assets, opportunities and universal education. Moreover, economic growth does not always benefit poor people and reduce poverty (Jackson, 2011). Naila Kabeer (1994) says, "Human needs go far beyond the ability to afford daily nutritional needs, but can be extended to living a healthy and active life and participating in community activities" (p-139).

The *capabilities approach*, *participatory poverty assessment*, and the *'hierarchy of needs' approach* all go beyond human economic needs and promote social aspects of human life. For example, the capabilities approach developed by Amarta Sen (1984) explores endowments and entitlements (means) of functioning achievements (ends) for the poor. This approach talks about means and ends (social inclusion) and it appears to respond to economic growth which fails to benefit (trickle down to) the poor. Economic growth fails to meet all people's essential needs: water, sanitation, shelter, clothing, public health, and transportation. The advantages of this human capabilities approach are the focus on monitoring basic achievements across country borders, gender relations, and gender inequalities. Although the capability approach is inclusive of social aspects, intangible social conditions are not quantifiable.

The capability approach tailored to the Human Development Index (HDI) of UNDP includes income, life expectancy and educational attainment as human development measurement. The benefits of HDI are the measurement of basic achievements across the country and the focus on gender inequality.

UNDP also monitors the gender inequality index (GDI) which uses three indices of HDI, but GDI focuses on gender inequality. GDI helps to identify gender inequality and low status of women, and promotes change. This gender-based approach helps to identify the human rights approach to social welfare. It further defines social entitlements as a right of citizenship.

Another multidimensional poverty assessment is the *Participatory Poverty Assessment (PPA)* that explores the cause and effects of poverty in a specific context. It looks at the experience of poverty from the poor people's perspective. It is a bottom-up approach to measure poverty. The advantages of PPA are: it looks not only at the basic needs but also the security, accumulation, social standing, and self respect. It also includes unskilled labor and social networks. Hence the capability approach, HDI, and participatory poverty assessment are more important in addressing poverty at the local level; much more so, than the poverty line approach.

Feminization of poverty is the phenomenon that women represent disproportionate percentages of the world's poor. UNIFEM describes it as "the burden of poverty borne by women, especially in developing countries". Feminization of poverty is a terrible ordeal both in LDCs and DCs. International poverty can be thought of as a mosaic of social elements. Any comprehensive analysis must stress, as a core concern, gender inequalities: the unequal access to assets, opportunities, and status that women experience, compared to men, in most of the world, and particularly in many Southern countries (Langdon, (1999). Crucial antipoverty element is gender equity and equality; this priority is not just to counter the discrimination that prevents contributions from women and men from being fairly recognized in society; but the effort against poverty, especially women and child poverty, requires a major focus on the inequality that women experience. Bangladesh has been leader with its emphasis on micro credit for rural women economic and social development through Grameen Bank, BRAC and other NGOs.

In Bangladesh more than 70% of rural women live below the poverty line. In Canada, 37% of single mothers live below the income poverty line. The women's nurturing activities and household responsibilities devalue them and leave them vulnerable to exploitation. The growing poverty rates give them no choice, voice, value, power, or status in society. Rather, they are exploited by upper class people and employers. For example, industrialized jobs are currently filled by females and thus, increasingly more exploitative" (Kabeer, 2003: p. 69). The global feminization of poverty represents a profound moral crisis for new generations. Many scholars see global poverty as a fundamental threat to human existence. The injustices of mass poverty especially feminization of poverty will effect to future political and social instability in the world. In order to challenge the global poverty and develop local poverty eradication programs, people should be able to participate vibrantly in shaping what is happening to their communities and neighborhoods. At the same state should develop macro-economic and social policies leverage to local economy and local development.

Patriarchal societies favor and give power via customary laws to men. This has a negative effect on women. All these factors are responsible for rural female poverty. However, the Dollar & Gatti study (1999) finds gender inequalities had a significantly negative impact on economic growth. Gender equality has positive effects on per capita income in society (Kabeer, 2003: p. 40). Hence gender equality would be one of the approaches to address the issue of the feminization of poverty.

There are many other poverty relief strategies developed by different scholars and institutions including: *Poverty Reduction Strategy Papers (PRSP), Gender Responsive Budgets (GRB), and Sectored Strategy for Poverty Policy (SSPP) and Gender Management System (GMS).* All of these programs are useful in macroeconomic policy. For example, PRSP deals with a country's macro-economic structural and social policies to promote economic growth and reduce poverty. Although PRSP explores opportunity for poverty reduction, it has rapidly become an integral component of aid-cooperation agencies. It is heavily influenced by the World Bank/IMF. Furthermore, it is heavily reliant on external technical advice. It expands global rules of trade and global market expansion that is regulated by bi-lateral and multilateral trading agreements (Kabeer 2003, p. 211).

The *Hierarchy of Needs approach* developed by the Fraser Institute uses an absolute approach. This hierarchy of basic needs pyramid theory suggests that "for poor people, the notion of self-esteem itself might be more closely tied to the ability to feed their children than to middle class, which would hamper their survival strategies" (Kabeer, 1994, p. 140). Although this is not a direct measurement tool for poverty, this ideology provides just another social theoretical framework from which sociologists examine the issue of poverty.

From the above definitions and approaches to poverty, it is clear that the economic and social theoretical viewpoints directly affect how policies are developed in recognition of these pressing issues. Therefore, poverty analysis and solutions should be considered both at the universal and local levels to define and to solve the poverty different components.

Now the paper is going to discuss the Grameen Bank (GB) micro-financing program that deals with poverty that is based on a combination of economic and social dimensions at the local level. Grameen Bank pioneered 'micro credit', giving funds to poor women once considered unbankable, and allowing them to engage in agriculture, commerce and food processing businesses. Through Grameen Bank, BRAC, ASA, NIjera Kori and many other micro-financings institutions (MFIs), many of the women engaging in microcredit etc. have less children and want less children; fewer children will also help get out of the cycle of poverty. The *Grameen Bank group based micro-credit approach* is a local solution to address poverty in Bangladesh.

Although Bangladesh is not out of the grip of extreme poverty, young women are working in garment factories in inhumane working conditions and are low-paid, these young women are trying to earn income and contribute to their families and to the Bangladesh economy. Although the author finds the garment workers are suffering in exploitive sweatshop job environments where these women are working, at the same time they (garment workers) talked about their greatest opportunity for their empowerment in Bangladesh. For example, they could imagine being able to save surpluses from their pay, manage their own income, have their own rooms, and choose when and whom to date and marry, choose when to have children, and use their savings to go back to school. According to Jaffrey Sacks (2005) this is the first step on the ladder out of poverty for Bangladesh.

Neither economic nor social viewpoints alone are enough to address poverty. Rather a combination of the two is needed. Most meaningful solutions to poverty work are at the local level. Even international aid, which is delivered globally, must eventually be administered locally. Grameen Bank is a very good example of an integrative approach. GB extends its collateral free banking service, which caters primarily to rural women in Bangladesh, and mobilizes the poor. It is a 'self-sustaining process' and makes its members work both individually and collectively to move up the social and economic tiers. Grameen Bank provides $16.7 billion in credit to 8.6 million rural landless in Bangladesh (Grameen Dialogue-93, 2014). GB narrows down its poverty measurement to the borrower level. It uses ten indicators to measure poverty for its members (Appendix-1). Here a combination of social and economic holistic development drives the Bangladeshi rural poor towards self-employment, independence. They are encouraged to make decisions on behalf of families, plan and save for the future, and alleviate the burden of poverty from their lives and their children's. Grameen Bank Statistics 2006) state that 58% of its borrowers have successfully graduated from poverty through the use of Grameen loans.

Microfinance is not designed to support large companies at the national or international levels. Rather, its success is entirely local, through improving local conditions for residents, teaching them to manage money, and plan for their lives beyond a day-to-day subsistence. Grameen Bank is an example which demonstrates that the concept of microfinance is rooted in local conditions. The loans are small and given to individuals who are rooted in local villages. They then use the loans to create small businesses which serve the local population.

Microfinance is part of the framework of *interventionism* as it is defined as the "need for intentional development alongside capitalism in order to *ameliorate the disordered faults of progress*" (Thomas, 2002, p.28). Interventionism looks to combine state and market forces. Microfinance is an intentional attempt at development using the capitalist methodology. Through borrowing small amounts of money, GB borrowers become entrepreneurs and owner-operators of small enterprises that conduct business independently in their communities. In this way, they increase their family income and savings, educate their children and plan for their future. GB helps to mentor businesses within their local market by providing a supportive community and teaching basic business management skills.

A key part of Grameen Bank is the strategy of bringing women together on a weekly basis not only to pay their loans, but also to share experiences, support one another's business, and to hear from bank staff about how to keep their family healthy and prepare for natural disasters.

Microfinance schemes are targeted at those people who are normally excluded from mainstream banking services, training programs, and business development advice. Their goal for each person is that they help the poor for their self-sufficiency and self-confidence. Only when an individual gains these important qualities can they pull themselves out of the depths of poverty for good.

Microfinance institutions aimed at the poor require some kind of a *means-test* to identify the extremely poor (Gibbons, 1994, pp. 116-117). Means-tests are also used in Canada to evaluate the assets and income of welfare recipients. Credit unions in Canada are local solutions to mobilize the poor and facilitate networking among them. They are local solutions that promote local small businesses and work to meet their banking needs.

Although the World Development Report (1990) says "Reducing poverty is the fundamental objective of economic development" (p-24), safe and sustainable environmental policy, programs and projects are also vital for poverty eradication and human development. Several NGOs and many international organizations are attempting to address poverty, but they are working piecemeal and often cancel out each other's efforts. An inclusive poverty definition and an integrated program for income development, education, health, and legal services for poor women at the village level are urgently needed. For poor women, their poverty is not just an issue of nutrition and basic needs, but of justice, voice, choice and fundamental human rights.

A globally-unified poverty definition and a uniform global poverty reduction strategy may not be appropriate for all poverty pockets in the world because the depth of poverty and causes of poverty differ from society to society. Therefore, we need to identify the *poverty headcount* of both absolute and relative poverty (Slayter, 2003, p. 297). At the same time the public policy should be reviewed and updated, and poverty-related trends and conditions must be monitored. This plays a crucial role in giving people the ability to develop their potential as well as to convert available resources into an economically and socially advantageous small business.

11.0. Conclusion

From the above discussions/arguments, the paper draws conclusion poverty is depriving poor people of access to resources to achieve anything beyond fulfilling their basic needs. It is one of the most important issues to be examined in development studies because the world has become an increasingly unequal place, as the gap between the haves and the have-nots has widened. Poverty, injustice and inequality are worst in capitalism. Because capitalism and globalization of the free market economy makes poverty global and the third world more impoverished. It is advantageous to wealthy nations, but developing countries have less wealth and significant social problems that are not encouraging to resource creation. Over fifty countries are now poorer than they were ten years ago (Bibby & Shaw (2005). The world is increasingly becoming globalised. However, people living in poverty are citizens who have rights to the benefits of development. Currently many thinkers are questioning is there no turning back from the social and economic impoverishing process.

Many development thinkers are suggesting for traditional cooperatives management by marginalized people could be an alternatives for their poverty eradication because cooperatives are based on social and ethical values and on the principles of democracy and self-help; however, many developmental practitioners consider *traditional cooperatives are like an 'old furniture model for development'* because this alternative developmental model unable to function properly in many countries including Bangladesh in the present. Therefore, Barbara Slyter (2003) suggests for an approach to address poverty, which should be considered that closely analyzes its causes and implications to address issue of poverty (p. 286).

To reduce poverty and to promote the Brundtland Commission's *human need-centered nine conditions could be considered- justice, sustainability, inclusiveness, gender equity, good literacy, human security and reduce poverty* (in Thomas, 1996, p-99), the state should deregulate free-trade within their country to protect its local products and businesses from imported competition. Moreover, UDCs need to work on a sustainable development agenda that "meets the needs of the present without compromising the ability of future generations to meet local people's own need" (Allen & Thomas, 2000, p. 158). UDCs should be solely dependent on overseas 'aid and assistance'; the government policy for poor should not be provide relief to them for their livelihoods rather provide assist them to run business for their income.

In Bangladesh, PKSF and its affiliated local MFIs//NGOs have been providing micro credit and offering business training for supporting the bottom people to run their business in Bangladesh. The Government of Bangladesh also develops strategies and makes separate budget and projects for the poor for eradicating poverty and for their development. Currently the Government of Bangladesh is not dependent on 'foreign aid' for assisting the poor. Rather the government beliefs it is effective to mobilize local resources for the poor and allocate local resources to them. The result is promising. Therefore, it is important to identify poverty issues locally; find resources/alternative paths that are suitable to marginalized people in their local context as well that are adaptable to marginalized people to uplift them from their sufferings of poverty, injustice and misery.

12.0. Bibliography

Ahmad, Mokbul, M. (2001). *Understanding the South.* Ireland: Social Science Council

Allen, T. and Thomas, A. (2000). *Poverty and Development into the 21st Century.* New York: Oxford University Press Inc.

Bangladesh Profile. (2001). Retrieved on June 08, 2005 from http://www.southasiafoundation.org/saf/bngladesh/banglastats.asp

Bibby, A. and Shaw, L. (2000). *Making a Difference: Cooperative Solutions to Global Poverty.* Cooperative College 2005. UK

Boserup, E. (1970). *Women's Role in Economic Development.* London: Earthscan Publications

Calmeadow Foundation (2005). *Annual Report 2005.* Toronto

Chappell, R. (2001). *Social Welfare in Canadian Society.* Canada: Nelson Thomson Learning

Bibby, A. and Shaw, L. (2005). *Making a Difference Co-operative Solutions to Global Poverty.* London: Cooperative College

Daley-Harris, S. (2002). *Pathways out of Poverty.* Connecticut: Kumarian Press

Desai, V. and Potter, R. (2002). *The Companion to Development Studies.* New York: Oxford University Press Inc.

Daily Star. (2006). *Bangladesh Poverty Statistics.* Dhaka: Daily Star, 2006, October 14)

Dickson, D. (1997). *Development and International Relations, Cambridge*: Polity Press

Dollar, D. and Gatti, R. (1999). Gender inequality, income and growth: Are good times good for women? Washington, DC: World Bank

Gasper,D. (2004). *The Ethics of Development: From Economism to Human Development.* Edinburgh: Edinburgh University Press

Gibbons, D. S. (1994). *The Grameen Readers.* Dhaka: Subarna Printers

Hick, S. (2004). *Social Welfare in Canada-Understanding Income Security.* Toronto: Thomson Educational Publishing, Inc.

Human Development Report (1995). *Human Development Index.* UNDP Bangladesh

Grameen Bank (2008). *Impact of Grameen Bank on Local Society.* http://www.rdc.com.au/grameen/impact/htm

Jackson, T. (2011). *Prosperity without Growth: Economics for a Finite Planet.* London: EarthScan

Kabeer, N. (1995). *Reserved Realities-Gender Hierarchies in Development Thought.* London, Great Britain, Biddles Ltd.

Korten, D. (1995a). *When Corporations Rule the World,* West Hardford CT: Kumarian Press, and Berrett-Koehler, San Francisco

Korten, D. (1995b). Steps toward people-centered development: Vision and strategies, in Heyzer, N., Riker, j. V. & Quizon, A. B. (eds.) *Government-NGO relations in Asia: prospect and challenges for people-centered development,* pp. 165-189

Langdon, S. (1999). Global poverty, democracy North-South change. Toronto: Garamound Press

National Council of Welfare (2002). *Factsheet.* Ottawa: National Council of Welfare.

O'Neill, J. (2007). *Markets, Deliberation and Environment.* Routledge eScholarID:4b2487

Penz, P. (1998). *Political Ecology: Global and Local.* New York: Routledge

Penz, P. (1997). Global Justice, Global Democracy. Fernwood

Polanyi, K. (1957). *The Great Transformation: The Political and Economic Origins of Our Times,* Boston: Beacon Press

Rouf, K. A. (2017). While poverty is a global problem resulting from global issues, its definition and solution can only be found locally, *International Journal of Research Studies in Management,* Vol.6(2), pp. 39-52

Rouf, K. A. (2015). Peasant socio-economic scenarios and technology use dynamics in Bangladesh. *Global Journal of Human Social Sciences,* Vol. 15(1), pp. 40-55

Sen. A. (1984). *Resources, values, and development.* Oxford: Blackwell

Sen, A. (1981). *Poverty and Famines: an Easy on Entitlement and Deprivation,* Oxford: Oxford Press

Shragge, E. (1997). *Community Economic Development-In Search of Empowerment.* Montreal: Black Rose Books

Slayter, B. (2003). *Southern Exposure.* Bloomfield: Kumarian Press.

The Islamic Tribune (2006, October 16), Toronto, Vol.1 *(2)*

Thomas, A. (1996). What is development management? *Journal of International Development*, 8(*10*), pp. 95-110

National Council of Welfare (2002). *Welfare Incomes*, Ottawa 2003. http://www.ncwcnbes.net

Wolf, M. (2004). *Why Globalization Works*. London: Yale University Press

Wong, W. A. (2002). *The Poor Women- A Critical Analysis of Asian Theology and Contemporary Chinese Fiction by Women*. New York: Peter Lang

World Development Report (1994). *World Development Index*. Washington, DC. World Development

Yunus, M. (2013). *Building Social Business: A New Kind of Capitalism that serves Humanity's most Pressing Needs*. New York: Public Affairs

Appendix-I

Grameen Bank Borrowers' Poverty Measurement Tools

1. Each individual of the household is able to take three meals a day
2. Children go to school
3. Live in their own houses
4. Winter clothes are available
5. Ability to afford health services and buy necessary medicine
6. Use safe drinking water
7. Have no loans or mortgages
8. Use mosquito nets
9. Pay regularly their Grameen loans and pension schemes unless affected by natural disasters
10. Access to literacy opportunities and higher education

The Advantages of Micro-credit Lending Programs and the Human Capabilities Approach for Women's Poverty Reduction and Increased Human Rights in Bangladesh

Abstract

More than fifty percent of people all over the world are suffering from a lack basic needs. Even poor women are denied their equality of human rights. Equality of rights for these women would mean access to food, clothing, shelter, and credit as well as liberation from exploitative forms of income generation such as domestic work, child labour and trafficking. Women in Bangladesh suffer from inequality of rights on quite an unimaginable level and their socio-cconomic development has been largely impeded. Thus, these poor women depend on others to survive. Human capability services like education and skills development services are not generated nor tailored to them particularly at the village level which affects the basic human rights of these women. Without educational, health, economic and social services at the village grass-roots level, poor people suffer most in Bangladesh.

Although the Constitution of Bangladesh appears to strongly approve gender equality and positive action that guarantees women's full participation in social, economic and political life, it is clear that full support is absent.

Ironically, the disadvantaged poor people specifically are struggling to fulfill their basic human needs and are aware of their basic human rights. Although some steps have been made to reduce gender inequality, some laws still lag behind and many discriminatory practices are found in the customary laws, which still remain in force.

A solution that has offered to assist poor women in Bangladesh through micro-credit organizations (MFIs) like Grameen Bank micro credit services that create opportunities for these women to help educate themselves and overcome poverty in Bangladesh. However, human rights education at the grass roots level is very nominal. Hence focus on human rights education extension programs are urgently required to establish basic human rights.

Key words: Grameen Bank, human rights, women human rights, micro-credit, feminization of poverty, participatory development and women empowerment.

Acronyms: Bangladesh Rural Advancement Committee (BRAC), Canadian International Development Agency (CIDA), Grameen Bank (GB), micro-finance institutions (MFIs) Millennium Development Goals, (MDGs), non-governmental organizations (NGOs), Palli Karma Shayak Foundation (PKSF), Structural Adjustment Policy (SAP), United Nations (UN), World Trade Organization (WTO) and World Health Organization (WHO).

1.0. Introduction

The "feminization of poverty" has been a growing concern in low-income countries such as Bangladesh. In this essay, the feminization of poverty refers to the burden placed on poor women in Bangladesh to feed, clothe and nurture their families and themselves. Poor women are denied access to credit. The development of women has been largely impeded, and women in Bangladesh suffer from inequality of rights on quite an unimaginable scale. Equality of rights for these women would mean access to food, clothing, shelter, and credit as well as liberation from exploitative forms of income generation such as domestic work, child labour and trafficking. There is a major lack of resources to support women in their struggle to work, take care of their families and survive. This struggle is often the result of macro- and micro-economic gender divisions, which reflect current political practices and the norms, customs and culture of the patriarchal society. Therefore, the 50% people suffer from a lack of basic needs. Human capability services like education and skills development services are not generated and tailored at the village level which affects basic human rights. Without educational, health, economic and social services at the village grass-roots level, poor people suffer most. Rich people exploit the poor and hinder their human rights and other legal rights. The effects of colonialization and globalization have also contributed to the poor conditions in Bangladesh, first with British rule and then the Pakistan regime from 1947 to 1971.

Although there are several international organizations and programs designed to help combat these injustices, often their techniques are not applied uniformly, and thus civil society has less power to lobby for the necessary changes in the legal system (Quadir, 2003). A promising new strategy, first introduced by Mohamed Yunus, brought to Bangladesh the concept of micro-credit. Micro-credit has proved successful thus far in providing poor women with the ability to generate income while developing human capabilities. The positive effects associated with such activities have helped reduce poverty in many rural areas, as well as increase women's equality and human rights. However, micro-credit and human capabilities development can only thrive in conjunction with successful implementation, government support and services, and international involvement. Thus, this essay will argue that the "feminization of poverty" in Bangladesh can be reduced through the development and successful implementation of micro-credit lending programs that increase human capabilities and provide a means of achieving gender equality and human rights for rural poor women.

2.0. Problems

Poor women in Bangladesh do not have basic human rights. Basic human rights in this essay will include food, clothing, shelter, health, education, justice, voice and choice of their rights. With no food, clothing and shelter, women are forced to beg, or borrow money or do maid servants jobs with poor wages in the wealthy peoples' houses both in rural and urban areas in Bangladesh and abroad. Borrowing money from money lenders leads to great debt, which in turn leads to landlessness and vulnerability in society.

3.0. Context

Currently, Bangladesh has 164.4 million people within a 147, 570 square kilometer range. The density of the population is 763 people per square kilometer and the per capita income is $370. Many studies before 2000 show in Bangladesh 51% poor people live under the poverty line. This rate is highest in South East Asia. The poverty rate of rural areas in Bangladesh is higher than the national average of 51%. The *Bangladesh Human Development Report 2000* reported that during the period between 1992 and 1996 the rural poverty line declined by about 1% per year and had dropped from 53% to 51%. Yet, a population growth rate of 2.3% per year was not considered in this estimation, thus, despite this decline, rural poverty is still higher in South East Asia.

Poor Bangladeshi women are not provided state enough resources, their human rights are seriously hampered, as well as other social civil rights like freedom of choice, freedom of speech, and opportunities in society.

Approximately 86.6% of the population of Bangladesh is Muslim. Therefore, Bangladeshi society is a highly patriarchal Muslim dominated society where all household family decisions are made by men. Men control women's labor, women's choice of marriage, access to resources, and legal, social, health, economic and political institutions are mediated by men. Rural women have no autonomy in their life from childhood into adulthood and old age. Public and private institutions underpin gender subordination and dependence. Women are treated as an unpaid reproductive agent for the family and are involved in unpaid family subsistence agricultural work. Women are discouraged by their 'male guardians' not to participate in public or private paid employment outside of the home. Public and private sector job opportunities are very limited. Thus, Bangladesh has a high unemployment rate of approximately 52.5%. However, it is important to stress that employment opportunities for women in particular, are required so that unmarried and widowed women can provide for themselves and their families.

Furthermore, there is no value associated with domestic work such as, housework and even social reproduction. Less wage work results in women's low economic status. Poor women do not have access to credit from formal financial services to do business. Some of them become street beggars after losing all that they own through the mortgaging of their assets.Consequently, these women are left with no rights and no power in the society.

In addition, women who lack education cannot develop the proper skills that could help them find employment. In fact, the adult female literacy rate is 43% (Bangladesh Human Rights Report, 2000). However, the rural female literacy rate is far lower than the national average. If women are unable to find jobs, they cannot provide modest food, clothe, housing, and medicine etc. for themselves and their families. Educated women in Bangladesh are more aware of their poor conditions and are better equipped to lobby and fight for their rights.

Only 30% of the total population has access to basic health services, and 76% of all households are deficient in calorie intake (CIDA, 2001). Without access to health care, poor women face malnutrition and death. This makes them very weak, perhaps even too weak to work and provide for themselves and their families. In addition, malnutrition leads to the spread of diseases, which can affect the entire country and not just marginalized sections of the population.

Lack of fundamental resources, affords these women no power and therefore, they are unable to exercise their human rights. Naila Kabeer (2003) states that in order to establish gender equality and female empowerment as well as reduce female poverty, Bangladesh needs to close the gender gap in education, increase women's employment and wages, and increase women's participation in parliament.

4.0. Causes

Before 1947, Bangladesh was a part of India, and then from 1947 to 1971 it was under Pakistan regime. The effects of Pakistan rule in Bangladesh will be discussed later in more detail.

The birth of new social classes (petty bourgeoisie) in Bangladesh before 1947 was the result of the destruction of the old social economy and superimposition of new social policies by the colonial rulers (Alam, 1995). British imperialism created a new class structure, which was absent in India. Although presently it appears that a democratically elected civilian authority governs Bangladesh, it is really governed by the petty bourgeoisies, who are now a ruling class comprised of an emerging middle class, the rich business class, and the military and bureaucratic forces.

In addition, there is a history of dependency on foreign capital that exists within the government of colonial powers (Novak, 1993). This government is unable to contribute to a sustainable economic development project for the poor. Therefore, the country is experiencing hegemonic crisis and political instability. Consequently, as Foucault would argue, the notion of power and knowledge related to 'participatory development' is inherently anti-nature and anti-women in Bangladesh (Shiva, 1988). As such, although the ruling class in Bangladesh receives foreign aid, the funds are not used for the welfare of poor people. The ruling class would rather use the money for their own interests. This produces misery and inequality in the society (Alam, 1995).

It is clear that British colonialization in Bangladesh has had a negative effect on macro-and micro-economics in terms of gender divisions in labour and within social contexts. These kinds of societal organizations have only supported ideas of subordination and encouraged the birth of many forms of inferiority. Class relations are an important contribution to this discussion because it is often the money lenders that poor women turn to for 'support'. Poor women in Bangladesh are being exploited by government macro-economic policies and money lenders (*Mohajan*), and therefore, are not afforded the basic human rights discussed above. Thus, poor, uneducated women depend on others to survive.

To maintain the family, poor people sell their labour in advance for one, two or even five years. The need to provide food and clothing to children forces poor women to become domestic maids in the homes of rich people. Poor people are forced to move from small rural villages to urban areas for survival. These people live in shanty slums that are in miserably low and unhygienic conditions. A majority of them are suffering from lack of Healthcare. They ultimately end up without food, clothing, shelter, health, education, security, and no choice. They become victims of malnutrition and deadly, crippling diseases. Some brothels take advantage of the troubled times of poor people and begin to traffic and prostitute desperate women and children. The result is an increase of injustice, inequality, and exploitation, which has an even worse impact on their lives.

Another important factor to consider is the maintenance of the male dominated patriarchal society in Bangladesh. Although Bangladesh declared itself a secular state, Muslim religious values dominate the society. These Islamic values are linked with politics in Bangladesh and often, political representatives lobby for their own political interests.

Thus, when fundamental Islamic religious leaders become powerful in politics, women's rights are affected. This is because Islam values *Sharia Law* which encourages male dominated patriarchy. Parvin Paidar (2002) notes the patriarchal nature of Islam and its subsequent oppression of women in Iran as well. Therefore, in Bangladesh, gender inequality and development discourse needs to acknowledge the contradictory affects of religious customary and legal laws that are often at the expense of women's human rights.

In addition, as Lourdes Beneria (2003) notes, with globalization and industrialization, trade became more commercialized, which made profit the motivating factor for work. Market forces in the formal and informal sectors of the economy are also important to the understanding of the feminization of poverty because, as previously discussed; women's work goes largely unnoticed in these sectors as does their unpaid labour and reproductive contributions. Dollar and Gatti (2003) and Seguino (2003) provide some interesting findings about the division of labour throughout their respective studies. These will be discussed later in further detail with a focus on macro- and micro-economic policies and their impact on gender-divisions.

The impact of globalization and commercialism can best be illustrated with a discussion of British Imperialism in Bengal and its post-colonial effects. The British East India Company first introduced British rule in Bengal in 1750. Its purpose was to build a trade market between India and England. Shortly afterward, this company introduced the idea of private ownership similar to the west, and land became an important commodity. A new upper class of 'landlords' (*Zamindars*) emerged who were revenue collectors during the Moghal Emperors (Karim, 1976). In 1773, the British introduced the Permanent Land Settlement Act. This new system introduced and forced farmers into cash crop production and commercialized agriculture. British metropolises remained linked to India by establishing metropolis satellite structures (Frank, 1970). They diverted agriculture in order to supply raw materials to industries in England, which transformed Bengal into a market for finished products for England. As Ester Boserup's (1970) literature would suggest changes in the production of agriculture effects women and the land, their roles, and the decline of women's equality from pre-colonial to colonial times. Thus, the conflict between gender and class relations becomes more apparent. Although Bangladeshi women contribute to the majority of agricultural production as well as within the informal sectors of the economy, they are still suffering from non-paid and undermined informal household and farming labour.

Another important contribution to the discussion on gender and class relations relates to the British educational policy that created a Hindu educated middle class in Bengal known as "gentlemen" *(bhadralok)*. According to Antonio Gramsci (1971) this class would fall under the category of "organic intellectuals." Organic intellectuals are involved in various bureaucratic and professional duties that are necessary to mediate British rule in India. Muslims in India refused to collaborate with the British and rejected learning English as Muslim religious leaders declared the English language the language of "kafirs" (infidels). Therefore, in Bengal, Muslims are behind in education when compared to Hindus. This Hindu-Muslim differentiation later resulted in separate religious sentiments, movements and nationalism to preserve Indian Muslim culture. Thus, in 1947, this division led to the Pakistani acquisition of Bangladesh (East Pakistan).

With new rule, Pakistan introduced development projects which favored West Pakistan's own interests. This generated class and regional inequalities between West and East Pakistan. Once Bengali petty bourgeois articulated nationalist discourse on the basis of economic and political exploitation, they started to identify political and economic discrimination in the Pakistan public. As a result, in 1971 East Pakistani people revolted, and East Pakistan became Bangladesh.

The development programs in Bangladesh created a parasitic class, who misspent public funds and caused the entire country to become impoverished. Huge foreign aid poured into Bangladesh in the name of public projects, but these funds were mishandled by the corrupt ruling class. This exacerbated the already terrible conditions for poor people.

A third factor contributing to the feminization of poverty today is globalization. Free market capitalism, globalization, democracy and technology are not worthwhile in Bangladesh, and worsen poverty, especially for women. This is because, macro-policies and programs are bureaucratic in nature (top down), and do not consider globalization's exploitative processes on Third World nations.

The invasion of multinational corporations is similar to the process of colonization. Multinationals come into the country of their choice, and exploit the people, the government and the resources, in the name of business. Like colonization, this changes the role of women in society and affects their human rights. Although the multinational corporations create some jobs in Bangladesh, these corporations care only about profits, which results in uneven economic growth in the country. For instance, in order to increase profits, multinationals find cheap labour and resources. Small businesses fail as they cannot compete with multinational products. In addition, multinational corporations ruin the environment and therefore, people have no lands for agriculture, which is needed for survival. As Patricia Stamp urges, "We should not pressure nature for human benefit" (Stamp, 1989). Human rights are also affected by multinational corporations. People are left to live in poverty, with no options for fighting against multinational corporations. In particular, women have no right to complain about work or complain about poverty and injustice as they have no power. Unfortunately, the Bangladeshi government relies on the money of multinational corporations and so they do not want to be rid of them.

Globalization literature (also referred to as "modernization literature") ignores traditional values. Third World countries are often depicted as falling behind. Patricia Stamp disagrees with such literature and argues that it is not a question of whether such Third World societies are "behind," but rather, modernization imposes Westernized views that are not tailored to consider the economic, political and social practices of traditional Third World societies. Edward W. Said (1978) has noted that "Orientalism" (the erroneous Western tendency to view all Middle Eastern and Asian cultures as a kind of homogenous whole and to place them within a false framework that is opposed to our own) is man-made for the West. The relationship between the Occident (Britain and the U.S.) and the Orient (Middle East and East Asia) is a relationship of power, a domination of hegemony. The interaction between the ruling classes and the state is the end result of a historical process to keep the country undeveloped (Said, 1978). This is very true as I note the effects of western capitalist goals with respect to modernization.

Diane Elson (2003) provides some insight into becoming gender-aware in macro-economic policies and government budgets. She notes the importance of unpaid reproductive labour and the dynamic between gender inequality and capitalist markets. Macro-economic policy developments need to be evaluated and adjusted to reorganize gender differences with respect to economic growth.

5.0. Attempted Solutions

The Bangladeshi Constitution calls for equality of all citizens before the law and no discrimination against any citizens on grounds of religion, race, sex, or place of birth; right to protection of the law; protection of right to life and personal liberty; freedom of speech, profession or occupation; rights to property; and enforcement of fundamental rights through courts of law. Any laws and enactments inconsistent with fundamental rights are void. The constitution of Bangladesh guarantees equal rights for women and men. However, there is still a large gap between the law and its actual implementation.

Article 25 of the Bangladeshi Constitution is vital to this discussion because it addresses the fulfillment of basic needs. Everyone has the right to a standard of living, adequate for the health and well-being of himself and of his family, including food, clothing, housing, medical care and necessary social services. However, in the constitution a provision for the same is made in Article 15 that the fulfillment of these basic needs is not a matter of rights, but rather, a state responsibility, which was unfortunately not included in the fundamental rights chapter of the Constitution. The above points illustrate that the constitution provides for the fundamental rights of its citizens, but fundamental needs are not fully recognized as rights of citizens. In addition, Article 10 of the Constitution notes, "Steps shall be taken to ensure participation of women in all spheres of national life" (BMSP, 1997). Ironically, the bottoms 50% of disadvantaged poor people specifically are struggling to fulfill their basic human needs.

Although the Constitution of Bangladesh appears to strongly approve gender equality and positive action that guarantees women's full participation in the social, economic and political life, it is clear that full support is absent. There is a separate ministry for women's affairs and although some steps have been made to reduce gender inequality, some laws still lag behind and many discriminatory practices are found in the customary laws, which still remain in force.

A solution that was offered to assist poor women in Bangladesh began with Professor M. Yunus. Yunus is the founder of the Grameen Bank. This organization argues that welfare or handouts do not help poor people (Yunus, 2002). Instead, the poor remain unskilled and continue to live in poverty. Grameen Bank credit creates opportunities for poor women in Bangladesh to help poor women educate themselves and overcome poverty.

Grameen Bank, a locally initiated model, provides credit to rural poor women without collateral. They serve 8.6 million families and provided 14.5 billion US dollars to its borrowers across Bangladesh.

The credit recovery rate is 97% (Grameen Bank, 2015). It has not only had tremendous success in generating income to the bottom 50% disadvantaged women, but it has also empowered them to make choices, have a voice, and gain opportunities and bargaining power. It views credit for self-employment as a fundamental human right, which is a powerful weapon that grants access to other resources. Grameen Bank has helped poor women break out of the cycle of poverty by increasing the income of its borrowers. Grameen clients are able to overcome the deprivation of basic human needs and fundamental human rights.

Following the Gramen Bank model, other micro-credit organizations (Bangladesh Rural Advancement Committee BRAC), Association for Social Advancement (ASA), PRISHIKA, PKSF) in Bangladesh are also now providing credit to poor village women for income generating activities. Various studies in Bangladesh show that credit programs have a positive impact on the reduction of poverty. Kofi Annan (2005), the former Secretary General of the United Nations, said on January 15, 2005 that micro finance has proved its value in many countries as a weapon against poverty and hunger. It really improves peoples' lives, especially the lives of those who need it most (Annan, 2005). Therefore, it is very important for poor women to have an economic income base that can open the door to other social and political rights for women, equality, freedoms, as well as struggle against the violations of their human rights and social injustice.

International organizations also play a vital role in helping to reduce the feminization of poverty. One such organization is the United Nations (UN). The United Nations has helped the world become more aware of this problem. A new strategy has been proposed by the UN that will include trying to implement development programs through the government. For instance, the Millennium Development Goals (MDGs) were agreed upon at the United Nations Millennium Summit in 2000 and in 2015 include: (1) to half world poverty by 2015; (2) to achieve universal primary education and (3) to promote gender equality in order to help empower women. However, as previously discussed, some corrupt government bodies divert funds for their own preferences. Furthermore, rural poor people are not considered a priority in the government fiscal budget agenda. Poor people are suffering from the disadvantages of national budget resources. However, women's equal access to financial resources is a human rights issue.

Other international organizations include, The World Bank, International Monetary Fund (IMF) and the World Trade Organization (WTO). These organizations took Third World countries and tried to push structural adjustment policies (SAPs) without tailoring the SAPs to each country. SAPs were intended to help the economic disturbances in Third World countries like Bangladesh. However, foreign debt adjustment did not consider gendered responsibilities in and outside the home. The World Bank promotes economic progress in developing countries. They try to raise productivity to help people live better lives. However, their priorities are at the macro-level, but have less impact at the micro-level. IMF monitors international finance, encourages financial cooperation between countries, lobbies for state exchange rates and assists governments with debt. However, IMF does not specifically address women's issues. It does not focus on poverty reduction and its main concern is economic growth. Equal economic growth is also not addressed. IMF does not provide hands–on assistance. Their SAPs are designed only to correct maladjustments in their balance of payments. The WTO was formed in 1995 and its basic principle is that all 125 member countries must abide by WTO rules. Rules include barriers on tariffs, intellectual property rights, and investment and trade relations. However, the WTO does not address worker's rights and poverty.

A proposal offered by the World Bank and the IMF was the greater funding and implementation of non-governmental organizations (NGOs) through apex funding. The involvement of apex funding was required in order to help monitor the activities of NGO's. Otherwise, there would be an overlap of resources in some areas, leaving other areas with nothing. The autonomous apex funding body in Bangladesh is called the Pally-Karmar-Foundation (PKSF). They take funding and distribute it to NGO's those are involved in delivering micro credit in Bangladesh; it coordinates and monitors MFIs and NGOs activities. The advantages of this model include, less government control, and funds go directly to NGOs. NGOs provide services directly to the people. Some NGOs are working for mass education, some are involved in primary health care services, some provide agricultural support services and some promote women's human rights. The majority of NGOs are now involved in micro-credit programs, which target poor rural women and promote income-generating activities. Through diversified NGO activities, village people are connected to various development programs. The Ain-O-Salish Kendra undertakes a variety of programs to improve people's awareness of legal and human rights. Mohila Samity (Women Association) runs various programs to help women achieve self-reliance. In particular, in Bangladesh, many NGO's work with women, this is a massive thrust toward women's equality and progress.

Two international organizations born in the west (North America) include the Canadian International Development Agency (CIDA) and the US Agency for International Development (USAID). CIDA supports sustainable development in developing countries. They hope to help reduce poverty and make the lives of poor people more secure and equitable. CIDA also supports democratic development. Its program is based on the Millennium Development Goals (MDGs) developed by the United Nations. CIDA has 4 main priorities: 1. social development; 2. economic well-being; 3. environmental sustainability; and 4. governance. There is a greater emphasis on human rights issues, democracy and good governance to help reduce corruption by governments. Also, equitability between men and women is promoted and supported by CIDA. The CIDA approach is more appropriate for Bangladesh in order to increase gender equality, human rights and human capital development of poor women.

On the other hand, US foreign assistance has always had the twofold purpose of furthering America's foreign policy interests in expanding democracy and free markets while improving the lives of the citizens of the developing world. USAID appears to be very general and vague about their policies and work in developing countries. Their policy objectives focus on economic growth, trade and democracy, and conflict prevention. USAID is unclear about how it helps economic growth and eradicates poverty. They do not focus on women's human rights and equity. They focus on terrorism and weapons of mass destruction. Oddly, education is not a priority even though education is a basic requirement for human capital and for human rights. Thus, it is clear that CIDA support is more oriented to promoting human rights, reducing poverty, and macro- and micro-level social and economic development in developing countries. Conversely, USAID is more concerned with US interests like foreign policy, commercialism, trade, globalization and an emphasis on capitalist democracy within a US context.

The purpose of these organizations is to stabilize currency and ensure free trade. Yet, none of these organizations have yet emerged as key contributors in Bangladesh civil society (Quadir, 2003). The big three (World Bank, IMF and WTO) reflect the interests of the capitalist powers. In fact, there is public opposition against some World Bank policies. Not only do people feel that these institutions develop devastating SAPs which negatively affect the poor, but feminist scholars also believe that the World Bank ignores women's issues and maintains gender inequality. Currently, a piecemeal system exists between NGOs and civil society. They need more coordination so that a complete package is implemented at the grass-roots level. Therefore, Bangladesh needs a national NGO who solely deals with the village people to counsel, advocate and lobby for women's human rights, stand against dehumanization, and work for victims assisting them in legal issues and prosecution.

6.0. Directions for the Future

As public and private sector formal jobs are limited, government resources and support for the villages is bleak. Rural poverty is increasing at an alarming rate in comparison to its population growth. Therefore, an independent income program, a universal education program and strong law enforcement can create the potential to enhance women's income, awareness, capabilities and status at home and in the community. Income and gender specific programs can benefit women because "micro-finance is a vital means for income generation, social inclusion, and empowerment" (Chowdhuray, 2005). The Grameen Bank program has proved the success of micro-credit. Distressed women are provided with education, skills, training, credit, and other support services for income generating purposes. This leads to economic progress, a boost in family and social status, independent decision-making, and the development of self-confidence that empowers them. Women's empowerment may lead to government participation at the local level. This participation is important for achieving the goals associated with women's human rights.

Increased human capabilities have a positive impact on both gender equality and economic growth (Nassubum, 1988). Studies conducted by Dollar and Gatti (2003) and Seguino (2003) illustrate a positive relationship between gender equality, efficiency and economic growth. In addition, Seguino (2003) suggests that there is a trade-off between gender equality and economic growth. Therefore, investment in human capital will improve efficiency and will inevitably have a positive impact on economic growth. Grameen bank micro credit contributes to its clients' human capital, economic capital and social capital development.

Micro-level programs, such as micro-credit, will help eradicate social discrepancy, gender inequalities, and other social catastrophic activities, which affect the poor women in rural Bangladesh. However, programs such as Grameen Bank (GB), along with other micro-finance institutions, only serve 27 million rural people composed of GB 8.6 million, PKSF 6.2 million, Bangladesh Rural Advancement Committee (BRAC) 5.9 million, and others 5.00 million and therefore, a large population still has no access to financial services. Therefore commercial banks and other financial institutions need to be government regulated to simplify collateral conditions and reduce banking bureaucracy.

Raising awareness through legal education and reform can challenge existing public policies and laws to empower victimized women. As Paulo Freire (1981) would suggest, ignorance leads to unequal power and exploitation. Thus, the government should promote and execute universal compulsory primary education with a special emphasis on female education. This will help poor women develop human capabilities and human dignity.

Besides education, the government needs to initiate greater support at the social, economic, and political micro-level. For instance, rural poor women are involved in informal agricultural and non-agricultural work. Their work is not included in the country's economic production and social reproduction goes unnoticed. Because of the domestic (household) nature of this work, it is stereotyped as 'women's work' which leaves poor women out of the fiscal budget. Therefore, the government should develop labour intensive special income generating projects in the rural areas for these poor women so that their activities will be included within the development programs.

In addition, deficient macro-policies can easily limit the development of poor women. A micro-economic policy framework for maintaining poor women's development may be more conducive to sustainable development and poverty reduction. Social mobilization is a pre-condition for improving the access, equity and equality of public services available at the local level. The government of Bangladesh can implement a massive social mobilization program to encourage rural communities to solve their own common concerns and share any available local resources among themselves.

A special judiciary bench may be established at the district level to deal with violence against rural poor women and to enforce laws regarding trafficking, dowry, rape, forced prostitution, and acid throwing. BRAC has a wing to deal with violence against rural poor women. Courts at the local level need to criminalize and penalize the traffickers, syndicates and operators. At the same time, the victims of these crimes need to be empowered in order to help them rebuild their lives. This can be accomplished through rehabilitation in health and the provision of other social services. Men should be made to take responsibility for their sexual behavior and so the courts need to strictly enforce the existing laws with the help of honest law-enforcing personnel. The good news is currently courts are serious penalizing/ criminalizing rapists.

Margaret Shuler's "Strategy Matrix" provides techniques to work with the structural components of the law, so that we may find a strategy to assist women in Bangladesh who face violations of human rights. Strategies need to improve women's access to the legal system and services. The gender network committee at the upzilla (sub-district level) can be set up to monitor legal actions and enforcement of legal laws for establishing women's human rights.

At the same time the international community should also come forward and create pressure to governments to take serious action and to eliminate poor women's human rights violations. The Millennium Development Goals are an example of such action. However, without the development of women, Bangladesh will not be able to successfully accomplish their MDGs. Therefore, if a country wants to address the feminization of poverty, it also needs a clear definition of who constitutes poor women (bottom 50%) so that any projects or programs designed to assist poor women can be exclusively created for the bottom 50% of women. Grameen bank targets only poor women in Bangladesh to provide its services to them.

Although this essay covers all three MDGs as well as their targets and indicators, below I want to stress the urgent need to include another target under the first MDG. That is to establish poor women's human rights by promoting income generating programs and self-employment through the provision of collateral free micro-credit. The urgency of this proposition is important as poor women often go unnoticed in the development agenda, as they are invisible in society (Hick, 2004). For instance, the MDG that promotes universal primary education is too general, and does not specifically target poor women. Without being clearly targeted, women will be left out of education because of extreme poverty. Although the Bangladesh government has a good policy with respect to increasing literacy rates, this policy will only reach the poor with good governance and strong support for such national strategies. Good governance and government support is essential for ensuring that poor women are enrolling in vocational training and technology programs and continuing universal education.

7.0. Conclusion

The researcher believes that an independent income program can create the potential to enhance women's status at home and in the community. The Grameen Bank program has proved this opportunity through its micro-lending program. As Kabeer (2003) notes, by increasing women's income, women can have an increased number of choices, networking, greater household decision- making power, greater social status, and greater sense of confidence and independence. Women's empowerment can enable women to oppose authoritative patriarchal power structures through collective action.

Empowering women through education is a big key to change. Otherwise, their human capabilities will not develop, and rich people will eat the fruits of the economy while exploiting and abandoning the poor people. Therefore, there must be opportunities and choice provided for them. This will help to develop their human capabilities and help reduce poverty among women.

Other social, economic and political support at the micro level can assist poor women in the development of their human capabilities. For instance, the rural population needs to operate a variety of self-employment activities. Access to capital via diverse micro-credit and micro-enterprise with other socio-economic programs targeted loan schemes helps to remove the credit constraint and hence accelerates the exits out of poverty. Grameen Bank proofs that micro-credit can create economic and social capital among the rural poor women in Bangladesh (Dowla, 2001). These programs can help to eradicate social discrepancy, gender inequalities, and other social catastrophic activities that affect the bottom 50% of women in rural Bangladesh.

Women's human rights development discourse differs between developed and developing countries. There are various approaches discussed by different authors within the literature. Their literature helps us to understand problems and the position of women in Third World countries. However, I am inclined to agree with Patricia Stamp (1989) and Chandra Mohanty (2003) when they stress the importance of analyzing the use of the literature in development discourse. More specifically, the literature should be used to promote poor women's human rights in Bangladesh, but in such a way that accepts that not all the traditional values of Bangladesh are a constraint to development discourse and practice, and not all Western ideologies can be applied to Bangladesh without considering local contexts. As Lourdes Beneria (1970) would suggest, development relates to Third World countries, gender and globalization, economic adjustment and feminist economics. These themes should be examined as interrelated dimensions that are relevant to external factors affecting the Bangladesh poverty process and inequality. Freire (1981) notes that through constant dialogue and praxis we can free each other and free ourselves from oppressors. Therefore, people must work together to a find permanent freedom.

Margaret Schuler (1986) offers us a method for understanding and challenging the current legal system. Her concept of the structural component of society (i.e., courts, administrations and law enforcement) should be challenged through advocacy. Building networks and organizing public and private protests and rallies can help to fight against women's exploitation. In addition, activities such as seminars, conferences, workshops, community banking, green and social businesses, community education, mass media campaigns, publication of scholarly works, and dissemination of information through popular literature, comic books, posters, dance, brochures, theatre, and poetry can initiate programs for women designed to help them claim their inherent rights.

Furthermore, the laws should be reformed in order to allow women freedom to claim their property rights, and freedom of choice. At the same time, the law needs to raise awareness through legal education to reform unequal power for social justice in the society. Greater government intervention and less government corruption are also needed to assist these women.

All over the world, poor women are living such inhuman lives and are exploited by government and the powerful elites. Therefore, it is urgent that we work to establish basic human rights for the poor women. It becomes a question of morality and thus, our duty to help these disadvantaged people survive in society. Empowerment and autonomy of women and improvement of women's social, economic and political status is essential for the achievement of both a transparent and accountable government, as well as sustainable women human rights in Bangladesh.

Figure-1: **Human Rights Diagram for Bottom 50% Poor Women in Bangladesh. The figure below summaries a human right framework for the empowered of marginalized women in Bangladesh.**

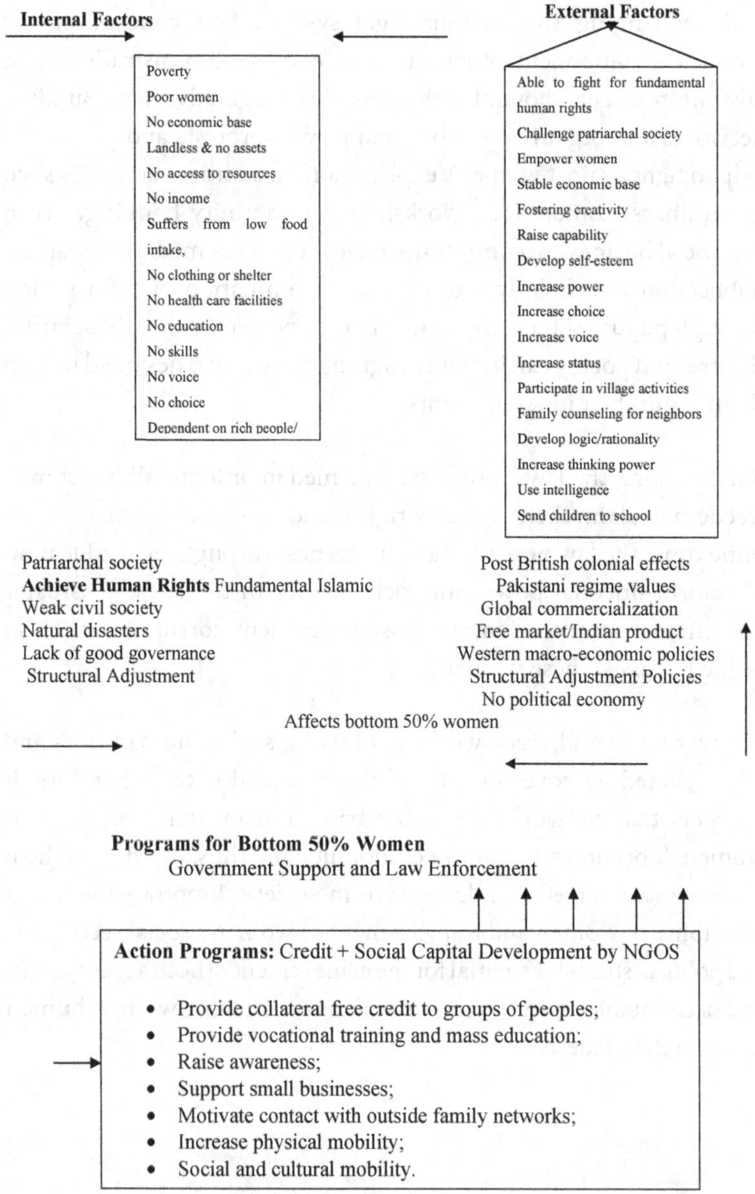

8.0. References

Alam. S.M.S. (1995). *The state, class formation, and development in Bangladesh*. New York: University Press of America, Inc.

Annan, K. (2005). *Grameen Dialogue #60, January 2005*. Dhaka, Bangladesh: Grameen Trust

Beneria, L. (2003). *Gender, development and globalization: Economics as if people mattered*. New York: Routledge

BIDS. (2005). Fighting human poverty: Bangladesh human development report 2000. An overview of the study prepared by the *Bangladesh Institute of Development Studies (BIDS)*. Retrieved June 17, 2005, from http://www.sdnbd.org/sdi/issues/sustainable_development/bd

BMSP. (1997). *State of Human Rights Bangladesh*. Dhaka, Bangladesh: Manobadhikar Samonoy Parishad (BMSP)

Boserup, E. (1970). *Women's role in economic development*. London: Earthscan Publications

Bangladesh Rural Advancement Committee (BRAC). (2005). *BRAC information*. Retrieved July 06, 2005, from http://www.brac.net/

Canadian International Development Agency (CIDA). (n.d.). *Development goals*. Ottawa: International Development Research Center. Retrieved June 5, 2005 from http://www.acdi-cida.gc.ca/whatwedo.htm

CIDA (2001). *Gender profile: Bangladesh*. Retrieved June 5, 2005, from http://www.acdi-cida.gc.ca/cida_ind.nsf/0/60/3ea7adbb8d592e85256b1b007403ef?OpenDocument#1

Chouwdhury, A. (2005). *Grameen Connections*. Newsletter, Vol. 7(4). Washington, USA. The Grameen Foundation

Dollar, D., & Gatti, R. (2003). In N. Kabeer, *Gender mainstreaming in poverty eradication and the millennium development goals* (pp. 39-44). Ottawa: International Development Research Center

Dowla, A. (2001). *Grameen Dialogue #60, January 2005*. Dhaka: Grameen Trust

Elson, D. (1998). Talking to the boys: Gender and economic growth models. In C. Jackson & R. Pearson (Eds.), *Feminist vision of development: Gender analysis and policy,* (pp. 155-170). New York: Routledge

Elson, D. (2003). Gender justice human rights, and neo-liberal economics politics, In Molyneux, M. & Razavi, S. (Eds.), *Gender justice development, and rights* (pp 78-114). New York: Oxford University Press

Frank, A.G. (1970). Dependence, imperialism and underdevelopment. In J. Cockcroft, A. Gunder Frank & D. Johnson (Eds.), *Dependence and Underdevelopment: Latin America's Political Economy,* (pp. 3-17). New York: Doubleday & Company, Inc.

Freire, P. (1981). *Pedagogy of the Oppressed.* New York: Continuum

Grameen Bank. (2005). *Grameen Dialogue #60, January 2005.* Dhaka, Bangladesh: Grameen Trust

Gramsci, A. (1971). The Intellectuals. In Q. Hoare & G. N. Smith (Eds.), *Selections from the prison notebook,* (pp.4-23). New York: International Publishers

Hick, S. (2004). *Social welfare in Canada-understanding income security.* Toronto: Thomson Educational Publishing, Inc.

International Monetary Fund (IMF). (n.d.). Retrieved June 17, 2005, from http://www.imf.org/external/pubs/ft/aa/aa01.htm

Kabeer, N. (2003) *Gender mainstreaming in poverty eradication and the millennium development goals.* Ottawa: International Development Research Center

Karim, A., & Nazmul, K. (1976). *Changing society of India, Pakistan and Bangladesh.* Dhaka: Nawroze Ketabistan

Miers, Maria (2005).*Search for a new vision,* Dhaka: Narigrantha Prabartanas

Mohanty, C. (2003). *Families without borders: Decolonizing theory, practicing solidarity.* Durham: Duke University Press

Nussabaum, M. (1988) Women's capabilities and social justice. In Molyneux, M. & Razavi, S. (Eds.), *Gender, justice, development and rights* (pp 45-74). New York: Oxford University Press

Natsios, A. S. (2005, April 22). Democratic opportunity and the Islamic World. Speech presented by Andrew S. Natsios on behalf of the

Centre for the Study of Islam and Democracy. Retrieved June 2, 2005, from http://www.usaid.gov./press/speches/2005/sp050422.html

Paider, P. (2002) Encounters between feminism, democracy and reformism in contemporary Iran. In Molyneux, M. & Razavi, S. (Eds.), *Gender Justice Development, and Rights*, (pp 78-114). New York: Oxford University Press

Pally Karma- Sahayak Foundation (PKSF) (2005). *PKSF profile*. Retrieved July 07, 2005 from http://www.pksf-bd.org/aprm_summit_new_list_workshops_panelists.htm

Polani, K. (1978). *The great transformation*: Frankfurt: suhrkamp

Quadir, F. (2003). How "civil" is civil society? Authoritarian state partisan civil society and the struggle for democratic development in Bangladesh. *Canadian Journal of Development Studies*, Vol. 24(3), pp. 425-438.

Rouf, A. K. (2012). The Advantages of Micro-credit Lending Programs and the Human Capabilities Approach for Women's Poverty Reduction and Increased Human Rights in Bangladesh. *International Journal of Research Studies in Management*. Vol. 2(1), pp. 25-36.

Said, E.W. (1978). *Orientalism*. New York: Penguin Books

Schuler, M. (Ed.). (1986). *Empowerment, and the law: Strategies of Third World women*. Washington, D.C.: OEF International

Seguino, S. (2003). In N. Kabeer, *Gender mainstreaming in poverty eradication and the millennium development goals* (pp. 39-44). Ottawa: International Development Research Center

Shiva, V. (1988). *Staying alive: Women, ecology, development*. London: Zed Press

South Asia Foundation. (2001). *Bangladesh profile*. Retrieved on June 08, 2005, from http://www.southasiafoundation.org/saf/bngladesh/banglastats.asp

Slayter, Barbara (2003). *Southern exposure*, Bloomfield, CA: Kumarian Press nc.

Stamp, P. (1989). Technology, gender, power in Africa. Ottawa: International Development Research Centre

Trainer, F. 91989). *Developed to death: Rethinking Third World development*, London; Green Print

United Nations. Department of Public Information. (2000). Gender Equality, Development and Peace for the Twenty First Century. *Women 2000: Beijing.* Proceedings of a conference on Women's rights. New York. 5-9 June 2000. Retrieved June 17, 2005 from, http://www.un.org/womenwatch/daw/followup/session/presskit/fs1.htm

US Agency for International Development (USAID). (n.d.). Retrieved June 17, 2005 from http:///www.usaid.govt/about_usaid/

Novak, J.J. (1993). *Bangladesh reflection on the water.* Bloormington: Indiana University Press

World Bank. (n.d.). *Data and statistics for Bangladesh.* Retrieved June 17, 2005, from http://www.worldbank.org/

World Trade Organization (WTO). (n.d.). The future of the WTO. Retrieved June 17, 2005, from http://www.wto.org.

Yunus, M. (2010). *Building social business*, New York: Public Affairs

Yunus, M. (2002). *Grameen Dialogue #52, October 2002.* Dhaka, Bangladesh: Grameen Trust.

Yunus, M. (1997). *Banker to the Poor.* London: Arum Press.

Grameen Bank Women Borrowers Non-formal Adult Learning Transformation in Bangladesh

Abstract

Grameen Bank (GB), a micro credit organization in Bangladesh, targets adult women to serve them for their economic development who were illiterate, using non-formal adult learning techniques. GB's adult learning information has in 'Sixteen Decisions' which inculcate the socio-economic expectations aimed at improving the social-economic well-being of GB borrowers. It is important to know the efficacy of adult learning strategies that has used by GB to create this paradigm shift and transformation in local communities. How does the GB adult learning process enables GB's women borrowers to mobilize group solidarity, leadership development and apply the sixteen decisions in their daily life? How can other NGOs and other countries benefit from GB's women adult learning procedures? These questions are answered in this paper which uses the available literature on adult learning, literature on GB as well as the author's personal working experiences with GB to interrogate the application of non-formal adult learning which creates transformation shift in socio-economic well- being on women borrowers life. The objective of this study is to present the impact of GB non-formal adult learning on the socio-economic development in local communities. The study finds GB non-formal adult learning programs impacted upon GB women borrowers' socio-economic development in Bangladesh. Exponential improvements in literacy is happening, (100%) of GB borrowers are able to sign their names on the documents which show signs of achievements in adult learning. However, if GB non-formal adult learning strategies could streamline, this would generate more non-formal adult learning social justice reforms among the borrowers of GB in Bangladesh.

Key Words: Grameen Bank Sixteen Decisions; Grameen Bank seven-day workshops; Non-formal adult learning; and women empowerment.

1. Introduction

Grameen Bank has run its group-based collateral free micro-credit and savings schemes, and campaigning sixteen discussions–through forming groups, centers, chairmen, center chiefs and issuing loans to its women borrowers (Ahamed & Hakim, 2004). All these activities are done by oral face-to-face non-formal adult trainings and communications by GB twenty five thousand field staff to GB 8.6 million borrowers across Bangladesh. GB borrowers' adult learning is similar with Susan M. Brigham and Patricia A. Gouthro (2006) concept andragogy-learn in more individualized contexts (p. 84). Adult learning is about useful knowledge that helps create a more equitable world at individual, family, community and societal levels (Ahamed, 1999; 2002a; 2002b). It is about to build a more stable, safe and just society for the disadvantaged (Nesbit, 2006, p. 17). It also assists people development of their personality (Jung, 1954). GB credit transactions trainings, signatures learning and GB "Sixteen Decisions" campaigning among GB women borrowers through face-to-face group training, weekly center meetings, seven days workshops, exchange visits, annual gathering festivals and other action programs enhances socio-economic development to its borrowers in order to empower them in their family and in their community (Rouf, 2011). GB disseminates information that solicits women borrowers to become social actors and economic actors in Bangladesh. GB non-formal oral face-to- face adult trainings, communications and campaigns are effective for empowering marginalized people in Bangladesh.

2. Objectives

1. To study the operational practices of GB adult trainings and learning, communications and campaigns tools and processes for educating its borrowers on Grameen Bank "Sixteen Decisions" and its loan transactions in Bangladesh;
2. To explore the role of GB adult learning practices in exposing socio-economic and environmental messages to GB borrowers;
3. To examine the implications of Grameen Bank adult learning in GB borrowers daily life, family decision making practices and civic engagement in their community?; and
4. To explore and identify limitations of GB adult learning strategies and critical thinking ability among GB borrowers.

Through these questions, the study identifies factors that deter women borrowers' ability to participate fully in family spaces and public spaces within Bangladesh society.

3. Statement of the Problem

GB deals with illiterate, semi-literate adult clients. Hence it is important to know GB adult learning tools, procedures and strategies that has been practicing; what outcomes have happened at the grassroots levels because there has not been enough study on GB's adult learning and its influence to women's borrowers' private space and public space issues in Bangladesh. Therefore, author research focuses upon GB adult learning strengths and weaknesses for transforming GB non-formal training impact to empowering women's family space and public space development in patriarchal Bangladesh.

4. Research Questions

The study seeks to address the following two research questions (1) Does the Grameen Bank trainings/communications/adult learning process able for GB's borrowers in transforming group solidarity, center leadership development and apply sixteen decisions in their daily life. (2) Are they are able to challenge and critical thinkers in Bangladesh? These questions are important in Bangladesh context because Grameen Bank's goals are not simply about financial credit, but it has a broader view of changing the role of women in Bangladesh. Its objective is not only to make marginalized women become economic actors, but also to empower women to participate as equals in the family decision making process and engage in public settings (Henry, 2006; Joan, et al., 2006; Yunus, 2008)

5. Bangladesh Adult learning Context

The Adult literacy rate (15 years and above) is 41.6 percent (Bangladesh Bureau of Statistics, 2001; Chowdhury et. al 2002; Government of Bangladesh, 1990). However, three years the literacy rate for the adult population 15 years and over is 38.8% (Education Watch 2005).

Table 1.1: Literacy rate by age and sex

Age	Sex			Difference (Female-Male)
	Females	Males	Both	
11-14	56.9	55.5	56.2	1.4
15-19	60.8	67.6	63.8	-6.8
20-24	44.0	62.1	51.6	-18.1
25-29	31.4	46.8	38.2	-15.4
30-34	31.1	42.3	36.3	-11.2
35-39	27.6	35.7	31.6	-8.1
40-44	21.0	38.8	30.3	-17.8
45-49	15.9	41-7	28.4	-25.8
50-54	10.3	40.9	17.9	-30.6
55-59	7.3	33.0	20.7	-25.7
60-64	6.7	39.4	23.4	-32.7

65-69	2.5	32.0	19.4	-29.5
70-74	4.6	21.2	14.2	-16.6
75 and above	2.0	25.6	16.1	-23.6

Source: Education Watch National Survey (2002).

Literate rate was highest for the age group 15-19 years, at 63.8 percent, with decreasing rates for the older age-groups. The low level literacy is a barrier to better productivity and earning. This situation suggests the need for an emphasis on the functionality of literacy skills and linking literacy activities with specific efforts to improve productivity and earning of people.

The non-governmental development organizations (NGOs) have been running literacy centres since 1960`. The state also has spent substantial resources in literacy activities in the last two decades. The most prominent public sector literacy program is known as the Total Literacy Movement (TLM) carried out on a large scale in the second half of the last decade (Hussain, 2000; The Daily Star, 2002). However, non-literate by different levels of literacy skills in gender gap also exists in Bangladesh. Females lagged 12 percentage points behind their male counterparts (35.6 percent vs 47.6 percent (Education Watch 2005; UNIECF, 1992). In the rural areas non-literate rate is 53% females 56.5% and males 48.5%. Urban non-literate females are 34.8% and male's 25.2%. (NABBEIS, 2000) The below Table-2 data reflects different levels of non-literate in terms of reading, writing and numeracy varies.

Table-2: Literacy rates in rural and urban areas in Bangladesh

Assessment areas	Rural Bangladesh		Urban Bangladesh	
	Females	Males	Females	Males
Reading	41.4	48.3	63.4	72.9
Writing	25.7	34.3	50.6	62.9
Numeracy	24.0	39.8	48.2	66.6
Applications of all	21.2	37.6	45.5	65.0

Source: Education Watch 2002

The Education Watch (2005) findings on literacy do indicate a major national failure-failure in seriousness of effort, in setting priorities right, in applying professionalism to management and decision-making in education, and in lacking a vision and understandings of how literacy and non-formal education programs work (Nath, 2002). Therefore the teaching learning process needed to be transformed in order to get better results (Haq & Haq, 1998). The reason is the very poor quality of mainstream primary education is serious obstacles to better literacy outcomes, since one-third of those who complete primary education still remain illiterate (Education Watch, 2002).

6. Methods of the Study

The paper used author`s own personal working experiences with GB and uses GB secondary data and reviews GB literatures. Author's past experience working with different MFI programs and the application of the Sixteen Decisions has influenced writing this paper. This paper enlarges readers about Grameen Bank adult learning strategies and knowledge.

7. Background of the Study

A key part of GB's strategy is bringing adult women together on weekly basis not only to pay their loans, but also to share experiences, support one another's business, inform sixteen decisions and their applications, and to hear from bank staff about how to keep their family healthy, keep the environment safe and prepare for natural disasters (Rouf, 2011). GB informs and provides these services through face-to-face dialogues between GB borrowers and GB staff. This adult learning process helps GB borrowers to be involved in familial activities, the family decision making process and community engagement, acquire literacy skills, and engage in family as well as community leadership skills so that they may represent themselves in the family and in the community and to be critical to their challenges. This non-formal adult education builds women borrowers' human capabilities and opens opportunities for them. It stimulates and empowers people to participate meaningfully in their own development. The GB Sixteen Decisions consciousness raising campaign and adult learning socio-economic leadership development process occurs through knowing and implementing the Sixteen Decisions; attending the group and center weekly meetings bridges the gap between the public and the private realms (Bouchard, 2006; Burton & Point, 2006; Todd, 1996; Welton, 1995).

8. Literature Review

Adult literacy is a process of developing skills and knowledge and adult people applying these in their life rather than an event that ends with awarding a certificate (Selman & Dampier, 1991). It is an effective literacy involves the integration of speaking, listening and critical thinking with reading and writing (Dawkins 1991; Fenwick, 2006). Adult literacy is part of the process by which illiterate people become aware of their personal situation- and learn to do something about improving it. People who learn to read and to write can play a role in making their world a better place to live. It creates critical thinking among adult learners about their situation and develops consciousness about power, privileges and to challenge them. Moreover the critical adult education can lead to change in the way power is distributed in society (Parlo Freire, cited in UNESCO, 2000; 1997).

According to Draper (1998), Illeris (2002), and Nesbit (2006) adult education context allows organizationally encompassing the three main and enduring traditions of adult education. (1) A set of unyielding social purpose, informed by passion and outrage and rooted in a concern for the less-privileged; (2) A systematic and sustained philosophical and critical analysis that develops the abilities to connect immediately individual experiences with underlying societal structures; and (3) A keen attention to the specific sites, locations, and practices where such purposes and analysis are made real in the lives of people (Freire, 1973,

1972, 1970; Nesbit, 2006). English & Gillen (2000); and Leona English (2006) finds adult learning helps to know issues like power, identity, the subject and discourse and how these issues relate to and plays out in adult education. Sue Scott (2006) takes adult learning–the concept of transformation and explores its relevance to change at both personal and social levels.

Sawchuk, P. (2006), Becker, G., (1993), and Bouchard, P. (2006) link human capital theory with adult education where he finds the application of human capital theory in adult education could result adult learners to economic and social responsibilities; learners could be able to relate between issues, and work and employment. Moses Coady (1939), pioneer of adult education, in his Book 'Master of their own destiny' finds that adult learners enlightened and gained power and act to change their life situations through adult education. For example, the United Farmers of Alberta, Canada and the Saskatchewan Grain Growers Association (SGGA) build an educative democracy (Ibid, p. 25; Henson, 1946). Farmers learned democracy by actively participating in meetings where they learn to speak and act confidently. The farm local was a key educative form through lectures, study clubs, speakers, networks, farm newspapers, and the annual convocation. Through these social learning processes, individuals combined their intelligence (Tomkins, 1921). They used the dialogical methods in their just learning society. Hence adult education is the holistic learning society frame, whose purpose is to foster a more just and self-conscious learning process (Grace, 2006; and Selman, 1998).

Wendy Burton and Gwen Point (2006) narrative about Indigenous education methodology is look, listen and learn. It is context specific and avoids imposing ones will on another. Storytelling is an essential feature of the lifelong learning of adult members of Aboriginal communities. Ceremonies play an essential role in imparting lessons and the further education of specialists (Poonwassie, 2001). Wendy Burton and Gwen Point (2006) mention that the grassroots activism of the 1960s resulted in community development such as leadership training, and consciousness raising which led to the development of Indian rights organizations-the National Indian Brotherhood.

Elizabeth A. Lange. (2006) believes that adult educators should be aware and critical as part of reflective thinking and reasoned inquiry. Through the process of adult learning, marginalized peoples can collectively uncover the power relations and hegemonic ideologies that disguise the true nature of social relations that prevent them from fulfilling their aspirations. GB sixteen decisions campaigns enlightened GB borrowers towards wellbeing life. This enlightened education attempts to resists the deepest levels of oppression and enhances ethical thinking of people (Foucault (1984).

Leona M. English (2006) studies Canadian Association for the Study of Adult Education (CASAE) from 1990 to 2004 and finds that adult education affects adults thinking, views of practice and perspective transformation. It embraces creative responses. Andre P. Grace. (2006) believes that critical adult education has predominantly concerned itself with advancing social and cultural forms of education focused on life, learning and work for adults. Moreover, Sue Scott (2006) believes that adult education includes engaging and analyzing adult change in progressive, positive ways. It helps adults to learn critical thinking and develop consciousness skills that can facilitate understanding of what is happening. Lifelong learning was advocated- particularly by UNESCO –as a model that would promote a better society and quality of life and allow people to adapt to and control change (OECD, 1996; UNDP, 1999; UNESCO, 2000; and WCEFA, 1990). Hence it can be concluded in general, education and training are still based on raising an individual's competitiveness and human capital, and his/ her capacity for innovation and entrepreneurship. According to Kjell Rubenson and Judith Walker (2006) lifelong learning and new economy made connection between learning and earning.

Adult learning also includes environmental non-formal education. Public environmental education (EAE) is about individual small change, expert knowledge, being with a deficit model-full of challenges (Clover, 2003; and Darlene, 2006). Hence UNESCO environmental education includes awareness raising, information sharing, and individual behavior and attitude change. Here the key is to promote individual actions. GB 4th slogan is campaigning for planting plants and grow vegetables throughout the year that GB borrowers do. Moreover, GB borrowers are careful about environmental degradation.

9. Adult Education Programs in Different Countries

After Second World War, many newly independent nations launched mass literacy programmes/campaigns or eradication of illiteracy. One of the most widely publicized mass literacy campaigns was launched in Cuba in January 1961. Fidel Castro declared Cuba to be a: 'Territory free from literacy' on December 1961 (Jennings, 2000). The Nicaraguan Literacy Crusade also receives world attention. A total of 80,000 literacy teachers were trained for the campaign (Deneer, 1981). After the Communist takeover of power in China in 1949, a campaign was started to achieve universal literacy. Thus the five countries including the Soviet Union reportedly made drastic reductions in the national illiteracy rate. The most well-known mass adult literacy programmes in the developing world was initiated by Dr. Frank `Laubach, an American missionary working in the Philippines called: "Each One Each One," whereby volunteer tutors each taught an illiterate, who in turn would teach someone else.

The Experiential World Literacy Programme (EWLP), UNESCO launched in 1967 that included adult education, which earlier called fundamental education. EWLP basic idea was to combine literacy and numeracy with a program of education in basic vocational skills directly linked to the occupational needs of participants. This life-oriented literacy program not only concerns with economic, but also on health, nutrition, family planning, and other concerns related to daily living. The Total Literacy Campaign (TLC) in India was launched in 1988, has been undertaken in over 550 districts with a target of making 100 million people literate in a decades in the age group of 15-35 years. Freirean concretization influences can be seen in the Action Aid education projects (Action Aid, 2000) in Bangladesh and other South Asian and African countries named Regenerated Freirean Literacy through Empowering Community Techniques (REFLECT).

10. GB Micro-credit Program and Sixteen Decision Campaign

Grameen Bank 'Sixteen Decisions' is a socio-civic ecologial consciousness raising program and GB's group and center formation by-laws have leadership practices built-in. Grameen Bank group based micro credit operation meetings, campaigns, and trainings directly address their poverty issue (Rouf, 2011). Now in GB 97% are women borrowers. Majority women borrowers (75%) are below the poverty line (Yunus, 2011). However, women's economic growth cannot ensure women's free voice, choice and liberation from their male dominated families and communities. Hence GB designed Sixteen Decisions for borrowers for informing them for their wellbeing.

11. GB Sixteen Decisions

GB's field employees voluntarily discuss different issues and Sixteen Decisions, which are related to GB women borrowers social, economic, cultural, environmental and civic public space exploitation with clients in different venues, including the client's mini meetings, orientation meetings, open house meetings, weekly center meetings and especially in face-to-face informal group training sessions before clients receive their loans. GB has developed women's civic consciousness-raising program through following the Sixteen Decisions by its clients. Although all sixteen decisions are designed and stated in a simple way, few of them have direct tangible messages to create awareness among borrowers about socio-civic and economic issues. For example, among GB's sixteen decisions the 4th, 5th, 7th, 8th, 9th 11th, 12th, 14$^{th, 15th}$ and 16th decisions are directly related to women's private and public space development in the community. Some sixteen decisions principles have intangible social messages that contribute to creating positive spaces for women in their family and public space. For example, the 11th slogan is to initiate dowry-free marriages among borrowers and their children, the 12th slogan is that borrowers shall not inflict any injustice on anyone, neither shall they allow anyone to do so. Among GB's sixteen decisions, the 12th, 14th, 15th and 16th decisions are directly related to women civic rights consciousness-raising and promote a rights-based approach. Although all GB programs are targeted to women's socio-economic development, but its 'Sixteen Decisions' campaigns, workshops, and trainings are aimed for their familial and community development. A study conducted by Kazi Rouf (2011) shows that 87% GB borrowers able to take decisions by all family members together. Although GB sixteen decisions don't have direct campaign for taking family decisions jointly; however, it is the transformation of GB adult learning outcomes that has resulted family violence reduces among GB families. However, still in some questions exist are all GB borrowers able to be self-critical, challenge status quo, and achieved their full potentials and self-empowerment in the community?

12. Different Strategies for the GB Sixteen Decisions Campaign

In 1984-1999, GB distributed the Sixteen Decisions' flyers to each center and asked borrowers to discuss them in groups in the weekly center meetings and other leisure time. GB field officials participated in the dowry-less marriages if borrowers invited them. Moreover, borrowers showed their center schools, vegetable plots, orchards, sanitary latrines and improved stoves to the GB field staff that they had grown and constructed. Borrowers also made separate savings for their children's education and children's wellbeing. This demonstrated that the different GB workshops, training programs, meetings, discussions and development programs have influenced the socio-economic life of the women borrowers of Grameen Bank.

12.1. GB Borrowers Seven Days Workshop

GB women once attended seven-day workshops and one-day workshops where women borrowers exchanged information, and follow-ups to the different workshops were conducted in 1979-1999. These workshops were conducted at the branches. Here, every participant had the chance to speak their life stories and build confidence, creating an atmosphere of warmth. These discussions were about the realities of women borrowers' lives such as discussions around their past suffering from poverty with children. The Grameen Bank women borrowers seven days workshops gave GB women borrowers new energy, brought out their own creativity, added new life skills knowledge and drove them to improve the male domination status quo (Bashin, 1991).

Usually one female borrower per center participated in the seven-day workshops and one-day workshops of Grameen Babk. In each workshop, thirty-five GB women borrowers from thirty-five centers would participate. Breakfast and launch were served in the workshop from the bank. In addition, the bank distributed fruits/timber samplings, vegetable seeds, ORS packets, Alum packets and ideodized salt packets to the participants. Two women program assistants facilitated each workshop. Different posters on women's liberation, women's health, children's health, balanced diets, vegetable production, homestead gardening, backyard poultry, community forestry, and adult literacy were displayed in the workshop room. In the workshop, GB also demonstrated how to prepare oral saline at their home for diarrhoea prevention, sanitary latrines, safe child delivery, cooking, soil improvement, stoves, solar energy, and biogas plants etc.

Moreover, in the workshops different subject specialists' resource persons came from outside; like medical doctors from public hospitals, educationalists, nutritionists, nursery planners, agriculturalists, livestock officers, fisheries officers, cottage industry officers. They talked about primary health care, women's health, children's heath, child nutrition, child education, livestock vaccination, crop production, and integrated pest management (IPM) in the workshops and deliver lecturers. Moreover, GB high officials like zonal managers, area managers, program officers and branch managers of Grameen Bank also talked in the workshops. Workshop facilitators, GB officials discussed in detail the 'themes and benefits of the Sixteen Decisions' to the participants. GB officials explained the effects of dowry, teenage marriage, the benefits of using sanitary latrines, women's unity etc. Workshop participants arranged dowry-less marriages in the workshop and GB praised those who arranged dowry less marriages and discouraged teenage marriage. GB field employees discussed those initiatives in the weekly center meetings too. It is important to note that workshops lectures avoid one way delivering lectures in workshops sessions, rather enhance interactive dialogues that are more effective to workshops' participants.

Kanud Illeris (2002) finds adult learning is the building blocks of human development in the areas of cognition, emotion, and social interaction. In these perspective, although the GB Sixteen Decisions campaigns do not exactly follow the strategies and themes of the western type of consciousness-raising discussions like women experiencing violence from their male partners, sexism, mothering, women housewification, discrimination of gender division of labour, women's subordination, women's abuse and domestic violence, personal is political; however, GB officials discussed the process of women's marginalization, women's exploitation, injustice and oppression process by the elites, money lenders and landlords. GB always gave advice to its borrowers to see their daughters and sons as equals, not to discriminate on children based on sex, rather to give them all an education. GB advises its clients to instead of spending money on a dowry for their daughter's wedding rather to spend money on her education so that she could become exposed and aware of her different rights, and issues in the family and in the community.

12.2. GB Follow-up Workshops

Grameen Bank also organized follow-ups to the seven-day workshops where participants share their ideas, skills and knowledge with their center members immediately after the workshops. Moreover, GB women clients conducted one-day picnic gatherings within their neighbourhoods after three months of the workshops where they cook together, eat together, play together, discuss together about their groups, center and identified problems and issues for solving collectively. In this gathering, GB employees also joined and discussed and reviewed the center performances.

12.3. GB Exchange Visit Program

Paulo Freire in his book *Pedagogy of the Oppressed* (1970) and *Education for Critical Consciousness* (1973) uses the term consciousness, understand what one reads and to write, creates and recreates an attitude-a self-transformation producing a stance of intervention in one's context (Freire, 1973, cited in Jennings 1990). The critical consciousness transformation applications can also see through exchange-visit programs of Gramen Bank where center chiefs stayed in other branch centers clients' houses for three days. Then hosted center chiefs stayed in guest center chiefs' houses of the other branch for three days. At the 7th day both women borrowers' and branch mangers sit together and reviewed borrowers' observations and experiences in the review session. Borrowers discussed what they observed and learnt from the exchange visits to other branch centers: Women borrowers' loan utilizations and their businesses status, children's education, housing, whether the Sixteen Decisions were followed by the borrowers individually, and collectively in centers, balanced diet preparation, harmonious relationships with the family members, used sanitary latrines, drank pure drinking water, grew and ate vegetables, mentioned center discipline, integrity among center members etc. Through this exchange visit program, GB women borrowers identified each one's positive and negative features of the Sixteen Decisions, their loan performance portfolios and the respective centers' discipline. Women borrowers this physical movements to other centers in other branches, attending different center meetings as guests drove them to develop their psychological development and social mobility in their life by networking among neighbouring branches' women borrowers; it helped them to share, exchange and learn ideas from homogeneous likeminded women borrowers. However, now these excellent programs are closed in GB because of funding and GB field staff overloaded with loans transactions.

12.4. GB Borrowers Annual Gatherings

Sue M. Scott. (2006) identifies individuals intend to learn from events and messages. This theory implication can be found in GB annual gatherings. GB women borrowers' gathered annually (*Barsha Purti*) and celebrated their business fairs in every branch every year until 1995. In this annual gathering, 1500-3000 borrowers gather together in their locality; chat and interactions each other and sell their products in these gatherings. Children jointly showed their parades, gymnastics, dance, songs and theatre in these occasions. Sometimes, Muhammed Yunus participated and celebrated these annual festivals fairs and children's games along with borrowers. These annual gatherings had an impact on borrowers' lives, and their family members. For example, they feel they are not alone or isolated, rather they assumed they are important people and are united in the community. Moreover, the rural elites saw these events and saw that these people had awakened and were participating in the social-economic life of the community. These annual gathering festivals have multiple impacts in borrowers' leadership development in their private and public life; however, now this program has closed because bank branches need a long time and a large budget to organize such events every year. The field employees find it is now difficult for them to manage time to organize such huge events in addition to their huge loan disbursement and loan collection jobs. A bank worker now deals with 600 borrowers' different types of loan proposals-flexible loans, education loans, and micro-enterprise loans, collect pension schemes money, selection of children for scholarships etc., loan disbursement, loan collection, savings collection, and group training.

12.5. Grameen Bank Women Borrowers Leadership Skills Development

Moreover, GB's group, center leadership practices built in Grameen Bank peer lending credit program has been trying to develop their leadership development and to empower them to develop their decision making abilities within their families as well as in the public space. Borrowers' understanding of GB's by-law and Sixteen Decisions slogans can help them remove barriers in empowering women against male domination in family spaces and public spaces in the villages. When these barriers are understood by women, it is easier for them to address the issues of women's empowerment and leadership development in private and public spaces. For example, GB borrowers stand against and protest against GB dismantled government policy in Bangladesh in 2013. Now Government of Bangladesh withheld GB dismantle policy.

Through center meetings discussions and interactions among them, GB borrowers become exposed to various issues and are informed about different developmental information, interact with their centre members resulting in the development of a harmonious relationship among centre members and develop social solidarity, integrity, and promote cohesion and women's awareness about their various human rights issues. GB borrowers' weekly meetings have implications to women intra-household power relations, 'family partnerships', their cognitive development and adult learning dialogue engagement sensitized them about their deprivation. These adult learning dialogues develop their confidence, reinforce and nurture them to achieve gender equality; however, still patriarchy hurts them, confuses them, and makes them inferior, invisible, disempowered and oppressed women in the family and in the community context.

Bangladeshi many scholars realize that patriarchal oppressions are unacceptable and uncomfortable for them (Abdullah, 1973; Jahan, 1995; Mahamud, 2004; Rathgeber, 1990) because husbands, fathers and brothers are controlling their wives, daughters and sisters respectively; women are not free from patriarchal dominance in their society. Although GB borrowers are not challenging patriarchal values and norms where they are living; however, GB sixteen decisions adult learning campaign has created aware them about this issue. As a result, the patriarchal values and norms are melting down as their logical arguments cautions to their mates and community elites.

13. GB Adult Learning is working for GB Women Borrowers' Financial and Non-financial Development

GB has initiated several projects for marginalized women's income generation and environmental projects for increasing their self-employment and paid-employment and to raise awareness about various issues that are related to marginalized women in the villages in Bangladesh. GB orients these programs to its borrowers through non-formal adult learning training, discussions and dialogues that mentions earlier in the paper. GB different literatures mention that GB is successful to implement is different schemes like micro-credit, savings mobilization, education loans, housing loans, latrine loans, handloom loans, crop production loans, agricultural projects for irrigation, seed production, seed preservation, distributing vegetable seeds, oral saline (ORS), alum distribution for pure drinking water, crop processing machines, community forestation, fortified yogurt plants for eradication of child malnutrition, eye hospitals, rural pathological clinics, paramedic clinics, livestock development, poultry development, rural children's education center, cell phones, nursing training, rural garments, mini bio-gas plants, home solar system, and improved stove distribution (Todd, 1996). All these tangible material development projects and intangible projects (civic development, leadership development, critical thinking and challenge status quo), ideas disseminate and organized and conducted by face-to-face workshops, trainings and meetings. GB provides information on public health, nutrition, adult education, women's rights, immunization, vaccination for livestock, integrated pest management (IPM), and homestead gardening for GB borrowers in the centers (Ibid, 1996).

Several NGOs and many international organizations are attempting to address the feminization of poverty, the dowry issue and to empower women in Bangladesh, but they are working piecemeal and often cancel out each other's efforts. Therefore, NGOs alliance with an inclusive women's collective action awareness empowerment project and campaign needs to be included, which should be an integrated development program that includes income-generation, education, health, agricultural and legal services for poor women at the village level. This is urgently needed because for poor women, their poverty is not just an issue of increasing income, and fulfilling basic needs, but fulfilling their fundamental human rights (Collins, 2006), abolishing dowry, teenage marriage, gender division of labour, sex discrimination, the devaluation of women's domestic chores, and the abuse of women in the family spheres and public spheres still are concern too.

14. Revision of the Sixteen Decisions and revitalizing the Sixteen Decisions Adult Learning Awareness Campaign

Currently, GB is not organizing Sixteen Decisions awareness campaign workshops to explain the significance of the Sixteen Decisions to women. Now, GB has begun printing the Sixteen Decisions on the backside of the borrowers' loan pass book and borrowers themselves can read these sixteen decisions and possibly reflect on how they might impact the socio-civic-environmental issues they face. The campaign through printed material supply strategy is not enough to raise awareness among the borrowers of the challenges and opportunities they face for socio-economic development for marginalised people (Bhola, 1984). However, GB women borrowers fell free and comfortable to visit GB offices, and to work with GB employees. For example, Majeda, a GB borrower says,

> "My husband is alive. To do public functions, it requires interactions with males, but religious leaders' are against it and claim that women are breaking Purdah. Society may treat me badly unveiled and I might be unaccepted in my society. However, in GB, we women can retain our purdah because there is a separate restroom for women in grameen bank offices. Moreover GB officials respect us. I don't care village whispering."

GB Sixteen Decisions campaign and its implementation by GB women borrowers follows the *Sustainable Development Approach* too because GB women borrowers not only encompasses income-generation, and bring money in their family but the 'Sixteen Decisions' campaign is also a process that incorporates people-centered development (Joan, 2006; Korten, 2003; and Sen,1996) where massive women have participated in this 'Sixteen Decisions' campaign for their socio-economic and cultural development. Moreover, GB adult learning different principles and slogans are socially, environmentally and economically sound, follow sustainable business practices and promote stewardship of the local social economy.

GB borrowers are gradually moving to make their space in all local councils, regional councils, and national councils; and participate in the public decision making processes. Elites people now counts them, sit them in elites meeting, or any other public occasions and events. Previously these disadvantaged people were used to work as labors in elite' lands, houses; now they become their colleagues in the councils. For example, in 2008, there were 79 Grameen Bank women borrowers running for Upzilla vice-chairmen for the first time in Bangladesh. In each of the constituencies of the Upzilla vice-chairmen, there are 250-300 Grameen Bank centres. These GB borrower candidates visit the centres and campaign and borrowers also campaign for them. This networking process helped these 79 women vice-chairmen win the elections (25% of the total seats) and they are now representing marginalized women. This statistics indicate that gender changes are happening as women are becoming successful in representing their family and holding public offices in patriarchal Bangladesh. Although many borrowers are not yet formal councillors, they are nevertheless invited by their respective formal elites or informal village elites to attend the hearing committee meetings. Now, if village elites make an unjust decision against marginalized women, the Grameen Bank borrowers who participate in the meeting protest against the injustice or suggest an alternative solution. For example, Sophina says:

> "If I am not present in my community hearing committee, the Union Parishad member (Councillors) shall wait until I arrive before making the decision."

14.1. GB Women borrowers' opinion of their engagement in community activities

In this regards a research report (Rouf, 2011) finds that two-thirds of participants' say that they like to participate in community activities. Borrowers' regular visit to Grameen Bank office, center schools, attending workshops enhances their public space development. For example, Halima, borrower of GB says:

> "By joining in GB, my mind has opened, my intelligence, experience and ability to speak to different people has also increased. I distribute relief and senior's allowances to my neighbours. Moreover, I have developed my family decision-making skills."

GB borrowers have also determined for their children education. They do not want their daughters to suffer from illiteracy. Hence

GB women borrowers encourage their daughters and sons to pursue higher education. For example, one GB borrower Shajeda says:

> "I sent my first son to Cyprus and I shall send my second son abroad for studying higher education". This is implication of 5th slogan of the sixteen decisions.

15. Implication of the paper

The end product of this paper encourages Grameen Bank women to be able to use the knowledge for the improvement of personal life and citizenry development in their communities. This paper discovers GB non-declared adult learning and its implication to borrowers' social life.

16. Limitations of the study

The study measures GB women borrowers' family space and public space development through knowing and following the Sixteen Decisions, but do not measure their economic development and micro-enterprise development that is also significant. Without verification, the researcher recorded participants' self-reported statements during the interview. The paper does not have primary survey data on the impact of GB borrowers in their life. The study only reviews GB Sixteen Decisions adult learning campaigns and adult women center meetings outcomes.

16.1. Validity

This paper has intrinsic validity because it defines and reviews non-formal learning skills from adult educators and adult learners' perspectives and contexts. The paper has external validity too through careful review and analysis of GB adult learning strategies and implementations. The GB sixteen decisions adult education campaign lenses from Freirean literacy through empowering GB borrowers' by GB adult learning different techniques and events (seven days workshops, exchange visits and group training etc.).

17. Suggestions and Conclusion

17.1. Suggestions

The GB 'Sixteen Decisions Awareness Creation Campaign' through workshops, mini group sessions, and training has been reduced since 1999. Restarting the 'Sixteen Decisions Awareness Campaign' with a new approach is important. GB could focus on formalizing and streamlining its non-formal adult learning strategies, which could give way to more sustained adult learning that more effectively responds to the needs of GB borrowers' context and to their family members and also other disadvantaged groups in Bangladesh. GB could provide adult training to its field staff following non-formal learning principles, which could be used more effective ways for adult learning. The GB efforts to adult learning could be looked at by other MFIs/ NGOs and receive lesions from it and apply in their programs whatever applicable in Bangladesh.

The author agrees with Education Watch (2005) flexible way with contextual mass adult literacy education program through involvement of adult learners in development activities, including income generations activities, numeracy and financial literacy, public health education, mother and child health education and other specific skills learning programs are important(Becker, 1993; Bouchard, 2006); Ontario Public Health Association & Frontier College, 1989). GB could develop non-formal learning reading materials and written materials with attractive audio video films, cartons, pictures (visual arts) and technical support tailor to the local conditions and with local cultural expressions could make available to GB borrowers' families and other adult learners in Bangladesh.

17.2. Conclusion

As GB borrowers graduate and achieve some of their basic socio-economic and civic issues, Grameen Bank organizes workshops and seminars against male chauvinism and gender discrimination in the family and in the community. Also, it is very important that GB should advocate for law enforcement for dowry violence, teen age marriage at both the macro level and grass roots level. The GB credit and non-credit programs can have a more positive impact on Bangladesh, if the Grameen Bank adult learning facilitates and works more on following two-way dialogue style communication adult learning strategies. These actions would develop women's critical thinking development and leadership development so that they may cope with the existing social norms and values in their communities.

References

Abdullah, T. A., & Zeidenstein S. A. (1982). *Village women of Bangladesh: Prospects for change*. Oxford: Pergamon Press

Action Aid (2000). *REFLECT Condition Unit Annual Report 2000*. London: Action Aid

Ahmed, M. (1999). Literacy and National Education: Overlap and Divergence. In D. Wagner et al (Eds.), *Literacy: An International Handbook*, Colorado: Westview Press

Ahmed, M. (2002a). *Confusion about Literacy: Can it Help Fight poverty?* Dhaka; The Daily Star, 28, April 2002

Ahmed M. (2002b). Lifelong learning and the Learning Society. In M. Singh (Ed.), *Institutionalizing Lifelong Learning*. Hamburg: UNESCO Institute for Education

Ahmed, S. and Hakim, M. A. (2004). *Attacking poverty with micro credit*. Dhaka: The University Press Ltd.

Grace, A. P. (2006). Critical Adult Education: Engaging the social in theory and practice. In Contexts of adult education: Canadian

Perspectives (Eds.), Tara Fenwick, Tom Nesbit, Bruce Spencer, (2006). Toronto: Thompson Educational Publishing, Inc.

Bangladesh Bureau of Statistics (2001). *Population Census 2001. Preliminary Report,* Dhaka: Bangladesh Bureau of Statistics

Becker, G. (1993). *Human Capital,* Chicago: The University of Chicago press

Bhola, H.S. (1984). *Campaigning for Literacy.* Paris: UNESCO

Bouchard, P. (2006). Human Capital and the knowledge economy. In Contexts of adult education: Canadian Perspectives (Eds.), Tara Fenwick, Tom Nesbit, Bruce Spencer. (2006). Toronto: Thompson Educational Publishing, Inc.

Brigham, S. M., & Gouthro, P. A. (2006). Cross-cultural Teaching and Research in Adult Education. In Contexts of adult education: Canadian Perspectives (Eds.), Tara Fenwick, Tom Nesbit, Bruce Spencer. (2006). Toronto: Thompson Educational Publishing, Inc.

Burton, W. & Point, G. (2006). Histories of Aboriginal Adult Education in Canada. In Contexts of adult education: Canadian Perspectives (Eds.), Tara Fenwick, Tom Nesbit, Bruce Spencer. (2006). Toronto: Thompson Educational Publishing, Inc.

Chowdhury, A., R., Nath, S. R., & Chowdhury, R. K. (2002). Enrolment at Primary Level; Gender Differences Disappears in Bangladesh. *International Journal of Educational Development,* Vol. 22, pp. 191-203.

Clover, D. E. (2003). Environmental adult education: Critique and creativity in a globalizing world. In H. L. Hill and D.E. Clover (Eds.), *Environmental adult education: Ecological learning., theory, and practice for socioenvironmental Change* (pp. 5-16). San Francisco: Jossey-Bass

Coady, M. (1939). *Masters of their own destiny.* New York: Harper and Row

Collins, M. (2006). The critical Legacy: Adult education against the claims of capital. In Contexts of adult education: Canadian Perspectives (Eds.), Tara Fenwick, Tom Nesbit, Bruce Spencer. (2006). Toronto: Thompson Educational Publishing, Inc.

Darlene, E. C. (2006). Environmental Adult Education in Canada. In Contexts of adult education: Canadian Perspectives. Eds. Tara

Fenwick, Tom Nesbit, Bruce Spencer. (2006). Toronto: Thompson Educational Publishing, Inc.

Deneer J. T. (1981). The Nicaraguan Literacy Crusade. *Journal of Reading*, Vol. 25, pp. 118-25

Draper, J. (1998). Introduction to the Canadian Chronology. *Canadian Journal for Studies in Adult Education/RCEEA*, Vol. 12(2), pp. 33-43

Education Watch (2005). *Literacy in Bangladesh-Need for a New Vision.* Dhaka: Campaign for Popular Education

Education Watch (2002). *Literacy in Bangladesh-Need for a New Vision.* Dhaka: Campaign for Popular Education

English, L. M., & Gillen, M. A. (2000). A postmodern approach to adult religious education. In A. I. Wilson and E. Hayes (Eds.), *Handbook of adult and continuing education* (pp. 523-538). San Francisco: Jessey-Bass

English, L. M. (2006). Postfoundationalism. In Contexts of adult education: Canadian Perspectives (Eds). Tara Fenwick, Tom Nesbit, Bruce Spencer. (2006). Toronto: Thompson Educational Publishing, Inc.

Fenwick, T. J. (2006). Work, learning and adult education in Canada. In Contexts of adult education: Canadian Perspectives (Eds.), Tara Fenwick, Tom Nesbit, Bruce Spencer. (2006). Toronto: Thompson Educational Publishing, Inc.

Freire, P. (1970). *Pedagogy of the oppressed.* New York: Seabury Press

Freire, P. (1972). *Pedagogy of Oppressed.* Harmondsworth: Penguin

Freire, P. (1973). *Education for Critical Consciousness.* London: Sheed and Ward

Foucault, M. (1984). "What is enlightenment" In P. Rabinow (Ed.), *The Foucault reader* (C. Porter, Trans.; pp.32-50). New York: Pantheon Books

Government of Bangladesh (1990). The Education (compulsory) Act, 1990. *Bangladesh Gazette.* Vol. 5, Additional Issue, 13 February 1990. Dhaka: Government of Bangladesh 9in Bangla)

Grace, A. P. (2006). Critical Adult Education: Engaging the social in theory and practice. In Contexts of adult education: Canadian Perspectives (Eds.), Tara Fenwick, Tom Nesbit, Bruce Spencer, (2006). Toronto: Thompson Educational Publishing, Inc.

Haq, M. & Haq, K. (1998). *Human Development in South Asia 1998.* Karachi: Oxford University Press

Hussain, S. (2000). *Total Literacy Movement (TLM): Learning through Experience.* :Proshikhyan, Vol. 8(2), pp. 1-10

Henry, S. (2006). *How MFI's and their clients can have a positive impact on the environment. Good practices in business development services: how do we enhance entrepreneurial skills in MFIs clients?* Paper presented at the *Micro Credit Summit* Halifax held in November 2006. Toronto: Alterna Savings

Henson, G. (1946). *Provincial support of adult education in Nova Scotia: A report by Guy Henson.* Halifax, NS: King's Printer

Illeris, K. (2002). *The three dimensions of learning: Contemporary learning theory in the tension field between the cognitive, the emotional, and the social.* Frederiksberg, Denmark: Roskilde University Press

Jahan, R. (1995). *The elusive agenda: Mainstreaming women in development.* Dhaka: The University Press Ltd.

Jennings, J. (1990). *Adult Literacy: Master or Servant?* Dhaka: University Press Limited

Joan, H et al. (2006). How MFI's and their clients can have a positive impact on the environment. Paper presented in the *Micro-credit Summit Campaign.* Halifax

Jung, C. (1954). *The development of personality* (R. F. C. Hull, Trans.), Princeton, NJ: Princeton University Press

Korten, D. (2006). *The great turning from empire to earth community.* Connecticut: Kumarian Press Inc.

Lange, E., A. (2006). Challenging Social Philosophobia. In Contexts of adult education: Canadian Perspectives (Eds.), Tara Fenwick, Tom Nesbit, Bruce Spencer. (2006). Toronto: Thompson Educational Publishing, Inc.

Mahmud, S. (2004). Microcredit and women's empowerment in Bangladesh. In S. Ahmed & S. Hakim (Eds.), *Attacking poverty with microcredit* (pp. 148-153). Dhaka: The University Press Limited

NABBEIS. (2000). Bangladesh Education Statistics (at a glance) 2000. Dhaka: Bangladesh Bureau of Educational Information and Statistics (BANBEIS)

Nath, S. R. (2002). *Education Watch 2002; Literacy Situation in Bangladesh; Instruction Manual for Interviewers (in Bangla).* Dhaka: BRAC Research and valuation Division

Nath, S. R. & Chouwdhury, A. R (Eds.) 2001). *A Question of Quality-State of Primary Education in Bangladesh. Volume 11 Achievement of Competencies.* Dhaka: Campaign for Popular Education and University Press Limited

Nesbit, T. (2006). Introduction. In Contexts of adult education: Canadian Perspectives (Eds.), Tara Fenwick, Tom Nesbit, Bruce Spencer. (20060. Toronto: Thompson Educational Publishing, Inc., pp. 13-22

Ontario Public Health Association & Frontier College (1989). *Literacy and Health Project, Phase one: Making the world healthier and safer for people who can't read.* Toronto: Ontario Public Health Association, Frontier College

OECD. (1996). *Lifelong Learning for All.* Meeting of the education committee at ministerial level, 16-17 January 1996. Paris: Organization for Economic Cooperation and Development

Poonwassie, D. (2001). Parental involvements as adult education: A microstrategy for change. In K. Binda and S. Calliou (Eds.) *Aboriginal education in Canada: A study in decolonization* (pp. 155-165). Mississauga, ON. Canadian Educators' Press

Rathgeber, E. (1990). WID, WAD, GAD: Trends in research and practice. *Journal of Developing Areas,* Vol. 24(4), pp. 489-502

Rouf, K. A. (2014). Grameen Bank women borrowers' non-formal adult learning transformation in Bangladesh. International Journal of Research Studies in Education. Vol. 3(4), pp. 1-16

Rouf, K. A. (2011). Grameen Bank women borrowers familial and community relationships development in patriarchal Bangladesh. *International Journal of Research Studies in Psychology,* Vol.1 (1), pp. 17-26

Rubenson, K., & Walker, J. (2006). The political economy of Adult Learning in Canada. In Contexts of adult education: Canadian Perspectives (Eds). Tara Fenwick, Tom Nesbit, Bruce Spencer. (2006). Toronto: Thompson Educational Publishing, Inc., pp. 173-186

Scott, S. M., Spencer, B. and Thomas A. M. (Eds.). (1998). *Learning for life: Canadian readings in adult education*. Toronto, ON: Thompson Educational

Sawchuk, P. (2006). Frameworks for Synthesis of the field of adult learning theory. In Contexts of adult education: Canadian Perspectives (Eds.), Tara Fenwick, Tom Nesbit, Bruce Spencer. (2006). Toronto: Thompson Educational Publishing, Inc.

Selman, G. (1998). The foundation of adult education in Canada. (2nd ed.). Toronto, ON: Thompson Educational Publishing, Inc.

Selman, G. and Dampier, P. (1991). *The foundations of adult education in Canada*. Toronto, ON: Thompson Educational Publishing, Inc.

Sen, A. (1995). *India: Economic Development and Social Opportunity*, Delhi, Oxford University Press

The Daily Star. (2002). Special Supplement Education for All Week. *The Daily Star*, Dhaka, April 22, 2002

Todd, H. (1996). Women at the centre: Grameen Bank borrowers after one decades. Dhaka The University Press limited.

Tomkins, J. (1921). *Knowledge for the people*. Antigonish, NS: St. Francis Xavier University.

UNDP. (1999). *Human Development Report*. New York: Oxford University Press

UNESCO. (2000). *The Dakar Framework of Action*. Paris: UNESCO

UNESCO. (1997). *Final Report of Fifth International Conference on Adult Education*. Paris: UNESCO

UNICEF. (1992). *Assessment of Basic Competencies of Children in Bangladesh: A status Report*. Dhaka: UNICEF

WCEFA. (1990). *World Conference on Education for All: Meeting Learning Needs*. Jomtien, Paris: UNESCO

Welton, M. (2003). De-coding Coady: Masters of their own destiny under critical scrutiny. *Studies in Continuing Education*, Vol. 25 (1), pp.75-93.

Welton, M. (Ed.) (2003). *In defence of the life world: Critical perspectives on adult learning*. Albany: State University of New York

Welton, M. R. (1995). The critical turn in adult education theory. In *defence of the life world: Critical perspectives on adult learning* (Ed.), Welton, M. R. (pp. 11-38). New York: State University of New York

Yunus, M. (2008). *Creating a World without Poverty*. Dhaka: Subarna Publications Ltd.

Debates and analysis of integrated micro-credit verses single-minded micro-credit

Abstract

This paper debates and analyzes different approaches of microcredit and reviews the book "What's wrong with microfinance?" edited by Thomas Dichter and Malcolm Harper (2007). Many articles of the microcredit criticize different approaches of microcredit especially Ditcher and Harper edited book articles criticize different micro-credit programs in the world and make sociological analysis and interpretations. Many writers connect micro-credit with other societal problems such as capitalism, commercialization of micro-financing, high interest of rates, peer pressure coercive loan repaying provisions and profit making neo-liberal agenda affect the poor through micro financing. The paper reviews the articles from the author's integrated micro-credit working experience in terms of people's quantitative (economic) growth and qualitative (social livelihood improvement) development. The easy also reviews debates issues raised by different writers in many micro-credit books and addresses missing points found in the articles. Moreover, this paper draws attention micro finance programs need public and private financial supports to increase loan disbursement size with less interest rate for micro-entrepreneurs' micro-enterprise development. The micro finance programs should emphasize and run with human economics instead single minded profit making economics. In addition, the business incubation/ mentoring support and citizenry skills development services are essentials for quantitative and qualitative development of the micro-borrowers. Moreover, rehabilitation schemes in crisis period can assist micro-borrowers especially delinquent borrowers to revive their businesses when their business is in crisis.

Keywords: Commercialization of microfinance; Capitalism; Grameen bank; Group lending; Handouts; Integrated micro-credit; Interest rate; Micro-borrowers; Micro-entrepreneurs; Micro finance institutions (MFIs); Neoliberalism; Poverty; Self-employment; and Single-minded micro-credit.

1.0. Introduction

There is a continued debate within the microfinance sector as to whether minimalist credit or the provision of credit integrated with other programs is most effective. This of course raises the question of how success is to be judged or measured and how microfinance programs are evaluated. This paper is about analyzing different scholars' views and incorporating my experiences working in different micro-finance institutions in different countries.

2.0. Integrated microcredit and single minded micro-loan debates

Some of the strongest advocates for minimalist credit (Otero & Rhyne, 1994; Adams, 1998; Robinson, 1998; Gibbons & Meehan, 1999; Drake & Rhyne, 2002, Yunus, 1980) promote microfinance as the most effective form of assistance to the poor and suggest that aid efforts should be concentrated on expanding micro credit financial services. They challenge that a social welfare approach, handout approach is not consistent with the delivery of efficient microcredit programs and question whether charity NGOs are the most suitable institutions for the delivery of microcredit (Otero & Rhyne, 1994, Abugre, 1994). Charity NGOs/MFIs are seen to be reluctant to charge the high interest rates that will make programs sustainable and more forgiving of arrears or defaults than are financial institutions. Therefore, the minimalists see specialized financial institutions as the most appropriate vehicles to address the needs of low-income entrepreneurs (ASA, Bangladesh).

The concept of the cost of money is still a strange one for many charity NGOs, including the big ones. Many times one comes across large credit funds managed by entirely unprofessional and untrained staff, the schemes themselves unprofessionally conceived, designed and implemented, generating an enormous waste and all these together leading to either the indebtedness of the poor or their increased dependency on external support (Abugre, 1994: 67). In my observation, I find many micro-credit programs are running like formal banking office system in Africa and in North America.

Vijay Mahajan (2007) in his article *'From micro-credit to livelihood finance'* suggests for integrated micro-finance services for promoting sustainable livelihoods for the poor. He recommends for inclusion of savings, credit, insurance, investment in human development; agricultural and business development services like productivity enhancement, risk mitigation, local value addition, and alternate market links in MFIs etc. (p. 245). Many micro-finance institutions like BancoSol, Grameen Bank, BRAC, NABARD India, and SEWA India already have these multiple services through their programs that he covers. MFIs have proved through their practice that appropriate micro-credit programs are effective tools for poverty eradication and micro-enterprise development in different communities. However, according to Vijay Mahajan (2007) these programs are fatal assumptions that limit micro-credit. His notes about fatal assumptions are debatable: (1) credit is a financial service needed by the poor, (2) credit can translate into successful micro-enterprises, (3) credit can create self-employment, (4) MFIs are not serving people who are above the poverty line as they have no assets, and (5) the last assumption is micro-credit institutions can all become financially self-sustaining (p. 245). Now micro-credit is not an assumption rather it is a practice-proved tool for community economic development, micro-enterprise development and a poverty-eradication tool for the poor. Although Mahajan (2007) emphasises that livelihood finance requires large amounts of funds (p. 246); however, he does not give solutions on how MFIs can mobilize resources.

Wright (2000) insists that banking should not be a sideline and that those NGOs that move into the microfinance sector should concentrate on it exclusively. A number of programs have in fact shifted from offering integrated programs to minimalist strategies. K-Rep in Kenya is one such example (Mutua, 1999). Otero and Rhyne (1994) emphasize the importance of scale and self-sufficiency in operating efficient MFIs. They, and others, suggest that donors should demand institutional sustainability, encourage partnerships between MFIs and the commercial banking sector and focus attention on reforming and expanding financial institutions (Otero & Rhyne, 1994; Adams, 1998). Donors can then assume the role of guarantors, brokering partnerships between MFIs and commercial banks.

The proponents of the minimalist strategy suggest that other poverty alleviation measures or social programs should be left to NGOs working in specific areas. However, as more and more donors support the microfinance sector; this may reduce the resources available for other types of poverty alleviation programs. On the other hand, the proponents of a credit-plus, or integrated approach, argue against the emphasis on credit to the exclusion of other issues such as the health care, training in small business development, gender equity, education, land reform, etc. Some favour collaboration between specialized MFIs and NGOs working in the social welfare or social justice fields. Others maintain that credit works most effectively when one institution is able to offer a combination of credit plus education around health care, technical training or social mobilization (Dawson

& Jeans, 1997; Hulme and Mosley, 1996; Rabinson, 1998; Sabharwal, 1999; Morduch, 2000).

Johnson and Rogaly (1997, p. 53) identify three types of integrated approaches commonly taken by NGOs.

1. groups form to function as social organizations as well as for the provision of credit (this may involve a process of community empowerment and capacity building to address other local issues such as improvement of water access, etc);
2. microcredit groups provide ancillary development activities such as health education or literacy programs;
3. business and financial skills training is provided in conjunction with microcredit services.

A number of large NGOs (ACTIONAID, Oxfam, Care, Freedom from Hunger, BRAC< Grameen Bank Bangladesh etc.) are combining microcredit programs with related development work such as literacy and health programs, technical training, skill development in a variety of fields, and housing programs. For them, the integrated approach provides a more realistic alternative to poverty alleviation. Some NGOs have added microcredit projects to existing programs while others such as Freedom from Hunger (FFH), Yunus Center Bangladesh have added health and nutrition programs to microfinance initiatives. Yunus Center initiated social business equity financing services to low-income people in Bangladesh. FFH'S "Credit with Education Program" combines village-banking services for women with education sessions on health issues, nutrition and business practices. Local credit unions finance the loan portfolio while Freedom from Hunger supports the technical assistance and education costs (Stack & Thys, 2000). Research carried out by Freedom from Hunger indicates that women's health, income and nutritional status has improved as well as the nutritional status of their children (McNelly & Dunford 1999 in Stack & Thys, 2000; Yunus, 2006). A survey on the Grameen Bank micro-credit services in Bangladesh conducted by Mahbub

Hossain in 1982 finds grameen borrowers food intake have increased per day and their living conditions become modest than worse before. All these above mentioned researchers also concluded that it was more efficient for the NGO to partner with credit unions rather than set up a separate infrastructure. However, Muhammad Yunus runs Grameen Bank and Grameen America independently in Bangladesh and US respectively. However, Yunus thinks it is better run micro credit institutions and micro-credit plus service institutions separately instead put all programs in one organization.

Among those who favor integrated approaches, there has been some recognition that training in business development may be one of the most difficult strategies to undertake successfully and often it is more effective when offered through a separate institution (Harper, 1998; Mutua, 1994; Mayoux, 1995). Usually MFIs/NGOs may lack the skills to survey markets, develop a product, train workers and undertake marketing. Many MFIs/NGO efforts at establishing small businesses have failed, particularly those that involve cooperative enterprises. While people may be motivated to meet in order to obtain credit, they may be less inclined to participate in a co-operative business venture (Johnson & Rogaly, 1997). Grameen and BRAC experimented with group loans for the provision of deep tube-wells and community employment initiatives. These initiatives did not prove to be financially viable and as a result some borrowers lost assets or suffered income reductions (Hulme & Mosley, 1997).

There remain exceptions to this general trend. Some institutions such as Bank Rakayert Indonesia (BRI) have developed businesses (for example, poultry rearing) that are able to offer employment to poor women. Pro-Mujer in Bolivia maintains an integrated approach in order to serve both the economic and social needs of poor women. They have been successful in combining microfinance with business development, health training and basic health services, stressing the need for sustainability of their clients not the institution (Natilson, 2000). Grameen Bank sixteen decisions have socio-economic development messages that GB micro-borrowers are committed to memorize and follow.

Proshika, one of the largest NGOs in Bangladesh, is firmly committed to integrating microcredit within a larger social development approach that offers training in trades and community mobilization. In a study, Hedrick-Wong et al., (1997) differentiated between social empowerment indicators (literacy, health education and awareness, family planning, infant mortality, empowerment of women, environmental awareness and practice, access to public resources, participation in local institutions) and economic empowerment indicators (indicators of assets and indebtedness, income, savings, investment, market mobility and power). Credit repayment is not interpreted as an indication of overall empowerment. Using the above indicators, Hedrick-Wong et al. (1997) found that compared with non participants, a higher proportion of Proshika women used family planning, birth-rates and infant mortality rates were lower, they were more likely to have dowry-less marriages, and the incidence of physical abuse was lower. Overall, women's decision- making power within the family was greater.

Linda Mayoux (1995) views the minimalist approach to microfinance as being synonymous with a market approach that "focuses on integrating women within existing structures rather challenging the structures themselves". It is a method for bringing women into the market place and using them as a vehicle for poverty alleviation. She stresses the importance of an empowerment approach that encompasses gender equity as a necessary part of development.

Different study results on integrated microcredit show this program is more effective and is inconclusive and at times contradictory, although it is clear that minimalist credit can achieve greater outreach than integrated programs. Evidence from Bolivia, indicates that there is little difference in poverty impact and recovery rates between institutions that provide a 'minimalist' approach and those that offer an 'integrated' approach (Mosley, 2001). Other researchers have identified the need for additional in-depth social impact studies (CCISC, 1998). While the minimalist approach may be more effective in reaching large numbers, it does not challenge structural inequities and may in fact lead to more acceptance of the status quo, the operations of the market economy, and global economic forces.

3.0. Analysis of micro-credit different notions and views

Below I am reviewing the book *"What's wrong with Microfinance?"* that contains twenty articles edited by Thomas Dichter and Malcolm Harper. Although the book asks many questions and poses issues around micro-credit; its articles miss evidenced and positive results of micro-credit in different societies. These results have informed the micro-credit movement across the world. Many articles in the book note that single minded MFIs (profit making motive only) are carrying a neo-liberal agenda to poor people. They claim it also exploits disadvantaged people through single minded micro-credit projects, because MFIs charge high interest to micro-borrowers. There are also claims around MFIs replacing moneylenders, because their single minded loans are still costly. MFIs, however, are the development agent in the local community and they enhance local living economics as evidenced in several micro-credit studies. Hence this book review debates issues raised by different authors in the book and addresses missing points found in the articles.

For decades, poor people were unable to access loans for their starting and running their businesses, now MFIs are providing loans to micro-entrepreneurs. Micro-borrowers use these loans in their businesses and earn income. The micro-credit program is very simple and its purpose is straightforward. There are not any hidden agendas in MFIs; however, many writers relate single minded micro-credit to other societal problems such as capitalism which can affect the poor via MFIs. In reality, the poor see micro-finance as an opportunity for them to acquire business capital because MFIs are joint risk-takers with micro-borrowers. It is not a chicken-and-egg dilemma rather; MFIs provide soft loans to poor for their business development. Integrated MFIs (socio-economic agenda inclusive) take on the risk of bad debt loan losses and rehabilitate delinquent borrowers by offering them extra loans for their business rehabilitation. Grameen Bank has rehabilitation program for the delinquent clients and disaster affected clients in Bangladesh. Grameen Bank incorporated 'Grameen Pension Scheme' for its borrowers where they can deposit their monthly premiums at the weekly center meetings. Delinquent borrowers can borrow flexible loans from GB and re-schedule the loan instalments with the bank.

Dichter (2007) comments that "Credit relationships in business are complicated" (p. 183), that are surprising to me. Dichter writes, "When mass access to formal credit comes on the scene, it is for consumption" (p. 187). This is debatable, because 99% of micro-borrowers use their loans for their businesses. I do not see any harm if a few borrowers use small portions of loans for consumption purposes in times of emergency. Many scholars treated micro-credit as consumer loan, but borrowers are taking loans for running business and earn income. Grameen Bank borrowers are deposit their weekly savings regularly in Grameen Bank. Clients may withdraw their savings for consumption. MFIs provide emergency loans to clients for buying food and to meet other critical needs buying witer clothings, repaire cyclone afftected damaged broken houses. Thomas Dichter's statements "Self-financing (savings) or borrowing money from a close social network has generally always been the case for business start-ups, at least from the early days of the Industrial Revolution" (p. 7.]. This may still exist; however, recent economic hardships in people's livelihoods result in many poor families being unable to make loans to their family and friends in order to start a business. Dichter's (2007) remarks may be true but the average poor person in the past is not an entrepreneur; when he or she has access to credit it is largely or consumption or cash-flow smoothing (p. 6). Instead, under integrated micro-finance program, the average poor person is an economic actor instead of a burden to the community. This is a great impact of micro-credit.

However, many of the articles in the book critique different micro-credit programs that are underway in different countries. They argue that micro-credit programs create micro-debtors in these communities (within neo-liberal society). However, my argument is that this is not the case, but that integrated micro-credit serves poor people to be self-reliant and build self-esteem in terms of development. It also creates independent living in society and empowers the marginalised poor. There is a constant demand among poor people for small loans to start or enrich business capital and for MFIs to meet the increasing demand of micro-loans to micro-entrepreneurs across the world. Although some authors like Aliaga, Irina and Paul Mosley (2007); Bateman, Milford. (2007), Mary Houghton & Ronald Grzywinski (2007), and Vijay Mahajan (2007) acknowledge micro-credit's contribution to local living economics in local communities; however, some articles' argument reflect that the poor are being dominated and losing their identity through the operation of micro-credit programs (Harper & Ditcher, 2007; p. 1, p. 3, p. 14, p. 18).

Authors in the book make general comments that everywhere debt has been seen as bad. For example, Thomas Dichter (2007) said, "The indebted person could end up feeling dependent on the constructs in a particular culture, unequal in stature, underpowered, diminished, and could even undergo a loss of identity. One possible result of this is suicide". (p. 14). Moreover, David Hulme (2007) commented that the indebted person ends up feeling a moral loss of certain values that occur as a result of credit use (p. 20). David Hulme also pointed out that there are no favourable results to poor peoples' lives using micro-credit (p. 19]. Even Dichter (2007) remarks that although micro-lending has led to the evolution of the micro-finance industry matching clients needs, but not all of them not have access to the types of micro-savings services that they desire (p. 186). This comment is contradictory to S. M. Rahman's (2007) study, which declares that MFIs incorporate savings products in their loan programs develops saving behaviours among poor borrowers (p. 197).

The first article *'Can micro-credit make an already slippery slope more slippery? Some lessons from the social meaning of debt'* written by Thomas Dichter critiques micro-credit negatively. For example, he says, "micro-credit has failed to see the slippery slope towards consumerism and the loss of certain values that may occur as a result of formal credit use (p. 16). Micro-credit creates debt among poor people that results in loss of respectability in the neighbourhoods, less independent in society and loss of their identity. This comment contradicts with many other micro-credit studies conducted by the World Bank (p. 30). With regard to micro-credit addressing the issue of poverty, Muhamad Yunus (2010b) and Sam Harris (2006), have said that *micro-finance* has proven its value, in many countries, as a weapon against poverty and hunger (p. 32). Now, it is recognized integrated micro credit as a sustainable development model for income-generation, self-employment that empowers disadvantaged women in Bangladesh (p. 19).

The second article *is 'microdebt good for poor people? A note on the dark side of microfinance'* written by David Hulme (2007) mentioned that MFIs have created the myth that poor people always manage to repay their loans because of their ability to exploit business opportunities (p. 19). He raises the cautionary that savings accounts are less available at MFIs. MFIs have been working in different countries with specified frameworks with built-in loans and savings that contribute to socio-economic development of the poor in different communities (p. 4). The scaling of contribution and return on investment may vary in different societies. MFIs cannot work against existing capitalist saturated markets where environmental and economic shocks are common (Ibid. p. 4). My questions are: why has this issue not been raised as compared to other macro-financial institutions other than Grameen Bank and why is the challenge of structural change within capitalist exploitation an issue solely for MFIs? MFIs don't have extra reserve funds that require permission from the central bank. Here, the government or international organizations could be guarantors to promote savings collection from the public. Micro-credit debtors might suggest to Government and to International financial institutions for guarantors of MFIs in different countries.

Author comments made by Hulme (2007) on MFI programs distort actual MFI achievements. Several studies show evidence that disadvantaged people receive benefits by using micro-credit (p. 13). However, David Hulme (2007) shared pessimistic remarks about MFIs virtually never working with the poorest, the mentally and physically disabled, the elderly, the destitute and refugees (p. 13). However, several studies conducted by the World Bank, USAID, and UNDP, ILO, Asian Development Bank (ADB) Africa Development Foundation etc. report that the greatest power of micro-finance is that it increases income for the poor. The poor become economic actors in the market instead of *handout receivers*. This lies in social network-institutional capital that is unleashed through the process of providing microfinance.

Community-based MFIs are serving the day labourers and micro-entrepreneurs in different societies. The reason behind Hulme's denial is debateable, because MFIs are designed to give the poor access to soft loans without collateral (p. 13). MFIs exclusively target the poor and create different forms of capital process like social capital-network with producers, consumers, and citizens. It creates hopes, builds inspirations and brings together a new culture of responsibilities and reciprocities among poor. However, many writers raise issues that fall outside credit services, e.g. micro borrowers face health problems that can be reduced if basic information and prevention services are available in the villages (p. 16). We need to remember that the neo-liberal free market economy is competes with micro-entrepreneurs businesses. MFIs are working within a minimalist micro-credit approach to minimize their costs. The author agrees with Aliaga & Mosley (2007) that the poor need other socio-economic, health and education supports (p. 1). Paul Rippy (2007) rightly articulates, in his articles *"Princes, peasants and pretenders: The past and future of African microfinance"*, that amazingly politicians, donors and programmes assume that the demand for credit is a need or even a right. Universal access to debt is treated with the same sort or urgency as universal access to primary education or to health care (p. 116). That's why Muhamad Yunus (1996) says, "Credit is a human right. Many public health institutions and private health practitioners' services are available in the community. It begs the question as to why these institutions do not accommodate poor people in their health and education programs currently. If MFIs perform these services, who is going to fund them?

All MFIs follow soft loan policies such as providing loans without collateral. However, I wonder about Paul Rippy's comments that the task of getting loans to people is not always easy (p. 116). MFIs provide loans with simple procedures for poor people to start up and run their businesses. There are not any preconceptions that exist in MFIs that differ from Paul Rippy's tips about financial institutions: knowing what is best for them, acting in a rational manner consistent with their long-term interests and consumers knowing what are best for them. General banking systems do not provide access to loans for the poor. Here, poor people buy financial services from MFIs to meet their needs and make their lives better through the utilization of loans.

Frances Sinha (2007), in his article *'Self-help Group (SHGs) in India: Numbers yes, poverty outreach and empowerment partially'*, raised the issue that records of accounts need to be well maintained with systems for verification and transparency in place. He noted that it is a complex job, but these are the mandatory rules for financial institutions, otherwise trust will be questioned. There is not any mercy here. Government agencies should have monitoring mechanisms (p. 26). The author is wondering how the local Indian government has decentralized NABARD through the Panchayati Raj system which vests local village councils with power, resource allocation (credit) and decision-making processes with SHG. The reason for this wonderment is loan transaction jobs are huge. It will be a large burden for field staff to carry multiple jobs. This would include GB health education, adult education, awareness creation, livestock development education, etc. that was brought forth during the 1980s. However, these multiple jobs hamper the smooth functioning of micro-credit operations which resulted in huge delinquencies in the bank. Hence the question is how will NABARD balance financial and non-financial jobs together in SHGs as an opportunity for social action and empowerment through women's involvement? The good news is Grameen sister organizations like Grameen Kallyan is providing health care clinical services, health education and nutrition education to them to GB borrowers and other poor people in Bangladesh.

MFIs take risks in forming partnerships and providing loans to poor people, which is typically absent in traditional banking. Mary Houghton and Ronald Grzywinksi (2007) in their article *'Opportunity and evolution for microfinance'* acknowledge that the conventional banking system does not fully take over the work of financing economic development activity at the 'bottom of the pyramid' (p. 252). It is true in the history of banking that banks never take the risk of partnership with the poorest 50%. Although they deal with rich businessmen, they have large claims in bankruptcy annually. They do not forecast their loan repayment rates or delinquency rates or delinquent loans writeoff amount publicly. Although they have delinquency problems and bankruptcy problems, they refer bankruptcies to the court, which does not seem to be effective. GB never refers its delinquency loans to courts for repayment. In Bangladesh, commercial banks' loan repayment rates are below 50%, whereas MFIs have a loan repayment rate of more than 98%. Where the commercial banks are unsuccessful in developing savings behaviours among their clients, MFIs are successful in maintaining the poor's credit worthiness and developing their savings behaviours. It has been possible, because Grameen believes in joint risk partnerships with clients; therefore, GB is a facilitator of clients' socio-economic development instead of solely being a loan provider (since 1979). These are the concrete positive attributes of MFIs.

It is not true that by definition, micro-credit is a single intervention. My question is why such critiques are attached to MFIs, why don't authors lobby for traditional banks and governments to provide some additional support services to MFIs, which may help to serve the poor more both via financial and non-financial services with fewer service charges. These supports are very essential to MFI survival, and sustainability. The good news is MFIs follow soft loan policies like soft loans without collaterals, and weekly/monthly mini loan repayment procedures etc. are incorporated in MFIs services. If loans receivers comply with the terms and conditions of the respective MFI project, it is easy to get loans from MFIs.

Hugh Allen (2007), in his article *'Finance begins with savings, not loans'* mentioned that of the 10,000 or so MFIs worldwide it is variously estimated that only 3–5 per cent have achieved full financial sustainability (p.2). This is not true. T Vijay Mahajan (2007) in his article *'From micro-credit to livelihood finance'* recognises that there is a huge demand for micro-credit in communities (p. 18). The same concern is also posed by Susan Johnson and Namrata Sharma (2007). They said that the pressure for financial sustainability of microfinance institutions over the last decade has meant that mainstream approaches to microfinance service provisions have created limited outreach to more remote and rural areas, especially in Africa (p. 15). However, MFIs are screaming for loan capital to meet client demand. Therefore, it needs to be recognized that MFI activities are labour-intensive and costly, hence they are unable to recover their costs. Here public and private institutions support can fill the loss and gap of deficit of MFIs. They emphasize savings collections from the poor and built-in savings and loans in their products; however the problems are that some countries' central banks are sceptical about the saving collection of MFIs.

4.0. Commercialization of micro-credit

Commercialization of micro-credit and its engagement with the mainstream financial sectors and aggressive loan repayment strategy is a burden for micro-borrowers. Malcolm Harper critiqued group lending programs. Malcolm Harper (2007); Prabhu Ghate (2007); and Susan Johnson and Namrata Sharma (2007) make the accusation that group lending programs create coercive loan repayment peer pressure for members instead of developing social capital and human capital (p. 15). They see the opposite side of the group constraints like regular group meetings, group fund accounts, etc. Harper thinks that group micro-finance methodologies are very useful for MFIs and banks themselves as opposed to clients. He concluded that MFIs are effectively full-service unremunerated retailers. However, MFIs help to bridge the wide information gap between their members and MFI staff by appraising fellow members' loan proposals. Although group members have been pressured to reduce meetings, higher repayment rates are directly associated with more frequent meetings. Peer lending works in NABARD partnerships in India: Therefore research is needed to explore the impact of group lending in India.

The concept of group peer lending is cooperation among group members. The intention is not to be coercive to each other of the group members or by the MFIs. Rather develop cooperation among GB group members and the exchange of information has resulted in a successful peer-lending program in Bangladesh. However, Harper's (2007) comments that MFI group members are taking a risk in repaying their delinquent borrowers' (neighbours) loans (p. 9). The statement lacks evidence. Moreover, Rahman (2007) expressed that MFI employees use savings for loan repayment without borrowers' authorization (p. 23). These are unusual and unacceptable practices in MFIs.

Grameen Bank's credit delivery system is labour-intensive and the economies of scale from services are through groups rather than individually. The group based microfinance concept follows the cooperative ideas of mutual help and social capital leadership development among disadvantaged people. Here my question is what the percentage of such malpractices is in MFIs. Financial institutions never accept such illegal practices if any. Few unusual practices cannot deny the positive impact of micro-credit: clients become self-employed, independent, developed self-esteem among them and minimize their vulnerability in the community.

Micro-credit is complex, labour-intensive work in the competitive corporate market world. MFIs are working to empower small business people, as well as micro-enterprise development in local communities. Harper (2007) mentioned that members who borrow less than the average, generally the poorest, are at risk for adverse effects and have few opportunities for investment. They are effectively providing free money for their colleagues who borrow more (p. 42). This is not true. For example, GB initiated a special program called hard core poor (beggars' loans) loans that involve nurturing and mentoring the poorest clients by providing them both financial and non-financial services. Harper misses GB's group fund abolition information that was removed in 2001. Now GB only has basic loans, educational loans, housing loans and flexible loans for clients since 2000.

Many authors such as Dichter, Thomas (2007); Harper, Malcolm (2007); Hulme, David (2007); Mahmud (2007); Rahman,); and Susan Johnson and Namrata Sharma (2007) mention that MFI loan costs are very high (p. 23). This is true because MFIs visit vulnerable clients weekly and monthly at their doorstep and provide different types of counselling services: family counselling, financial literacy and non-financial counselling services to them. They collect loan instalments from clients' neighbourhoods weekly; therefore, MFI operation costs are higher. Commercial banks invest more money to few clients whereas MFIs invest fewer amounts of loans to more borrowers. For example, commercial bank can invest above one million dollars in loans to 1-3 people; however, MFIs need 200 clients to invest $1 million. Here MFIs deal with 200 people, which need 200 times more stationeries, more time, and more resources than to deal with only 1-3 people. Therefore, MFIs operational costs are higher than commercial banks and MFIs are not receiving loan funding from the government, or other donors. They run their programs from borrowing funds from the market and wholesale loan refinancing agencies. Therefore, MFIs cannot serve their micro-borrowers for free or lesser prices. Although government has a commitment to people; state agencies do not support MFIs. Social scientists, IT specialists and researchers need to find ways for MFIs to help them reduce their workload, operational costs and to disburse more loans to micro-borrowers.

There is no denying that MFIs have multidimensional, positive impacts in different societies evidenced by different professional MFI studies. However, Milford Bateman (2007) said, "MFIs are anti-industrial quasi-banking institutions (p. 214). They place emphasis on financial return instead of social return (p. 254). We have to remember that in the past, the poor have always been out of the orbit of banking facilities to receive loans for their businesses. Even thirty five years before, they were unable to get access to loans from the bank. In Bangladesh, the Grameen Bank Project (GBP) was first initiated to provide micro-loans to the poor without collateral- in 1979. Micro-loan recipients have proved that they are creditworthy through their loan transactions. GB 14 billion dollars in micro-credit reaches directly to 8.6 million poor in Bangladesh (Grameen Bank Updates, 2016, p. 31). Now, this message/model has spread across the world and more than 10,000 MFIs are serving mini-loans to the poor without collateral. MFIs are social business organizations that have been served with a social and economic mission to provide for the disadvantaged poor (Harris, 2011, p. 32). All over the world, these institutions provide micro-credit to 175 million poor that help them to be involved in micro-business and earn money. MFIs have *solely targeted the poor,* which is absent in many public, private and NGOs who do not solely focus on poor people. The micro-credit summit in 2006 confirmed that MFIs are able to target and serve the poor directly and that this is its greatest success (Harris,

p. 12). There is not any middle man in between them, no middle class people and no rich people to take undue benefit from these financial institutions. Hence MFIs solely serve low-income people in the world (Harris, p. 25).

MFIs are successful in transforming poor people in becoming micro-entrepreneurs and economic actors, savers and social actors - instead of receiving handouts or simply remaining day labours throughout their lives. However, Harper Malcolm (2007) and S.M Rahman (2007) debate and interpret that MFIs regular savings program are a loan for poor women as savings products are tied into a loan program with high interest rates (p. 22). Through the loan transaction process and savings deposit, borrowers develop their banking behaviours. Through the whole process micro-borrowers are able to reduce their poverty (Ibid, p. 30). However, it is curious that Rahman (1997) has an oppositional critique: micro-borrowers' mini savings and interest are a load for poor people (p. 197). Here the point is that MFIs can reduce their loan interest rates if they can receive low-cost loan fund capital and reach many clients for investment. Grameen Bank has reduced its interest rates to 16% from 20% in 2009, because now GB can be sustainable with the 16% service charge to its investments. As GB calculates interest rates in the diminishing methods, clients actually pay 8% interest, which is missed in Harper's (2007) descriptions (p. 1). MFIs believe that if women in the family can receive loans and are exposed to different developmental ideas through the program; it can have multiple effects for the borrowers' families.

Moneylenders only give loans informally to their neighbours with high rates of interest and cruelly take back the loans with interest. If loan receivers do not repay the loans, moneylenders forcibly take assets from the loan-receivers. MFIs do not only offer loans to the poor, but they also exchange other social values with people like empowerment, leadership and cooperation among them. They also provide financial and non-financial literacy to clients that benefit them in attaining their socio-economic and environmental mantra. Hence,

Kim Wilson's comments (2007) on MFIs as moneylenders are not true. If MFIs are cruel like moneylenders, their program cannot continue in the community even if governments allow MFIs to work with the poor. Kim Wilson and Muhammad S. Rahman instead of articulating the positive side of the micro-credit, they are critiques to it (p. 29). Now micro-borrowers are free from money-lender exploitation like competing to work in money lenders' farms with fewer wages or with handouts.

5.0. Handouts versus Micro-credit

Canada's safety net program helps marginalized people with welfare assistance in critical periods and it is a good strategy. This handout concept can be found in generous religious donation and gifts to poor people. For example Christianity's, Islam's and other religions' purported foundation is upon gifting and redemption. With Christianity specifically, redemption is through the death of Jesus Christ – that is the ability to apologize and forgo past sins and to ask God for forgiveness for eternal life. Gifting is a part of that redemption. Many of the agencies that exist today in Canada and OECD countries have a Christian foundation (Salvation Army, Good Will). Traditionally, the role of the Church was to help 'the needy'. Those who donated participated in their own salvation – that of saving their own soul. The receiver of the donation feels blessed that he or she was able to receive this gift from God via the donor.

Therefore both feel as if they have a right to salvation; however, the problem of this model is that it is inconsistent, casual and for the most part people can 'give' in residual amounts and give only when they feel like they are obligated (through their own bad acts) or when they see those in dire need. In the late 1980s Catholic Relief Services (CRS) joined the micro-credit industry in parallel to their charity (p. 97). The program has had huge positive benefits to low-income people and the repayment rate is also excellent, but the problem was in a lack of funding and continuous commitment to the program. In charity there is no need for continuous services and monitoring, but in micro-credit programs large mentoring support services involvement is needed which was lacked at CRS. A key principle of CRS micro-credit was to include a savings feature, the only sure way for clients to accumulate assets (p. 104). However this self-sufficiency mantra of best practices mandated a more competitive approach, because the internal account (group fund) competes with CSR loans. Borrowers tap their own group fund loans than they borrow from CSR. To avoid such problems CRS is dismantling the group fund (p. 104).

Grameen Bank has not had a group fund operation since 2000, but the article '*The Money Lender's Dilemma*' mentioned that the internal account (group fund) competes with borrowers' own loans (Kim, p. 104). Maccolm Harper (2007) wrongly asserts that members have to leave if their payment rotation exceeds two weeks at Grameen Bank (p. 42) is not correct. Grameen bank members must attend weekly meeting and deposit their weekly savings in their GB recorded accounts and apply for loans at the center meeting. There is no strict rule to expel members or that one need to leave the group if no transactions with the bank are made. The principle is that group members themselves make decisions about their group membership's registration. This is not done by the Grameen Bank employees.

Kim Wilson (2007) noted, "Micro-credit seemed irrelevant to the lives of the poor in the times of our success – when we were profitable – and very relevant in the times of our failure – when we ran a sloppy ship." (p. 106). However, several micro-finance impact studies do not agree with this statement. For example, Grameen Bank, Association for Social Advancement (ASA), BRAC in Bangladesh and SEWA India have run their own micro-loan programs for profit and benefit to clients for years. If clients do not benefit from micro-credit programs then MFIs cannot survive. Clients' numbers do not increase just to receive loans from these community economic development agencies.

Paul Rippey (2007) asserted, "Asian micro-credit models replicated to Africa and failed" (p. 109). I worked in Africa, as well as evaluated three micro-credit programs in Namibia (COSEDA and CDI) and Lesotho (TKMA) in 1997-2000. It is not that the micro-credit phenomenon failed in Africa rather the problem is the armchair short-term consultants/program designers who designed credit programs without considering local context and customizing products tailored to the poor's comfort. The consultants quit the project after finishing their contract. Moreover, the projects hired inexperienced, young, urban employees who were absent in the locality. Moreover, CEOs of the projects were corrupted. They used project resources for their own interests and misused project money. Also, there is no ongoing monitoring by the government or the donors. Although micro-entrepreneurs need soft loans, the credit delivery design needs to be customised and simple.

Milford Bateman (2007) acknowledged that the microfinance model that is very much seen as a 'quick-impact' poverty reduction policy would provide a modest cash income to the 'entrepreneurial poor'. An expanding micro-enterprise and SME sector was expected to gradually constitute the dynamic core of a revitalizing Bosnia & Herzegovina (B&H) economy (pp. 210-211). He also mentions that the expansion of the micro-enterprise and SME sector in B&H has had a number of fairly distinct and inter-related characteristics. First, the overwhelming majority of new entrants were found to be operating in the informal sector (p. 211), but now the overwhelming majority of new entrepreneurial initiatives established in B&H after 1995 have turned out to be very a simple easy-entry. Poor people in B&H take this opportunity and that's why Bateman said, "The rate of micro-enterprise entry has been impressive (p. 212). However Thomas Dichter (2007) in his article: *The chicken and egg dilemma in microfinance: An historical analysis of the sequence of growth and credit in the economic development of the 'north'* separates rich business people from the micro-credit borrower and finds the vast majority of today's micro-credit programme borrowers are more or less straightforward in their behaviour – they want to payback their loan or get rid of the debt (p. 183). This proves that the poor are credit-worthy across the world and they reduce their poverty by using micro-credit. Although MFIs are social enterprises, their first job is providing loans to marginal entrepreneurs.

This is the principle, values and impact of micro-credit in many communities. However, I disagree with Milford Bateman interpretations that very little evidence has emerged in Bosnia and Herzegovina (B&H) to suggest that the commercial microfinance model actually possesses the required 'transformative capacity' to secure genuinely sustainable poverty reduction, through genuinely sustainable local economic and social development (p. 220). Moreover, Milford Bateman, in his article *De-industrialization and social disintegration in Bosnia,* said that most microfinance in B&H has overwhelmingly gone into establishing tiny, informal, non-industrial ventures, with almost nothing directed towards financing potentially sustainable small-scale industry-based ventures. He comments that the micro-finance model contains an 'adverse selection' of anti-industrial bias and that this bias works in filtering out those potential entrepreneurs wishing to work in the industrial sector (p. 214). The author is not sure how the author finds micro-credit is anti-small-scale industry-based ventures and the microfinance model actively destroys social capital through individual entrepreneurial success (p. 218). Here, Bateman should consider that MFIs have actually solidified its activities in Bosnia since 2000. Hence, it is too young for MFIs to reach across B&H words and have an intensive impact on the nation. Grameen Bank, ASA, BRAC, K-rep in Kenya, Bank Rakayat Indonesia, BancoSol Bolivia and KASF Foundation Pakistan are MFIs that run their micro-credit program for profit. However, MFIs need a 3-5 year incubation period to scale up their programs for profit. In Bosnia, poor people lost their houses, businesses and farms. The Bosnian micro-credit program replicated its work using Grameen Trust technical support after the war in 2000. Currently, local staff started to serve its

10,000 clients and they are doing well; however, B & H needs to wait for its micro-credit impact on society-at-large.

Imran Matin, Munshi Sulaiman and Saleque (2007), Bangladeshi researchers wrote the article *'Imagining microfinance more boldly: Unleashing the true potential of microfinance'* acknowledged micro-finance's contribution to the social network and institutional capital development (p. 16). They mentioned that the process of the microfinance provision creates three forms of 'process capital': Social capital emerges from the new trust-based social contract, network capital creates new hopes, aspirations and brings poor together within a new culture of responsibilities and reciprocities; and institutional capital emerges from the ability of micro-finance to provide institutions with the capability to manage large scale delivery systems. Even the dominance of microfinance discourse chooses to focus on the output component of microfinance- the provision of financial services (Ibid, p. 24). I agree that many MFIs in Bangladesh are working with a minimalist approach to provide credit-only instead of an integrated approach. The reason is that MFIs do not have extra financial resources for services in health, nutrition, and providing education to the poor. Sectored programs can serve these services by respective specialised institutions. In order for MFIs to deal with all of these socio-economic services to the poor, they would require extra resources and specialise people.

The Self-Help Group (SHGs) program works for people who live way below the poverty line under the National Bank for Agriculture and Rural Development (NABARD) and ICICI bank in India. These banks developed partnerships with NGOs and developed a partnership with SHG models in India (Harper, 2007, p. 167). The SHG program has been linked with savings and credit programs. People can open savings accounts in the banks and can receive more loans against savings. Fairly substantive outreaches to the poor (half of SHG members are below the poverty line) are clients of NABARD (Ibid, p. 75). Frances Sinha (2007) and Prabhu Ghate (2007), in their articles, confirmed that

MFIs are working for poor people through SHG in India. Although all over the world there are 10,000 MFIs that exist, only 3-4% of MFIs are financially sustainable (p. 49). Moreover, Johnson & Sharma (2007) claim that MFIs have limited outreach to more remote and rural areas, especially in Africa (p. 15). The reasons are that MFIs are suffering from insufficient donor funds, public funds and other public supports. MFI borrowers do not have ownership in their MFIs except Grameen, BRI and BankcaSol and few other organizations.

Malcolm Harper's (2007) commented in his article *Microfinance and farmers: Do they fit?* that micro-loans are unsuitable for on-farm investment, activities or businesses (p. 93) are debatable because Grameen Bank provides 85% of its loans to borrowers that are using for agricultural activities: irrigation, crop production, raising livestock, and poultry, homestead gardening, and buying agro-machines. Alterna Savings Toronto provides loans for trimming and cutting grass, community gardening, and nursery businesses. However, Malcolm's (2007) interpretations of the 'old paradigm' rural development financial institutions have for the most part disappeared, and others have been converted into what are effectively specialist microfinance institutions (p. 10). Again he asks question around the new paradigm of microfinance effectively addressing the needs of farmers (p. 83). Moreover, Malcolm Harper (2007) asserts that there are some fundamental differences between farming and other income-generating activities; that most farming products are a means of survival, farming tends to be an ancestral activity etc, but in the short term it declines in value if it is not used (p. 84). It is true that annual reports of GB reflect a percentage of agricultural loans have decreased since 2000 as compared to 1980s micro-credit investments in agriculture and livestock. MFI principles include that clients are free to make choices as it relates to their loans and utilize their loans by themselves. Although currently rural people's livelihoods have diversified, farming is still the most important single source of income for most rural people, in kind and in cash.

Irina Aliaga and Paul Mosley (2007) narrated a case study of micro-finance in a crisis situation in Bolivia. The authors mention three MFI projects names: Crecer and ProMujar and BancaSol that have been giving credit in Bolivia since 2000s. Both Crecer and ProMujar have credit plus programs, health, livestock development services, produce and subscribe to the 'village bank' (banco communal) model of organization (p. 1). They had stronger mutual support mechanisms than other organizations. This social capital represented an asset that could be drawn on in case of need (p. 1). The writers also mentioned that in the crisis situation, they helped clients develop a flexible payment plan, shopping for food and other essential services – helping clients who were suffering. Alike Grameen Bank has a loan rescheduling program. It provides food loans and has a loan rehabilitation program too. For example, it has frozen loan collection during natural disaster periods like flood, hurricane, and cyclones since 1988. In addition to this, Grameen employees provide water purification tablets, nutritional dry food, primary health care services, and post- flood rehabilitation loans for agriculture inputs, crop production and buy livestock in post-flood periods. These activities help clients quickly regain their agriculture and rectify social and economic loss with these post-flood actions.

J.D. Von Pischke (2007) divided MFIs into three categories: Type-1 MFIs follow commercial minimalist approach in their loan operation; this Type-1 follow financially sustainable model through serving huge clients receiving funds from international finance institutions (IFIs). The type-11 MFIs depend on subsidy for their survival with alleviate poverty mission (p. 144). These social enterprises usually depend on donor funds following holistic approach one-stop- shop or social welfare services; however, they cannot serve across the nation because of shortage of funds. Type-111 follows cooperative laws and joint-stock corporations' principles (p. 146). Nevertheless, the Type-111 has limited clients because they depend on external loan funding and become blocked at some pint. For example, Bangladesh Rural Development Board (BRDB) and Milk Vita Bangladesh eschewed their program because of fund crisis and conflict among members and employees. The micro loan program has multiple effects in disadvantaged people's lives; however, the quantitative evaluation only measures economic (income) factors, but hard to measure other social and environmental effects. The qualitative research methods, social accounting and social auditing method can incorporate in MFIs impact evaluation to identify the social and economic development impact of MFIs on clients' lives.

S. M. Rahman (2007) in his article *A practitioner's view of the challenges facing NGO-based microfinance in Bangladesh* says loan rescheduling is generally not allowed in micro finance agencies (p. 196). Here Rahman misses GB flexible loans products that reschedule clients' loans in its Phase-11 if required. Even Alterna Savings reschedules repayment instalments for its delinquent borrowers upon client requests. Moreover, loan collection flexibility exists in MFIs in Pakistan, Philippines, India, and Africa. Although many MFIs have not yet not been able to incorporate their borrowers to be members of the organizations; Grameen Bank, Bank Rakayat, BancoSol, Grameen Americas and Alterna Savings have provisions that their clients can be members. This is something that Rahman denies. Moreover, Rahman (2007) mentioned that MFI savings withdrawal rules are difficult, agreed loan amounts are often reduced by complicated deductions and fees, loan pricing is not carefully thought out, etc. (p. 23). These statements are not supported by evidence where MFIs are violating savings and loan disbursing roles. Every MFI registered by the government should follow the statute that is incorporated in registration documents.

6.0. MFIs neoliberal governentality politics

Lamia Karim (2011) in her book *Microfinance and discontents: Women in debt in Bangladesh* debates on micro-finance activities in Bangladesh. She thinks micro-credit is the extension of neo-liberal notion that is working for the poor in Bangladesh at the expense of their cost. Microcredit is an economic program for the poor, but it has social little mission. Microcredit is questionable to uplift the socio-economic conditions of poor in Bangladesh. It has little contribution to political economy and social economy in Bangladesh even in the world. There is no political economy in MFIs programs. Karim asserts that microfinance NGOs promote the idea that the borrower knows best, and that the state should withdraw from the sphere of economic activities, leaving it to the unseen hand of the market. Microcredit is the extension of small loans to poor to start income generating businesses out of their homes. In the 1990s, the term microcredit was replaced by microfinance. Microfinance refers to a broad range of financial services to the poor such as credit, savings, insurance and pensions. However, these two terms are fundamentally equivalent. She thinks both are instruments of finance capital, and both promote the idea of entrepreneurship over investments in the public. In development circles, the excitement over microfinance is exhilarating because "it promises to achieve what previous models of development could not attain" and "mark an important turning point in human history (Fernando, 2007). In fact, it can be argued that microfinance as a tool of poverty alleviation has taken on a religious fervor among its advocates. This excitement is akin to a "new wave of evangelists for microcredit" (Wood & Sharif, 1997). In the 1990s, the Consultative Group to Assist the Poorest (C-GAP) and donor agencies made microfinance is a major donor plank for poverty alleviation and gender strategies (Mayoux, 2002). In 1997, when the first Microcredit Summit was launched in Washington, DC, a research was presented in support of the notion that microfinance institutions are not only profitable and self-sustaining, but they are also capable of reaching and empowering large numbers of poor women.

In 2006, the Noble Peace Committee legitimized the microfinance model as a key to women's economic and social development. These endorsements have resulted in an unprecedented escalation in funds promoting microfinance in development (Yunus, 2006). Poor as a category refers to families that live on less than ".5 acre of cultivable land or assets with a value equivalent to less than 1.0 acres of medium quality land" (Hashemi & Morshed (1997). They (Hashemi and Morshed) shared the microcredit model popularized by Grameen Bank, based on group formation, joint liability for individual loans, savings schemes and strict fiscal discipline with minor variations. Moreover, they (MFIs) had close ties with international aid organizations and multinational corporations and operated within neoliberal notions of privatization and profit maximization. Lamia Karim's (2011) analysis of microcredit impact has influenced by three authors- Michel Foucault, on governmentality, David Harvey on neoliberalism, and Arturo Escobar on development as discourse. Lamia Karim terms NGOs governmentality that regulates, manipulates social relations of micro-borrowers to regulate the financial behaviour of individual borrowers to create wealth for the NGOs. According to Foucault, the role of modern governments is the management of populations. Governmentality is the creation of a set of rules, conducts and procedures that aim to achieve selected goals through the supervision of targeted populations. This concept articulates with the work of NGOs that govern rural populations, particularly women, through a range of tactics, instrumentalities, and programs; but most notable among these practices is the regulation of microfinance as an instrument of power between a resource-rich institution NGO) and its poor clientele.

This concept of governmentality is closely linked to the politics of neoliberalism. Harvey's theorization of neoliberalism was instructive in comprehending the unfolding of microfinance policies in Bangladesh (Harvey, 2005).

As noted earlier, neoliberalism is the withdrawal of the state from the economic and social lives of its citizens. The Western-aided NGOs stepped in to provide credit, education, healthcare, road reconstruction and other essential services to rural populations. The goal of neoliberalism is to align people to a deregulated market as efficient producers and consumers. Within this economic arena, neoliberalism subjects citizens to act in accordance with the 'market principles of discipline, efficiency and competiveness'. And microfinance NGOs have adopted these norms to shape the conduct of their borrowers as entrepreneurial subjects. But people live in parallel social worlds where other forces, such as kinship norms, encroach on their behavior. It is at the intersection of these different worlds that Lamia Karim's micro financing analysis occurs.

The insights of Escobar (1995) on development are used by Lamia Karim for analyzing her micro-financing discourse. Escobar things that knowledge operates as a form of development to act in accordance with those principles that promote particular ends and visions. For example, in Bangladesh the poverty discourse is conveyed by a plethora of studies, statistical surveys, conferences and brochures with pictures of happy rural women- all held together by the discursive power of research aligned with the development industry. Lamia Karim's first analysis stands how NGOs have operationalized rural codes of honor and shame to manufacture a culturally specific governmentality (Rahman, 1999). Rural life is guided by the proper conduct of women, and women are the bearers of family honor. When loan defaults occur, and they do so regularly for poor people, the NGOs use the group of women to shame the defaulting women and her family to recover the outstanding loan. In the face-to-face community of rural Bangladesh, public shaming results are heightened strife and dishonor for the women. This fear of shame by NGOs haunts rural men and women, and they regulate their fiscal behavior accordingly. Lamia Karim termed the economy of shame.

Second Lamia Karim (2011) analyses a trend to which studies have paid little attention on how the NGO operates as a shadow state, and how this signals the privatization of state functions in many areas. How NGOs and their Western sponsors have privatized the Bangladeshi state by developing the NGO sector as an alternative provider of services to the poor. In rural economy, NGOs are the key providers of necessary services. They offer rural employment through their development programs. Moreover, NGOs are the primary institutions of rural credit. These relationships of dependencies between NGOs and their rural clients help to inaugurate the NGO as a quasi-sovereign shadow state. However, the language of neoliberal efficiency that is invoked by donors and NGOs alike obscures the withdrawal of the state from public life, a process that has enormous implications for the country.

Finally Lamia Karim examines how development knowledge is produced within the cultural and hierarchical context of Bangladeshi society. There has been no study on microfinance that has examined the cultural production of NGO knowledge itself. In Bangladesh, NGOs, their Western sponsors, and a small coterie of NGO researchers circumscribe the discourse of development, and determine what can be made intelligible to the public. This small group of researchers determines the rules of NGO research, and they function as the gatekeepers of knowledge production. Hence the construction of development knowledge itself has to be culturally examined.

Richard L. Meyers (2007) in his article *'Measuring the impact of microfinance'* asked the question does micro-credit lift people out of poverty (p. 20)? Moreover, in his article, he discusses the limitation of micro-credit impact analysis. According to him, the key concepts and problems of quantitative impact analysis are: poverty proxies, counterfactual control and comparison groups (getting harder to find those unaffected by micro-finance), and borrowers' displacement from one place to another over time. Present micro-credit empirical impact studies focus on current versus past clients (successful graduates) achievements, attrition, and differential impact by poverty level. Micro-credit evaluators use several control variables, but still there remains bias in interviewees' selection in the survey. Moreover, problems can be found in identifying, collecting and analysing the data and in statistical analysis. Meyers interprets that empirical evaluators face greater difficulties in employing robust techniques (quantitative method), partly due to the large methodological difficulties in undertaking impact analysis (p. 237). Therefore it is very important use both empirical methods, qualitative case study methods and use social accounting techniques for micro-credit impact analysis. Moreover,

Meyers (2007) finds that there is dissatisfaction with the cost and complexity that has prompted two new directions in impact analysis (p. 20). For example, he says that randomized control procedures are emerging as a way to resolve some of difficult counterfactual problems in quantitative microfinance impact analysis. Hence according to him the impact analysis represents an opposite response to the question of analytical rigor. Therefore, Meyers suggests eradicating these problems, evaluators should be prompted to search for more user-friendly methods (Unspecified) of impact analysis (p. 237).

7.0. Why MFIs have high interest rates

Policy makers in Asia and the Pacific are increasingly critical of the high interest rates that microfinance institutions (MFIs) charge. Some policy makers have suggested that ceilings be introduced on microcredit interest rates to ensure that poor households have access to affordable credit. Fernando, Nimal A. (2006) in his book *'Understanding and dealing with high interest rates on microcredit: A note to policy makers in the Asia and Pacific region'* talks and analyse the interest of MFIs in different countries.

Charging prices high enough to cover costs is an essential practice for any business enterprise that intends to continue its operations beyond the short-term. Many MFIs have adopted cost recovery interest rates on microcredit. Significant numbers of such institutions have been able to expand the depth and breadth of their operations. The nominal interest rates charged by most MFIs in the region range from 30% to 70% a year on a reducing balance basis. The effective interest rates are even higher because of commissions and fees charged by MFs. Other factors-such as compulsory deposits for obtaining a loan, frequency of repayments and the systems adopted to collect repayments–also raise the effective interest rates. The Government of Sri Lanka recently introduced interest rate ceiling on a number of microcredit schemes operated through the National Development Trust, the government-controlled apex agency in the industry.

Fernando A. Nimal (2006) raises question why microcredit rates are so high. He finds there are four key factors determine these rates: The cost of funds, the MFI's operating expenses, loan losses and profits needed to expand their capital base fund expected future growth. As MFIs main objective is to provide poor and low-income households with an affordable source of financial services. Interest charged on loans is the main source of income for these institutions and because they incur huge costs, the rates are correspondingly high. Although micro-lenders receive loan funds at concessional rates, they must cost these funds at market rates when they make decisions about interest rates to ensure the sustainability of the institution's operations. Donors provide concessional funds for a particular usage only for a limited period, as do some governments. However, concessional funds cannot be considered a permanent source of funds for MFIs, and provision must be made through interest rates to sustain the lenders' operations. Micro-lenders have two kinds of operating costs: Personnel and administrative. Because micro lending is still a labor-intensive operation, personnel costs are high. However, microcredit interest rates are often compared with those charged by both commercial banks and excessively subsidized lending organizations. I think such comparisons are inappropriate.

In Bangladesh, the Grameen Bank charges annual interest rates of 20% (currently GB interest rate is 16%) on a reducing-balance basis on its main credit product. Because this rate was below cost recovery levels, the Grameen Bank incurred losses for many years, and these losses were underwritten by the big subsidies it received in 1980s and 1990s. Thus, Grameen Bank's interest rates should not be compared with those of an MFI has not received subsidies (Fernando, 2006).

8.0. Conclusions

From the above discussions, many authors of the books and articles are columnists of micro-credit, armchairs scholars and consultants (not directly involved as micro-credit practitioners). Although many of them raise several intuitive issues in their articles; none of them provide solutions to overcome problems like how to reduce loan transactions costs, how to mobilise government and formal financial institutions to develop resources to serve micro-borrowers and make them joint risk-takers with MFI. Every country has banks for the rich, but there are not any banks for the poor. Although MFIs are committed to serving micro-credit to their communities; they are screaming for loan funds and suffering from a lack of legal support to collect and use savings from the public, which are very essential. Hence public and private financial supports are needed to increase loan disbursement size with less interest rate for micro-entrepreneurs. Besides these, integrated micro credit rehabilitation schemes can assist delinquent borrowers revive their businesses when their business is in crisis.

In Canada, micro-finance programs are suffering from a lack of public and private institutional supports. Therefore, municipal governments and other quasi-public institutions can initiate small business incubation programs to incubate their local micro-entrepreneurs. The financial and non-financial support services can mentor micro-enterprises to grow and to contribute to socio-economic development in the community. Hence, government can provide IT support services, accounting services, legal aid services, monitoring resources and extension workers to MFIs to reduce MFI operational costs. Throughout my grass-root micro-finance working experience in Grameen Bank and different countries and reviewing different micro-finance literature, I strongly believe the above mentioned financial and non-financial support services along with a strong powerful leadership lobby is urgent in order to mentor MFIs and to support their clients' businesses. This is rather than simply saying that MFIs provide multiple services to the community without providing resources to them. Therefore, social scientists, academicians, and lobbyist should lobby for a separate bank for the poor for the interest of incubating, mentoring micro-enterprises, engage them to be economic and social actors in the community in order to reduce poverty, reduce marginalized youth unemployment, enhance green and social businesses and develop self-reliance and dignity among marginalised people in society.

9.0. References

Abugre, Charles (1994). "When Credit is Not Due" in *Financial Landscapes Reconstructed: The Fine Art of Mapping Development*. Bouman, F.J.A. and Otto Hospes (eds.). Boulder Colorado: Westview Press

Ackerly, Brooke A. (1995). Testing the Tools of Development: Credit Programs, Loan Involvement, and Women's Empowerment. *IDS Bulletin*. Vol. 26 (3), pp. 56-68

Adams, Dale (1998). "Altruistic or Production Finance? A Donor's Dilemma" in *Strategic Issues in Microfinance*. Mwange S Kimenyi, Robert C. Weiland and J.D. Von Pischke (eds). Aldershot, U.K. Ashgate Publishing Company

Aliaga, Irina and Mosley, Paul. (2007).Princes, peasants and retenders: The past and future of African microfinance. In Thomas Dichter and Malcolm Harper (Eds.), *What's wrong with microfinance* (109-120).Warwickshire: Practica Action Publishing

Allen, Hugh.(2007). Finance begins with savings, not loans. In Thomas Dichter and Malcolm Harper (Eds.), *What's wrong with microfinance?* (49-60). Warwickshire: Practica Action Publishing

Bateman, Milford. (2007). De-industrialization and social disintegration in Bosnia. In Thomas Dichter and Malcolm Harper (Eds.), *What's wrong with microfinance* (207-224)? Warwickshire: Practica Action Publishing

Dawson, Jonathan and Andy Jeans (1997). *Looking Beyond Credit: Business Development Services and the Promotion of Innovation Among Small Producers*. London: Intermediate Technology Publications

Dichter, Thomas and Harper, Maccolm. (ed.) (2007). *What's wrong with Microfinance*? WarWickshire, UK: Intermediate Technology Publications Ltd

Ellerman, David. (2007). Microfinance: Some conceptual and methodological problems. In Thomas Dichter and Malcolm Harper

(Eds.), *What's wrong with microfinance* (149-162)? Warwickshire: Practica Action Publishing

Ditcher, Thomas. (2007). The chicken and egg dilemma in micriofinance: An historical analysis of the sequence of growth and credit in the economic development of the 'north'. In Thomas Dichter and Malcolm Harper (Eds.), *What's wrong with microfinance (179*-192)? Warwickshire: Practica Action Publishing

Ditcher,Thomas.(2007). Can microcredit make an already slippery slope more slippery? Some lessons from the social meaning of debt in Thomas Dichter and Malcolm Harper (Eds.), *What's wrong with microfinance? Pp.* (9-18).Warwickshire: Practica Action Publishing Gibbons, David S and Jennifer Meehan (1999). The Microcredit Summit's Challenge: Working towards Institutional Self-Sufficiency while Maintaining a Commitment to Serving the Poorest Families. Paper for the *Microcredit Summit Meeting of Councils*. Abidjan, Coite d'Ivoire

Ghate, Prabhu. (2007). Learning from the Andra Pradesh crisis. In Thomas Dichter and Malcolm Harper (Eds.), *What's wrong with microfinance (pp.* 163-178)? Warwickshire: Practica Action Publishing

Grameen Bank Annual Report (2016). *Grameen bank updates*. Dhaka Grameen Bank

Hashemi, Syed M. (1996). NGO Accountability in Bangladesh: Beneficiaries, Donors and the State in *Beyond the Magic Bullet: NGO Performance and Accountability in the Post-Cold War World*. Michael Edwards and David Hulme (eds.). West Hartford, Connecticut: Kumarian Press

Hashemi, Syed M. (1997). Those Left Behind: A Note on Targeting the Hardcore Poor in *Who Needs Credit: Poverty and Finance in Bangladesh*. Geoffrey Wood and Iffath Sharif (eds.). London: Zed Books

Hashemi, Syed M, Sidney Ruth Schuler, and Ann P. Riley (1996). Rural Credit Programs and Women's Empowerment in Bangladesh, *World Development*. Vol. 24(4), pp. 635-653

Hashemi, Syed M and Lamiya Morshed (1997). Grameen Bank: A Case Study in *Who Needs Credit: Poverty and Finance in Bangladesh.* Geoffrey Wood and Iffath Sharif (eds.). London: Zed Books

Harper, Malcolm (1998). *Profit for the Poor: Cases in Microfinance.* London: Intermediate Technology Publications Ltd.

Harper, Malcolm (2007). What's wrong with group? In Thomas Dichter and Malcolm Harper (Eds.),*What's wrong with microfinance?* (pp. 35-48).Warwickshire: Practica Action Publishing

Harper, Malcolm. (2007). Microfinance and farmers: Do they fit? In Thomas Dichter and Malcolm Harper (Eds.), *What's wrong with microfinance (83-96)*? Warwickshire: Practica Action Publishing

Harper, Malcolm. (2007). Some final thoughts. In Thomas Dichter and Malcolm Harper (Eds.),*What's wrong with microfinance* (257-259)? Warwickshire: Practica Action Publishing

Harper, Malcolm (1998). *Profit for the Poor: Cases in Microfinance.* London: Intermediate Technology Publications Ltd.

Harris, Sam Daley (2006). Pathways Out of Poverty: Innovations in Microfinance for the Poorest Families. Connecticut: Kumarian Press Inc.

Hendriks, Maaike (1994). Trade Arrangements and Interlinked Credit in the Philippines in *Financial Landscapes Reconstructed: The Fine Art of Mapping Development.* Bouman, FJA and Otto Hospes (eds). Boulder Colorado: Westview Press

Hossain, Iftekhar, Javed Sakhawat and Ben Quinones (2000). Bangladesh: The Pioneering Country in *Microfinance and Poverty Alleviation: Case Studies from Asia and the Pacific.* Joy Remenyi and Benjamin Quinones (eds.). London: Pinter. 2000

Hossain, Mahabub (1993). The Grameen Bank: Its Origin, Organization and Management Style in *The Grameen Bank: Poverty Relief in Bangladesh.* Abu Wahid, (ed.). Boulder, Colorado: Westview Press

Hossain, Mahabub (1993). "Operating Costs of the Grameen Bank" in *The Grameen Bank: Poverty Relief in Bangladesh.* Abu Wahid, (ed). Boulder, Colorado: Westview Press

Hulme, David and Paul Mosley (1996). *Finance against Poverty.* London: Routledge

Hulme, David and Paul Mosley (1997). Finance for the Poor or Poorest? Financial Innovation, Poverty and Vulnerability in *Who Needs Credit: Poverty and Finance in Bangladesh*, Geoffrey Wood and Iffath Sharif (eds.). London: Zed Books

Hulme, David (2000). Impact Assessment Methodologies for Microfinance: Theory, Experience and Better Practice. *World Development*, Vol. 28 (1), pp. 79-98

Hulme, David. (2007). Is microdebt good for poor people? A note on the dark side of microfinance. In Thomas Dichter and Malcolm Harper (Eds.), *What's wrong with microfinance?* (pp. 19-22). Warwickshire: Practica Action Publishing

Houghton, Mary and Grzywinski, Ronald. (2007).In Thomas Dichter and Malcolm Harper (Eds.),*What's wrong with microfinance* (pp. 251-256)? Warwickshire: Practica Action Publishing

Johnson, Susan and Ben Rogaly (1997). *Microfinance and Poverty Reduction*. Oxford: Oxfam

Johnson, Susan (1997). Gender and Microfinance: Guidelines for Good Practices, Bath: Centre for Development Studies, University of Bath

Johnson, Susan and Sharma, Namrata. (2007). 'Institutionalizing suspicion': The management and governance challenge in user-owned microfinance groups. In Thomas Dichter and Malcolm Harper (Eds.), *What's wrong with microfinance* (pp. 61-72)? Warwickshire: Practica Action Publishing

Karim, Lamia (2011). *Microfinance and discontents: Women in debt in Bangladesh*. Minneapolis: University of Minnesota Press

Matin,Imran.Sulaiman,Munshi. and Saleque, M.Abdul. (2007). Imagining microfinance more bodly: Unleashing the rue potential of microfinance. In Thomas Dichter and Malcolm Harper (Eds.), *What's wrong with microfinance?* (pp. 23-34).Warwickshire: Practica Action Publishing

M-Cril (2003). *Microfinance Review*, M-Cril, Gurgaon

Mahajan, Vijay. (2007). From microcredit to livelihood finance. In Thomas Dichter and Malcolm Harper (Eds.), *What's wrong with microfinance* (pp. 241-250)? Warwickshire: Practica Action Publishing

Mahmud, S. (2004). Microcredit and women's empowerment in Bangladesh. In S. Ahmed & S. Hakim (Eds.), *Attacking poverty with microcredit* (pp. 148-153). Dhaka: The University Press Limited.

Mayoux, Linda (1995). *From Vicious to Virtuous Circles? Gender and Micro-Enterprise Development.* Geneva: United Nations Research Institute for Social Development

Morduch, Jonathan (2000). The Microfinance Schism, *World Development,* Vol. 28 (4), pp. 617-629

Meyer, Richard (2007). Measuring the impact of microfinance. In Thomas Dichter and Malcolm Harper (Eds.), *What's wrong with microfinance* (pp. 225-240)? Warwickshire: Practica Action Publishing

Mosley, Paul and David Hulme. (1998). Microenterprise Finance: is there a Conflict Between Growth and Poverty Alleviation? *World Development,* Vol. 26 (5), pp. 783-790

Mosley, Paul (2001). Microfinance and Poverty in Bolivia" in *The Journal of Development Studies,* Vol. 37(4), pp. 101-132

Mutua, Albert Kimanthi (1994). The Juhudi Credit Scheme: From a Traditional Integrated Method to a Financial Systems Approach in *The New World of Microenterprise Finance: Building Healthy Financial Institutions for the Poor.* Otero, Maria and Elisabeth Rhyn (eds.). West Hartford, Connecticut: Kumarian Press

Nimal A. Fernando, (2006). *Understanding and dealing with high interest rates on microcredit: A note to policy makers in the Asia and Pacific region,* Manila: Asia Development Bank

Natilson, Nancy. In Their Own Words: Pro Mujer, Bolivia in *The Microbanking Bulletin.* Issue No. 5. Sept. 2000. Toronto: Calmeadow

O' Connell, S. (2004). *Credit, lass and Community: Working Class Belfast 1930- 2000,* University of Ulster, School of History and International Affairs, Ulster

Otero, Maria and Elisabeth Rhyne (eds.) (1994). *The New World of Microenterprise Finance: Building Healthy Financial Institutions for the Poor.* West Hartford, Connecticut: Kumarian Press

Rahman, Aminur (1999). *Women and Microcredit in Rural Bangladesh: Anthropological Study of the Rhetoric and Realities of Grameen Bank Lending.* Boulder Colorado. Westview Press.

Rahman, Atiur and M. Mahabub-ul Islam (1993). The General Performance of the Grameen Bank in *The Grameen Bank: Poverty Relief in Bangladesh.* Abu Wahid (ed.). Boulder, Colorado: Westview Press

Rahman, Atiur and Baban Hasnat (1993). Housing for the rural Poor: The Grameen Bank Experience in *The Grameen Bank: Poverty Relief in Bangladesh.* Abu Wahid (ed.). Boulder, Colorado: Westview Press

Rahman, Atiur, Abu Wahid, and Faizul Islam (1993). Impact of Grameen Bank on the Nutritional Status of the rural Poor in *The Grameen Bank: Poverty Relief in Bangladesh.* Abu Wahid (ed.). Boulder, Colorado: Westview Press

Robinson, Marguerite (1998). "Microfinance: the Paradigm Shift from Credit Delivery to Sustainable Financial Intermediation" in *Strategic Issues in Microfinance.* Mwange S. Kimenyi, Robert C. Weiland and J.D. Von Pischke (eds). Aldershot, U.K. Ashgate Publishing Company

Paul Rippey (2007). Princes, peasants and pretenders: The past and future of African microfinance. In Thomas Dichter and Malcolm Harper (Eds.), *What's wrong with microfinance* (pp. 110-120)? Warwickshire: Practica Action Publishing

Rahman, S.M. (2007). A practitioner's view of the challenges facing NGO-based microfinance in Bangladesh. In Thomas Dichter and Malcolm Harper (Eds.), *What's wrong with microfinance* (193-206)? Warwickshire: Practica Action Publishing

Rouf, K. A. (2012). Integrated micro-credit vs single minded microcredit? Bingley UK: Emerald Group of Publishing limited. Vol. 28(4)

Rouf, K. A. (2012). Green microfinance promoting green enterprise development. *International Journal of Research Studies in Management.* Vol. 1 (1), pp. 85-96

Rouf, K. A. (2012). The advantages of micro-credit lending programs and the human capabilities approach for women's poverty reduction and increased human rights in Bangladesh. *International Journal of Research Studies in Management*. Vol. 1 (2), pp. 25-36

Sabharwal, Gita (1999). *From the Margin to the Mainstream: Micro-Finance Programmes and Women's Empowerment: The Bangladesh Experience.* Thesis for MSc in Economics in Development Management, Centre for Development Studies, University of Wales, Swansea

Sobhan, Rehman (1997). The Political Economy of Micro Credit in *Who Needs Credit: Poverty and Finance in Bangladesh*. Geoffrey Wood and Iffath Sharif (eds). London: Zed Books

Stack, Kathleen and Didier Thys (2000). "A Business Model for Going Down Market: Combining Village Banking and Credit Unions" in *The Microbanking Bulletin*. Issue No. 5. Toronto: Calmeadow

Sinha, Frances. (2007). SHGs in India: Numbers yes, poverty outreach and empowerment, partially. In Thomas Dichter and Malcolm Harper (Eds.), *What's wrong with microfinance* (pp. 73-82)? Warwickshire: Practica Action Publishing

Thorndike, E. L. (1920). Psychology notes on the motives of thrift', *Annals of the American Academy of Political and Social science,* Vol. 87, pp. 212-18

Von Pischke. (2007). Methodenstreit and sustainability in microfinance: Generations describing institutional frameworks. In Thomas Dichter and Malcolm Harper (Eds.), *What's wrong with microfinance* (pp. 137-148)? Warwickshire: Practica Action Publishing

Wahid, Abu (ed). (1993). *The Grameen Bank: Poverty Relief in Bangladesh*. Boulder, Colorado: Westview Press

Wahid, Abu (1993a). The Socioeconomic Conditions of Bangladesh and the Evolution of the Grameen Bank in *The Grameen Bank: Poverty Relief in Bangladesh*. Abu Wahid, (ed). Boulder, Colorado: Westview Press

Wahid, Abu (1993b). The Growth and Progress of the Grameen Bank in *The Grameen Bank: Poverty Relief in Bangladesh*. Abu Wahid, (ed). Boulder, Colorado: Westview Press

White, Sarah. (1999). NGOs, Civil Society, and the State in Bangladesh: The Politics of Representing the Poor, *Development and Change* Vol. 30(2), pp. 307-326

Wilson, Kim. (2007). The moneylender's dilemma. In Thomas Dichter and Malcolm Harper (Eds.), *What's wrong with microfinance (97-108)?* Warwickshire: Practica Action Publishing.

World Bank (1996). *Impact of Grameen Bank in Bangladesh.* Washington D.C.: The World Bank.

Yunus, Muhamad (1996). *Credit is a human right.* Dhaka: Grameen Bank

Yunus, Muhamad. (2010b). *Building social business: A new kind of capitalism that serves humanity's most pressing needs.* New York: Public Affairs.

Commonalities of Mondraon Corporation Cooperativa (MCC) Spain, The Grameen Bank Bangladesh and The Big Carrot Cooperative Social Ventures Canada

Abstract

This paper compares and contrasts the Evangeline Cooperatives in Canada, The Big Carrot in Toronto, Mondragon in Spain and the group based microcredit Grameen Bank in Bangladesh in the lens of cooperative movement in Canada, Spain and Bangladesh.

Key words: Micro-credit, Cooperative, Mongragon, Social Enterprise, Social Venture and Big Carrot.

Acronyms: Arctic Co-operatives Limited (ACL), Bangladesh Rural Development Board (BRDB), Grameen Bank (GB), Mondragon Corproacion Cooperativa (MCC), Profit-Making-Businesses (PMB), Social Business Enterprises (SBE).

1.0. Introduction

Evangeline Cooperatives in Maritime Canada, The Big Carrot in Toronto, Mondragon in Spain and The Grameen Bank in Bangladesh are examples of cooperative movements that promote local employment and contribute to local community economic development. They are not charities, rather cooperative social enterprises that follow democratic decision making processes, share economic and social missions with local people, and operate without government grants and subsidies (Quarter et al. (2009). At the same time these groups contribute to local living economies and promote long-term sustainable development in their communities. They are all alternatives to profit-making-businesses (PMB). These organizations have changed the way that business is done in their areas of the world. This paper looks at what they have in common, what makes them work in their settings and how they have been and could be replicated in other areas of the world.

2.0. Meaning of co-operative

A cooperative is an autonomous association of persons united voluntarily to meet the common economic, social and cultural needs and aspirations through a jointly owned and democratically controlled enterprise (International Cooperative Alliance, Geneva). Cooperative values are based on the values of self-help, self-responsibility, democracy, equality, solidarity and caring for others. They are an alternative to market based individualized capitalism in that they promote community development. These programs have a combination of social and economic objectives. Cooperatives are creative, innovative, productive and aspiring social enterprises that create social purpose and have social return on investment. Childcare centers, funeral services, Acadian Co-operative Enterprises and Eva Print are examples of social enterprises in Canada. These groups commonly combine the passion of a social mission with an image of business-like discipline, innovation, and determination (Dees, 1998). For social entrepreneurs, the social mission is explicit and central. The social entrepreneur aims to promote socio-economic local context culture and values (Bornstein & Davis, 2010). Below are discussions about the common features and societal contributions of Mondragon Corproacion Cooperativa (MCC), The Grameen Bank (GB), Evangeline Cooperatives and The Big Carrot cooperative social enterprises.

3.0. Compare and constrast Mondragon Corproacion Cooperativa (MCC) Spain, The Grameen Bank Banglsadesh, Evangeline Cooperatives and The Big Carrot Canada

Mondragon Corproacion Cooperativa (MCC), The Grameen Bank, Evangeline Cooperatives and The Big Carrot are all community-based cooperative social enterprises that follow a cooperative model and were initiated by individuals. The initiators of these social enterprise cooperatives combine cooperatives with social collective businesses and emphasize a social mission. Usually these innovative localized social venture cooperatives are successful within their local areas. Father Jimmy Tompkins and Moses Coady initiated The Evangeline Cooperative, a part of the *Antigonish Movement* in Nova Scotia in 1940 (Wilkinson & Quarter 1996). Don Jose Maria, a priest in Basque, initiated Mondragon through organizing a technical school without government sponsorship in 1956. Now it is call Mondragon Corproacion Cooperativa (MCC), a workers cooperative enterprise. Don Jose Maria's idea considered the collaboration of the labour-union movement, cooperative movement and progressive political movement (MacLeod 1997). Muhammed Yunus began the Grameen Bank in Bangladesh in 1979 (Yunus, 2003). Nine individuals began The Big Carrot in Toronto in 1984 (Big Carrot 2011). None of these cooperatives used government funding.

These social enterprises emphasize creating wealth through group effort rather than solely through consumption. This is grounded in the belief that each person is weak, but individuals united as a group become strong a concept that has been proved through practice (MacLeod 1997). All work in team spirit and believe in human capacities, creativity and need instead of treating human beings as a unit of labor. They have common goal; to improve the lives of low-income people and a focus on the primacy of community. Their missions are different from capitalist corporations where the goal is profit for the owners.

Above all these cooperatives exercise their autonomy and independence in their program operations, have democratic accountability and follow the seven principles of cooperatives which are: (1) voluntary and open membership, (2) democratic member control, (3) member economic participation, (4) autonomy and independence, (5) education, training and information, (6) co-operation among co-operatives, and (7) concern of community (International Co-operative Alliance's ICA). Their priority is people where satisfaction of their clients forms a part of the enterprise. For example the Grameen Bank clients are not handout receivers; instead they become economic actors in the community by using micro loans in Bangladesh. The Grameen Bank, Evangeline and The Big Carrot also promote agricultural production and agricultural marketing through their programs; however, Mondragon produces and sells non-agricultural products like automobile parts and other industrial products. All of these groups follow social value cooperative principles.

Like Mondragon, the Grameen Bank and Evangeline follow open admission to members, democratic decision process, sovereignty of people, and self-management policies. They believe in group cooperation. Like Evangeline cooperatives, the Arctic Co-operatives Limited (ACL) is a service federation of 31 community-based cooperatives in Nunavut, the North West Territories, and Northern Manitoba. This organization is the largest employer of

Aboriginal people outside of the Canadian government. They have a commitment to the community and work for the well-being of the local communities. Mondragon and the Big Carrot social enterprise cooperatives share their surplus among workers where the Grameen Bank and Evangeline Cooperatives share their loss and profits with their members. MCC, The Big Carrot, and The Grameen Bank are social businesses that compete directly with profit making businesses.

4.0. Social business Mondraon Corproacion Cooperativa (MCC), The Grameen Bank and The Big Carrot

Mondraon Corproacion Cooperativa (MCC), The Grameen Bank and The Big Carrot follow social business model in their respective country. These cooperatives follow a social business model where a non-loss dividend is distributed to their members and reused for businesses expansion. These social businesses make revenues and profits to pay back their investor's money and to support the long-term social goals. They are running their businesses in self-sustaining ways. Although Mondragon, The Big Carrot, GB, Evangeline cooperatives follow community- based social venture principles, some contrast can be found among them. Below is the discussion of the degree of similarity and contrast of the general common features among them.

The Grameen Bank and Mondragon both believe in and use modern technology for development. For example, Mondragon workers' cooperatives use high tech machines in their factories and produce auto parts and other machineries that provide income to Mondragon. Similarly, the Grameen Bank provides cell phones, power tillers, tractors, and oil extruders to its borrowers for use in their income generating businesses. These services have a major impact on individual life and promote collective social and economic values.

Mondragon Corproacion Cooperativa (MCC) and the Big Carrot are more similar than the Grameen Bank and the Evangeline social businesses cooperatives. MCC and the Big Carrot are both workers cooperatives, but the GB and Evangeline are community-based open membership cooperatives. The Big Carrot borrowed the Mondragon worker-owned co-operative collective model in their wholesome and organic food workers co-operative business. Each cooperative member of these two organizations receives a share of the profits commensurate with the time s/he has worked in these cooperative businesses and factories. Each worker-member is a shareholder and has a right to vote at the Annual General Assembly held once a year and approves the operational plan. Their Board of Directors is elected every 2-4 years. Both Mondragon and the Big Carrot present their operational plans to their respective assemblies for approval. A Management Council is the head of the key departments of these two organizations.

Employees' wage disparity is limited in MCC and The Big Carrot workers cooperatives. For example, in Mondragon no one person is allowed to earn more than six times what another person earns. Any profits that remain after salaries and other expenses are then divided up into funds and the members (profit sharing). In the case of The Big Carrot, the wage ratio is 3:1 ratio between the highest and lowest paid. Any profits which remain after salaries and other expenses are then divided up in a typical division: 10% to the Social-Cultural Fund, 20% to the company reserve fund, 70% to the workers-members account. The individual worker receive the sharing money in his/her account only upon retirement or when leaving Mondragon (MacLeod, 1997). Such policy is also found at the Big Carrot. For example any year-end surplus is divided as follows: 10% for the community, 20% for a collective reserve, 70% labor dividends to be divided according to hours worked. The collective reserve is placed in capital accounts and is reinvested in the business (The Big Carrot 2011). Labor dividends are paid out as cash flow allows. However one concern is that because cooperatives include the role of members approving other members this can lead to forms of discrimination. In the Big Carrot to be a new member you require 80% members' approval in the General Assembly.

Mondragon Corproacion Cooperativa (MCC) and Evangeline Cooperative: Mondragon and Evangeline are both local cooperatives that have a federated cooperative council that coordinates the cooperatives, provides guidelines, and is involved in management decisions. Both cooperatives started with a vision as a social movement to create an alternative to capitalism that would be controlled through communities and a decentralized democratic structure. Mondragon's entire system is unified under one umbrella organization called the Congress. Similarly Evangeline cooperative council, a second tier Evangeline co-operative development, encourages thinking regarding the overall welfare of the Maritime Canadian region (Wilkinson & Quarter 1996).

Mondragon and Evangeline both have links with credit unions for funding. Credit unions strengthen the ability of the primary organization to provide its service rather than to serve the broader objective of developing the local community. For example, the Evangeline Credit Union provides loans to different cooperatives in Maritime Canada (Wilkinson & Quarter, 1996). The Baie Acadienne Venture Capital Group makes equity financing to new community enterprises. In Mondragon, the role of Caja Laboral Popular (credit union) utilizes local financial resources and invests them in the creation of new enterprises for the development of the Basque region with a social mission (MacLeod, 1997). The Antigonish Movement has had much influence in Maritime communities in forming co-operative credit unions and co-operatives stores. Acadian Co-operative Enterprises formed in 1978 to work on manufacturing and selling local arts and crafts with funding from the Canadian Employment program but it was not sustained (Wilkinson & Quarter, 1996). Evangeline promotes the local culture, values and community welfare. This political empowerment decentralizes responsibility and empowers people through both ownership and control of economic structures in their community. For example, it follows Antigonish tradition using adult education techniques where kitchen table meetings preserve the Acadian way of life and follow the comprehensive cooperative model through which communities develop and strengthen themselves (Wilkinson & Quarter, 1996).

However, Sally Hacer, a feminist critic of Mondragon points out that generally the men are at the top and women are at the bottom of the management in MCC. Although these cooperatives are working for the common good of the community, cooperatives always have experienced a threat from social change. For example, the Evangeline threat is disappearing quickly and has been taken over by pragmatism. Many of its cooperatives are management run and far from the ideal of an active membership who participates in policy decisions. The same thing has happened in the Bangladesh Rural Development Board (BRDB), a government managed cooperative in Bangladesh. Huge conflict and bureaucracy in BRDB have destroyed its activities in Bangladesh.

The Grameen Bank has taken lessons from BRDB Bangladesh and has developed a modified version of cooperatives, where individual and collective responsibility is distributed among group members like in Mondragon. The Grameen Bank is kept completely away from government influence until 2011. Every year the GB group leaders change. It enables small producers to enter into local markets and capture more of the value chain. This cooperative system assists in capital accumulation through using micro credit and providing weekly small savings to the poor. It plays an important role in empowering people to participate in civic and local decision making processes and enabling them to get ahead. However, the problem with complete sustainability is high interest rates and aggressive loan repayment techniques.

5.0. Differences in Mondragon and the Grameen Bank

The major point of difference of Mondragon and Grameen Bank is that Mondragon workers elect a Board of Directors through a General Assembly. Mondragon promotes cooperative paid employment and provides facilities to its employees whereas GB promotes self-employment in Bangladesh. Worker development is enhanced through skill improvement training, rotation of jobs, and continuing education in MCC (MacLeod 1997). However, GB places less importance on employees' vocational skill development. In Mondagon, employees are representatives in the congress and have a decentralized organizational structure. GB borrowers are the owner of the bank and their representatives are the Board of Directors who is making decisions for the bank.

The social business enterprises (SBE) have a commitment to the community. The Grameen Bank and its other umbrella organizations are examples of social businesses; their surplus is reused for the expansion of the community development program. The Grameen Bank has shared asset networks with its umbrella organizations. It has created many other SBE companies like Grameen Renewable Energy, Grameen Health, Grameen Phone, Grameen Telecom, Grameen Agriculture, Grameen Fisheries and Livestock, and Grameen Communications etc. They are independent from The Grameen Bank; however, their missions are also to serve the needs of the poor through the supply of solar panels, health services, phone services, crop production, livestock development and various IT services respectively. The Grameen Bank extends its managerial, advisory and funding support to these organizations. For example, it gave an endowment of $3.16 million of its revolving loan fund to Grameen Health (Grameen Statistics: 2002). The Grameen umbrella stakeholders share their services and help to channel more services to the rural poor in Bangladesh.

6.0. Replicable

The Caixa in Valencia first replicated the Mondragon research and development wing's model through a cooperative called EI Group Empresarial Cooperativ Valencia (GECV) and through a community bank or credit union called the Caixa in Valenca (MacLeod 1997). The

Modragon model works well in Spain. The Big Carrot replicates the idea of Mondragon worker's democracy, but on a smaller scale and with a non-community-development focus. It is unable to massively expand in Canada and is rather limited to its one-spot-shop in Toronto.

The Grameen Bank financial system has been used among the very poor throughout the world. Its group lending model has been replicated in 143 countries all over Asia, Africa, Europe, Australia, and the Americas. Most replicators adopt small group lending and collateral free loans. For example, group micro lending method has replicated in low-income neighborhoods in the United States and in Canada. However, micro-credit in Canada is not popular as a way to address unemployment and to eradicate poverty. Despite this, several initiatives develop in the Northern regions of Canada in 1990s. However, they do not replicate things like extra services other than loans, and weekly savings. Particular socio-economic-political conditions are necessary for successful replication of any borrowing cooperative model.

From the above discussions it is clear that in social business cooperatives people are able to help each other voluntarily to achieve their mutually desired goals. They offer an alternative development strategy where businesses, commerce and economic development tie with social and ethical collective values along principles of democracy and self-help. Hence Kofi Anan (2005) says," Cooperatives play a crucial role across a wide spectrum of human aspiration and need." They promote local cultures and values, collective economic participation provide employment, vital health, housing, and banking services, promote education, social inclusion and protect the environment." (Cooperative College, UK). So cooperatives make a significant contribution to reaching the millennium development goals in the community. All these cooperatives stimulate the local democratic structures and collective self-fulfillment that are important for sustainable development.

7.0. Conclusion

Undoubtedly, above co-operatives are the practical demonstration of locally controlled economic activities that meet the need of the local communities although some are facing challenges sustainability and effective replication. All of the above co-ops generate income through employment or by services and contribute to improving the quality of life for low-income people and their families (Shragge & Fontan, 2000). Today economic power and wealth is increasingly becoming concentrated within a small number of multinational corporations. To counter this hegemonic economic power, it is vital to create alternative economic forces, where social enterprise cooperatives can play an active role in socio-economic development, and address the issues of poverty. The idea of corporate responsibility can be shifted by a cooperative movement and become the heart of its value system. New social stock markets with social enterprise cooperatives can accelerate investment in social enterprise cooperatives to promote employment, sustainable development and to reduce poverty. It is important that this process should be free from government influence, control and regulations.

8.0. References

Anan, K. (2005). *Grameen Dialogue 2005*. Dhaka: Grameen Trust.

Big Carrot (2011). *The Carrot-Searching for Nurture's Finest.* Retrieved from http://www.thebigcarrot.ca/?id=14 dated August 20, 2017

Bornstein, D. and Davis, S. (2010). *Social entrepreneurship: What everyone needs to know*: New York: Oxford University Press

Dees, J.G. (1998). Enterprising non-profits. *Harvard Business Review* (Jan.-Feb.): pp. 55-67

Dees, J. G. (2003). *Social entrepreneurship is about innovation and impact, not income.* Skoll Foundation. [Online]. Available at: http://www.fuqua.duke.edu/centers/case/articles/1004/corner.htm

Grameen Statistics (2002). *Grameen Bank Bangladesh*. Dhaka: Packages Corporation ltd.

MacLeod, G. (1997). *From Mondragon to America: Experiments in Community Economic Development*. Sydney, NS: UCCB Press

Mendall, M. & Neamtan, N. (2010). The Social Economy in Quebec: Towards a New Political Economy. in (eds.) Laurie Mook, Jack Quarter & Sherida Ryan (2010). *Researching the Social Economy.* Toronto: University of Toronto Press Incorporated

Mook, Quarter and Ryan (2010). What's in a Name in (eds.) Laurie Mook, Jack Quarter and Sherida Ryan, (2010). *Researching the Social Economy*. Toronto: University of Toronto Press Incorporated.

Rouf, K. A. (2011). Commonalities of the Mondragon Corproacion Cooperativa Spain, the Grameen bank of Bangladesh. *International Journal of Research Studies in Management*. Vol. *1* (1), pp.25-30

Shragge, E., and Fontan, J., M. (Eds.). (2000). Introduction. In E. Shragge and Fontan, J. M. (Eds.), *Social Economy; International Debates and Perspectives*, pp. 1-21. Montreal: Black Rose

Wilkinson, P., and Quarter, J. (1996). *Building a Community –Controlled Economy; The Evangeline Co-operative experience*. Toronto: University of Toronto Press

Yunus, M. (2003). *Banker to the Poor; Micro-lending and the Battle against World Poverty*. New York; Public Affairs.

Grameen Bank services to Women in Development (WID), Women in Business (WIB), Gender and Development (GAD), Women and Development (WAD), Women in Cultural Development (WCD) and Women in Environment Development (WED) approach in Bangladesh

Abstract

The patriarchal ideology influences and shapes the sexual division of labor where their work and status is determined by sex, within the home, outside the home and workplace; and limits their access to economic, socio-economic, activities and community resources. Gander and Development (GAD), Women in Development (WID), Women and Development (WAD), Women in Cultural Development (WCD) and Women in Environmental Development (WED) are different approaches to instituting women's equality, empowering them, to fulfill their basic human needs and to establish the basic human rights of women in society. The Grameen Bank (GB) is working towards increasing and maintaining poor women's economic development (WID). The paper examines is Grameen Bank successful in applying the WIB,

GAD, WAD, WCD and WED approach to women-centered development in Bangladesh. The paper uses literature review; critically analyze Grameen Bank services to women for their socio-economic development.

Key Words: Grameen Bank (GB); Gender and Development (GAD); Women in Business (WIB); Women in Cultural Development; WCD); Women and Development (WAD); and Women in Environmental Development (WED).

1. Introduction

Women in Bangladesh are extremely disadvantaged in terms of socio-economic and human development. Violence, discrimination, barriers to banking services, religious disparities, and injustice towards women and girls, in domestic and public domains, remained unabated. These injustices are acute to bottom women, ethnic minority. Bangladeshi women are suffering from gender-based vulnerabilities. Muslim customary laws and Hindu Customary Laws deprived women from equal rights getting resources, put them low status in the family and in the public space and other benefits in community. Their low status and exploitation is due to patriarchal ideologies, religious and cultural values and attitudes in the society. The patriarchal ideology influences and shapes the sexual division of labor where their work and status is determined by sex, within the home and workplace and limits their access to economic and other community resources. In addition to limited access, women experience the direct disadvantage of being exploited and subordinated by men. Women are increasingly used instrumentally by men to exert control over family property or other assets. Furthermore, women's mobility and participation in various income-generating activities has become threatening to male-dominated society. Violence against women is not the pathological behavior, rather it is an extended system of practices and laws that sanction men's rights to regard women as their property and therefore to keep them under their (male) control.

Moreover, women who are harassed or killed, regardless of their age and occupation are systematically denied access to justice at all levels particularly bottom disadvantaged rural and slum women in Bangladesh. This denial of justice to women and their families in fact reinforces the acts of those causing violence against women. Some enforcement of women rights are taking place through some NGOs intervention, but unless and until women in Bangladesh attain economic progress and independence, education and exposed to various women rights, direct legal action and legal aid are essential to liberate them from patriarchy.

Recently feminist activities continued to pressure the government to lift up the disadvantaged women in Bangladesh. However, institutional support and law enforcement and governance formally, informally, privately and publicly is essential to overcome women exploitation, fulfill vulnerable women basic needs, women deprivation of equal access resources, equity problem and eradication of violence against women in Bangladesh. Bangladesh is the member of Convention on the Elimination of Discrimination of all forms against Women (CEDAW). The UN declaration on the Elimination of all forms of Violence against Women adopted in 1993 and identified eight different rights of women in Article 3 of the Declaration Bangladesh sign on this protocol. The women eight rights are:

1. The right to life
2. The right to liberty and security of person
3. The right to equal protection under the law
4. The to the highest standard attainable of physical and mental health
5. The right to just and favorable conditions of work
6. The right not to b e subjected to torture, or other cruel, inhuman or degrading treatment or punishment
7. The right to equality
8. The right to be from all forms of discrimination.

Gender and Development (GAD), Women in Business (WIB), Women in Cultural Development (WCD), Women and Development (WAD), and Women in Environmental Development (WED) are different approaches to instituting women's equality, to fulfill their basic human needs and to establish the basic human rights of women in society. All of the aforementioned are the elements of women's movement, struggle by women against sex division and inequality in society (Peggy 2004: p.10). The Grameen Bank (GB) is working towards increasing and maintaining poor women's economic development (WID), gender equality (GAD) and empowering them in different decision-making processes such as, participation in different development activities (educating children, joining local councils, earning more by improving skills, and uplifting living standards) (WAD). Moreover, Grameen Bank claims that it encourages women to be more involved in people-centered business development and sustainable environmental development (WED) by providing direct green loans to poor women. Therefore, the paper examines whether the Grameen Bank is an example of successful use of the WID, GAD, WAD, and WED approach to women-centered development.

2. Implication and significance of the study

The manuscript discusses women development different approaches and theories of WID, GAD, WAD, WCD and WED with examples of implementation of different agencies particularly Grameen Bank and its sister organizations services in Bangladesh. The paper also identifies different features women development different theories, identifies gaps of these theories and finds out the challenges women development agencies are facing using women development different approaches in different society. Therefore, this paper generates a new knowledge of different approaches of women development and their implication in different places. Reading this article, readers can be familiar with women development different approaches and their different features.

It is important to develop programs and services for women for their total development. Eradication of feminization of poverty is very urgent and essential to free women from their deprivation of sufferings. Although environmental activism constitutes one of the most visible and effective civil society initiatives in Bangladesh; however, bottom disadvantaged women are victims of environmental degradation and pollution. International, national and local NGOs are active to provide services to marginalized women for their liberation, social development and environmental development. Feminists usually analyze how women are deprived of their rights in their family and community. The *feminization of poverty* describes a phenomenon in which women represent a disproportionate percentage of the world's poor. This trend is not only a consequence of lack of income, but also of lack of opportunities due to gender biases and fixed gender roles in some societies. Therefore, the paper critically examines Grameen Bank different programs and services contribute to feminization of poverty, women development in Bangladesh using women development different approaches. Grameen Bank activities are helpful to setup green businesses that are environmentally friendly sustainable and convenient for their green environment development. This manuscript could enhance readers' knowledge of women development different approaches and their applications in Bangladesh. Moreover, the paper can contribute to women development agencies to get thoughts of women development different approaches-WAD, GAD, WED, WCD, and WIB as well as might assist implementing agencies tailor their holistic services to disadvantaged women in society.

First, the paper discusses the definitions of the WID, GAD, WAD and WED approaches. And then it shows how Bangladeshi women are exploited in the society, the origin of the Grameen Bank, its methodologies and activities; and finally, examine how GB activities has affected different approaches to women's equality, meanwhile highlighting other aspects of socio-economic development in their life.

3. Women Development different approaches and their implementation

The issue of women's inequality was first raised in the Women in Development (WID) approach developed in the early '70s with the objective of integrating women into the discourse of development. WID liberal feminists advocates for integrating women's policies into the mainstream policy framework. Kate Young (1997) in her article "Gender and Development" talks about WID strategies that concentrate on women's access to cash income, usually via the market either as individuals or members of some form of collectivity (p.52). Marxist feminists support the Women and Development (WAD) approach. They analyze dependency theory, and place emphasis on improving women's working conditions. The GAD approach focuses on how macroeconomic policies highlight the economic empowerment of women; and also pursue poverty alleviation without regarding their socio-political empowerment. Gender is socially constructed, which determines social relations between men and women. WED ideology is people-centered sustainable development that meets the needs of the present without compromising ability of the future generations to meet theirs. In the early 1960s, an interest in women and their connection with the environment was sparked, largely by a book written by Ester Boserup entitled *Woman's Role in Economic Development*. Starting in the 1980s, policy makers and governments became more mindful of the connection between the environment and gender issues. Changes began to be made regarding natural resource and environmental management with the specific role of women in mind. According to the World Bank in 1991, women play an essential role in the management of natural resources, including soil, water, forests and energy...and often have a profound traditional and contemporary knowledge of the natural world around them. Whereas women were previously neglected or ignored, there was increasing attention paid to the impact of women on the natural environment and, in return, the effects the environment has on the health and well-being of women. The gender-environment relations have valuable ramifications in regard to the understanding of nature between men and women, the management and distribution of resources and responsibilities and the day-to-day life and well being of people.

3.1. Context analysis of women development different approaches

Bangladesh has 168 million people within a 147,570 square kilometer area (Bangladesh profile, 2014). Half of the population is female. The majority of Bangladesh's citizens live in rural areas. 67% of women live below the poverty line, which is significantly higher than the national average of 51% (Human Rights Report: 2000). Therefore, a majority of rural poor women are suffering from absolute poverty, marginalization and discrimination in the society. The reasons are that they have limited access to and choice of state resources. Poor women are responsible for working, serving and caring for rich families at extremely low wages. These rich people treat them as a burden on the society, undermine them for their poverty and regard them as poor who are not interested in improving their lot. However, these rich people forget that women are an integral part of the work force and that they have the potential to develop their own life. Besides this invisibility and marginalization women are continually abused, especially under the dowry system. Therefore, income-generating policies, programs and projects are urgently needed to improve the conditions of rural poor women. Grameen Bank initiated its loan activities through the efforts of Muhamed Yunus initiatives who extended banking facilities to landless poor women, without collateral, on a pilot basis in 1976.

GB clients proved that given financial and non-financial support poor women are capable of bringing about incredible change in their lives by becoming involving in different economic, social, cultural and environmental activities. This initiative was a flashlight to the Jobra poor women with little credit. Its aim was to improve the well being of the poor and to empower them in society. Now it has increased its client's services cumulative to 8.6 million where 96% of them are women across Bangladesh (GB report: December 2014). Involvement of women in business for their income generation is an example of women in business (WIB) notion.

3.2.1. Grameen Bank (GB) group-based micro-credit methodologies: GB developed some parameters that are key pillars to the success of its objectives to make women more visible in the society. These parameters are: GB's target group is exclusively rural poor women. It follows group-lending procedures with a peer support system where no gender mixes within the same group, which adds consistency among members. This group formation system adds homogeneity to the make-up of centers and allows members to interact freely among each other. To maintain equal opportunity and to address issues of participatory management, and empowerment to all members of Grameen, the positions of Centre Chief, Group Chairman, and Group Secretary change every year. By this process all members of the center get a chance to be Center Chief, Group Chairman, and Group Secretary by rotation. This practice helps to enhance leadership qualities and decision-making skills among borrowers and adopts a community participation approach to empower women. This women empowerment process fulfills the notion of gender and development (GAD).

3.2.2. Women development different approaches implementation

It is important to find out application of women development different approaches whether these approaches benefit women for their socioeconomic liberation. The paper examines and analyses Grameen Bank activities in the lens of women development different approaches- WAD, GAD, WCD, WED, and WIB.

Over the years development programs have been criticized for ignoring gender roles and the impact it has on women in the global south. However we see a shift to integrate women into development programs in hopes of eradicating poverty and low social economical status. There are six main theoretical approaches towomen development are: "(1) the welfare approach; (2) women in development (WID); (3) women and development (WAD); (4) gender and development (GAD); (5) the effectiveness approach (EA); and (6) mainstream gender equality (MGE). Martinez tries to understand the various outcomes and effectiveness of all 6 development theories.

Despite the effort to reinforce gender mainstreaming into society we still see a vast number of gender inequality especially in the developing world. Women make up the 70% of individuals living in poverty and in sub-Saharan Africa 57% of HIV infected individuals are women. This also includes the disproportionate ratio of women to men in the job market and at leadership position, low level of education among women, and low socio-economic status among women.

The term "Women, Gender and Development" could be seen a discipline much like ever other area of knowledge. However, what sets it apart from various disciplines is that, its major contributors are individuals that raise issues and concerns, concerning women, gender and development. These are academics, feminist activists and development practitioner.

Women in development (WID) approach, was originated as a result of three major feminist moments/waves concerning feminine conditions. The first two were due to the feminist waves. The first wave also known as women's suffrage movement, originated in the North America back in the late 19th century, when women fought for the equal right to vote and participate in politics. The second-wave of feminism sought to deal with the remaining social and cultural inequalities women were faced with in everyday affair i.e. sexual violence, reproductive rights, and sexual discrimination and glass ceilings. The second wave was very controversial; however, the women's movement was very influential that the UN organized the first global conference on women back in 1975 at Mexico. The conference sought to address nations role on fighting gender inequalities and support women's right. The third was influenced by Ester Boserup (1970) publication on "Women's Role in Economic Development". The book sent a shock wave through northern development agencies and humanitarian organization (p. 93). She states and gave empirical results of how increasingly specialized division of labor associated with development undermines or neglects the value of women's work and status especially in the developing world. The WID approach helped to ensure the integration of women into the workforce and increase their level of productivity in order to improve their lives. However some have criticized this approach as being very western. Since it is a perception of the global south from global north perspective, as it fails to acknowledge the collective and cultural concerns of women in the developing world. This approach has been tagged as being rather cumbersome on women, as it fails to understand the dynamics of the private sphere but focus solely on the public sphere.

The women and development (WAD) approach originated back in 1975 in Mexico city, as it sort to discuss women's issues from a neo-Marxist and dependency theory perspective. Its focus was to "explain the relationship between women and the process of capitalist development in terms of material conditions that contribute to their exploitation" (pg 95). WAD is often misinterpreted as WID; however, what sets it apart is that, WAD focuses specifically on the relation between patriarchy and capitalism. The WAD perspective states that women have always participated and contributed towards economic development, regardless of the public or private spheres.

The Gender and Development approach is originated by socialist feminism in the 1980s. It serves as a transitioning point in the way in which feminists have understood development. It served as a comprehensive overview of the social, economic and political realities of development. It origin relates back to the Development Alternatives with Women for a New Era (DAWN) network, when it was first initiated in India. The DAWN program was then officially recognized in 1986 during the 3rd UN conference on women in Nairobi. The conference brought about activist, researcher and development practitioners globally. As the conference discussed about the achievements made from the previous decade's evaluation of promoting equality among the sexes, and a full scope of the obstacles limiting women's advancements, especially in the developing world. The forum discussed about the effectiveness of the continuous debt crisis and structural adjustment program implemented by the IMF and the World Bank, and how such concept of neoliberalism tend to marginalize and discriminate women more in the developing countries.

The diversity of this approach was open to the experiences and need of women in the developing world. Its two main goals were to prove that the unequal relationship between the sexes hinders development and female participation. The second, it supports to change the structure of power into a long-term goal whereby all decision-making and benefits of development are distributed on equal basis of gender neutrality. The GAD approach is not just focused on the biological inequalities among sexes: men and women; however on how social roles, reproductive roles and economic roles are linked to Gender inequalities of: masculinity and femininity.

The Effectiveness Approach (EA) also originated in the 1980s. Its ideas are linked to the concept surrounding WID, which was the inequalities women faced and how societies fail to acknowledge the impact of women in economic development. However EA sort to not just include women into development projects but also reinforce their level of productivity and effectiveness in the labor market. So this required the development of infrastructure and equipment that aided to increase women's earnings and productivity (especially women in the rural areas).

Mainstreaming Gender Equality (MGE) approach also commonly referred to as gender mainstreaming is the most recent development approach aimed on women. Gender mainstreaming ensures that all gender issues are address and integrated in all levels of society, politics, and programs. It originated in 1995 at the 4th UN conference on women in Beijing, China. At the forum, 189 state representatives agreed that the inclusion of both women and men in every development project was the only way to succeed and progress in a nation economic growth and development. The WID approach had been drop by various aid agencies like CIDA, due to it negative interpretation from supporters as being too feminist and brought about hostility from men towards such programs. So basically organization like CIDA now has to include men and women in their annual development report concerning the allocation of funds spent towards education, health care, and employment of both sexes.

Culture is to describe the beliefs and practices of another society, particularly where these are seen as closely linked with tradition or religion. But culture is more than that. Culture is part of the fabric of every society, including our own. It shapes "the way things are done" and our understanding of why this should be so. This more comprehensive approach is proposed in the definition of culture adopted at the World Conference on Cultural Policies (Mexico, 1982) and used in ongoing discussions on culture and development: "Culture... is... the whole complex of distinctive spiritual, material, intellectual and emotional features that characterize a society or a social group. It includes not only arts and letters, but also modes of life, the fundamental rights of the human being, value systems, traditions and beliefs."

Expectations about attributes and behaviours appropriate to women or men and about the relations between women and men–gender– are shaped by culture. Gender identities and gender relations are critical aspects of culture because they shape the way daily life is lived in the family, but also in the wider community and the workplace. Gender (like race or ethnicity) functions are like as an organizing principle for society because of the cultural meanings given to being male or female. This is evident in the division of labour according to gender. In most societies there are clear patterns of 'women's work' and 'men's work', both in the household and in the wider community– and cultural explanations of why this should be so. The patterns and the explanations differ among societies and change over time. While the specific nature of gender relations varies among societies, the general pattern is that women have less personal autonomy, fewer resources at their disposal, and limited influence over the decision-making processes that shape their societies and their own lives. This pattern of disparity based on gender is both a human rights and a development issue.

Peggy Antrobus (2004) believes 'Women, Culture and Development' (WCD) approach would help resolve some of the dilemmas within women's movements by addressing the following issues:

- Issue of class, race,/ethnicity and nationality
- The links between production and reproduction
- Issue of power, conflict and the larger social, cultural and political contexts of women's lives
- The centrality of family, community and religion in women's lives
- Women's agency' that may not just perpetuate inequalities but also challenge them.

Kum-Kum Bhavnani (2003) argues that in integrating production with reproduction alongside women's agency, a WCD approach can interrogate issues of ethnicity, gender, religion, sexuality and livelihood simultaneously; thereby, providing a nuanced examination of social processes...that may provide clearer ideas for a transformative development that attends to aspects of people's lives beyond the economic.

Societies and cultures are not static. They are living entities that are continually being renewed and reshaped. As with culture more generally, gender definitions change over time. Change is shaped by many factors. Cultural change occurs as communities and households respond to social and economic shifts associated with globalization, new technologies, environmental pressures, armed conflict, development projects, etc. For example, in Bangladesh, changes in trade policies allowed for the growth of the garment industry, which drew large numbers of women into the urban labour force. This process has involved a reinterpretation of the norms of purdah (female seclusion) by the women entering this employment and by their families. The much greater visibility of women in cities such as Dhaka is also influencing public perceptions of possible female roles in the family and the workplace.

Change also results from deliberate efforts to influence values through institutions activities, changes in the law or government policy, often due to pressure from civil society. There are many examples of efforts to influence attitudes about race relations, the rights of workers and the use of the environment, to name three areas in which cultural values shape behaviour. Efforts to reshape values about women and gender relations have focused on concerns such as the number of girls sent to school, women's access to paid work, and public attitudes to domestic violence.

Development is about positive change. Development initiatives (by governments, NGOs or development agencies) are investments in promoting social and economic change. Some development initiatives aim to change values and practices that shape social relations – consider, for example, the investments made in family planning and what this implies about family structures. Development models also incorporate cultural values – consider; for example, the concern with the transition to market economies, and the support for private property as a cultural value. Other types of initiatives less obviously concerned with culture nevertheless have impacts on the social relations that characterize a culture. Consider, for example, the possible impacts of an improved road network linking rural and urban areas. New roads allow greater mobility of people and goods. Many villagers could benefit from better access to markets for farm products, to health services and to schools for their children. This could lead to an increase in rural-urban migration. This could result in more households where men are absent and women take charge of farms and families or women leaving villages for employment in urban areas.

Decisions made in planning an initiative that shape the type of impact that it will have on culture. Even if gender equality is not explicitly considered, decisions made in the planning process will have an effect on gender equality.

To address this, CIDA's Policy on Gender Equality requires explicit consideration of gender equality issues in the planning process and a decision-making process that supports progress toward gender equality. Partner countries agree on the gender equality goal, as noted below: Strategies that support women's empowerment can contribute to women's ability to formulate and advocate their own visions for their society–including interpretations and changes to cultural and gender norms. CIDA's Policy on Gender Equality emphasizes the importance of women's empowerment to the achievement of gender equality. It provides a definition of empowerment and indicates a role for development cooperation: "Empowerment is about people – both women and men – taking control of their lives: setting their own agendas, gaining skills, building self-confidence, solving problems, and developing self-reliance...outsiders cannot empower women: only women can empower themselves to make choices or speak out on their own behalf. However, institutions, including international cooperation agencies, can support processes that increase women's self-confidence, develop their self-reliance, and help them set their own agendas." UNDP's 1995 Human Development Report mentioned the 'engendered approach,' that highlights the importance of women's empowerment to social and cultural change: "The engendered development model, though aiming to widen choices for both men and women, should not predetermine how different cultures and different societies exercise these choices. What is important is that equal opportunities to make a choice exist for both women and men."

GB micro credit has women in businesses (WIB) produced a greater impact on extreme poverty (Khondaker 2003). It can play a vital role in attaining Millennium Development Goals (MGDs) and SMDGs. That is why Kofi Anan, UN Secretary General, says that Grameen Bank microfinance has proved its value, in many countries, as a weapon against poverty and hunger. Now it is recognized as a development model for women's development, increasing income generation, self-employment and the overall empowerment of disadvantaged women (Grameen Dialouge-60, 2005).

Ester Boserup (1970) in her book 'Women's Role in Economic Development' states that women's roles were important in agrarian societies where they had equal status in the family; however, women lost their equal status when society moved from agrarian to urban industrial. In agrarian societies people survived on subsistent agricultural production where women had egalitarian status in the family. Women in development are an approach of development projects that emerged in the 1969s, calling for treatment of women's issues in development projects. It is the integration of women into the global economies by improving their status and assisting in total development. This approach mainly advocated chiefly by the World Bank, smart economics is an approach to define gender equality as an integral part of economic *development* and it aims to spur *development* through investing more efficiently in *women* and girls. According to Gita Sen and Caren Brown (1987) in their article "Systemic crisis, reproductive failures and women's potentials", women are also the main producers of food crops in agricultural societies. They are the food processors and the main persons who collect fuel woods and water for the family. They are the managers of intra-household food distribution; but they eat after men, consuming less. Beneria, L. and Sen, G. (1997) called it *reproductive crisis*. Women's work is neglected in modern agricultural, patriarchal, capitalist society because the macro policies of states tend to exclude women.

Several different feminists claim that development fails to appreciate women's non-economic social reproductive work; but rather undermines their contribution to the family and society. Development in neo-liberalism has given top priority to the relationship between people and things, not gender relation and things. In this situation WID feminists' slogan is "level the playing field" for women's equality. The WID approach fails to address the need for women's autonomy, and the ability to gain control over their lives, bodies and sexuality. Here is an unequal power relation between men and women as a major cause for women's subordinate position within the family and the society. According to Irene Tinker (1990) macro policy has given little attention to WID policy in practice.

GB realizes the shortcomings of the WID approach and develops credit delivery tools exclusively for poor women at the village level and works for them to improve women's economic condition, because it is essential to improve their efficiency in earning income within the household. Hence, GB provides credit to poor women that create home based, self-employment business opportunities within the family. GB weekly savings products promote the development of savings behaviors among women and help them create wealth (Khandoker & et al., 1995, p.82. These home based family businesses open the door of different income generation opportunities among villagers, but it does not directly challenge male dominance over women in Bangladesh because GB works within the existing social structure. It works towards gradually reducing gender inequality over time in the society. It believes that this gender gap will decrease if women become economically active within their households. Thus, GB minimizes this inequality gap by increasing women's income-generating activities in the family. However, women's economic liberalization is still a question in neo-liberalism. Rounaq Jahan, a feminist in Bangladesh (1995) mentioned that by passing even elucidate from WID policies and measures, although *women agenda setting approach* is clearly defined in Bangladesh constitution (p. 3).

Women's equal rights issues are guaranteed in the Bangladeshi constitution, article 28(10, 28(2), 28(3) and proactive sanctions in favor of women. However, government officials and national public and private institutions are bypassing women's issues in their national developmental planning, policies and budgets. Grameen Bank, Bangladesh Mohilla Samity, National Women Council, Narri Pakk, and different NGOs are demanding separate projects, budgets and law enforcement for women, which could explicitly give women's rights and development first place in the society. However, these organizations do not challenge women's subordination in gender relations and in other power relations with regards to race and class. They only focus on the productive role of women while ignoring their reproductive roles. These feminists do not challenge the existing power structure of the society; but rather, they believe in reformist maintenance of the status quo. Hence, GAD feminists are struggling to develop alternative strategies to eradicate the oppression of women and sex-role discrimination in society.

The Gender and Development (GAD) approach focuses on the socially constructed differences between men and women and the need to challenge existing gender roles and relations. This approach was majorly influenced by the writings of academic scholars such as Oakley (1972) and Rubin (1975), who emphasize the social relationship between men and women. These relationships, they argue, have systematically subordinated women. GAD departs from WID, which discussed women's subordination and lack of inclusion in discussions of international development without examining broader systems of gender relations. Influenced by this work, by the late 1970s, some practitioners working in the development field questioned focusing on women in isolation. GAD challenged the WID focus on women as an important 'target group'and 'untapped resources' for development. GAD marked a shift in thinking about the need to understand how women and men are socially constructed and how 'those constructions are powerfully reinforced by the social activities that both define and are defined by them.' GAD focuses primarily on the gendered division of labor and gender as a relation of power embedded in institutions. Consequently, two major frameworks 'Gender roles' and 'social relations analysis' are used in this approach. 'Gender roles' focuses on the social construction of identities within the household; it also reveals the expectations from 'maleness and femaleness' in their relative access to resources. 'Social relations analysis' exposes the social dimensions of hierarchical power relations embedded in social institutions, as well as its determining influence on 'the relative position of men and women in society.' This relative positioning tends to discriminate against women.

Unlike WID, the GAD approach is not concerned specifically with women, but with the way in which a society assigns roles, responsibilities and expectations to both women and men. GAD applies gender analysis to uncover the ways in which men and women work together, presenting results in neutral terms of economics and efficiency. In an attempt to create gender equality, (denoting women having same opportunities as men, including ability to participate in the public sphere; GAD policies aims to redefine traditional gender role expectations. Women are expected to fulfill household management tasks, home based production as well as bearing and raising children and caring for family members. The role of a wife is largely interpreted as 'the responsibilities of motherhood'. Men however, are expected to be breadwinners whom are associated with paid work, and market production. In the labor market, women tend to earn less than men. For instance, 'a study by the Equality and Human Rights Commission found massive pay inequities in some United Kingdom's top finance companies, women received around 80 percent less performance-related pay than their male colleagues.' In response to pervasive gender inequalities, Beijing Platform for Action established gender mainstreaming in 1995 as a strategy across all policy areas at all levels of governance for achieving gender equality.

Caroline Moser developed the Moser Gender Planning Framework for GAD-oriented development planning in the 1980s while working at the Development Planning Unit of the University of London. Working with Caren Levy, she expanded it into a methodology for gender policy and planning. The Moser framework follows the Gender and Development approach in emphasizing the importance of gender relations. As with the WID-based Harvard Analytical Framework, it includes a collection of quantitative empirical facts. Going further, it investigates the reasons and processes that lead to conventions of access and control. The Moser Framework includes gender roles identification, gender needs assessment, disaggregating control of resources and decision making within the household, planning for balancing work and household responsibilities, distinguishing between different aims in interventions and involving women and gender-aware organizations in planning.

In the late 1980s the women's movement created new paradigms from WID to gender and development (GAD). GAD represents a transition to "not only integrate women into development, but to also look for the potential in development initiatives to transform unequal social/gender relations and to empower women (Canadian Council for International Cooperation, 1991, p, 5). GAD's main objective is to remove all social, political and economic inequalities that could hinder benefit to women and men. In this context Grameen Bank firmly believes and is actively involved in promoting gender equality because it has identified that at the grass roots level, gender inequality impedes women's well being and progress. Grameen Bank finds that women are key actors in child rearing, maintenance of household, food preparation, resource management, and to the overall well being of the whole family. Momson has termed this "social reproduction" (2004: p.47). Gender inequality not only retards economic and social development but also promotes injustice and violence in the family. According to Naila Kabeer (1994), in Bangladesh gender discrimination is institutionalized in patriarchal ideologies, repressive laws, and violence toward women.

GB targets rural disadvantaged landless women not only to alleviate their poverty, but also to socially empower them and create public space for them within society by offering loans for education and housing in addition to its general loans. Moreover Grameen Bank creates facilities for its clients to participate in different workshops, and council meetings.

Although eradication of poverty and provision for employment are the two main objectives of Bangladesh development planning and receives over billions of dollars in foreign aid every year for the implementation of gender development projects, it does not have a direct program for the promotion and well being of gender development in Bangladesh. Gender discrimination has been labeled as a feminist issue. The poverty alleviation activities of the GB are mainly conducted at a grass roots level. These initiatives serve GAD goals because they focus on the economic emancipation of poor village women and promote poor women's participation in different socio-economic activities in the village. However, it is essential for GB that men and women work not in isolation but collectively in utilizing credits; although GB gives loans directly to poor women for income generation. It organizes women's workshops on the creation of gender awareness to further aid in empowering them. The GB's gender awareness program at the village level, its loan services and savings products has been an integral part of its operations which provide opportunities for poor women to become involved in different craft works, bamboo and cane basket making, mat and fan making, growing vegetables and fruits, raising livestock and poultry on their premises. All these activities open the door for poor women to generate income and also possibly improve husband-wife relations in the family. Now husbands are able to count their wives' production and social reproduction in the family as well as their opinions and decisions.

GB also promotes gender equality in relation to property rights. Bangladesh is a Muslim and Hindu dominated society in which women have no equal rights to inherit properties and lands. For example, in orthodox Hindu religion daughters have no rightful claim to their father's property. In Islam a widow can only own 12.5% of her husband's property (Sharia Law). In practice, widows cannot own their husband's property. Here Grameen Bank reverses the pattern. For example, GB housing loans have enabled women to become legal landholders of their properties because GB provides loans to women who can build their houses on their own lands. Although GB does not challenge the existing customary laws or advocates for changing the male biased property law, this GB policy compels husbands to purchase lands in their wives' names as well as their own. GB places special emphasis on women's property rights, and so has separate organizations for women in the hopes of helping them create public space in society.

Professor Muhammed Yunus and other feminist in Bangladesh like Rabeya Bhuya, Farida Rahman, and Simeen Mahamud emphasize the need for separate women's organizations for female participation at local and national levels. Local level women's participation in different councils can strengthen awareness and lend support to gender empowerment in the family. This micro level awareness program pushes male biased macroeconomic policies to women centered policies in Bangladesh. It is for this reason that Jahan's *agenda setting approach* (1995) demands for primacy to women's agency (p. 127). Although Rounaq Jahan's agenda setting approach is based on macro level policy, local level gender development activities and projects like GB and other NGOs together accumulate women production and reproduction value and contribute to national development in Bangladesh.

GB believes that women's inclusion and participation in income generation, education and community participation (capability approach) is important for women and development (WAD), which the UNDP called human development and tailored it to the gender development index (GDI) that includes women's life expectancy, standard of living and educational attainment. The Commonwealth Secretariat, on the other hand, emphasizes gender empowerment measures (GEM). However, women's preferences are sometimes excluded from policy making; however, Grameen Bank targets disadvantaged women and serves them directly.

Although GB-type group based credit delivery systems place emphasis on women's empowerment, eradicate poverty and improve gender relations in the family, it has less direct implication in breaking down regular patriarchal values and no direct intervention against religious fundamentalism. Therefore the GB model must be customized to recognize constraints of religious aspects like *purdah,* a strict veiling system that keeps women in the private realm, and can be viewed as a male dominating trap to exploit women. Contrarily, GAD approach should look at both macro and micro level women agenda because global restructuring (SAP) adversely affects the whole issues of women empowerment and participatory decision making in macro gender policy. GAD does not fundamentally question the assumptions of the dominant development paradigm itself that is firmly rooted within the logic of modernization, and the economic growth model. Hence there is an urgent need to give preference to including women into different socio-economic policies; programs and budgets where WAD approach can directly impact gender development. In addition, it works to free them from patriarchal domination over women.

WAD feminists see women situation as a working class (proletariat) is being exploited in the society. Clients' participation in businesses, weekly centre meetings, local councils, visits to GB offices, health clinics, community centers, and following the sixteen GB decisions, move them to achieve egalitarian status in the community. Instead ofbeing exploited in the society as a proletariat class, women have become self-employed owners and bosses ofbusinesses. WAD strategies aim to build women's capacity for change in leadership development. Although WAD demands for separate programs and policies for women, they (like GB) do not challenge patriarchy. Moreover, global institutions like the IMF, World Bank, and donor institutions like UDAID and CIDA need to restructure their gender policies and transfer their resources based on the principles of women's equality, justice and fairness (Jahan 1995, p.130).

Grameen center meetings are a place where 30-40 women gather weekly in their neighborhoods to repay their loans, discuss their family problems, exchange business information, and other concerns. So GB centre meetings are catalysts for networking among clients. Through these Grameen activities poor women are more visible in the society. They improve their living women's living standards and their egalitarian status in their community. 96% of GB's clients are women and it is working for both financial and non-financial development, creating awareness among them regarding their human rights, and for their empowerment. GB advocates for social justice for women; therefore, GB activities are an integral part of WAD and women's movements as well as social movements in Bangladesh. As Peggy says (2004), "Any organization work for women's development is part of women's movements" (p.13). She also mentions that, "all these diverse activities are elements of social movement" (p.24). So from this point of view Grameen Bank comply with WAD concept.

Grameen Bank clients earn money and save money by utilizing loans result asset creation among borrowers; therefore, GB members are not the chattels of their men but rather, they are assets for the family because now they bring cash income to the household. Now they are able to sustain themselves such as providing their basic needs: food, clothing, shelter, health and education. As a result improve their health and nutritional statuses, reduce child mortality and pregnancies. Thus, GB services are on the track of WAD.

GB also provides tube well loans for safe drinking water, solar panels, and biogas plants for renewable energy supply to homes. These facilities reduce the time women spend in food processing and instead manually compound crops. These facilities reduce the time spent in domestic work and shift it to time to develop their businesses. However, GB clients do double jobs in the family although they have increased their choice in their reproductive rights. GB clients have both productive and social reproductive roles in the family, but now their husbands recognize their contributions in the family because now they contribute tangible income to the home.

GB is proactive in implementing pro-women development. It gives due importance to women's voice in the decision-making process. GB policy encourages the egalitarian status of women, participation in environmental development programs, and recognizes women's work and achievements. Although Grameen Bank believes that economic freedom is a precondition to empowering women; it does not mean that they do not consider the social issues of women. It has "sixteen decisions" Annexure-1 that guides and encourages women to participate in socio-cultural, political and environmental development programs in the villages. For example, members plant trees, grow organic vegetables and build sanitary latrines, activities, which are intended to address environmental issues. GB clients own 94.34% of its shares by buying share certificates and thus become partial owners of the bank. The board of directors is comprised of 13 members, nine of whom are elected by the borrowers. They make bank policies and decisions (GB Annual Report 2005). All of GB's activities and policies work towards the sustainable development of women. So it is the accomplishment of the WED approach.

Ecofeminism is seen as the connection between the environmental movement and the feminism movement. It is one of the only movements that combine multiple social movements. Academics and activists like Vandana Shiva (India), Ariel Salleh (Australia), Maria Mies (Germany) and Gloria Goldstein (United States), ELlie Perkins (Canada), Ronuk Jahan (Bangladesh) are regarded as important representatives from ecofeminism. However, critics like Rosi Braidotti (1994) and Bina Agarwal (1998) argue that ecofeminism has focused too much on ideological arguments and failed to address power and economic differences which also contribute to differentiation among women, and that ecofeminists also tend to overestimate the idea of harmonious, ecological, and traditional societies. Grameen Bank is promoting the idea of ecofeminism through its social and green business engaging women in ecologically friendly businesses, exposing them about women's contribution to environment.

Women, particularly those in poor countries, are affected differently by climate change than men. They are among the most vulnerable to climate change, partly because in many countries they make up the larger share of the agricultural work force and partly because they tend to have access to fewer income-earning opportunities. Women manage households and care for family members, which often limits their mobility and increases their vulnerability to sudden weather-related natural disasters. Drought and erratic rainfall force women to work harder to secure food, water and energy for their homes. Girls drop out of school to help their mothers with these tasks. This cycle of deprivation, poverty in focus: gender equality and inequality undermines the social capital needed to deal effectively with climate change. Therefore, Amarty Sen *says, "Advancing gender equality may be one of the best ways of saving the environment, and countering the dangers of overcrowding and other adversities associated with population pressure. The voice of women is critically important for the world's future – not just for women's future."*

The Beijing Declaration and Platform for Action identified three strategic objectives in the critical area of women and the environment:

- Involve women actively in environmental decision-making at all levels. Integrate gender concerns and perspectives in policies and programmes for sustainable development. Strengthen or establish mechanisms at the national, regional and international levels to assess the impact of development and environmental policies on women.

A group of Grameen officials attended the Beijing Declaration and Platform for Action Summit. They narrated how they work for women environmental development in Bangladesh through engaging rural poor women in green businesses. They urge for women's active engagement in environmental programs, request for promoting women green sustainable businesses by all other organizations in Bangladesh.

Following the 5-year review of the Beijing Platform for Action, major achievements in the field of women and the environment are:

- A positive, albeit tentative, trend towards greater participation and involvement of women in environmental decision-making positions
- Steps to incorporate a gender perspective in (inter) national and local environmental activities, policies, plans and legislation, as well as in institutional arrangements. Increase in women's capabilities in the environmental field, including their knowledge, skills, and organization
- A growing quantity and quality of gender-sensitive environmental research and data
- A more holistic approach that incorporates poverty eradication and women's economic empowerment in environmental conservation and management

However, during Beijing+5 also a number of obstacles to further progress on women and the environment were identified. These include:

- Low participation of women in environmental protection and management, and in the formulation, planning and execution of environmental policies
- Insufficient numbers and inadequate influence of women in responsible positions and a male monopoly in the management of environmental resources
- Under-representation of women in research and teaching in the natural sciences
- Lack of gender-sensitive environmental policies, programmes and research

- Absence of deliberate strategies to ensure women's participation in decision-making, including lack of funding and monitoring
- Low level of management and technical skills among women and Women's limited access to resources, information, education and training.

The Grameen Bank targets women as recipients of development assistance and the development of the environment. GB believes that women are the key engines of development in the family. GB strongly supports women's role in the household economy, food security, resource management (production), childcare and linkages with kinships. Monson calls them women's social reproduction. GB provides loans for agriculture, livestock raising, poultry farming, fish cultivation, tree planting, and provision of solar energy, wind pump building, and the construction of bio-digester plants. It supplies vegetable seeds, organic fertilizers and other inputs for agriculture. It supplies oral dehydration saline (ORS) and vitamin capsules to clients and encourages women to join immunization camping. All these activities together promote environmentalism and sustainable development (WED) in the society because these home-based businesses help women to earn money at home, fulfill their basic needs and upgrade their socio-economic conditions.

GB has deliberately targeted women, realizing that their participation in various cultural, social, religious rituals, and carrying social reproduction, are all necessary for their socio-economic and cultural development because of their primary role in maintaining collective familial values, providing health, education, and nutrition to children (social reproduction). However, women have been neglected by development projects, which have removed them from economic growth, and the social development process. As women are poorer than men, GB actively promotes their membership more than men within the Bank. In addition, Grameen Bank micro financing services help the rural poor women to utilize their productive means and generate income on a sustainable basis.

Now the rich cannot exploit women's labor by paying them low wages. They are united and have become visible in the society. They create their public spaces outside the home by attending weekly centre meetings, joining village councils and participating in different community activities. Religious fundamentalists cannot dominate and abuse them by unethical emotional religious faiths and customs. They participate in different religious rituals and cultural events. GB respects women, their familial rituals, local cultures and community norms. So the bank is also working for women's cultural development (WCD). Although GB activities empower women and respect their cultures (WCD), promote environmentalism (WED) at the micro level; village women's cultures are affected by western globalization.

GB activities are holistic in their approach. The lending process initially impacts on the woman's income, allowing them to fulfill basic needs. The indirect beneficial result is a revival of women's egalitarian status in the family because their husbands come to realize their worth. GB social development programs like center schools, creation of awareness of human rights, movement against dowry, developing networks among members, practicing leadership through group chairmanship and joining local counseling sets out guidelines to borrowers. All of these activities help to develop women's self-esteem, social and human capital. Hence, GB services not only accomplish WAD objectives but also fulfill WID, WIB, GAD, WCD and GED paradigms of women's wealth creation, equality and empowerment. However, their small businesses are struggling to survive in capitalist free markets. The structural adjustment policy (SAP) and trade liberalization affects their business and life. For example, poor people take health services from private clinics and receive education from expensive private schools.

Micro credit services equip women to be active in decisions about loan use, and in the control over incomes from loan investment. Robin Isserles (2003) study also confirms that women are considered to be better credit risks and they are thought to use money to care for their family better than men. (p. 47). However, sixteen percent of women experience an increase in verbal and physical violence from their husbands because of their reception of loans and their subsequent refusal to hand over the money (p.49). This is a sure indicator that patriarchy is still very prevalent and that gender inequality has not reached a zero gap.

Although GB claims to be a social benefit institution it operates on a profit motive as a private bank. It made a profit of $6.03 million dollars in 2005. This net profit transferred to rehabilitation funds for the purposes of giving aid to members affected by natural disasters (GB annual report 2005, p.54). GB's long-standing success is due to its entrepreneurial development (women in business WIB); however, each and every borrower cannot become a successful entrepreneur. Isserle says, "It is a neo-liberal notion of individualism that supports Grameen Bank" (p.54). Although GB primarily responds to the needs of the poor women and helps them to run their business and earn money, the World Bank researcher Shahid Khandaker (1995) examine GB borrowers' business markets and he found that GB does not have marketing promotion components for its borrowers. Therefore he suggests that GB extend its services to clients' product promotion ad vocational training to increase their vocational skills. UNDP has SME promotion programs which include vocational training, teaching marketing and business management skills that are not included in GB loans services for its members.

Trade businesses are extended to remote villages through GB loan services, so consumerism extended in the rural areas. For example, if we compare GB annual reports 1995 and 2005, it can be found that loan disbursement on agriculture and forestry is 9% in 2005 whereas it was 28% in 1995; livestock and fisheries is 19% in 2005 whereas it was 31% in 1995, but its investments increased in trade to 28% in 2005. These data show that GB investments are gradually reducing on environmentally friendly businesses. GB environmental sustainable businesses are decreasing. Therefore, it should reverse its loan investment policy towards agriculture and livestock for the promotion of environmentalism in rural Bangladesh.

Simen Mahmud (2004), a Bangladeshi researcher, in her article "Micro credit and women empower in Bangladesh" examines the relationship between micro credit program participation and the process of empowerment in Bangladesh. Her findings show that women have good access to credit and these credit facilities impacted their household income, involvement in household decision making, strengthen their voice and choices in reproductive rights, control over household income and ownership of assets, improved literacy, and schooling, health and nutrition, and birth rate control. These services open the public space for the village women by increasing women participation in agriculture and livestock labor forces in the villages. These activities decrease women's unemployment and thereby resulted in increased wellbeing. All together, these factors contribute to building economic capital, human capital and social capital among credit recipients. These harmonized gender relations in the family and increase women's status in the society.

Feminist consciousness-raising is an important first step towards the identification and 'naming' of female subordination. Without this, activism can remain abstract, a purely intellectual notion of 'oppression' that fails to translate into lived experience and serious commitment to challenge female subordination. Although consciousness-raising is associated with 'white, middle-class housewives' in North America and Europe, it is far more widespread than that. Consciousness-raising is experiential learning: through reflection on the personal experience of gender-based oppression, women can gain a deeper understanding of the experience of other forms of oppression based on class, race, ethnicity, culture and international relations. The process of consciousness-raising is an important tool in feminist organizing; making the link between one's own experience and the experience of the others based on other categories of exclusion can be powerful analytical tool, a stimulus to action that benefits oneself and others. Women of bottom class, race, and minority group can identify with the experience of structured exclusion, marginalization and alienation within patriarchal society that they can identify with the exclusion, marginalization and alienation of others on the basis of class, minority group, race, culture, religion, geographic location, age, physical ability, etc. This consciousness raising program is very effective for gender and development. Grameen bank in general talks how bottom people become economically and socially exploited, discriminated by the elites of society; however, it has no program for bottom women consciousness raising against elites exploitation and patriarchy. Therefore, Grameen bank could include consciousness-raising program and story-telling program for the bottom women and facilitate bottom women consciousness-raising sessions at their locations.

Coalition and alliance building among women organizations at neighborhoods, villages, Upzillas, district and national level has been an important strategy for the global movement. The understanding of the linkages between the social, political,, economic and cultural concerns of women, intersectionality can links women's experience at the personal and micro-level of the community to the common policy framework of neo-liberalism, has facilitated and encouraged the formation of alliance and coalitions. Coalitions and alliances may be formed with other women's networks, as well as with NGOs/MFIs in Bangladesh working on common issues. Coalitions and alliance of women organizations with NGOs/MFIs are essential to massively campaign for gender and development program in Bangladesh because gender justice is economic and social justice.

4. Conclusion

Development in capitalist societies is a tactic that favors modern men that allow them to practice patriarchy over women and exploit them. Therefore development needs to be redefined beyond male dominated economic growth. Sustainable development should be economic growth plus egalitarian rights for both sexes. GB is pulling rural poor women to become involved in different income generating activities in addition to various social, cultural and environmental programs in order to increase gender equality, overcome poverty, and reduce the discrimination and abuse they experience in the society. Consciousness-raising on patriarchal values domination, group storytelling, bottom women's coalition and alliance-building, campaigns for women liberation, advocacy, mainstreaming and networking often linking them are essential for bottom women development and get-rid of patriarchal value domination over women. Grameen bank could organize bottom women to protest against patriarchy and include some of these programs for its borrowers. Peggy Anthobus (2005) thinks for GAD, WAD, and WCD the most effective strategies are those that combine political with professional and counter-cultural approaches, i.e. paying attention to cultural elements through spiritual growth, consciousness raising/conscientization, solidarity and networking; political elements such as lobbying, advocacy, caucusing, coalition-alliance building including using insider/outsider approaches; and technical-professional elements i.e. sound research and analysis. Alliance and coalition building must start with women before reaching out to the wider civil society, otherwise women advocating change may find them isolated from or de-legitimized by other associations of women. Therefore multiple strategies are necessary for women development, gender development.

Although different approaches to women and development have different paradigms based on different feminists' perspectives, all these approaches seek for women's socio-economic and political development in the society (Peggy, 2005, Winnipeg). Therefore, GB's financial and non- financial components (social reproduction) all encourage poor women to participate in different social, cultural, economic and environmental development program that fit WID, GAD, WAD WCD and WED feminists' approaches.

5. References

Beneria, L. and Sen, G. (1997). Accumulation, Reproduction and Women's Role in Economic Development: Boserup revisited in *the Women, Gender and Development Reader.* London: Zed Books

Bhavnani, Kum-Kum. Foran, J, and Kurian, P. (2003). *Feminist Futures: Re-imaging Women, Culture and Development.* London: Zed Books

Braidotti, R. Charkiewicz, E., Hausler, S. and Wieringa, S. (1998). "Women, The Environment and Sustainable Development" *The Women, Gender and Development Reader* Visvanathan, N., Duggan, L., Nisonoff, L., and Wiegerersma, N. (eds.). London: Zed Books

Habn, F. (1996). "Feminization through Flexible Labor" in *Homeworkers in Global Perspective: Invisible No More.* London: Routledge Inc.

Gra,meen Bank (2015). Impact of Grameen Bank on local society.: http://www.rdc.com.au/grameen/impact/htm

Internatonal Forum on Globalization (2004). "The Unholy Trinity" in *A system in Crisis.* San Francisc: Berett-Koethler Publishers, Inc.

Isbister, J. (2003). *Promises not kept: Poverty and the Betrayal of Third World Development.* Bloomfield: Kumarian press

Jahan, R. (1995. *The Elusive Agenda: Mainstreaming Women in Development.* Dhaka: The University Press Ltd.

Kabeer, N. (1995). *Reversed Realities: Gender Hierarchies in Development Thought.* London: Verso Inc.

Mizan, A. (1994). *In quest of Empowerment: The Grameen Bank Impact on Women's Power and Status.* Dhaka: University Press Limited

Momsen, J. (2004). *Gender and Development*, London: Routledge Inc.

Peggy, A. (2004). *The Global Women's Movement: Issues, Strategies and Challenges.* London: Zed Books

Rathgeber, E. (1990). WID, WAD, GAD: Trends in Research and Practice, *The Journal of Developing Areas*, Vol. 24(4), pp. 489-504

Rouf, K. A. (2016). Grameen Bank services to Women in Development (WID), Gender and Development (GAD), Women in Business (WIB), Women and Development (WAD) and Women in Environment (WED) approach in Bangladesh. *International Journal of Research Studies in Management*, Vol. 5(2), pp. 11-20

Sen, G. and Grown, C. (1987). *Development, Crises and Alternative visions: Third World Women's Perspectives.* New York: Monthly Review Press

Tinker, T. (1999). The making of a field: Advocates, practitioners, and scholars in *the Women, Gender, and Development Reader.* Visvanathan, N., Duggan, L., Nisonoff, L., and Wiegerersma, N. (eds.). London: Zed Books

Visvanathan, N. (1997). *The Women, Gender and Development Reader.* London: Zed Books.

Grameen Bank is working for poverty, not for citizenry skills development in Bangladesh

Abstract

Grameen Bank (GB) is famous for group-based micro credit delivery to poor women in Bangladesh. Many studies document that Grameen Bank micro-borrowers' income has increased by using its micro-credit in their businesses and many of them overcome their poverty. GB is successful in economic determination and is a pioneer in collateral free micro credit delivery services in Bangladesh. However, many studies challenge Grameen Bank women borrows socio-economic development particularly their citizenry skills development in their families and in their communities. Hence, this paper debates on Grameen Bank is working for poverty, not for citizenry skills development in Bangladesh because GB micro-borrowers citizenry skills development is very important for their social and political liberation in Bangladesh. The paper concludes GB can initiate a pilot project on the advocacy of citizenry and political skills awareness development program within its existing structure or could create a separate organization and acquire experience in citizenry advocacy programs. This initiative can then is followed by other micro finance institutions (MFIs) and inspire them to become involved in civic engagement programs in Bangladesh.

Key terms: Citizenry skills development; Grameen Bank; micro credit patriarchy, gender development; women empowerment.

1.0. Introduction

It is widely known that Grameen Bank (GB) is successful in economic determination and is a pioneer in collateral free micro credit delivery services in Bangladesh. However, GB has no citizenry objectives in contrast to other major MFIs in Bangladesh. Badruddin Umar (2001) stated that Grameen Bank and other NGOs preach a kind of economism instead of a politically progressive consciousness. Their goal is the extension of credit instead of socio-political development. In this way the political outlook has been hijacked. Therefore, it needs to synchronize their economic determination program with political determination in order to promote civic wellbeing and empowerment of women in Bangladesh. This is urgent because women's human rights are seriously violated in Bangladesh. Men make household decisions, control property rights, participate in and rule in all village matters and public spheres. Women are stereotyped as passive, docile, and silent. They have no voice and choice either in the family or in society. This stereotype keeps women invisible and as objects of the ruling social organization (Bannerji, 1993: p.149). Kabeer says, "The denial of women's autonomy is everywhere in Bangladesh" (Kabeer 1983:8). Therefore rural women are imaged negatively, becoming the invisible and faceless in the society thus occupying the lowest levels in the society and are exploited/robbed of their equal rights. Therefore, despite the success of Grameen Bank in poverty alleviation, it fails to advocate for greater social equity facilitating a balance in the power relations between men and women in Bangladesh.

This paper examines the extent to which micro credit programs, as represented by the Grameen Bank, affect the power relationships in Bangladesh? With this aim, the paper first discusses how GB credit perpetuates violence against women. Secondly, it examines the empowerment of women through credit services. Thirdly, why it moves to profit motive instead retains its original objects. Fourthly, why citizenry is important; and why the plans of the GB for citizenship skills development for low income women important in Bangladesh.

Lastly, the paper makes some recommendations and come to a conclusion. The whole paper also looks for how Grameen Bank is successful in economic determination. It seeks to answer whether or not economic determination is enough to empower women in political skills development and violence against women in patriarchal Bangladesh.

Microcredit is a provision of small-scale loans to the poor and more recently microfinance includes credit, savings, insurance, and remittance management. The majority of micro financial interventions have been targeted towards off-farm small and microenterprises (SMEs) (Hulme & Moore (2006). Grameen Bank is a 'micfro-finance-minimalist bank' that offers a wide range of financial products, and limited organizational support. In 2001-2, all Grameen Bank branches began to operate the new, simpler and much more flexible 'Grameen Generalised System' (also called 'Grameen II), which offers four types of loan products: basic, housing, higher education and struggling members (beggars) loans. Although the GB phase- 2 changes its credit delivery system to adapt to the new changing situation and included new financial products since 2001; it does not included citizenship education in its core program which is crucial for women empowerment in Bangladesh.

2.0. Poor women socio-economic position in Bangladesh

In Bangladesh, men work outside, earn money and provide financial support to the family. They are involved in politics and hold the power; while women are responsible for domestic obligations. Society stereotypes men as the breadwinners and women, the homemakers. Domestic work is stereotyped as'women's work' and has no value in comparison to that of their men. Women are the main exploited, marginalized and invisible group in the society. Undisputedly, it goes to the advantage of men since the division of labor is organized in a manner that confines women at home with unpaid domestic chores.

The dichotomy of public and private realm in Islam underpins gender subordination and dependence. Women are dependent upon men due to the rigidity of the Purdah system, which restricts them from participation in economic activities outside the household (Kabeer, 1988:108). Patriarchy is given all the power and denies women any equal rights. Women's subordinate status is almost an established fact in Bangladesh (Begum, 1988). Men of all classes benefit from women's unpaid labor in the home and therefore, they enjoy a higher status in society (Mead et al. 1979, p. 417). One reason given for this, as Abdullah (1974) mentions, is that there has hardly been any attempt on the part of the government or NGOs to examine how far the victims (women) think and feel about their exploitation and subordination in patriarchal society. To challenge this traditional male dominated custom, rural women must be recognized equally for their economic contributions and their work must be rewarded accordingly.

The denial of women's basic human rights is a major cause of poverty. When women have equality in society it has a huge positive impact upon the system as a whole. But it is not just about resources or services. Changes to beliefs and behaviors that discriminate against women are also necessary. To end global poverty and injustice, the most important things are to help secure women's rights and equality. When these rights are respected, women will be healthier, better educated and better paid. This will lead to more sustainable development in their lives. Therefore, lobbying and advocating for women policy changes at the micro-mezzo and macro levels are necessary.

Currently, Bangladesh has 16.4 million people; half of the population is female (Bangladesh profile 2016). Individual per capita income is $670. Only 30% of the total population has access to basic health services, and 76% of all households are deficient in calorie intake (CIDA, 2001). More than 25% of people living on less than $1 a day are women (World Bank, 2005). Each day 1,400 women die in pregnancy and childbirth. Without access to health care, poor women face malnutrition and death. 37% of women live below the poverty line, which is significantly higher than the national average of 27% (Human Rights Report, 2016). Women's positions are so bad in Bangladesh that one cow is being smuggled in at the same price of two women smuggled out (State of Human Rights, 1994, p. 9).

3.0. Tension and anxiety of women micro borrowers in Bangladesh

Now below the paper discusses how GB credit provisions perpetuate violence against women. GB believes that income-generation for women could create the potential to enhance their power and status at home. Its initial objectives were (1) to reduce poverty through creating self-employment by using group based loans; (2) to organize women into groups for raising their collective consciousness, strengthening their group solidarity through weekly meetings and assisting them to attain greater socio-economic empowerment in society, and enable networking among them. However, several studies indicate that although GB has contributed to poverty eradication and created self-employment, its activities have yet not been able to empower women to fight against patriarchy in Bangladesh (Rahman (1999); Goetz & Sengupta (1996); Karim (2001); Isseriles (2003); and Mahamud (2004).

Instead, loan liabilities raised tension and anxiety within borrowers' households and increased violence against women. For example, Rahman's (1999) study reports that 70% borrowers confessed to increased violence and aggressive behavior in their household because of their involvement with the bank (p.74). Moreover, his study mentions that men are users of more than 60% of women's loans (p.75). Karim (2001) finds that ninety percent of the loaned money went to men. She remarks that women are the bearers of the credit although not its users. The NGOs use women's social vulnerability and powerlessness but do not support them in the direct fight against patriarchy (Karim, p.100).

In addition, findings of Anna Maia Goetz and Sen Gupta study (1996) mentions that only 18% women have full control over their loans including marketing, partial control 24.1%, and no involvement at all is 21.7%. Male dominance to loans hampers women's independence loan use. For example, Goetz and Sengupta's (1996) study mentions that 63% of women's loans are controlled by male family members. They concluded their study on the note that the lending process often victimized female borrowers and contributed to their disempowerment. Although this data is not sufficient to understand women's control over their loans; it does indicate that more than 60% of loans are managed by their husbands or by their male relatives. Thus women are basically in the dark where businesses and loan transactions are concerned. As women are not directly involved in marketing of their business, they remain dependent on men to grow their businesses.

Women encountered violence because of their refusal to turn loans over to men or for challenging men's proposals to use loans for personal benefits. Aminur Rahman (1999) remarks that female borrowers are not only conscious of their increased violence, but a few in the study village are also gaining power by controlling their loans and resisting men's violence against them (p.75). The same conclusion was reached by Isserles, R. (2003) where he mentions that although GB has seen many success stories of women who have been emancipated through micro credit, he cautions that many women are still dominated by their husbands and do not actually reap the benefits of the financial gains through their investments. In many cases their husbands receive the credit (p. 41). Muhammed Yunus admitted to some defects of the bank's lending practices in addition to the rigidity of the system. Therefore, he made several fundamental changes in it's' operations in 2000 and called this new stage Grameen Bank Phase -11. He stated that, "Poor people are not trouble makers for the institutions, rather, the design of the institutions and rules make trouble for them" (2002). Therefore, now the questions are posed to GB: (1) do micro credit projects help to empower women within households or increase their vulnerability, or (2) do their micro credits lead to increased tension and violence for these same women?

David Hulme and Karen Moore (2006) asserts that Grameen has been foundational in creating a global image of microfinance as a policy that can appeal to both right of centre and left of centre ideologies. Its talk of micro-entrepreneurs, micro-enterprise, investment, loans; not grants and cost recovery garnered support from those who see private sector development as the pathway out of poverty: this was much better than social grants and welfare. On the other side of the political spectrum, its talk of the agency of the poor, group formation, participation, empowerment and women's rights met with the approval of those who believed social change was the way forward.

Grameen's activities have been credited for having a positive impact on women's economic lives in Pitt and Khandker's (1995) World Bank research. This study concludes that women were empowered in households where they had received a loan. Hashemi's study (1996) Grameen and BRAC found that participation in credit programs contributed significantly to the likelihood of women being empowered in terms of a number of the indicators: ability to make small and large purchases, involvement in major family decision-making, participation in public action, and physical mobility within some public offices. Hashemi's study did also conclude that participation in a credit program reduced the likelihood of a woman being beaten by her husband. However, Schuler (1986) concluded that if women were involved in micro credit programs, her husband might not beat her, as he would worry that this fact would become known in the village.

4.0. Grameen Bank meeting basic needs of its clients

GB thinks that it is almost impossible for people to learn new skills, and to participate in protest when they are worried about where their next meal will come from. Basic needs must be met first. It assumes that economic determination would help them to overcome their poverty as well as relieve them from violent males. In addition, there is the need for physical security and other social services such as education, health, and citizenry and so on. However, poverty reduction also involves removing barriers that prevent particular power and politics in the labor market. Unfortunately, several of the above mentioned studies confirm that Grameen Bank borrowers are still not free from their male partners' dominance in their loan transactions. The husbands control the loans and other property within the family. Even a recent research conducted by Isserles (2003) suggests that 57% of women experienced a rise in verbal aggression from their husbands after they received loans (p. 49). Women are marginal decision-makers in loan use. Kabeer (1998) identifies that lack of voice in the household decision-making process was typically a result of male appropriation of their loans and their investment in businesses in which women had little or no role. Patriarchy is systemic and very powerful in Bangladesh in so far as its deep roots are interconnected among class, gender, religion, and education; and thus women are far away from their empowerment.

Microcredit is a form of small loans to poor people with the objective of engaging them in small businesses for earning income. Although different writers use micro finance as an alternative term for micro credit; microfinance has various commercial products other than credit, such as savings, insurance and other investments with a profit motive. Now all micro credit institutions are called micro finance institutions. Grameen Bank has succeeded as a community economic development program which has created local living economics in the rural area. It is successful in working in the community as an insider and following the bottom up approach because it finds that top down policy contradicts with local values. Its credit transactions circulate money within the community. The World Bank recognizes that the GB micro credit system has had a great impact on extreme poverty (Khondaker 2003) and admits that it plays a vital role in attaining Millennium Development Goals (MDGs). In the words of Kofi Anan (2005), UN Secretary General, "GB microfinance has proved its value in many countries that it is a weapon against poverty and hunger. Now it is recognized as a development model for income generation, self-employment and empowers disadvantaged women" (Grameen

Dialouge-60, 2005). However, women's leadership and their voice have yet to influence the public sphere.

5.0. Male violence over women borrowers

Below the paper examines whether or not credit services empower women and make sustainable development available to them. Women's empowerment is the process of gaining power over their lives, in terms of increasing welfare and reducing subordination to men through the expansion of their choice and voice in the decision making process. According to Lamiya Karim (2001) the Grameen Bank has provided the world financial community with the seductive information that: the poor are credit worthy, the poor are willing to pay a high price for their debt, and the bank goes to the doors of the poor. There is no need for the poor to come to the bank office for money. But the high repayment rate 99% does not tell the reader how money is recovered from its poor borrowers. She finds that money is often recovered through intimidation, force and violence against poor female members (p. 95). Simeen Mahamud (2004) asserts that although women have good access to credit, the norms and practices put them at a definite subordinate position to men, which means they have little power in the decisions and processes that shape their discrimination and make them vulnerable in the society.

Another ideological problem in practice is that microcredit is based on the notion that anybody can become self-reliant and successful if he or she works hard enough. Therefore, if success does not result from one's attempts, then the implication is that that individual did not work hard enough and is responsible for his or her situation. As Isserles (2003) put it "this is merely a policy version of bootstrap theory, or the economic individualism so prevalent in the U.S. political ideology" (p. 43). So, credit is unable to address the issue of patriarchal discrimination in gender power relations and property rights. Hence public concern and activism about property rights discrimination, violence against women and women in poverty, can encourage a positive political response as an initiative against patriarchy. Campaigns by NGOs in alliance with International NGOs against issues such as women's ownership of property, and violence against women, can encourage and support women in challenging these types of discrimination and exploitation issues.

6.0. Enlightening the political will of women micro borrowers

Enlightening the political will to implement women's equal rights, participation in public space and the overall enhancement of women's socio- economic and political empowerment in the society are necessary through community engagement. Hickey and Mohan (2004) recommend that community participation by both individuals and institutions is central to ensure local leadership development and the promotion of social cohesion and mutual help. Regular consultation, and communication with clients/communities and NGOS can enhance the ability to meet the needs of the women and men that they are supporting and help them to organize themselves to access their rights and entitlements in the society, to create a voice for women's human rights and provide access to community resources. Ilan Kapoor (2002) mentions that PRA campaigns for local knowledge and puts forth a methodology aimed at enabling local people to take power over their own lives.

Ultimately these strategies can help form an understanding of the power and politics and other social and bureaucratic structures and processes such as: how exploitation processes are going on in the society, who are the key players, how one can build relationships with key players like Mullahs, rural elites, money lenders and land lords (Quadir, class discussion: April 2007). Community participation can be promoted more if NGOs can mobilize beneficiaries with political/citizenship skills and literacy to increase civic engagement and awareness in power and politics. However, Grameen Bank has no broader notions of social and political investment like creating human, cultural, political and social capital that are equally important to economic, social and political well-being. It only focuses on economic support of the people.

Therefore Grameen Bank and other NGO programs on 'Civic Engagement' are very essential in Bangladesh to mobilize citizenry because strong and caring communalities start with the citizen as the base of their development. Civic engagement or broad participation in decision making is a prerequisite for achieving sustainable development. So MFIs should include a focus on mobilizing people for political participation in their community. Moreover, they need to include a focus on community problem solving strategies because it is a process of finding a solution appropriate to the community. Muhammad Yunus realizes it and took the initiative to be involved in politics in 2007; however, he did not continue his commitment to be engaged in politics. Other NGO leaders did not respond to his new mission and neither did the Grameen Bank take up the challenge of activism for citizenry.

Women's voices can support and promote gender equality; increase awareness of rights and can hold government and agencies more accountable to fair commitments while providing a base for sustainable development. To develop gender equality through women's leadership development each year the center chief for GB community groups is changed, which is an opportunity to develop each borrower's leadership qualities. Yunus says that, "The same person can not be elected twice until other members of the group have had their chance" (1997, p.13). It is a system by which the center develops poor women's leadership in rural Bangladesh and raises their self-confidence (Chandler, 1993). However, Aminur Rahman (1999) discovered that one or two influential members had real control over the decision-making process of the center (p.74). Center chiefs hold *de facto* power as they decide almost every issue of the center. Perpetuation of such power relations in the loan centers is contradictory to the Grameen Bank ideology because although new center chiefs are elected every year, influential people still tend to dominate (p.74). My response to this information is that Grameen Bank field staff is sometimes silent in this regard because they feel it is too risky and controversial for them to address the issue of patriarchal men domination over women borrowers and run the center smoothly although GB B*iddimala* does not permit it.

Feminization of poverty occurs when women have no accessibility to resources and usually results in unequal power relations, in which women are permanently marginalized, vulnerable and are dependent on male patronage. Poor women can benefit greatly from service delivery programs offering food, credit, health care, and education; but these programs can not address the deeper systematic roots of their vulnerability: the lack of independence to make decisions within the family and society because of patriarchy (Wood, 2003; and Kamat, 2004). The qualitative change brought about by citizenry empowerment programs are not mirrored in GB, rather, its credit delivery program is popular to poor people because they can use small loans along with their own ability and get quick economic tangible return from it. Conversely political mobilization results are intangible, time consuming and hard to achieve for the poor.

Therefore, the question remains on GB's sustainable development accomplishments because according to Bill Hopwood, Mary Mellor, and Geoff O'Brien (2005) sustainable development is an attempt to combine growing concerns about a range of power and politics issues with economic issues. It concentrates on sustainable livelihoods with well-being, rather than well-having. However, GB considers sustainability development from economic fulfillment of basic needs like food, clothing and shelter perspectives. It is working and maintaining the status quo without any fundamental changes to power relations within society. So its development concept is identified with economic growth. GB has a weak commitment to socio-political sustainability because its credit delivery approach has lack of equity in political power. It does not locate the root of the problem in the society. Along with other MFIs, the Bank believes that income, and the accumulation of resource/things will change the challenges to poverty and exploitation. However, GB's main focus is on credit and economic return (Hopwood et al., 2005, p-45).

Political economists use sustainable development in a boarder way where they include the rights to a sustainable livelihood, to basic social services, to life and security, to an identity and to be heard. Gender inequality is a driving force for women's economic independence as their reliance on men renders them vulnerable and makes them more prone to be victims of violence, and thus unable to enjoy and protect their basic human rights. So women are in high-risk assault in private and public places in their life. To reduce this dichotomy, GB has an intensive socio-economic program called the Sixteen Decisions, instigated in 1983 that helps women to promote a group peer support lending system. This creates social collateral among GB borrowers. These Sixteen Decisions act as social collateral that helps GB to use it instead of material collateral. The sixteen decisions provide women with a space to meet with each other and discuss various social development issues like health, education, environment, agriculture, and village events as well as pay installments. The Sixteen Decisions represents the social development agenda. Grameen centre is a place for creating social solidarity among women. Yunus says that, "Each center tries to ensure that all its members are guided by the Sixteen Decisions in their daily life" (Yunus, 1997, p.19). However, Rahman (1999) interprets this collective social collateral which should enhance social solidarity, as a strategy for ensuring high repayment rates, and which actually escalates violence towards female borrowers (p. 72). This could be attributed to the fact that GB borrowers have less experience with human capital development. However, in the 1980s GB initiated center schools for its borrowers to increase their literacy and numeric skills. Therefore, it is not true GB has been working and solely concentrated to economic development of its borrowers, rather it is working for clients socio-economic and environment. Unfortunately all center schools closed because bank workers did not have extra time to look after these schools. There is also a facility for larger small enterprise loans, credit plus services like education, health care, renewable energy etc. through its sister organizations. For example, Grameen Shikka (GS) established in 1997 to promote the education of non-literate Grameen Bank members; provide financial support in the form of loans and grants for education; and use and promote new and innovative ideas and technologies for educational development. Although GB has little support for vocational and business management skills development program; however, Grameen Shikka, a sister organization of Grameen Bank, has been serving educational services, providing vocational training to poor youths in Bangladesh.

7.0. Grameen Bank has shifted to a profit motive

Bebbington and McCourt (2005) asserts that it is clear that microfinance in Bangladesh at least reaches a significant population of otherwise disadvantaged people and here has been a tangible enhancement of their capabilities. On balance the evidence suggests that this is the case, particularly through asset enhancement, but also via positive effects on the socio-economic environments in which the poor work and live. However, Grameen Bank shifted to a profit motive drift mission instead of retaining its original objects. Recently GB has begun to emphasis on to a financial, self-sustaining agenda. This profit-making focus diverted employees not only to credit disbursement and repayments rates, but also turned them away from social and citizenship development discussions. However, the fact that GB had objectives of creating organizational solidarity and networks among the poor and bringing groups together in co-operative activities, as well as using joint efforts for the solution of problems. This system has led to more opportunities for women to show leadership. However Anne Maria and Rina Sengupta (1996) challenge this and infer that GB focuses on dispersal of credit and repayment it, but is unable to create solidarity among women.

The GB field program is designed in such a way that GB field workers go to the clients' doors, and not the other way around (not office-based). This field visit system provides the opportunities for workers to discuss and share ideas on social issues like education, health, personal hygiene, child nutrition, homestead gardening, and the rural exploitative process with their clients. Rahman (1999) remarks that Grameen Bank has a really good objective; but now there is a gap between its original goals and field realities. In 1992, the GB made a slogan for profit agencies in the microcredit market for the sustainability of MFIs. The Bank of Rakyat Indonesia and the BancoSol in Bolivia also follow the same slogan and are advocating for commercialization of micro credit services for the poor. However, field staffs are now more focused on loan disbursement, loan collection, deposit mobilization, pension and other investments. To do these jobs, field staffs now have no time to look at other socio-political and environmental issues of the clients.

Christen and Drake (2002) concluded that instead of helping to eradicate poverty MFIs are involved in doing high profit business. Although Muhammad Yunus of Grameen Bank cautiously makes an important point in that the development finance community must continue to innovate in the areas of targeting tools, products, service delivery and operations in order to reach the full range of low income families. However, a focus on financial sustainability encourages MFIs to place a greater emphasis on making profit than on the well-being of clients as this has a negative impact on borrowers' lives (Goetz and Sen Gupta, 1996; Morduch, 1999; Rahaman, 1999; and Woller, 2002). Therefore there is still need to broaden and deepen the outreach of MFIs. For example, GB made a profit of $6.03 million dollars in 2005 (Gramen Bank annual report 2005, p. 54). Although it claims to be a social benefit institution, it now operates on a profit motive as a private bank. Therefore, the Grameen Bank credit operation is totally different from Yunus's above statement.

Now financial sustainability has become an important goal in the agenda of the GB. In the words of Muhammed Yunus, "a sustainable system can be built only on the basis of users' undertaking responsibility" (1995, p.13). This has led the bank to operate its micro-credit program on cost recovery and profit making. For example, GB charged 16% interest rate until 1991 and then it raised it to 20% interest rate; and this rate is continuing now. This is like a commercial bank's high interest rate, which is too much for poor people. However, in the 1980s the Bank's operations were not so based on profit making. This new step to financial suitability helps the bank to be self sustained with its own financial income. Rahman says that, "Now investment has become primary and members are becoming secondary" (1999, p.79). He concluded that now GB's initial objectives have been diluted by emphasizing on quantitative success. It is now a successful financial institution lending to poor women; which is a contradiction to the original objectives of the Bank (Ibid. p.79). Thus, GB follows the capitalism approach by charging interest and making profits from its investment (Awal, 1994). However, the introduction of the profit motive into micro credit degrades MFIs organizations' commitment to the very poor. Such types of MFI banks are more available in Latin America (BANcoSol). This commercialization of the microfinance concept detracts from the achievement of political mobilization for clients and others being served. Although lot of change has made by the bank; however, group-based micro-financing, weekly center meetings, Sixteen Decisions slogans are still remain same those are serving clients for forming their social capital, cultural capital, citizenry capital and green business capital.

The GB success in high volume lending, loan repayment rate and high profit is well-liked among development practitioners. Grameen Bank operates nation wide through 2,185 branches. The repayment rate has been highly satisfactory (99%) since 1979. The majority of (97.9%) patrons are female borrowers. The Bank serves a total of 6.8 million borrowers through 130, 000 rural landless associations in 70,370 villages in Bangladesh. The total loan disbursement has been $14.65 billion since its inception. Of them $9.00 billion has been repaid. Current borrower savings are $4.2 billion. To date, its monthly loan disbursement is $58.00 million and 100% of loans are financed from borrowers' deposits. It has 22,000 staff members working at the village level nationwide (Grameen Updates 20016). It runs on its own internal funds and investment incomes, recover its costs from its incomer and that makes it economically sustainable. However, Isserles (2002) challenges that the Bank's high repayment rates do not indicate high efficiency; but he fails to point out the increase in the quality of women's lives.

Microcredit is unlikely to be automatically empowering for all women. At best, it can create an environment or provide credit resources which are most likely to help many women to be empowered through earning money. GB credit services to women have expanded all over Bangladesh and it creates a flow of money to low income women and promotes the creation of small businesses as well as opportunities for self-employment among poor women. Many other economic changes have occurred in rural Bangladesh. Naila Kabeer (1998) concludes that the last few decades have seen major social changes in Bangladesh, creating what has been called a 'quiet revolution' in gender relations and in the level of awareness about gender issues. Women's increased access to credit is an effect of this revolution, but the micro credit has also helped to contribute to women revolution (p. 69). Microcredit organizations have allowed the many women who have the talent and capacity to manage enterprises to utilize their talent in a way that society has not permitted them to do before (Ibid. p. 69).

8.0. Grameen Bank must consider why citizenry is important for its clients

One must consider why citizenry is important and what role the GB plays in citizenship skills development for low income women in Bangladesh. If we consider empowerment as 'the process of challenging existing power relations, and of gaining greater control over the sources of power' then it gives conflicting information. For example, the Kabeer (1998) study '*The Small Enterprise Development*

Program (SEDP) of Bangladesh" draws the conclusion that some feel that microcredit programs have a positive effect, and some believe that it is largely men who benefit, as microcredit has done little to move toward a situation of gender equality. A negative study by Montgomery (1996) found that only 9% of first-time female borrowers reported that they were the primary managers of their loan-assisted activities, while 87% described the loan-assisted activities as a 'family partnership'. Hence Fahim Quadir says, "Current Bangladeshi MFIs/NGOs' are the credit providers to poor people and thus, they are not the actual facilitators of women's empowerment (Class lecture April 03, 2007) in Bangladesh.

However, Simeen Mahamud gives us an interesting finding in that female credit recipients visit more NGO offices, health care centers and use birth control more, and have greater access to household income more than non- participating women. Use of immunization programs is also higher in microfinance receivers. Her findings show that micro credit expands women's access to valuable resources like self-employment and physical mobility in certain public spaces. However, women's access to wage employment, social and psychological mobility in the male dominated public sphere is not increased. She stresses the need for improved their self-perception that can increase women's welfare and can reduce subordination to men. Recently, the World Bank recognized gender equality as an element for sustainable development. Therefore, Grameeen Bank and other MFIs might campaign for gender equality (men and women have equal rights campaign) and for rural women empowerment across Bangladesh.

The World Bank *Engendering Development Program* focuses on gender equality in rights, resources and voice. It realizes that gender inequality and gender based division of labor slows down a country's economic growth and hence, poverty reduction. This program empowers women to participate in education, community and national decision making processes. World Bank data suggest that women tend to view corrupt practices more negatively than men. It shows that if women are able to take a more active role in citizenry and governance, governments would be less corrupt (World Bank 2002). Grameen Bank has no objectives to work against power and politics that perpetuate poverty and injustice in society. Therefore it is unable to create a voice for freedom and justice against patriarchy and local authorities to address the problem of violence against women which is a result of the failure of positive social change in Bangladesh.

Nonetheless, the Bangladesh National Women's Lawyers Association, Coordination Council for Human Rights in Bangladesh (CCHRB), Bangladesh Human Rights Council, Nijara Kori, Unyanan Bilkalpa Nari Pakka (UBINIK) and PROSHIKA, challenge the male dominated customary law on property rights and violence against women. However, *Shura* (high level religious leaders) and Islamic organizations in Bangladesh united together to maintain *Islamic Family Law.* Some pro-citizenry NGOs like Nijara Kori, Proshika, Unnayan Bikalp, and Narri Pakka (UBINIK) focus on rights and human dignity. They work for women's leadership development, advocacy and are actively involved in promoting equity, campaigning for building awareness and the granting of legal status. Although Proshika and Nijera Kori have programs for political development among disadvantaged people, they face a lot of problems.

Lamiya Karim finds BRAC, PROSHIKA, Nijera Kori, and UBINIK have some radical ideas and actions about women power and politics. For example, Proshika has taken an active role in promoting a politics of the poor. It organized a female protest in Brammonbaria in June 1997; but they were attacked by the local madrassah teachers, students and other religious leaders. These religious people declared that women's rallies/protests are non-Islamic. The clergy objected the rallies and verbally abused them. They burned and looted BRAC, Grameen Bank, PROSHIKA and other NGO offices. Therefore, it is difficult for women to resist against this clergy because MFIs' main programs are credit delivery services; they have no citizen skills development program. Proshika was unable to be a savior of the poor from this abusive event.

The massive provision of credit program by NGOs takes away from their social mobilization programs. It is either due to pressure from donors or from NGO Affairs Bureau (NGOAB). In 1990 the government opened the NGO Affairs Bureau to oversee the flow of foreign funds to NGOs. NGOs were required to register with the NGO bureau. All MFIs work under the NGO bureau with the condition that they abstain from participating in politics because the Bureau is regulates and monitors the inflow of foreign donations in addition to regulating their choice of policies. Many scholars note that civil society has less power for lobbying the necessary change in the legal system in Bangladesh. Dannecker (2000) asserts that NGOs engaging in social mobilization programs find themselves under greater governmental scrutiny. Government repression and NGOAB's regulation of donor funds has been used to regulate the policy approaches of most NGOs, and especially to prevent these NGOs from engaging in social mobilization activities.

GB and other MFI's educated NGO workers have been working in close contact with the rural poor. It is estimated that NGOs employ 200,000 young men and women are working in the villages of Bangladesh. The educated NGO workers have daily contact with the villagers, visiting them in their homes. In the 1980s the staff of Grameen bank spent more time in the centers discussing various social issues with group members. Now, Grameen Bank workers are involved with different types of loan investments, housing loans disbursement, loan collection, and the collection of pensions and savings from the borrowers (Bernasek, 1992; Chandler 1993; Goetz and Sen Gupta, 1996). These activities, according to Hashemi, " This going to the poor breaks down some of the threatening distance between the educated NGO workers and the poor, that is so much a part of rural social stratification (Hashemi 1997b: p. 4). According to Karim, "These activities in reality, introduce a new power elite into the existing dynamic of rural social relations in Bangladesh" (2001, p. 96).

Lamiya Karim (2001) remarks that micro credit shifts borrowers' conception about their location in the society. For example, borrowers are now individual entrepreneurs and have become more individualistic attitudes in their networks of social relations. They are now engaged in income generating projects; they do not consider themselves as laborers, but rather owners of petty capital. NGO beneficiaries are less willing to engage in political activities that may disturb their income generating activities. Isserles (2003) concludes that the main problem of micro credit stem mainly from the neo-liberal notion of individualism, which supports the notion that the recipients of the loans are responsible for their own fate if they should not be successful in this program. The westernized style of GB's economic success is based on how fast a loan is re-paid, and does not indicate anything about the cultural implications for the quality of life for women in the community (Isserles, 2003, p. 55).

GB has a system to lead groups and centers where they belong to; this leadership system by women borrowers laid the foundation and arrangement that has given the female clients some honor and status in their communities. Moreover, GB clients own 94.34% of its shares by buying share certificates and thus becoming partial owners of the Bank. The board of directors is comprised of 13 members, nine of whom are elected by the borrowers. They make bank policies and decisions (GB Annual Report 2005).This is one aspect of clients' participation from the grass roots to the top levels of policy making. So it is a process to develop women's leadership. It is definitely an empowering process; however, although the Grameen Bank has been successful in delivering loans to poor women and bringing socio-economic changes to many of these women's households, Aminur Rahaman's (1999) findings indicate that there are still some hidden transcripts in GB like women clients are vulnerable and become victims of male violence and are trapped by the system. He mentions that, "The public transcripts of GB offers only a partial view of the process and is influenced by the desire to see success in equitable and sustainable development, hence it obscures a fuller understanding of the process" (p. 68).

Under the patriarchal religious-dominated society, women in Bangladesh do not have equal rights to inherit property. To reverse this order and to free women from male dominance and to enhance women propriety rights, the Grameen Housing Loan Program recently introduced a policy that house loans could only be disbursed to those female borrowers who have houses or land in their own name. Borrowers' husbands registered land in their wives name in order to get housing loans. As a result 3.6 million Bangladeshi rural women are able to have land in their own name (Grameen Bank 2006). However, patriarchy is still there. Therefore, strong advocacy program for women's human rights and property rights is urgently needed and this is unfortunately lacking in GB's activities.

Parpert and Staudt (2002) assert that good governance and the empowerment of citizens and groups can ensure responsibility and accountability in government and challenge patriarchal and political-economic inequalities (p. 24). MFIs applying bandages to deeply root and systemic problems are an insufficient response. Therefore, political awareness is very important in Bangladesh because it can create public accountability. Levine, Peters and Thomson (1990) discuss accountability in terms of bridging answerability, responsibility and responsiveness. Citizens want administrators to be held accountable for their wishes. In this way citizens make administrators responsible for their particular needs.

Bangladeshi NGOs/MFIs have no intensive long term political mobilization programs in Bangladesh; however, in West Bengal popular political mobilization successfully has led to pro-poor economic reforms. There the rural poor people were able to use local government as an alternative institutional channel for promoting their interests (Sengupta & Gazdar, 1998). Union council is a local government institution that has been involved in local political power in Bangladesh, but is less powerful in helping the local people in because many villagers see political participation at the local level as irrelevant to them because its people are involved in corruption. However, it can be useful to local people if local government institutions (union councils) can be activated. Muhammad Yunus recently tried to draw the government's attention to focus on this local institution, but GB is not directly involved in lobbying for citizenry. PROSHIKA leaders have been accused for the rallies of their clients. PROSHIKA and GSS face government repression that hampers their programs. GB has taken some examples from PROSHIKA. Lamiya Karim (2001) thinks GB and other apolitical service delivery NGOs avoid antagonizing the government and jeopardizing their ability to promote citizenry.

According to the Grameen Bank Annual Report of 2005, 58% of the families of Grameen Bank borrowers have crossed the poverty line. The remaining families are moving towards the poverty line. However if we compare Grameen borrowers electoral success with their economic achievement, we can draw an assumption that the social and political empowerment process has started among credit recipients; however, political achievement is not as strong as its economic achievement. Fahim (2007) identified the reason as being that micro finance institutions see and work with single elements of the segment of the problem.

My research on NGO's gives me the idea that their existing activities do not have core programs to address the issues of power and politics, patriarchy and the market that are barriers to moving forward and achieving democratic objectives. However, they do need to look at the power dynamics of the whole community and analyze the elements that are essentials for opening up new spaces for political action by all people to achieve equal choice and voice and have more opportunities in the community.

Pankaj S. Jain (1996) in his paper 'Managing credit for the rural poor: Lessons from the Grameen Bank', based on a detailed study of the Grameen Bank in Bangladesh, suggests that the credit policies of the Bank do not constitute a sufficient explanation for the Bank's success, and that its acclaimed policy of replacing individual collateral with group guarantee is in fact not practiced. The paper presents an alternate explanation for the success of the Grameen Bank. In addition, it explains how the Grameen Bank has been able to overcome typical problems of implementing development programs by sustaining good performance from its large work force, and keeping to a minimum the tendency of a few target beneficiaries to corner program benefits and flout organizational norms for their personal benefit. However, Jain's study overlooked micro borrowers' citizenry skills development and their political empowerment in Bangladesh. Therefore, Gramen Bank needs to introduce the citizenship education program for its borrowers for civic knowledge development and political empowerment.

Recently BRAC has initiated a targeting ultra-poor (TUP) program that re-engages social mobilization and advocacy programs. However it is in a small scale. Expansion of this program can help to create a voice of the poor that can help elites to change their attitude towards them. GB can initiate such an advocacy program that can help poor to have access to political institutions challenge and reform public policy. Fahim says, "If participation can do three things-creating new opportunities for people to political control, obscures local power in differences and incorporate initiatives to the poor - it can be seen as a new form of social, political and cultural parameter to enhance opportunities for all people having equal voice, and choice in community development" (Class lecture, April 03, 2007).

MFIs borrowers, their family members and children are developing their human capital, social capital and economic capital in their community. Such evidence can be found in Mark M. Pitt and Shahidur R. Khandker (1996) study. In their paper 'Household and Intra-household Impact of the Grameen Bank and Similar Targeted Credit Programs in Bangladesh' they mention that group-based lending programs for the poor have become a focus of attention in the development community over the last several years. This paper treats the choice of participating in credit programs in a sample of Bangladeshi households and villages as corresponding to a *quasi-experiment* conditional on all observed and unobserved village characteristics. Their study uses the same approach to help identify the separate effects of lending to female and male household members, making use of the fact that credit groups are single-sex and groups for both sexes are not available in all villages. The data were collected in a special survey carried out in 87 rural Bangladeshi villages during 1991-92.

The paper provides separate estimates of the influence of borrowing by both men and women for each of three credit programs (the Grameen Bank, the Bangladesh Rural Advancement Committee (BRAC), and the Bangladesh Rural Development Board's RD-12 program (BRDB) on a variety of household and individual outcomes. These outcomes include the school enrolment of boys and girls, the labor supply of women and men, the asset holdings of women, recent fertility and contraceptive use, consumption, and the anthropometric status of children. The author finds that credit is a significant determinant of many of these outcomes. Furthermore, credit provided to women was more likely to influence these behaviours than credit provided to men, and had the greatest impact on variables associated with women's power and independence. Therefore, in short, credit has a significant effect on the well-being of poor households in Bangladesh and this effect is greater when women are the program participants. However, Mark M. Pitt and Shahidur R. Khandker study does not mention the status of women micro borrowers' political position in their communities.

8.0. Conclusion

Oxfam works in different countries to increase women's capacity to promote and defend their rights, and be attentive to laws that promote gender equality. Canadian NGOs are diversified and are a vehicle for the engagement of citizens. There are many non-profit organizations such as the Ontario Coalition for Advocacy against Poverty (OCAP) which has been a lobbying organization and it is involved in protesting, marching, advocating and lobbying for human rights and women rights. Many other Canadian NGOs are influencing the Canadian government to change some policies although very few

NGOs are engaged in micro lending programs. Bangladeshi NGOs, especially Grameen Bank, the biggest grass-root organization in Bangladesh, can make radical changes if it lend, support and lobby to achieve people's civil and political rights, and to make sure their voices are heard. It is very important because rural women and other minorities need to support for their equal rights and status those are oppressed or marginalized.

There are several sister organizations of the Grameen Bank like Grameen Agricultural Foundation, Grameen Fisheries Foundation,, Grameen Check, Grameen Health, and Grameen Shikka Foundation which are involved in agriculture, ponds management, fish cultivation, rural handlooms management, rural health, and rural child schooling programs in Bangladesh. However, there is no Grameen sister organization that promotes citizenry skills development among rural poor women. Therefore, it is necessary that the Bank rethink including political activism agendas in its arena. It can create programs that include face-to-face counseling, lobbying and advocacy activities, emphasizing positive change. This is urgently needed in Bangladesh because women's dependency on male incomes makes them vulnerable and more subject to physical and sexual violence by men. A recent World Bank Gender and Development Policy (Policy 4.20) allows for assisting with gender plans of action. An approach to gender issues benefits both men and women. So there is a great space for GB to improve in advocacy for women's human rights development along with its investment credit products. Training on a power and politics basics, capacity-building in advocacy, lobbying, communication with different government agencies and elites are needed as a foundation in Grameen Bank services.

PRA based on equitable and respectful partnerships and collaboration between clients and institutions with due attention to local knowledge (Chamber, 1997; Crush, 1995' Escobar, 1995; and Friedmann, 1992). According to Amartya Sen's (1999) it is a process of developing individual capabilities through gaining education and skills in order to power individuals to fight for a better life, goals of good governance, democracy and economic liberalization. Grameen Bank and all other MFIs are working closely with grass roots marginalized people and following a community participation approach. Yunus has a strong network and influence in Bangladesh. He can lobby for poor people's inclusion in the political policy arena in Bangladesh that might assist poor to be close to the state power and for achieving their social justice and legal rights in Bangladesh.

Ilan Kapor (2002) mentions in his article 'The Devil's in the Theory: A critical Assessment of Robert Chamber's Work on Participatory Development' that the practice orientation of Robert Chambers' work on *Participatory Rural Appraisal (PRA)*, which aims at enabling local people and communities to take control over their own development, has received much attention in development circles. His article attempts to shift the emphasis away from PRA's practice towards its theoretical underpinnings. The article argues that PRA's practice/empiricist orientation causes it to be insufficiently theorised and politicised. As a result, questions about inclusiveness, the role of PRA facilitators, and the personal behavior of elites overshadow, or sometimes ignore, questions of legitimacy, justice, power and the politics of gender and difference. The article draws on arguments and debates involving Habermasian *'deliberative democracy'* and post-structuralist notions of power. From this point of view, MFIs are controlling the poor because they have power over the poor through proving credit. MFIs put rules and regulations of loan recovery over their clients. Here MFIs have no program 'deliberative democracy' for the MFIs clients in Bangladesh.

Puspa Raj Sharma (2007) studied 'Micro-finance and Women Empowerment' in Nepal. His paper examines the effects of women's participation in group-based micro-credit programs on a large set of qualitative responses to questions that characterize women's autonomy and gender relations within the household. The data come from a special survey carried out in hill and tarai in 2004-2006 of Nepal. The results are consistent with the view that women's participation in micro-credit programs helps to increase women's empowerment. Credit program participation leads to women taking a greater role in household decision-making, having greater access to financial and economic resources, having greater social networks, having greater bargaining power compared with their husbands, and having greater freedom of mobility. Female credit also tended to increase spousal communication in general about family planning and parenting concerns. Ecologically, the higher impact on women's empowerment was noticed in terai. The reason may be relatively lower social and economic status of terai women at the time of program initiation compared to that of hills. As a result, even a small change in their status would get reflected distinctly. However, Sharma study missed to tell readers what citizenry skills tarai people have, what kind political deficiency they are suffering from and how MFIs could empowered them politically.

However, different picture is found in Anne Marie Goetz and Rina Sen Gupta (1996) study. Anne Marie Goetz and Rina Sen Gupta (1996) in their paper 'Who takes the credit? Gender, power, and control over loan use in rural credit programs in Bangladesh' mention that Micro credit institutions in Bangladesh have dramatically increased the credit availability to poor rural women since the mid-1980s. Though this is intended to contribute to women's empowerment, few evaluations of loan use investigate whether women actually control this credit. Most often, women's continued high demand for loans and their manifestly high propensity to repay is taken as a proxy indicator for control and empowerment. Anne Marie Goetz and Rina Sen Gupta paper challenges this assumption by exploring variations in the degree to which women borrowers control their loans directly; reporting on recent research which finds a significant proportion of women's loans to be controlled by male relatives. The paper finds that a preoccupation with 'credit performance'- measured primarily in terms of high repayment rates- affects the incentives of fieldworkers dispensing and recovering credit, in ways which may outweigh concerns to ensure that women develop meaningful control over their investment activities. However, K. A.

Rouf (2011) survey on Grameen Bank women borrowers finds that 87% women are involve in public space activities in Bangladesh. Many of them ride local government elections and 4785 women borrowers elected as Local Union Councils' councilors and sub-district councils' councilors in 2009. If this statistics compare with 1997 election, it can be found that in 1997, out of a total of 4298 unions of Bangladesh, 7 GB members and 39 members of the family were elected to the post of Chairman. In the membership election in the union councils, out of 51,396 seats, 261 male and 1,343 female GB borrowers were elected by contest and 34 members were elected uncontested. In addition, 1,073 family members were elected as members of the union council (Grameen Dialogue 2001, p.16). However, this data is not as strong as its poverty success statistics. GB women borrowers' public space participation is increasing. This is a great achievement for GB borrowers in Bangladesh. This is one of the sign of women micro-borrowers empowerment in public space in Bangladesh.

In 1997 election, Proshika and Nijera Kori formed an institutional alliance which sponsored 44,138 women candidates for 12,894 Union Council seats and 12,822 of these candidates won. This huge win is one illustration of the triumph of feminization in the rural power structure. This statistics show that GB borrowers' and other MFIs borrowers' participation in the formal local councils is increasing although they have no core program for mobilizing citizenship rights for their clients.

Uphoff's (1992) concept of 'social energy' is applicable to the success of GB micro-credit program in Bangladesh. Yunus has a dynamic charismatic leadership quality and diffused his ideas through society gaining momentum and persuading individuals and organizations to take on different values and do things differently in Bangladesh. The spark of social entrepreneurship that Yunus set off has literally energized scores of other leading Bangladeshi social activists and thousands of others to try to get micro-financial and other services to poor people. The diffusion process has moved into the public sector through PKSF.

Now more than 20 million bottom people receive micro credit from MFIs in Bangladesh that inspired by Grameen Bank Bangladesh.

However, many micro credit programs are limited in their success to empower the female gender unless there is some change in men's attitudes towards women. Fahim Quadir says that, "NGOs can organize people as a countervailing force where they can construct a new form of politics through NGOs mobilizations" (class lecture April 04, 2007). Anne Maria calls for a policy response to improve women's control over loan use. Grameen Bank activity produces new forms of social and institutional dominance over many female clients in the program; however, it has no citizenry education program for its clients. Therefore, Grameen Bank could initiate a pilot project on the advocacy of citizenry and political skills awareness development program within its existing structure or could create a separate organization and acquire experience in citizenry advocacy programs. This initiative can then can be followed by other MFIs/NGOs and inspire them to become involved in civic engagement programs. GB can initiate this program in two folds: First by designing a citizenry program experimentally like the BRAC TUP program in Bangladesh; secondly through forming alliances with other NGOs for citizenry advocacy at the national level. This forum can examine different power and political institutions and their elements like patriarchal property laws, customary laws, and women's human rights and may provide a platform from which micro-borrowers can protest against gender-biased property laws, wages, violence against women, and other patriarchic discrimination, domination, and exploitation. At the beginning this platform may not directly challenge religious values and customs, but may rather start a dialogue with related stakeholders.

9.0. Bibliography

Abdullah, A. T. and Zeidenstein, S.A. (1982). *Village Women of Bangladesh Prospects for Change.* Oxford: Pergamon Press

Ackerley, B. (1995). Testing the tools of development: credit programs, loan involvement, and women's empowerment, *IDS Bulletin*, Vol. 26 (3), pp. 56-67

Bannerji, H. (1993). *Popular Images of South Asian Women. Returning the gaze: Essays on racism, feminism, and politics.* Toronto, ON: Sister Vision Press

Bebbington, A. and McCourt, W. (2005). Statecraft in the South: A framework for understanding public policy success in developing countries. Paper presented at the *ESRC Seminar on Policy Success in Developing Countries,* Institute for Development Policy and Management, University of Manchester, May 20, 2005

Bangladesh Institute of Development Studies (BIDS. (2005). Fighting human poverty: Bangladesh Human Development Report 2000. An overview of the study prepared by the *Bangladesh Institute of Development Studies (BIDS).* Retrieved February 16, 2006 from http://www.sdnbd.org/sdi/issues/sustainable_development/bd

Bill Hopwood, Mary Mellor, and Geoff O'Brien (2005). Sustainable development: mapping different approaches, *Sustainable development,* Vol. 13 (1), pp. 38-52

BMSP. (1997). *State of Human Rights Bangladesh.* Dhaka, Bangladesh: Manobadhikar Samonoy Parishad (BMSP)

Bangladesh Rural Advancement Committee (BRAC). (2005). *BRAC information.* Retrieved February16, 2006 from http://www.brac.net/

BRAC Research and EducationDepartment (2004). The elites, their perspectives of poverty and the Gram Shahayek Committee: Some early explorations. *CFPR?TUP Research Preview,* Vol. 7

Cain, Mead; Syeda Rokeya Khanam; Shamsun Nahar. 1979. Class, Patriarchy and Women's Work in Bangladesh, *Population and Development Review,* Vol. 5(3), pp. 405-538

CIDA (2001).*Gender Profile: Bangladesh,* CIDA Webpage

Daley-Harris, S. (2005). *State of the Microcredit Summit Campaign Report 2005* http://www.microcreditsummit.org/pubs/reports/socr/2005/SOCR05.pdf

Drake, Deborah and Elisabeth Rhyne. Eds., (2002). The Commercialization of Micro-Finance: Balancing Business and Development. Blomfield, C.T. Kumarian Press. Chapter 1, 2, and 6.

Devine, J. (2003). The Paradox of Sustainability: Reflections on NGOs in Bangladesh, *Annals of the American Academy of Political and Social Sciences*

Edwards, M. and Hulme, D. (1996). 'Too Close for Comfort? The Impact of Official Aid on nongovernmental Organizations', *World Development*, Vol. 24(6), pp. 961-973

Fuglesang, A. and Chandler, D. (1987). *Participation as process: What can we learn from Grameen Bank* . Oslo: NORAD

Hashmi, T.J. (2000). *Women and Islam in Bangladesh, Beyond Subjection and Tyranny.* London: MaCmilian Press Ltd.

Hashemi, S., Schuler, S.R., and Riley, A.P. (1996). Rural credit programs and women's employment in Bangladesh, *World Development*, Vol. 24(4), pp. 635-653

Hashemi, Sayed M. (1989). The NGO Non-Alternative in Bangladesh. Paper presented at *Jahangir-nagar University.* Bangladesh.

Hashemi, Sayed M. (1997b). NGOs and Popular Mobilization in Bangladesh: The Shift in Empowerment Paradigm. Paper resented at *Jahangir-nagar University.* Bangladesh

Hulme, David & Karen Moore (2006). *Why has microfinance been a policy success in Bangladesh (and beyond)?* Institute for Development Policy and Management, University of Manchester

Hulme, D. and Mosley, P. (1996). *Finance against poverty*, Volumes I and II. London/New York: Routledge.

Jain, P. and Moore, M. (2003). What makes microcredit programs effective? Fashionable fallacies and workable realities. *IDS Working Paper*, 177. Brighton: Institute of Development Studies

Isserles, Robin, G. 2003. Microcredit The Rhetoric of Empowerment, the Reality of Development As Usual, *Women's Studies Quarterly*, Vol. 3 & 4, pp. 38-57

Grameen Bank. (2005). *Grameen Dialogue #60, January 2005.* Dhaka, Bangladesh: Grameen Trust

Goetz, A. M. and Gupta, R. (1996). Who Talks the Credit? Gender, Power, and Control over Loan Use in Rural Credit Programs in Bangladesh. *World Development*, Vol. 24(1), pp. 45-63

Kabeer, N. (2002). We donít do credit: Nijera Kori social mobilisation and the collective capabilities of the poor in rural Bangladesh. Dhaka: Nijera Kori

Kabeer, N. (1995). *Revised Realities-Gender Hierarchies in Development Thought*. London, Great Britain, Biddles Ltd.

Kapoor, I. (2002). The Devil's in the Theory: A critical Assessment of Robert Chamber's Work on Participatory Development. *Third World Quarterly*, Vol. 23 (1), pp. 101-117

Kamat, S. (2004). The privatization of Public Interest: Theorizing NGO Discourse in the Neoliberal Era, *Review of International Political Economy*, Vol. 11(1), pp. 155-176

Karim, L. (2001). *Politics of the Poor? NGOs and Grass-roots Political Mobilization in Bangladesh*. American Anthropological Association.

Kevin P. Kearns (1996). *Preserving the public Trust*, Jossey-Bass

Khandker, S. R. (2005) Microfinance and poverty: evidence using panel data from Bangladesh. World Bank Economic Review, Vol. 19, pp. 263-286

Mahamud, S. (2004). Micro-credit and Women's Empowerment in Bangladesh in *Attacking Poverty with Micro-credit*, (Eds.), Salehuddin Ahamed and M. A. Hakim. Dhaka: Dhaka University Press

Moser, Caroline (1989). Gender Planning in the Third World: Meeting Practical and Strategic Gender Needs. *Word Development* Vol. 17(11), pp. 1799-1825

Matin, I. and Hulme, D. (2003) Programs for the Poorest: Learning from the IGVGD in Bangladesh. *World Development*, Vol. 31(3), pp. 647-665

Matin, I., Rutherford, S. and Maniruzzaman, M. (2000). *Exploring Client Preferences in Microfinance: Some Observations from SafeSave*, CGAP Focus Note 18

Mayoux, L. (1998). *Women's empowerment and micro-finance programs: approaches, evidence and ways forward*, Open University Development Policy and Practice Working Paper No. 41

Mayoux, L. (1995). *From vicious to virtuous circles? Gender and micro-enterprise development*, Geneva: United Nations Research Institute for Social Development

Levine, Charles H., B. Guy Peters, and Frank J. Thompson (1990). *Public Administration: Challenges, Choices, Consequences*. Glenview, IL: Scott, Foresman/Little, Brow

Nussabaum, M. (1988) Women's Capabilities and Social Justice. In Molyneux, M. and

Razavi, S. (Eds.), *Gender, Justice, Development and Rights*, (pp 45-74), New York, Oxford University Press

Pankaj S. Jain (1996). Managing credit for the rural poor: Lessons from the Grameen Bank, *World Development*, Vol. 24 (1), pp. 79-89

Parpart, Jane L, Shirin M. Rai, and Kathlen Staudt. (2002). Rethinking Empowerment, Gender and Development: An Introduction in Parpart, Jane L. Shirin M, Rai and Kathelen Studt, (eds.*), Rethinking Empowerment Gender and Development in a Global/local World* (pp. 3-12). London: Routledge

Pereira, F. (2001): "Women's rights to equality and non-discrimination" in *Human Rights in Bangladesh*. Dhaka. Ain Salish Kendra

PKSF (2004). Annual Report 2004, http://www.pksf-bd.org/annual_report2004/annual_report _cont.html

Puspa Raj Sharma (2007). Micro-finance and Women Empowerment, *The Journal of Nepalese Business Studies* Vol. 4(1), pp. 16-27

Rahman, A. (1999). Micro-credit Initiatives for equitable and Sustainable Development: Who pays? *World Development*, Vol. 27(1), pp. 67-82. Elsevier Science Ltd.

Rhyne, E. (2001). *Mainstreaming Microfinance: How Lending to the Poor Began, Grew, and Came of Age in Bolivia*. Bloomfield CT: Kumarian Press

Quadir, F. (2003). How 'civil' is Civil Society? Authoritarian state partisan Civil Society and the struggle for democratic development in Bangladesh. *Canadian Journal of Development Studies*, Vol. 24(3), pp. 425-438

Bill Hopwood, Mary Mellor, and Geoff O'Brien (2005). Sustainable Development: Mapping Different Approaches, *Sustainable Development*, Vol. 13(1), pp. 38-52

Sachs, J. (2005). *The end of poverty: economic possibilities for our time*. New York: Penguin.

Sanjay Sharma and Audun Ruud (2003). On the Path to Sustainability: Integrating Social Dimensions into the research and practice of Environmental management. *Business Strategy and the Environment*, Vol. 12(4), pp. 205-214

Sherri Torjman (1998). *Strategies for a carrying Society,* Caledon Institute of Social Policy, Canada. ISBN #1-859194-23-3

Schuler, M. (Ed.). (1986). *Empowerment, and the law: strategies of Third World Women.* Washington, D.C.: OEF International

Sengupta, S. and Gazdar, H. (1998). Agrarian Politics and Rural Development in West Bengal, in J. Dreze and A. Sen (eds) *Indian Development: Selected Regional Perspectives*, pp. 129-205. Delhi: Oxford University Press

Sen, A. (1999). *Development as Freedom*. New York: Anchor House

Shahiduzzaman. (1999). PKSF: A success story. *Bangladesh Observer,* 30 July 1999. http://www.pksf-bd.org/ass.html

Todd, H. (1996). *Women at the center: Grameen Bank borrowers after one decade.* Boulder: Westview Press

Uphoff, N.T. (1992). *Learning from Gal Oya: Possibilities for participatory development and post-Newtonian social science*, Ithaca: Cornell University Press

White, S. (1999). NGOs, Civil Society, and the State in Bangladesh: The Politics of Representing the Poor, *Development and Change,* Vol. 30 (2), pp. 307-326

World Bank (2002). *Integrating Gender into the World Bank's Work: a strategy for action*, Washington. D. C.: The World Bank. Chs. 1, 3 & 4

World Bank Report (1996). *Pursuing Common Goals,* Dhaka: World Bank Publications

Wong, Wai-Ching Angela (2002). *The Poor Women- A Critical Analysis of Asian Theology and Contemporary Chinese Fiction by Women.* New York: Peter Lang

World Bank (1996). *Impact of Grameen Bank in Bangladesh.* Washington D.C.: The World Bank

Yunus, Muhamad (1996). *Credit is a human right.* Dhaka: Grameen Bank

Yunus, Muhamad. (2010b). *Building social business: A new kind of capitalism that serves humanity's most pressing needs.* New York: Public Affairs.

Measuring training participants' changing performance using self-reporting method: Grameen Bank training evaluation experience in Bangladesh

Abstract

Transfer of learning through training contributes to clients, managers, and organizations' success in achieving organizational goals. Therefore, training learning gained in evaluations is very important to measures transfer of learning and skills development through training. However, to avoid training evaluation costs, institutions usually avoid evaluating its training performance by outside evaluators and consultants. Self-reporting training evaluation methods are popular to evaluate training participants' changing performance and their contributions to achieve institutional goals. This paper reviews different training self-reporting evaluation methods and their suitability of using Grameen Bank's training evaluation in order to measure learning achievement and skills development of the officials of Grameen Bank in Bangladesh. The paper also discusses prospective and retrospective self-reporting methods and compares them with other training measurement methods to find an appropriate training evaluation method for Grameen Bank.

Key words: Grameen Bank; response bias; self-assessment; self-reporting; and training evaluation.

1.0. Introduction

Self-reporting is a widely-used form of training evaluation, because of its simplicity, low–cost and convenience. It is one of the main approaches that can be used to measure training outcomes, especially learning gains. B. Mezzof (1981) reported that at least 80% of evaluation programs employ self-reporting as the measure of choice due to its ease and low-cost. Although self-assessment training evaluations can be measured in several ways with several benefits, self-assessment still has *response-shift-bias* that contaminates training evaluation test scores (Mezzof, 1981; Bray & Howard, 1980; Stufflebeam, 2005; Lam & Bengo, 2003; Taylor & Taylor 2009; and Hill & Betz, 2005). Moreover, other questions arise in the use of self-reporting methods such as: retrospective design problems in pre- and post-test design, validity concerns, subject response style effect and recall bias. Another question centres on whether the measurement of all of Kirkpatrick's four levels of training outcomes is necessary to accurately understand learning outcomes at the end of a training course. Therefore, the paper looks at the issues arising from using self-assessment in measuring Kirkpatrick's four levels of training outcomes in practice; discuss different methods of self-assessment and as an example, the suitability of using Grameen Bank's training evaluation.

2.0. Transfer of learning different theories

Transfer of learning through training contributes to everyone's success: clients, managers, and organizations. Therefore, training learning gained in evaluations is very important, because training measures learning and skills developed through training. Also, it measures the effectiveness of training to determine how much the trainees have learned. However, if training evaluation results are unreliable or invalid because of response-shift bias, or other errors, one cannot say how or if a program achieved its desired outcomes. Hence, evaluators are serious about finding appropriate training evaluation methods and are placing an emphasis on the validity of retrospective tests (Cook 1998; Meyers-Wall; 2000 in Hill and Betz 2005: p.501) to minimize response-shift-bias and other errors. According to J. H. Bray and G. S. Howard (1980) response-shift bias, a methodological source for contamination that confuses results of studies including self-report measures are looked at by training evaluation studies (p. 62). In this regard, the *Pre-Then-Post-Tests* (retrospective test) can improve training accuracy and can legitimately document the benefits of training. In retrospective tests, participants are asked to take a test of their skills and knowledge in order to judge their knowledge and ability in specific areas of evaluation prior to and following a certain (weeks / months) instructional period. This retrospective method helps training participants to reduce the responses that engender response-shift bias as compared to other evaluation methods like control groups and experimental groups, prospective tests, etc.

There are several models and methods that exist in training evaluation. This paper is not arguing different training evaluation models; rather it discusses prospective, retrospective self-reporting methods and compares them with other training measurement methods to find an appropriate training evaluation method for Grameen Bank.

Some common problems have been found with respect to subjective self-reporting strategies. One example is that pre-test scores can cause frustration, nervousness and trauma for trainees if they are asked to be tested on items that they have not yet learned. Training; however, provides subjects with more accurate information that can improve their understanding and can change their perception from their initial level of functioning. This weakens pre-and-post treatment comparisons and is the source of response-shift-bias, a source of contamination of the training outcomes. In order to minimize response-shift-bias, several training evaluation experts like Mezzof (1981); Stufflebeam

(2005); Darling & Gallagher (2003); Bray & Howard (1980), Taylor & Taylor (2009); D'Eon et al. (2008); Hill & Betz (2005); and Lam & Bengo (2003) use different prospective and retrospective self-reporting methods. Below section discusses different self-reporting issues, self-reporting methods and their pros-and-cons in training assessment.

B. Mezzof (1981) identified a major issue of self-reporting: The issue of response-shift bias (Mezzof 1981: p.3). He challenged the traditional prospective self-report training method and argued that a learning evaluation calculation based on a pre-test and post-test measurement is not able to provide accurate learning outcomes, because trainees reported using the traditional pre- and post-testing methods often underestimated or overestimated training benefits. Therefore B. Mezzof proposed a "then-test" to minimize what he described as response-shift-bias. The test process is called *'Pre-Then-Post'* testing where participants reflect back after training to their level of functioning prior to the training and re-state themselves in addition to the pre-post measure of traditional self-report. (p. 4). Mezzof (1981) uses a one-way analysis of variance (ANOVA) strategy to compare pre-then tests and then-post tests. His empirical study finds the pre-then-post (retrospective) testing eliminates response shift bias (Ibid, p. 5). A fictitious code number is used when testing participants in the then-post test, which allows analysts to anonymously compare the then-post tests with the pre-then tests. Although this method is easy to administer; it is important to develop appropriate self-reporting questionnaires to eliminate the instrumental error-response-shift bias. Moreover, T. Lam (2009), through his findings, suggest that self-assessment not be the only measure that is paid attention to in self-assessments (Lam 2009: p 4-5).

D. L. Stufflebeam (2005) also uses a self-reporting assessment method for evaluating learning outcomes by using the *Self-Assessment of Program Evaluation Expertise (SAPEE)* method. His study has three types of participants: Novice evaluators, experienced evaluators and experts. He compares these three groups through learning gains.

Participants' *Self-Assessment Mean Pre-test* and *Post-test* Scores are taken by novice participants and experienced participants (Stufflebeam 2005: p. 14). This in-depth study was designed for three weeks training for the novices and two weeks for experienced participants. The self-assessments included needs assessments so that the instructor could understand which areas needed more attention and to help participants know what they learned (Ibid, 2005: p.3). The results were converted to an average score and this result was compared with participant from other years' pre-and-post instruction results (Ibid, 2005: p.9). The study showed that the average gains in perceived evaluation expertise made by novice participants were substantially larger than those of the experienced participants. This is because (a) the novice participants received more instruction than the experienced participants, and (b) the novice participants had more room for improvement. This indicates that the extra week of training may be effective in closing the gap between experienced and novice participants (Ibid. 2005: pp.13-15). However, there were several limitations found in this study. An example is that participants inflated their rating of learning gains because of a desire to please the institution's staff members. Hence it needs further validation of this method.

3.0. Different Training Evaluation Methods

- Self-reporting (Solely) Method Self-assessment in combination with other methods other than self-reporting
- B. Mezzof (1981) Retrospective testing, identified response-shift bias
- S. Darling and P. A. Gallagher (2003) CSPD, Need Assessment, Multivariate analysis (MONOVA) of Bamberger (2004): Shoestring + project design, contextual factor, No control and Experienced. Groups
- D. L Stufflebeam (2005) method SAPEE, pre- and post- test
- Russ-Eft Taylor and H. Taylor (2009): Have clear wording, conventional and retrospective test

- W. A. Eckert's (2001) method is considered best training design that talks about situational factors analysis with checklists, use pre-and post-tests but using no control and experienced group
- D'Eon, M., Sadownik, L., Harrison, A., & Nation, J. (2008) training evaluation method called "Multilevel self-assessment training evaluation"
- T. Lam and P. Bengo (2003) method called HLM, compare conventional, retrospective and perceived change. This also has multilevel assessments + direct observation + Need assessment+ perceived change + program design
- R. R. Haccoun (2008) method contains "One group-pre-test and post-test design, ANOVA, IRS, Identify Type -1 Error and Type-2 Error."
- S. G. Hill and D. L. Betz (2005) training evaluation method compares prospective and retrospective test, effect size, prospective and retrospective test, Subjective self-report measure
- J.H. Bray and G. S. Howard (1980) retrospective test, IDEA, social content analysis to look for subject response style effects
- J. Mayne (1999) Performance measurement analysis, analysis of existing files, secondary data and case study
- Blanchard P. N. (2009) training valuation is about self –reporting, theory and practice;
- R. O. Brinkerhoff (2003) model is called "Success Case Method (SCM)"
- Hoogstraten, J (1982) training evaluation method is called "Seeing Problems Strategy (SPS), conventional and retrospective test, look at subject response style effect:,
- Jr., W. Aurther, P. S. Edens, S. Bell and Jr., W. Bennett (2003) training evaluation focus on need assessment + Meta Analysis of design + paper –Pencil test
- S. M. Jenkins and P. Curtin (2001) centered on "Job analysis method."

- G. Kaupins (1997) method called "Live Case Analysis, internship, and chalk board-display paper."
- S.M. Darling and P.A. Gallagher's (2003) study looked at the requirements for Comprehensive System of Personnel Development (CSPD) pre-service and in-service training for those living with disabilities in Georgia (p.2). This CSPD method has three stages of self-assessment: SA1: administered at the beginning of training and reviewed responses, SA2: overseen at the end of the training to self-reflect (p. 4) and in SA3 assessment questionnaires are mailed out with their certificates after three months. (p. 4). A repeated measure MANOVA (multivariate analysis of variance) with SPSS program uses in this experiment to determine the improvement of participants over time (p.5).

  This CSPD method also requires a needs assessment to verify and clarify issues like strengths and weakness for participants (Darling & Gallagher 2003: p. 2). During a 5-day training module a participant completes 15 self-assessments. Although the CSPD method is an in-depth study; it is time-consuming. SA3 should be avoided because it is administered too late to assess learning and provide feedback. It is unreliable, as the evaluator is subject to the trainee mailing back the information. Below the paper explores a retrospective self-reporting study that covers different types of subjects like instructor and student self-rating for self-reporting assessments.

- J.H. Bray and G.S. Howard's (1980) retrospective self-reporting test has five parts: instructor, student-rated progress, course evaluation, student self-rating and student demographic data (p.65).

Table 1. Different training evaluation methods

Self-reporting (Solely) Method	Self-assessment in combination with other methods	Methods other than self-reporting
Mezzof (1981) Retrospective testing, identified response-shift bias	Darling and Gallagher (2003) CSPD, Need Assessment, Multivariate analysis (MONOVA)	Bamberger (2004) Shoestring + project design, contextual factor, No control and Experienced. Groups
Stufflebeam (2005) SAPEE, pre- and post- test	Taylor and Taylor (2009): clear wording, conventional and retrospective test	Eckert (2001) Best training design, situational factors, Checklists, use pre-and post-tests, No control and experienced group
D'Eon (2008) Multilevel self-assessment	Lam and Bengo (2003) HLM, compare conventional, retrospective and perceived change, Multilevel assessments + direct observation + Need assessment+ perceived change + program design	Haccoun (2008) One group-pretest and post test design, ANOVA, IRS, Identify Type -1 Error and Type-2 Error
Hill and Betz (2005) compare prospective and retrospective test, effect size, prospective and retrospective test, Subjective self-report measure,	Bray and Howard (1980) retrospective test, IDEA, social content analysis to look for subject response style effects	Mayne (1999) Performance measurement analysis, analysis of existing files, secondary data and case study

Blanchard (2009) Self –reporting, theory and practice		Brinkerhoff (2003) Success Case Method (SCM)
Hoogstraten (1982) Seeing Problems Strategy (SPS), conventional and retrospective test, look at subject response style effect		Aurther, Edens, Bell and Bennett 2003 Need assessment + Meta Analysis of design + paper –Pencil test
		Jenkins and Curtin (2001) Job analysis method
		Kaupins (1997) Live Case Analysis, internship, chalk board-display paper

The method uses multivariate analysis for collected data analysis (Bray & Howard, 1980, p. 66). Participants rate themselves with regard to their knowledge just after training and as they were before the training. Then each is scored separately (Ibid. p. 64). G. S. Howard and his colleagues aimed at demonstrating the response–shift -bias phenomenon and the superiority of retrospective pre-tests over traditional pre-tests (Bray & Howard, 1980; Howard & Dailey, 1979; Howard et al., 1979; Howard, Schmeck and Bray, 1979, Birkenbach, 1986; Hoogstraten, 1982; and Hoogstraten 1985).

Bray and Howard's (1980) study looks at whether response-shift bias is a threat to internal or construct validity (p. 63), finding a solution in using retrospective pre-tests, comparing test data and then determining the self-rating impact assessment on training measurement. This method is a little different than Mezzof's. J. H. Bray and G. S. Howard (1980) use the instructional development and effectiveness assessment (IDEA) for student rating. Training was successful in the areas of teaching assistants' (TA's) self reports of teaching, actual teaching and student ratings of instruction (p. 66). Although the findings indicate several benefits such as teacher training programs as a way to improve teaching ability and effectiveness; the program has subject response style effects (memory distortion, social desirability, compliance with implicit demand characteristics, etc.) on retrospective pre-test ratings which can be a high contaminator (Bray & Howard 1980: p. 64). The perception of learning knowledge does not reflect an exact measurement.

D'Eon et al. (2008) concluded that change in performance self-assessment means from before to after a workshop can detect workshop success in there and other situations. In this commentary, their recommendation is refuted by showing that (a) self-assessments with balanced over-and underestimations are still biased and should not be used to evaluate workshops, even though the means of self-assessments and criterion measures are artificially equal; (b) participants' performance should not be attributed directly to training, even if the self-assessments are psychometrically valid and obtained prior to the workshop as well; (c) self-assessment findings should not be generalized to other situations without further analysis and caution, even if the participants' performance can be attributed to training. For clarifying the recommendation by D'Eon et al. to use ``aggregated self-assessments'' to evaluate workshops, analysis of multilevel data is explained and discussed. Finally, nine rules of thumb in using self-assessments for evaluating training are provided.

Howard & et al. (1979) also conducted a study on the validity of retrospective pre-test and concluded that retrospective pre-test and post-test comparisons yield more valid results than conventional pre-test comparisons, but the study informed pre-tests do not improve self-reporting accuracy. They found two possible causes of response-shift bias: (a) memory distortion (forgetting), (b) subject response-style effects (social desirability, subject acquiescence). To combat this, they recommended collecting self-reporting ratings of pre-intervention performance retrospectively rather than prospectively; as well as suggesting uniform standard measurement for both then-test and post-test ratings. Although several benefits can be found in this method, there was no information collected about the employees learning achievements, and student achievement measure information. Therefore the actual effectiveness of the trainers is not completely known and thus needs further study (Bray & Howard, 1980: p. 69).

D. L. Staffelbam (2005) describes the Self-Assessment of Program Evaluation Expertise instrument and procedure developed to help participants assess their learning gains in a 3-week evaluation institute. Participants completed the instrument in a pre- test and post-test format. To reduce both the threat of embarrassment from individual results and the temptation to inflate self-ratings, participants responded anonymously. Although each participant saw her or his individual results, only aggregated results were reported to the total group. The article reports on the self-assessment results of a group of recognized evaluation elders and participants in six annual evaluation institutes. The findings indicate that the instrument is sensitive to the respondents' changed perceptions of competency following instruction. Strengths and limitations associated with the procedure are discussed. The procedure is presented as a work in progress and could benefit from adaptation, research, and development. The instrument is available at http://www.wmich.edu/evalctr/ess/selfassess.html.

S. G. Hill and D. L. Betz (2005) looks at different training evaluation methods including self-reporting measure especially examining and critiquing J. Mayne's (2001) performance-based measurement for training analysis although Campbell et al., 1963, Shadish, Cook and Campbell, 2002 suggests for objective performance assessments that can considered superior to self-reporting (in Hill and Betz 2005 p. 502). Hill and Betz (2005) assert that performance-based measurement may be supplemented or replaced by subjective self-reporting measures. They (Hill and Betz) conduct a comparison study on retrospective assessment with prospective rating bias and show that in a prospective test program effect is underestimated, where it is overestimated in retrospective tests, which is different from the Stufflebeam study (2005).

Moreover, S. G. Hill and D. L. Betz (2005) have concerns about the validity of the retrospective method, which is a primary threat to program evaluation because there are some degrees of recall bias (distortion or degradation of memory) in all retrospective ratings. Hill and Betz (2005) place emotional biases under the category socially desirable or impression management responses (Paullus, 2002 in Hill & Betz (2005), p. 504). This finding is relevant to other program evaluation ratings made by Griffin & Kahneman, 2002; King & Bruner, 2000 in Hill & Betz 2005, p. 504; and Lam & Bengo, 2003). All of these studies find other cognitive biases in retrospective rating that are implicit theories of change. Aronson and Mills (1959) call this cognitive dissonance bias effort justification bias (Hill & Betz 2005, p. 505). On retrospective pre-tests, clients may be able to provide more accurate estimates of pre-treatment behaviours; however, in traditional pre-tests this may yield an underestimate of treatment effects or, even worse negative effects.

S. G. Hill and D. L. Betz (2005) also study Effect size (ES), the standardized measure of different scores between then-pre-test-post-test outcome variable. The findings say the pre-test-post-test ES is slightly larger .52 than ES reported from the program's experimental trial (p. 510). However, here the primary problem of the study is there are no objective criteria to which pre-test and post-test results can be measured against. They suggest for future research for incorporating objective criteria for more fine-grained analysis of pre-test-then-test differences. A well-designed research comparing both types of pre-test across multiple studies would provide a useful benchmark for exploration of pre-test–then-test differences. In this respect, T. Lam and P. Bengo's (2003) study is prominent.

T. Lam and P. Bengo's (2003) self-reporting data collection system includes a needs assessment, service utilization, and program processes (design) and uses them in different evaluation projects to determine pre-intervention status of knowledge and post –intervention status. Their study analysis has three self –reporting methods: the post and retrospective pre-test method, the post and perceived changed method, and perceived change method. Their study shows that teachers in the post and retrospective pre-test condition reported least change, but in the perceived change condition, participants reported the greatest change. Schwaz and Oyserman (2001) say that this significant in change scores is the intervention-related change (in Lam & Bengo 2003; p. 66). However, W. A. Eckert (2000) concludes that these tests designs have inherent validity threats, which are caused by self-reporting in the pre-test because a pre-test can have a lower internal validity by introducing a carry-over or practice effect. This results in post-test participants recalling their responses and inflating their performance on the post-test. T. Lam and P. Bengo (2003) call it the *carry-over-effect* that can minimize internal validity threats.

Tony Lam (2003) identified other drawbacks in pre-test models where trainees depreciated their pre-test scores to inflate their treatment-counterfactual estimation is also a concern in training evaluation. Therefore, T. Lam and P. Bengo (2003) suggest not using pre-tests prior to intervention in measuring self-reporting change. Within the literature, there is an indication that response-shift-change measurement obtained from post and retrospective pre-test methods are often more accurate estimates of change than those obtained from traditional, pre-test and post-test design (Bray & Howard 1980, Hoogstraten 1982, Howard & Dailey 1979, Howard et al., 1979a, 1979b in Lam & Bengo 2003: p. 69). However, Lam & Bengo's comparative study (2003) on three methods report that all have response-shift-bias differences. Therefore, T. Lam and P. Bengo ask for the use of multiple methods including social desirability measures in future research to avoid the false response in testing (p. 78). They suggest for the post-test only method for self-reporting estimation (2003: p. 69). However, T. Lam and P. Bengo do not explain the design of their retrospective self-reporting method. They do suggest further research that can substantiate this approach (2003: p. 66).

J. Hoogstraten (1982) identifies three causes of response-shift bias: initial lack of information, memory-effects and subject response style. He investigates the relative validity of self-reporting measures using two conventional pre-test-post-test designs and retrospective pre-test-post-test designs. Here subjects receive training in *Seeing Problems Strategy (SPS)* and are assigned to three conditions at random. The findings are the then-post scores reflect actual performance changes while conventional pre-post scores do not. Therefore, J. Hoogstraten (1982) suggested that the retrospective pre-test is a valid means to control for response-shift bias. However, this experiment did not allow researchers to determine the impact of these three causes on response shift bias.

Lam (2009) challenges D'Eon & et al.'s (2008) self-reporting assessment method and argues with evidence that aggregated self-assessments results both at the single level and multilevel analysis (*Hierarchical Linear Models (HLM)*) are not generalizable due to individual differences, contextual differences, assessment content and procedural factors (p 12). Lam says generalizability based on over- or under-estimates for both the self-assessment and criterion assessment is flawed (p. 12). To fully capture both over- and underestimation biases, he suggests evaluators should use both difference-in-means and correlation indices to determine the validity and subsequently the usability of self-assessments for measuring training outcomes and effects (Lam, 2009: p. 4). T. Lam says that D'Eon et al. (2008), by only using self-assessment, can only determine a participant's performance not overall training effectiveness (Lam 2009: p. 6). With regards to this, Lam proposes for further research on aggregated self-assessment for its validity effectiveness and to make it efficient and more professional (p. 12). He offers nine points to use self-assessment to determine workshop success (p. 12). He also suggests for multilevel analysis or Hierarchical Linear Models (HLM), a special regression analysis procedure that looks at the aggregation effect by using information from all levels. This multivariate analysis is more efficient and precise, but cumbersome. Moreover, the HLM method needs statistical advanced knowledge and is expensive for measuring learning gains.

Taylor, Russ-Eft and H. Taylor's (2009) research contains trained supervisors and untrained subordinate participants in tests. Conventional and retrospective pre-test self-reporting scores are compared using a correlated t test. The conventional pre-test ratings are typically found to be significantly higher than retrospective pre-test ratings and lead researchers to conclude that a *response-shift bias* has occurred. Training effects based on self-ratings are substantially larger (Taylor & Taylor 2009, p. 40). T. Lam and P. Bengo (2003) also found the same results. Participants indicated even greater changes when asked about the degree to which they have changed than when asked separately for retrospective pre-test and post-test ratings (in Taylor & Taylor 2009, p. 41).

Although retrospective pre-tests may prevent response-shift bias, they may introduce other biases that inflate intervention effects. For example, individuals may be motivated to exaggerate their improvement to reflect favourably on themselves. Similarly, they may be motivated to show a substantial improvement regardless of their actual improvement to justify the effort that they have expended in completing the program (Taylor & Taylor 2009, p. 32). Therefore, the problem is more likely in a retrospective pre-test design because individuals complete both pre-test and post-test ratings at the same time and are thus better to manipulate their pre-test ratings to show an improvement. Hence the use of retrospective pre-tests for any rating source could be suspect (Taylor & Taylor 2009, p. 34). To avoid this response-shift- bias, Russ-Eft Taylor and H. Taylor (2009) recommend it should be addressed through careful construction of clearly worded measures rather than using retrospective pre-tests.

The Canadian Society for Training and Development (CSTD 2009) uses three methods for training measurement: (1) The Immediate Impact Questionnaire (IIQ), (2) The Job Impact Questionnaire (JIQ), and (3) The Effective Practices Audit (EPA) of training evaluation to evaluate different trainings outcomes. The Job Impact Questionnaire (JIQ) evaluates the impact of a training program on job performance following the participants' self-report in light of four key questions:

applying the knowledge and skills; application of the learning for improving job performance, improved performance impacting business results, and difficulties faced by the participants to apply their learning on-the-job. This self-reporting training evaluation method is very simple and is widely-used in Canada. However, it is important that CSTD include 'evaluators' direct observation' while collecting participants self-reporting data as suggested by Tony Lam.

4.0. Compare and contrast self-reporting training evaluation methods and alternative training evaluation methods

Below the paper looks at other alternative training evaluation methods to compare status within self-reporting training evaluation methods. M. Bamberger, M. Church and L. Fort (2004), W. A. Eckert (2001), R. R. Haccoun and T. Hamtiaux (1994), and J. Mayne (1999) have different training evaluation methods, which do not use self-assessment training evaluation methods. For example, Haccoun and Hamtiaux (1994) use a simple procedure for estimating the effectiveness of training on trainee knowledge through the Internal Referencing Strategy (IRS) as compared to a traditional experimental evaluation (p 593). R. R. Haccoun and T. Hamitaux (1994) identify two types of errors: Type-1 and Type-2 errors in the study. To avoid these errors, R. R. Haccoun suggests parallel pre- and post-tests (p 597). However, IRS is still susceptible to type 2 errors and should not be used to replace more complex and rigorous designs (p. 603). IRS may not be used for behavioural or higher learning levels (p. 603). M. Bamberger, M. Church and L. Fort's (2004) *shoestring evaluation approach* collects training data without using a control group and baseline data for the project group, but it has six intensive steps. This method is used when working within time and budgetary constraints and limitations on data accesses (Bamberger et al., 2004: p. 6). Evaluators collected secondary data using participatory methods and used checklist for quantitative data. Although Bamberger's training evaluation finds solutions to the varied threats to validity and adequacy of evaluation designs (pp. 29-30); this method is very detailed, intensive, complicated, and expensive.

W. A. Eckert (2001) and J. Mayne (1999) do not believe in using the pre-test and post-test control groups and experimental groups for training learning and change behaviours. Rather, they emphasize on the best training evaluation designs, which can identify internal threats and address them (p. 186). W. A. Eckert (2001) places emphasis on the right setting or situational factors, regression analysis and uses a checklist to determine plausible threats to validity. Here Eckert's method's advantage is that the work offers a better application of designs not better designs (p. 192) and is less expensive. However, regression analysis cannot provide case-to-case participants variation results. J. Mayne's (1999) performance measurement attempts to program contribution analysis, which explores and demonstrates performance measures. Existing program files, secondary analysis, and case study evidence are used for program measurement. The features of the contribution analysis are: acknowledging the problem, presenting the logic of the program, identifying and documenting behavioural changes, etc. J. Mayne's logic model chart encourages programs to be more precise in program designs (1999: p. 9). However, here expert opinions and a structured survey need to give support evidence about the contribution of the program.

Throughout the above discussion, it is found that several training evaluation models and methods are developed by different training evaluators. The classical one is Kirkpatrick and his four levels of measurement. Others are Philips and Stone's (2007) five levels of training outcomes, G. Alliger's (1997) *Augmented Framework Training Taxonomy Model* (learning sub-levels), D. Eseryel's (2002) *ADAPT –IT instructional design* tool, K. Kraiser, Ford and Sales' (2002) primary classification scheme of learning outcomes-cognitive, skill-based and effective learning outcomes. The *Context, Input, Process and Product (CIPP)* model, and Alvarez et al.'s (2004) integrated models are also used for training evaluation.

All of these models suggest measuring more than one training outcome level like reaction, learning outcomes, behaviour change and results. However, Blanchard, Thacker and Ways (2000) share that not all companies need follow all these steps of training evaluation. The measurement of all training steps depends upon organizational demand, executives' interest, budget, time and manpower. P. N. Blanchard, J. H. Thacker and S. A. Ways (2000) argue that there is a difference for training evaluation academia versus practitioners' practices. Academicians are proponents of evaluating students' academic knowledge performance, but practitioners are interested to know their employees job performance and training learning outcomes.

D. Kirkpatrick's four-level training (p.2) to justify the worth in constantly improving training and prefer follow all levels of training evaluation, but practitioners tend not to follow all of Kirkpatrick's levels of training evaluation (p.3). P. N. Blanchard suggests there should be a balance among academics and practitioners. They should communicate with each other to discuss current training issues (Ibid, p.9). Blanchard's study shows that reaction is the most used for both management-employee and non-management-employee training (Ibid, p.4). More than half of companies are not evaluating training based on behaviour or results levels (Ibid, p.5). Hence, according to P. N. Blanchard, J. W. Thacker and S. A. Ways (2000) levels of evaluation should be conducted depending upon the client's objectives, despite the perceived need for all four.

5.0. Grameen Bank self-reporting training evaluation method and its suitability of using different training evaluation methods in Bangladesh

Below this section of the paper narrates how self-reporting can be used in Grameen Bank (GB) to better inform training practices and looks at how this model may apply to other microfinance institutions' training evaluation. In the GB context, measuring knowledge of learning gains on loan delinquency depends on various factors such as cliental situations, training budget and organizational policies. Even employees can perceive the problems from different perspectives. Therefore, trainees' responses in pre-then-post testing self-assessments will vary. Self-assessment is undoubtedly the most efficient data-collection method in training evaluation (Lam 2009: p.12). However, invalid self-assessment cannot be used to gauge training effectiveness and self assessment data with equal underestimates and overestimates are invalid. In this situation, S. G. Hill and D. L. Betz (2005) concisely recommend retrospective pre-tests for the examination of subjective experiences of program-rated change that can be used in GB to measure trainee learning gains.

Grameen Bank follows a minimalist decentralized training evaluation approach. GB's training evaluation data collection uses the pre-test and post-test control group and experimental group (Eckert method) and uses IRS with pre-post single group training evaluation design (Haccoun & Hamitaux, 1994), which involves many stages. Moreover, the use of J. Mayne's training performance validity measurement and Bamberger, Church and Fort's shoestring method incorporating checklists for quantitative secondary data collection will be complicated, expensive, and cumbersome and grassroots employees may feel uneasy and nervous to go through all the steps of training evaluation. Hence asking questions of trainees about learning gains following the retrospective method could be one method in the GB training measurement.

GB has conducted several delinquent loan recovery workshops for its employees and informally asked them about their perception of the delinquency problems and possible solutions for reducing loan delinquencies. Some participants realized the issue(s) after the workshop and shifted their self-assessment in comparison to how they did before the workshop (different mental yardstick). Now, I can anticipate a response-shift-bias with Grameen Bank (GB) trainees, employees and managers in their in-service pre-training and post-workshops, especially in measuring knowledge of learning gained on loan delinquency, which is dependent on various others factors such as cliental socio-economic situations. Hence, training levels and trainee responses in pre-then-post testing self-assessments vary from place to place and varied social contexts. P. N. Blanchard identifies this and provides an example where some respondents, using Kirkpatrick's levels in different ways, like an integrated strategic human resource system where the performance review process assesses employee behaviour and organizational effectiveness throughout the process. However, respondents using this system may not be able to answer all review questions (Blanchard et al., 2000: p. 7), but in the perceived-change method, questions are asked directly to trainees (how participants think they have changed as a result of an intervention) (Lam & Bengo, 2003).

Moreover, the distinction of uses of GB's relevant and irrelevant training content can identify training gained learning and gaps with respective to various items. In this context, S. M. Darling and P. A. Gallagher's CSP training evaluation strategy, D. L. Stufflebeam's shoestring SAPEE method, Bray and Howard's IDEA methods are all centralized training evaluation that have huge costs, require a lot of staffing and other resources needed for evaluating 30,000 employees at 2575 branches in Grameen Bank in Bangladesh. The above methods cannot give answers to GB's relevant and irrelevant items. Compared to all methods discussed, B. Mezzof's, simple framework for measuring the response-shift bias can help GB in a formal way to determine response-shift biases with some limitations. Internships program of Grameen Bank include job shadowing training strategies provide regular direct feedback to GB's relevant and irrelevant items.

Although there are many models and methods developed for the treatment of evaluation, to minimize counterfactual estimation, response-shift biases and effect size, Grameen Bank job shadowing could incorporate intensive observation while directly asking questions to interns using retrospective method. This can impact upon trainees and managers so that they can think intensively about the problems of loan delinquencies and their solutions. Hence, the paper recommends GB branch managers would prefer a decentralized, self-reporting training evaluation data collection method by directly asking questions to trainees at the end of their internships using the retrospective self-reporting method at the branch level until a refined training gains measurement that is tested may be published.

References

Alliger, G., & Janak, E. (1989). Kirkpatrick's level of training criteria: Thirty years later. *Personnel Psychology*, Vol. 42(2), pp. 331–342

Alvarez, K., Salas, E., & Garofano, C.M. (2004). An integrated model of training evaluation and effectiveness. *Human Resource Development Review*, Vol. 3, pp. 385-616

Arthur Jr., W., Edens, P. S., Bell, S. Bennett Jr., W. (2003). Effectiveness of training in organizations: A meta-analysis of design and evaluation features. *Journal of Applied Psychology*, Vol. 88(2), pp. 234-245

Bardella, I.J., Janosky, J., Elnicki, D.M., Ploof, D., & Kolarik, R. (2005). Observed versus reported precepting skills: Teaching behaviours in a community ambulatory clerkship. *Medical Education*, Vol. 39, pp. 1039-1044

Blanchard, P. N., Thacker, J. W., & Way, S. A. (2000). Training evaluation: Perspectives and evidence from Canada. *International Journal of Training and Development*, Vol. 4(4), pp. 295-304

Bomberger, M., Church, M. & Fort, L. (2004): Shoestring evaluation: Designing impact evaluations under budget, time and data constraints. *American Journal of Evaluation*, Vol. 25(1), pp. 67-87

Bray, J.H., & Howard, G.S. (1980). Methodological considerations in the evaluation of a teacher-training program. *Journal of Educational Psychology*, Vol. 72(1), pp. 62-70.

Brinkerhoff, R. O. (2003). *The success case method*. Barrington Research Group, Inc.

Campbell, D.T., & Fiske, D.W. (1959). Convergent and discriminant validation by multitrait-multi-method matrix. *Psychological Bulletin*, Vol. 56, pp. 81-105

Campbell, D. T., & Stanley,J. C. (1963). *Experimental and quasi-experimental designs for research on teaching.* Handbook of research on teaching. Chicago: Rand McNally

Cronbach, L.J. (1976). *Research on classrooms and schools: Formulation of questions, design and analysis.* Occasional Paper of the Stanford Evaluation Consortium. Stanford, CA: Stanford University

Darling, S.M., & Gallagher, P.A. (2003). Using self-assessments in early intervention training. *Journal of Early Intervention*, Vol. 25(3), pp. 219-227

D'Eon, M., Sadownik, L., Harrison, A., & Nation, J. (2008). Using self-assessments to detect workshop success: do they work? *American Journal of Evaluation*, Vol. 29, pp. 92-98

Eckert, W. A. (2000). Situational enhancement of design validity: The case of training evaluation at the World Bank Institute. *American Journal of Evaluation*, Vol. 21(2), pp. 185-193

Eseryel, D. (2002) Approaches to evaluation of training: Theory and practice. *Educational Technology & Society*, Vol. 5(2), pp. 93-98

Haccoun, R. R., & Hamtiaux, T. (1994). Optimizing knowledge tests for inferring learning acquisition levels in single group training evaluation designs: The internal referencing strategy. *Personnel Psychology*, Vol. 47, pp. 593-604

Hopkins, K.D. (1982). The unit of analysis: Group means versus individual observations. *American Educational Research Journal*, Vol. 19(1), pp. 5-18

S. G. Hill and D. L. Betz (2005). Revisiting the Retrospective Pre-test. *American Journal of Evaluation*. Vol. 26 (4), pp. 501-517

Hoogstraten, J. (19820. The Retrospective Pre-test in an Educational Training Context. *Journal of Experimental education*, Vol. 50 (4), pp. 200-204

George S. Howard, Jim Millham, Stephen Slaten, and Louise O'Donnell (1979). *Influence of Subject Response Style Effects on Retrospective Measures*, Huston: University of Houston

Jenkins, S. M., & Curtin, P. (2006). Adapting job analysis methodology to improve evaluation practice. *American Journal of Evaluation*, Vol. 27(4), pp. 485-494

Kaupins, G. (1997). Trainer opinions of popular corporate training methods. *Journal of Education for Business*, Vol. 73(1), 5-8

Kirkpatrick, D.L. (1977). Determining training needs: Four simple and effective approaches. *Training and Development Journal*, Vol. 31(2), pp. 22-25

Kraiger, K., Ford, K., & Salas, E. (1993). Application of cognitive, skill-based, and affective theories of learning outcomes to new methods of training evaluation. *Journal of Applied Psychology*, Vol. 78, pp. 311-328

Lam, T. (2009). *Do Self-Assessments Work to Detect Workshop Success? An Analysis of Argument and Recommendation* by D'Eon et al. *American Journal of Evaluation*, Vol. 30(1), pp. 93-105

Lam, T.C.M. (1990, October). A two-stage approach to assessing program effects. Paper presented at the annual meeting of the *American Evaluation Association*, Washington, DC.

Lam. T. C. & Bengo, P. (2003). A comparison of three retrospective self-reporting methods of measuring change in instruction practice. *American Journal of Evaluation*, Vol. 24 (1), pp. 65-80

Mayne, J. (2001). Addressing attribution through contribution analysis: Using performance measures sensibly. *The Canadian Journal of Program Evaluation*, Vol. 16, pp. 1-24

Mezzof, B. (1981). How to get accurate self-reports of training outcomes. *Training and Development Journal*, Vol. 35(9), pp. 56-61.

Miller, P.J. (2003). The effect of scoring criteria specificity on peer and self-assessment. *Assessment & Evaluation in Higher Education*, Vol. 28, pp. 383-394

Phillips, J., & Stone, R. D. (2007). *How to measure training results.* Toronto: McGraw-Hill.

Rouf, K. A. (2018). Measuring training participants' changing performance using self-reporting method: Grameen Bank training evaluation experience in Bangladesh, International Journal of Research Studies in Education, Vol. 7(2), pp. 41-51

Rouf, K. A. (2016). Despite the minimalist approach of Grameen Bank training program, similarities may be drawn between its practice and the models offered by Kirkpatrick and others. *International Journal of Research Studies in Education* 2017 January, Vol. 6 (1), pp. 105-114

Stufflebeam, D.L., & Wingate, L.A. (2005). A self-assessment procedure for use in evaluation training. *American Journal of Evaluation*, Vol. 26(4), pp. 544-561

Salas, E. & Cannon-Bowers, J. A. (2001). The science of training: A decade of Progress. *Annual Review of Psychology*, Vol. 52, pp. 471-499

Taylor, Russ-Eft, and H. Taylor (2009). Gilding the Outcome by Tarnishing the Past: Inflationary Biases in Retrospective Pre-tests. *American Journal of Evaluation*. 30 (31).

The Canadian Society for Training and Development (CSTD) (2009). *Invest in People's Project* Retrieved from www.cstd.ca/investing_in_people/tools.html dated June 2011.

Grameen Bank women borrowers' social development in Bangladesh and why does not social development through MFIs in North America

Abstract

The purpose of the study is to: (1) examine the degree to which women borrowers of the Grameen Bank are being empowered to participate in familial decision-making around the management of income and expenditures like food, children's education, dowry and teenage marriages; (2) to examine women borrowers' engagement in community activities such as the degree of freedom women are granted to visit public places like schools, local councils, banks and markets and to explore why does not social development of through MFIs in North America. *This study used a mixed-methods research design that included 61 GB women borrowers selected through purposive sampling. The findings indicated that 98% of GB women borrower participants are engaging in community organizations and 94% do not face problems with this engagement. In the 2009 UpZilla (Municipal Sub-district) Election, out of 481 seats, 114 Female Chairs (25% of the total) were elected from the GB women borrowers and their families. However, in Canada micro-financing programs are not doing well; however Grameen America is doing excellent job in USA.*

Key Words: Grameen Bank; GB Sixteen Decisions; Green Social Business; Community Organizations; Community Development; Dowry Marriages; Patriarchy; Leadership; and Women Empowerment

Acronyms: Grameen Bank (GB), Japan Bank for International Cooperation (JBIC), Ontario Institute of Studies in Education (OISE), Small and Medium Enterprise development (SME), Union Parishad (UP), United Nations Development Program (UNDP) and United Nations High Commissions for Refugee (UNHCR).

1. Introduction

The study attempts to understand whether the Grameen Bank (GB) Sixteen Decisions are enough to enhance GB women borrowers' social development as well as emancipate them from their male partners' dominance in their familial life and in their community life to address patriarchal chauvinism. Moreover, this researcher investigated whether these women micro borrowers are empowered to engage in their communities.Under this umbrella objective, the study explores the three research questions:

1. What are the development barriers that GB women borrowers experience in the family and in the community?
2. Are GB women borrowers able to transfer their center leadership skills to other public spaces?
3. What supports are needed for GB women borrowers to take part in decisions that pertain to family and community?
4. Is micro-credit fiunctioning in North American countries?

1.1. Context

Bangladesh is a patriarchal religious village-dominated country where non-agricultural paid employment is limited and the emancipation of women which took place in the Western world has not yet occurred.

Forty-nine percent of the total population lives below the national poverty line in the world (The Hunger Project, 2010) and in addition they are suffering from an abuse of their human rights. Worldwide, the feminization of poverty is one of the world's most pressing problems. For example, 67% of the world's women live below the poverty line. Asian women have only 1% of the wealth in the world, yet they do 66% of the work that is needed for human survival (Wong, 2002). The majority of women are suffering from poverty and their male partners treat them as secondary members of the family – meaning they have limited voice, choice and decision-making power within the family, and even less in the community where males are considered the primary members (Belal, 2008;and Jahan, 1995).

GB was initiated by Muhammad Yunus in 1976 and has been practicing its group-based microcredit operations in Bangladesh for more than 30 years. It provides credit to the poor women without collateral. Its aim is to improve the well-being of the poor and to empower them in their families and in society. Through utilizing GB loans, 8.6 million rural-poor borrowers in 83,967 villages in Bangladesh (GB monthly report June, 2017) increased their income, created assets for their families, and are reducing the cycle of poverty in Bangladesh. Women borrowers' familial and community relationship has developed in patriarchal Bangladesh (Ahmed & Hakim, 2004; Chu, 2007; Counts, 2008; Gibons, 1995; Khandker, 1998; and Yunus, 1994). The repayment rate of 97 percent has been sustained since 1979. 100 percent of loans are financed from borrowers' deposits. Moreover, fifty-eight percent of GB women borrowers have crossed the poverty line, as it is defined in Bangladesh. Kofi Anan (2005), the former UN Secretary General, says that microcredit has proved its value, in many countries, as a weapon against poverty and hunger. Hence Zeller (2004) comments that through microcredit, progress is being made in achieving the Millennium Development Goals (MDGs) such as eliminating poverty and promoting gender equality and women's empowerment (United Nations, 2000a).

The dominant patriarchal values; the rule of the men or the patriarch subordinating women, hampers women's empowerment in Bangladesh, and it effects half of the women; around 82 million (Bangladesh Profile, 2010). Although there have been many success stories of women who have been emancipated through Grameen microcredit, Isserles (2003) cautions that many women are still dominated by their husbands and do not actually enjoy the benefits from their financial gains or loan investments. In many cases their husbands use the loans to their own advantage. Isserles in her study mentions that 57 percent of women saw a rise of verbal aggression after they received loans for their households. In rural Bangladesh, where all GB women live, 67 percent of women experience domestic violence. In 70 percent of the cases, husbands were held responsible for the violence (Hossain, 2006). However, in recent years, in the 2009 UpZilla (Municipal Sub-district) Election, out of the 481 seats, 114 Female Chairs (25% of the total) were elected from the GB women borrowers and their families (Grameen Bank, 2009). In addition, the number of women borrowers serving as councilors has increased from 1,572 in 1997 to 1,950 in 2003; these data indicate that the number of women borrowers acting in formal leadership roles is increasing (Grameen Bank, 2009). This is evidence that GB woman borrowers' liberation at the familial level has not yet been fully achieved.

My personal working experience with micro-credit programs in Bangladesh, and abroad I had been involved in Grameen Bank Bangladesh's poverty reduction program that provided small loans to the rural poor for the last twenty-seven years. My work with Grameen Bank in Bangladesh, research on Grameen America and other countries helped me gain experience in micro financing and provided an understanding of how rural poor people become self-employed and empowered in Bangladesh. However, different scenario can be found in Canada.

In Toronto, I worked with the Toronto Social Services office where I saw many single mothers, widows and children suffer from poverty. There is a significant change in the availability of full-time employment, a shrinking pool of professional jobs and diminished employee-employer friendly relationships. In addition, large corporations relocate their facilities outside of Canada. Consequently, unemployed people rely heavily on part-time, temporary and other forms of contingent jobs. These factors increase inequality and create a gap in professional full time, high paying jobs which translate into few earners and low-paid earners.

However, micro businesses, through micro financing, have several benefits in eradicating poverty through community economic development; the promotion of local living economics and job creation in different countries of the world. Muhammad Yunus (2005), Founder of Grameen Bank Bangladesh says that the local economy becomes rejuvenated through microcredit programs. Therefore, millions of low-income people in Canada will benefit if micro businesses break into the mainstream policy formulation. Microcredit programs as tools to address poverty and inject energy into local living economics are not a part of the strategic plans of front-line service providers in Canada. As a proponent of microcredit, I feel that self-employment through engaging marginalized unemployed people in small business initiatives could be one of the options to address unemployment and poverty in Canada.

Calmeadow Foundation started group lending microcredit in Toronto in 1992 through 2000, but it is now closed. Then 2000, this program is attached with Alterna Savings Credit Union in Toronto. Alterna Savings has been working in the Greater Toronto Area for the last eight years and currently has ninety-five micro entrepreneurs who have received $387,000 CDN worth of microloans (November 2007). Through Alterna loans, many entrepreneurs become self-employed and expand their businesses in Toronto (Alterna Annual Report 2007). Yet this is not sufficient because many poor entrepreneurs are still seeking business capital and self-employment support services that need intensive nurturing services. Alison Bailey (1998) said cultivating virtue is a development process (p.38). They (poor entrepreneurs) need an alternative planning/strategy that are capable of disrupting/ resisting and challenging micro entrepreneurs against an oppressive business market in Canada. Despite these opportunities, unregulated microenterprises can create problems for the greater community and worsen nature through the destruction of natural protective barriers unless MFI practitioners ensure that this does not occur.

Micro business created 37,000 jobs or 11.6 percent of all jobs (the highest contribution by micro businesses) since the first quarter of 2005 in Canada (Industry Canada 2007). According to the 2001Census, 552,300 or 23% of all city residents had incomes below the Low Income Cut-off (LICO). Four out of five small business firms fail within the first five years. Currently almost 19 percent of adult women are below the low-income cut-off line in Canada (StatsCan 2006). Women are falling further and further into poverty (Hick, 2004: p. 277). In Canada, 4.4 million or 15.4 percent of the population live below the poverty line, including almost 1 million children (Statistics Canada 2006).

According to Statistics Canada (2002), self-employment and microenterprise development have been rated as the fastest growing segment of the economy for 18% of the Canadian workforce. A study done by Human Resource Development Canada in 1996 and the study showed that nearly 12,000 individuals participated in self-employment assistance programs with a business survival rate of 83% after the first two years (Graves & et al., 2000). According to Statistics Canada (2002), nearly 2.2 million individuals were self-employed in Canada in 2001. Calmeadow has created an awareness and acceptance that credit is an important tool in stimulating economic development for the disadvantaged in Canada. However, case studies brought out some structural, ideological and traditional differences and similarities in microfinance and microenterprise development between the developed and developing countries.

In the United States, 46 million people live in poverty. 34% female headed households live poverty; nearly 1 in 7 people live in poverty, 1 in 5 children live in poverty, and 1 in 6 underemployed. The federal government defines poverty as a family of four living on $23,500 or less. Many of these families work hard to make ends meet often employed at unpredictable minimum wage jobs. Even working full-time at minimum wage, individuals earn less than $15,000 a year. This mysterious issue was raised in US Presidential Election 2016.

1.2. Rationale of the study (Why micro micro-finance program for poor is necessary) and context

Many research studies suggest that in spite of economic advances, GB women borrowers' are still limited by patriarchal social structures in their family and community (Goetz, 2004). It is also important to understand the reasons why 47 percent of GB women borrowers in Bangladesh are still experiencing domestic violence from their husbands (Rahman, 1999). Rouf study in 2010 finds this number has reduced to 87%; however, still patriarchal dominance subordinate women in Bangladesh.

Microcredit institutions (MFIs) are not looking at these oppressive situations that affect women's self-esteem and civic participation and why these women are not accessing their full potential. Hence, Fahim Quadir (2003) states that currently Bangladeshi NGOs are the providers of goods to the poor rather than facilitators of the actual empowerment of women in Bangladesh. This is because they do not directly intervene with regard to these issues. Nevertheless, these issues need more exploration, as undertaken through this study.

1.2.1. Canadian socio-economic situation

Today, economic power and wealth is increasingly becoming concentrated within a small number of multinational corporations.

According to Professor John O'Neil of York University, capitalism is the production of wealth and poverty. Thomas Allen (2002) said, "It is part of a global crisis" (p. 16). Polany said, "This big transformation is self-destruction" (p-4). It is advantageous to wealthy nations. It is socially constructed. Vandana Shiva said post-colonization is process politics of disappearance of local knowledge systems and experience delegitimizing the politics that might arise from local experience (Julie Wuthnow 2002 (p.184). To counter this hegemonic economic power, it is vital to create alternative economic forces, where micro financing to small businesses can play an active role in socio-economic development and address the issue of poverty and environmental development. However, a microeconomics movement that is to become the heart of its very value system can shift the idea of corporate responsibility. In Bangladesh, micro-credit industries are huge and they are working to address the issue of poverty in Bangladesh. Now the poverty has decreased in Bangladesh. Poverty also exists in developed countries; however, some of their poverty issue strategy is different. Micro-credit service is not in priority in their state policy. For example, poverty is exists in Canada and it is increasing; however, micro-credit services are very limited. Although the paper is about Grammen Bank Bangladesh, I am narrating poverty situation in Canada for the readers in order to get ideas about depth of poverty in Canada and how poor people are struggling to survive in Canada.

Therefore, the shifting of microeconomics self-employment notion is very important even in Canada, especially in Toronto because according to Poverty by Postal Code report (2004), unemployment rate in very poor neighborhoods is 13% in Toronto. Many people are working in low-paying, part-time jobs. The largest poverty rate was in 2000 at 22.6% (p.17). A One in five family lives in poverty in Canada (Ibid, p.17). There has been a dramatic rise in the number of higher poverty neighborhoods in the City of Toronto during 1981-2001; it is just about doubling every ten years (Ibid, p.20). In 1981, just 17.8% of poor economic families resided in higher poverty neighborhoods. By 1991, it had climbed to 29.6%, and by 2001, it had reached 43.2% (Ibid, p.24). There is an astonishing 136.6% increase in the number of poor economic families in the former City of Scarborough in 1981-2001 (Ibid, p. 36).

In 1991, there were 80,590 children living in higher poverty neighborhoods in Toronto but by 2001, the number had increased to 160,890 - a 100% increase (Ibid, p.42-43). The size of the immigrant poor family population in the City of Toronto is increased by 125% between 1981 and 2001 Ibid, (p.46). Poverty is rising and deepening and the income disparity between rich and poor is widening. The increase of poverty makes children, single parents, newcomers and visible minorities vulnerable in Toronto (Poverty by Postal Code 2004). Poor neighborhoods cause increase in crime and abandonment by both residents and businesses (Poverty by Postal Code 2004). It is a challenge for human survival. However, Beck, Kunt and Levine (2005) argue that SME's expansion boosts employment more than large firm growth because SMEs are more labor intensive (p. 2000).

Between 1990 and 1999, self-employment increased dramatically by nearly 40% from 1.8 to 2.5 million Canadians. Approximately 15% of the Canadian labor forces are entrepreneurs. (Benjamin Tal, Self-employment in Canada-Trends and Prospects. CIBC, December, 2000). According to Statistics Canada, self-employed individuals for May 2007 increased by 5,600, while the number of employees in the private sector fell by 5,800. This is an example supporting the continuing trend of the rapid growth rate in self-employment (6.5%), compared to the sluggish employment growth in the public and private sectors (0.9%) and (0.4%) respectively) since October 2006 (Statistics Canada). Locally, there are about 147,000 Toronto residents that are self-employed, roughly 12% of the city's workforce in 2001 (City of Toronto). Looking at the numbers alone, self-employment plays a key role in providing job opportunities not only in Toronto but also across the country. Therefore, it is important to realize that as the manufacturing labor market decreases, self-employment serves as an important buffer for the economy (Destination Success, Ministry of Small Businesses and Entrepreneurship 2006).

There are more than 821,000 women entrepreneurs in Canada. Thirty-four percent (34%) of self-employed persons are women. They contribute in excess of Cdn$18.109 billion to the Canadian economy every year (Women Task Force Committee 2003). Since 1976, the average annual growth rate of self-employment for women has been 5.3%, compared with 2.2% for men. Half of self-employed women work at home (Statistics Canada 2003). Employment in small businesses has increased by more than 120,000 jobs in the fourth quarter of 2006 (Small Business Quarterly. Vol.9, No.1, May 2007, Industry Canada).

Many residents have suffered from the disappearance of well-paid manufacturing jobs, stagnating minimum wage rates, declining social assistance rates, limited access to employment insurance, and the extraordinary difficulty many recent immigrants are facing entering the labour market. Higher paying manufacturing jobs have disappeared. Manufacturing jobs in Toronto declined by 73,213- a loss of 30% Social Assistance benefits declined by 22% (Poverty by Postal Code 2004, p. 14). The wage rate for auto sector paid jobs is devastating. For example 157,400 auto jobs have been lost nationally and 141,000 jobs lost in Ontario. By 2014, the jobs that will be lost nationally are 269,000 in Ontario. These are red signals for the people of Ontario and the economy. If these three auto industries - General Motors, Ford and Chrysler production were to cease completely, 323,000 jobs would be lost immediately in Canada (Toronto Star, Dec. 16, 2008).

Of all the provinces, Ontario is the hardest hit from downsizing in auto industry jobs in 2008. Reshaped government policies, programs, and funding mechanisms are needed to better support all neighborhoods (Strong Neighborhoods). Currently the auto industry jobs situation is good in Canada; however, many people have no jobs that can cover their modest living cost.

In Canada, a few small, isolated microfinance organizations are providing microloans to micro entrepreneurs with tough terms, conditions, and high interest rates. They provide a maximum loan of $5,000 to first time borrowers, which is not enough for them to start their businesses. State agencies make policies, but are volatile in implementing self-employment policies. These agencies do not get involved in providing credit or urge banks and credit unions to provide small loans to micro entrepreneurs. In Canada, few small, isolated microfinance organizations are providing microloans to micro entrepreneurs but the terms and conditions are very tough and with high interest rates. Some community microloan funds exist; however, their functions are very limited. However, VanCity in Vancouver have been providing microloans to micro entrepreneurs since 1993 and have more than 5,000 clients who are self-employed, small business owners. However, the pay day loan industry is very large who is charging very high interest and is growing rapidly. According to the Canadian Payday Loan Association, more than 760 quick-cash operators' loan to about two million people each year (Lang, 2015). In the USA, the industry has a current annual loan volume of more than $28 billion. However, this is the injurious nature of payday lenders; 91% of their revenue comes from borrowers who cannot pay off their loans when they are due. The typical payday borrowers pay back $793 for a $325 loan and incur interest charges of 400%.

Not many community economic development thinkers advocate for community microloan funders and government at all levels must work together to promote self-employment in the neighborhoods to address the issue of unemployment and poverty. Neighborhood poverty has devastating human costs and damages the economic and social vitality of the neighborhoods and affects the quality of life for everyone in Toronto (Poverty by Postal Code 2004). However, microenterprise development has proven to have a significant impact on the larger Canadian economy and individual households. Microenterprise has played a key role in addressing unemployment, poverty and community economic development in Canada. Self-employment and small home-based businesses have been vital sources of community jobs and income, and self-reliance to them. Public funding safety net and social infrastructure development are decreasing day by day (Poverty by Postal Code 2004). Neighborhood poverty has devastating human costs and weakens the economic and social vitality of the neighborhoods and affects the quality of life for everyone (Poverty by Postal Code 2004). To face this severe poverty situation, it is clearly time for action to rebuild strong and healthy neighborhoods in Toronto. There is an urgent need to promote economic development strategies at the local and community levels. However, community microloan funders and government at all levels must work together to promote self-employment in the neighborhoods to address the issue of unemployment and poverty (Poverty by Postal Code 2004).

Furthermore, every year more than two hundred thousand immigrants are arriving in Canada and are looking for paid employment. The job market, however, is limited. The majority of these new immigrants accepts part-time and/or temporary jobs and receive minimum wage that is not enough to maintain a decent life. However, many of them, especially new immigrant women, are skilled in doing embroidery, sewing, wood craft, food preparation, nursing and childcare. These women are productive and can contribute to the local economy if they had the opportunity to become self-employed. If women had access to small amounts of business capital and small business management training, this would be possible. However, the growth of these small businesses is often stifled by a lack of easy access to capital as a result of a traditional banking sector, which ignores micro financing.

Varying literature indicates that microcredit and micro business development have been underserved in Canada, because public, private and other non-profit organizations are not serious about its development. Through my research I found that less attention has been given to microcredit by various public, private and NGO (financial and non-financial) agencies through policies, strategies, and programs in Canada. This is due to a lack of support from the state and various formal financial institutions. Moreover, there is not enough study/literature on microcredit to know a great deal about this industry. However, microenterprises are very important, because Lovins, A. and et al. (1999) warns us that the earth's sustainability is threatened by the corporate business world because they look only at exploitable resources of the ecosystem - its oceans, forests and plains. Therefore, environmentally friendly businesses are essential in the world.

Through microfinance, the Millennium Development Goals (MDGs) like eliminating hunger and poverty, promoting gender equality and women empowerment, and ensuring environmental sustainability can be achieved. In many countries, microfinance institutions that provide business capital, business management training, business mentoring services, marketing support, and networking, support microenterprises. According to Microcredit summit 2006, MFIs worldwide had reached 175 million clients. However, in Canada there are no consolidated MFIs statistics, even its MFIs do not publish the number of clients they serve. Many socially responsible funds and foundations like Calvert Foundation, CIDA, Ministry of Small Business and Entrepreneurship, eBay and other community micro investment agencies could implement 'soft' financing criteria for lending to MFIs.

2.0. Micro Financing and Community Economic Development

Before discussing the relationship between microfinance and community economic development (CED), it is important to define community and community economic development. A community is a group of people who know each other personally and who plan together towards a common goal, and work to overcome adversity (Shragge 1997). Shragge (1997) defines CED in the following way: "CED is a cooperative attempt by local people to take control of the socio-economic destiny of the community to respond to local needs" (p. 12). It is an attempt to democratize the economic lifestyle of the neighbouring communities (Ibid, p.103). Self-employment is a strategy for community economic development to promote local economic and social development in the high poverty neighbourhoods. It is a part of a solution to reduce unemployment and to address the issue of poverty in high poverty prone areas. In other words, CED is a socially directed approach in which individual groups devote their efforts towards meeting the basic needs of the others in the community. Here local communities work together at setting up businesses and promoting their own interests through economic expansion (Boothroyd & Davis, 1993, pp. 230). However, Chambers and Conway (1992) mentioned the integration of poverty-stricken people in the CED program are necessary elements of sustainable development that can contributes to the local economy, and provide sustainable livelihood at the local and national levels.

David Korten (1995) believes in 'people-centered development' that drives by CED. Amartya Sen (1999) emphasized *human-need centered development*. Escobar (1992) stresses positive social change in development. Rahnema 1997 sees development from humanitarian perspectives. MFIs have all of these features that generate CED. Micro financing is working with local currency to provide for the poor by creating self-employment through income generating schemes. This helps meet people's basic needs and build the local economy. It also accelerates small deposits and community savings, which will then be used to invest in community planning.

As I mentioned earlier, micro businesses, through micro financing, have several benefits like poverty eradication, environmental sustainability, community economic development; promotion of local living economics and job creation. Muhammad Yunus (2005), founder of Grameen Bank Bangladesh said that the local economy becomes rejuvenated through microcredit programs. Micro financing is very important for preserving the local businesses and sustaining business development, because green micro financing and micro business promote the notion of sustainable business development. In Canada, millions of low-income people will benefit if micro businesses break into the mainstream policy formulation. Therefore, I want to do research in people-centered, micro business development through microcredit institutions (MFIs) to peruse marginalized micro entrepreneurs empowerment.

Microenterprise development is important in Bangladesh, Canada, and many other countries in the world because it builds assets, increases income-earning capacity, reduces the severity of poverty, improves quality of life, improves household nutrition, promotes gender equality and empowers women. Microcredit service can reduce the spread of social exclusion for the disadvantaged. For example, in Canada many socially responsible funds and foundations such as Calvert Foundation, Trillium Foundation, Maytree Foundation, Ministry of Small Business and Entrepreneurship, eBay and other community micro investment agencies exist in Canada and they could include micro financing criteria for massive lending to MFIs for promoting community economic development in Toronto.

3.0. Definition of Key Terms

Microcredit is the provision of small loans to poor people with the goal of helping them engage in economic activities. In Canada, microenterprise is classified as a business with five or fewer employees that have business capital totalling $35,000 (Belcourt et.al. 1991). Micro financing is a small financing system, whereby; interested private entrepreneurs borrow money for running and maintaining small business ventures.

Microfinance sustainability is used interchangeably with financial sustainability of MFIs. According to Zeller and Meyer (2002), it is the ability of MFI to meet operating and financial costs over the long term. This means that the MFI collects its loans and cover all its costs well enough so that it can continue serving its poor clients, and be in a position to reach out to an increasing number of clients, even after it is no longer getting grants or soft loans from donors or the government (Gonzalez, 2005). In addition, if the microfinance institutions can attract sufficient capital and operate in a financially sound manner, they have the potential to become significant players in providing financial services and credit that can help foster demand for market innovations (Barr, 2004: p. 290).

Sustainable Development: According to Amarty Sen (1999), Jack Quarter (2007), Robert Schuman (2003) sustainable development should lead to poverty reduction, well-being and capability enhancements. Sustainable development promotes people-centered alternative development for social justice, and is inclusive of everyone (WCED (1987); Hopwood and et al. (2005); Korten (2006); Sen (1999); Rahmena (1997); Esbcobar (1992); and Dale (2003). Microcredit improves and uplifts lower-classed people from poverty and enhances sustainable development.

According to Brundtland's Report, 1987 sustainable development meets the needs of future generations. Sustainable development approach not only encompasses income generation but is also processes that are people centered (Korten (2003); Habermass (1999); and Cotla (2002). Cotla mentions that sustainable development approach rests on core principles that are "people-centered". According to Jeffry Scahs (1999), Haan & Zommers (2005, and Helmore and Singh (2001), it is the process building on the wealth of the poor. It is the fundamental building blocks of any development initiative and is the actual livelihood systems of the poor. Michele Schuman (2003) calls it natural capital development that constitutes both financial and non-financial assets.

The World Business Council for Sustainable Development (WBCSD) said business should be done with the poor in ways that simultaneously benefits the poor and benefits the company. UNCDF in its Voices of Microfinance (2004) affirms that microfinance aims at promoting sustainable livelihood options to ensure reduction in the vulnerability of poor households through asset creation and social security. Srivastava (206) challenged that the dominance of business perspective in microfinance sectors is not the only factor that limits its contribution to sustainable development.

4.0. Research methodology

The study used mixed methods (quantitative, qualitative, participant observation, literature review, secondary data, documents analysis, live experience and case study) approach to address the three research questions. There were two groups of participants: 61 GB women borrowers, 10 GB field employees. The GB borrowers were all active GB female clients for at least 10 years. The researcher developed a survey with both open-ended and close-ended questions and went to Bangladesh to collect the primary data. For the GB employees, semi-structured interviews were undertaken. The data collection period was from April to June 2010. Women borrowers were interviewed from three GB branches: Bashan Gazipur, Sadipur Munshigong, and Barera Chandina Comilla. The objective of the research was to measure GB women borrowers' empowerment in their family and community space.

5.0. Comparison of Microfinance and Microenterprise in the Developed and Developing Countries

Different studies indicate that microcredit and microenterprise development seem to be a phenomenon in developed countries, having been popularized by Muhammad Yunus by his Grameen Bank in Bangladesh. This concept is now replicated in developed countries and is used to address the issue of poverty, unemployment and the promotion of small businesses, especially for people on welfare that allows them to break their dependence on welfare and have independent lives.

Microcredit in Canada can be seen by the creation of *caisse populaire* in Canada in 1901, followed by the *Antigoinsh Movement* in Nova Scotia. This movement matured into microfinance services in the 1980's with the establishment of Calmeadow Metro Fund (Cheryl Frankiewicz 2001). According to Cheryl Frankiewicz, Calmeadow started its microcredit operation, *Native Self-employment Loan Program* in Wikwemiknog, Kettle and Schigo Lake in 1986. Although this program is now closed because of a realization that current microloan fund models are currently not viable in the Canadian context. However, the Jubilee Fund in Winnipeg provides loans or equity support for building community facilities such as day care centers, homes for seniors, special needs groups, employment training centers and recreation centers. *Peer Assisted Lending* pilot initiative (PAL) in Vancouver partnered with Royal Bank and transferred to VanCity Community Foundation and it is still working with microenterprise development in Canada.

Mary Coyle (1989) in The Atlantic Canada Opportunities Agency (2002) mentioned that one out of every three households in native communities received a portion of its income from a microenterprise. Calmeadow created Canada's first microloan fund, the First People's Fund but there was a problem of not getting enough clients among the First Nations people. By 1994 however, Calmeadow had served more than 300 clients in 20 Canadian Aboriginal communities in 5 provinces (Calmeadow, 2001). Calmeadow launched the Peer Assisted Lending pilot project initiative in Vancouver focused in an urban area. In 1994 Calmeadow opened offices in Toronto, offering both individual and peer loans. Peer lending proved difficult because of people's individualistic attitude. Therefore group commitments failed in this program. Cheryl Frankiewicz mentioned that the operating costs for MFIs were expensive as clients were not concentrated in one area of the city. The entrepreneurs faced complicated regulatory barriers and highly developed corporate markets where they had to compete with major big corporate suppliers of goods and services. Although Calmeadow failed, microenterprise development has been important in creating jobs in Canada (Canada Advisory Council on the Status of Women 1998). For example in 1988, small firms created three times the number of new jobs than that of large firms. In Canada, 150,000 new small businesses are launched annually, most of which are started by women. Although some organizations like *Alterna Savings, Vancity,* and *COADY* started micro financing for micro business funding, they do not expand massively on business financing for micro business promotion. In America, leading micro finance institution is Grameen America is following group-based micro financing models in USA. Detail information discuss later.

Community loan fund investing is a strategy for addressing unemployment, environmental degradation, economic restructuring, poverty, and social exclusion. It is a way of generating resources and opportunities for people and communities who are underserved by mainstream financial institutions.

6.0. Similarities and differences of micro-credit programs and other micro enterprise services to poor in Bangladesh and in Canada

There are ideological and traditional differences between the models applied in both Bangladesh and Canada contexts, although their mode of operation is not very different. In Bangladesh, GB mainly deals with poor, landless women, but Alterna Savings' main clients are welfare recipients, single mothers, Aboriginal people, and immigrants. Although microcredit is popular in developing countries; however, many the north countries also use Rotating Savings and Credit Associations (ROSCA). ROSCA is tailored to fit each community's needs, they all involve group or club formation - the fund is rotated among group members until all the members have a chance to receive loans and savings.

A significant similarity is that they are all aimed at the reduction of poverty for excluded, disadvantaged groups, especially women. Low-income people are willing to start small businesses, but they need credit. The microcredit system originated as a result of the failure of the mainstream formal banking sector to serve the needs of low-income people (Yunus 2005, Gibbon, 1995, Johnson 1997, Holis, A. & Sweetman, A. (1996), Rhyen 1994). Another similarity is that these programs provide social capital to microcredit borrowers. Johnson (1997) says this created social capital among micro entrepreneurs through the networks, norms, and trust that facilitated co-ordination and co-operation for mutual benefits among borrowers. This has not only ensured local economic wealth, but also local social health.

Metro Credit Unions, Maytree Foundation, and Alterna Savings Community Loan Funds program are aimed at developing financial capital for micro entrepreneurs. However, they do not streamline enough funds for micro lending to micro businesses. Although Canada is said to have one of the best self- employment development programs in the industrialized world, the country's enterprise development is not as developed as it is in US. However, Canada continues to play a significant role in the Canadian economy as well as in the lives of unemployed Canadians (SEDI, 2007).

Microenterprise in the developed countries is harder to start as compared to the developing countries because the informal sector is less appreciated in the developed countries than the developing opportunities. Marium, a client of Alterna Savings thinks that Canada gets more GDP from its mines and corporate worlds. There are other alternatives such as welfare and unemployment insurance that offer a safety net for the poor therefore micro business is not a priority in Canada. Moreover, there are lots of bureaucracies such as licensing and taxes; therefore a viable business plan is needed to satisfy the loan officers. These are some of the barriers micro entrepreneurs have to overcome to get optimum loans for their businesses. In developed countries, microcredit is mostly used by immigrant groups who face some prejudices (Ivan & Pham, 1997). In Canada, the costs of supporting clients are higher and clients are harder to reach as compared to Bangladesh where density of population is high. I myself work and visited many MFIs in Canada. The above facts indicate that Canadian MFIs are also contributing to address the issue social development in Canada although Canadian MFIs are not in front line in Canada. Similarly American MFIs are contributing to American society and MFIs like Grameen America is functioning well there.

In Bangladesh, GB is dominated by credit, savings and insurance products. However, in Canada, there is a debate Canadian MFIs are suffering from on capital accumulation or capital sources for microfinance programs (Johnson, 1997). Many microcredit programs in developing countries are mainly funded by international donors and supported by national programs. In Canada however, non-governmental agencies such as credit unions, women development agencies, churches and other local programs support MFIs. However, countries such as Bangladesh, Pakistan, Indonesia BRI, Bolivia BKK, BancoSol, *SEWA* India, *PRODEM* in Bolivia, *ADEMI* in the Dominican Republic, Mexico, French, Switzerland, and the USA support MFIs without government interference. Instead they help by supporting social sensitivity and cohesion (Lessons Learned and Learning Lessons p, 101). The Ontario government can also follow MFIs' supportive approach to address its unemployment and poverty issues.

7.0. Essentials Pre-and Post-Self-employment Counselling Services and Microcredit Services

Pre-counseling services to micro entrepreneurs: Micro entrepreneurs need referral services and to be linked with different business training agencies. Participants also need information on sources of obtaining small loans, eligibility and links with loan providing agencies.

Post-loan services to micro entrepreneurs: Post-loan services assist mentoring small businesses. Post-loan services are monitoring business progress, providing business mentoring services and networking services; organizing trade fairs, business products exhibitions, organizing microenterprise workshops and seminars.

8.0. Essential Viability Factors for Micro Enterprise Development:

Lack of capital funding is the primary barrier to micro business start-up and growth. Banks demand high ratios of collateral and personal guarantees for smaller loans, especially for working capital. Debt financing decisions place emphasis on credit score rating, business experience and track record. Banks need to review owners' equity and that they have sufficient cash flow in their businesses before approving a loan. Bank officers put more emphasis on the personal characteristics of the business owners and loan seekers.

Microenterprise strategy is the creation/expansion of businesses that help the clients become economically self-sufficient. Different agencies are seen as important strategies to help the poor get out of poverty and reduce levels of dependency. Access to credit and savings facilities has provided the poor with opportunities for self-reliance through starting and operating micro businesses. According to Hulme & Mosely (1996) and Johnson & Rogaly (1997), the success of microenterprise development depends on the provision of both financial and non-financial services such as training, savings services against risks and uncertainties, and insurance to manage specific risks. This helps the poor and marginalized groups make use of economic opportunities through business management training, group capacity building, and entrepreneurs' skills development. A combination of integrated financial and non-financial services can help entrepreneurs succeed by: building their self-confidence; increasing their income, productivity, and employment; and ultimately facilitating the personal growth of the entrepreneur.

9.0. Literature review

9.1. Grameen Bank philosophy and its operation strategies

Grameen Bank Bangladesh aims to improve the well-being of the poor and to empower them in society, both economically and socially. GB has encouraged women's inclusion and participation in income generation, their regular attendance at weekly meetings, their leadership of borrowers' groups and centers, their ability to understand the Sixteen Decisions and to follow them, and even their visits to the GB office, health clinics, livestock offices, school committees and other community activities. GB has designed some of its services exclusively for women so that they would be included in institutional policy and budgeting (Moser, 1993; Rathgeber, 1990; Todd, 1996). However, it has no mission to address the issue of women's equality in Bangladesh, which is urgent for women's empowerment in that country.

The Grameen center meeting is a place where 30-40 women clients gather and repay their loans, discuss their family problems, and exchange their business information and other concerns. Centre meetings are a catalyst for networking among clients. This group system helps clients interact freely among each other, receive and repay loans, and to address broader social concerns. To maintain equal opportunity and to address issues of participatory management, democracy and empowerment, the positions of Centre Chief, Group Chairperson, and Group Secretary rotate every year. By this process all members of the center have an opportunity to take leadership roles. This practice helps to enhance leadership qualities and decision-making skills among borrowers; it also develops their ability to exercise decision-making power within and external to the family. Borrowers are able to continue their interactions with each other beyond their groups and participate in center meetings, visit the GB office, and contribute to their community. However, it is not clear that the women's center leadership development is transferred to community activities.

9.2. Grameen Bank Sixteen Decisions

In the mid-1980s and 1990s, there were massive campaigns promoting the Sixteen Decisions cross Bangladesh, impacting non-GB neighbors. These individuals saw that GB borrowers were using sanitary latrines (9th Decision), using tube wells for clean water (10th Decision), growing vegetables (4th Decision), participating in sapling distribution (5th Decision), educating their children (7th Decision), keeping their families small (6th Decision), solving borrowers conflicts collectively (14th Decision), having dowry-less marriages (11th Decision), resisting injustices such as violence against women (12th Decision) and reinstituting centre discipline if a breach of discipline occurs (15th Decision). They saw that if anyone's home is damaged by a flood, cyclone or other natural disasters, centre borrowers would collectively assist them to rebuild their home (16th decision). However, there is a still a need to raise awareness about the necessity to combat such social ills as dowry, teenage marriage and violence against women, which are deeply rooted in patriarchal values. Women's human rights are often violated in the village and there is a need for women to collectively organize against these ills. There is also a necessity for other family members to be educated so that the men of the family support them more.

The female borrowers are able to benefit from the tangible aspects of the Sixteen Decisions like, building new houses, using sanitary latrines and growing vegetables. However, it has proven more difficult for them to implement dowry-less marriage and to ban teenage marriage as these are deeply rooted societal problems closely tied to patriarchy, an ancient system in Bangladesh.

The GB Sixteen Decisions are a combination of various socio-civic, economic, and environmental messages that mentioned earlier in the book. Central to the GB approach has been women's civic consciousness-raising through some of the Sixteen Decisions. These decisions are the focal point of GB's efforts to improve the economic plight of women and their families and community space development. These decisions promote *anti-dowry, anti-teenage marriages, environmentalism,* and *women's collective space development in their community.* Although the GB's main function is to provide microcredit to poor women in Bangladesh, the intensive social interactions that develop between GB employees and clients through loan transactions also have the potential to transform the lives of this group of women and their families. However, recently the Grameen Bank Sixteen Decisions Campaign strategies have shrunk because of the Bank's efforts to promote profit generation. This has hampered these micro-borrowers social development.

SMDGs developed by UN in 2015. These SMDGs goals are more narrowed and focused. Many SMDGs points are similar to GB Sixteen Decisions ideas. Grameen Bank and many other MFIs are contributing to SMDGs goals. SMDGs points are stating below:

SDG 1: End poverty in all its forms everywhere
SDG 2: End hunger, achieve food security and improved nutrition and promote sustainable agriculture
SDG 3: Ensure healthy lives and promote wellbeing for all at all ages
SDG 4: Ensure inclusive and quality education for all and promote lifelong learning
SDG 5: Achieve gender equality and empower all women and girls
SDG 6: Ensure access to water and sanitation for all
SDG 7: Ensure access to affordable, reliable, sustainable and modern energy for all
SDG 8: Promote inclusive and sustainable economic growth, employment and decent work for all
SDG 9: Build resilient infrastructure, promote sustainable industrialisation and foster innovation
SDG 10: Reduce inequality within and among countries
SDG 11: Make cities inclusive, safe, resilient and sustainable
SDG 12: Ensure sustainable consumption and production patterns
SDG 13: Take urgent action to combat climate change and its impacts

SDG 14: Conserve and sustainably use the oceans, seas and marine resources

SDG 15: Sustainably manage forests, combat desertification, halt and reverse land degradation, halt biodiversity loss

SDG 16: Promote just, peaceful and inclusive societies

SDG 17: Revitalise the global partnership for sustainable development

9.3. Gender Equality Issues in the Sixteen Decisions and in SMDGs

The SMDG 5th goal is to achieve gender equality and empower all women and girls in society. Although GB is working for its borrowers economic capital development and social capital development; however, Grameen Sixteen Decisions has no points on gender equality issues. However, GB women borrowers' understanding of the GB's by-laws and Sixteen Decisions can help to remove barriers in empowering women against male domination in family and community spaces in the villages. When these barriers are understood by women, it will be easier for them to address the issues of women's empowerment and leadership development in family and community spaces. However, the Sixteen Decisions are silent on gender discrimination and male aggression towards women. This silence limits the effectiveness of the Sixteen Decisions ability to empower women gender development. Therefore, the Sixteen Decisions are empowering women through awareness of male chauvinism, and of women's inegalitarian status within the family and the community. Hence many researchers (Amin, Becker, & Bayes, 1998; Goetz, 2001; Mahmud, 2004; and Mayoux, 2002) have argued that the GB must develop additional strategies to raising awareness of gender inequality and the injustice of male domestic violence, and also mobilize women to protest various social ills that afflict women. Actually GB has not been completely silent on these issues rather it has encouraged its members to work in their communities and to be involved in committees for schools and pavement, and to participate in local councils etc. However, Goetz (2001) asserts that the GB's approach is insufficient and it must specifically recognize how the constraints of religious customs like *purdah* (veiling) restrict women to the family realm.

10. Survey findings

Table 1 shows the study participants' of GB borrowers' demographic, socio-economic background information.

Table 1

Distribution of the borrowers' sample by age, marital status, family type, education, housing type, and number of children

Question	*N*	%
Age		
21-30	7	11.5
31-40	19	31.1
41-50	26	42.6
50+	9	14.8
Marital Status		
Married	55	90.2
Unmarried	0	0.0
Divorced	1	1.6
Widowed	5	8.2
Family Type		
Single	29	47.5
Extended/Joint	32	52.5
Borrower's Education		
No schooling	0	0.0
Centre schooling	20	32.8
Primary school	21	34.4
High school	20	32.8
College/university	0	0.0

Question	N	%
Housing Type		
Pacca	15	24.6
Semi-p	46	75.4
Acca		
Thatch house	0	0.0
Number of children		
No children	1	1.6
1-2	24	39.3
3-4	26	42.6
5+	10	16.4

Note: Dash indicates no response to category

10.1. Grameen Bank Housing Loan and Higher Educational Loan for its borrowers

GB's 3rd Decision is GB borrowers shall not live in dilapidated houses. The study indicates that 25% of the study's participants (GB borrowers) are living in their own concrete building houses and 75% have semi-pacca houses (floor and walls are concrete, but roofs are made of coagulated iron sheets). This is a tremendous change in borrowers housing type. Before the 1980s, the researcher observed that the majority of the housing of GB borrowers was classified as thatch, mud or tin-sheet roof; today few thatch houses or mud houses could be seen in rural areas. This is the result of the GB housing program as well as borrowers' economic improvement.

GB's 7th Decision is to encourage higher education for borrowers' children. To increase the likelihood of achieving this goal, the GB introduced educational loans for borrowers' children in 1998 and scholarships for GB borrowers' children in 2002. These two programs have encouraged borrowers and their children to pursue higher education. Remarkably, GB has provided $26.41 million in loans to 44,988 borrowers' children and $2.28 million of scholarships to 114,250 borrowers' children (GB Monthly Statement, June 2010). The GB student loans and scholarships program are meant to assist GB borrowers' second generation to pursue higher education. The survey data shows that all the children of the borrowers participating in this study are going to school. In addition, there is evidence suggesting that GB center schools help to develop borrowers' children's interest in schooling (Grameen Shikka, 2005). GB believes that education empowers women in their families and in their communities because it allows them to develop skills and knowledge; women with less education compared to male family members may participate minimally in familial decisions (Mizan, 1994). Although many GB women borrowers have not pursued higher education themselves, the GB 7th Decision on child education and the education loans and scholarships programs has created awareness about the importance of this objective. As a result, there is evidence that women borrowers are emphasizing their children's education, with many of them choosing to pursue higher education (Grameen Bank Annual Report, 2009).

10.2. Development barriers that GB women borrowers experience in the family and in the community

What are the barriers that GB women borrowers face in developing their spaces in their family and community? This question is very important for women liberation in Bangladesh.

10.2.1. Women borrowers facing barriers in their families

In spite of promising improvements, the response to some items in the survey suggests that GB borrowers still face substantial barriers, as shown in Table 2. With respect to decision-making, 41% indicated that male dominance is a barrier. In the 'Other' category, the barriers include: women having less practical experience to make decisions in the family, women being immature in decision-making, women lacking intelligence, women's lack of education. Domestic chores were also cited as another barrier as women had less time to think about making proper decisions for the family. Fifteen percent of women also identified 'ethnic family values' as barriers that they face. A large body of literature in Bangladesh shows that cultural religious practices are barriers for empowering women to participate in familial decisions (Ain-O-Shalishi Kendra, 2004). For example, it is difficult for a woman to go against the decision of dowry payment made by her male partner as it is a common practice in Bangladesh. However, rouf's survey finds only 5% of GB survey participants agreed with this concern, suggesting that women borrowers do not see religion as a barrier for empowerment in the family.

Table 2: *Percentage of Women Facing Barriers in Decision-making Process*

Barriers Women Face	N	%
Male dominance	25	41.0
Religious rituals	3	4.9
Ethnic family values	9	14.8
I avoid making decisions	-	-
Others	24	39.3

*Note a dash indicates that this response option was not chosen.

10.3. GB women borrowers' leadership skills to public spaces

As mentioned earlier, the study also looks at GB borrowers' community space development. Here findings specifically address the second research objective: Are GB women borrowers able to transfer their center leadership skills to other public spaces? A number of items in the survey relate to this research question. Table 3 indicates that only one third of the borrowers agreed with the question: Do you think male-dominated values, norms, practices and rituals are a hindrance to women's private and public space development?

Sajeda, one of the borrowers, stated:

> Before the 1980s, the rural religious leaders and rural elites were skeptical about women working outside the home, but now many young girls are studying in school and working in the garment factories. Religious customs are now changing. Males are not as rigid as they were previously.

This finding differs from what was expected and suggests that GB borrowers may have family arrangements that differ from the Bangladeshi norms. This change may be because of the GB program or it may indicate that women who borrow from the GB are from a less patriarchal environment. Also, in the last ten years, there has been a change in the culture due to the number of NGOs, media and women's awareness campaigns.

Table 3: *Percentage of Women Borrowers who View Male-Dominated Values as a Hindrance*

Question	N	Yes	No
Do you think male-dominated values, norms, practices and rituals are a hindrance to women's private space and public space development?	61	32.8	67.2

However, dowry is a cultural practice that violates women's human rights and many GB women borrowers realize this. For example, Safia says:

> Higher class people spend a lot of money on their daughters' weddings, giving gifts. This practice has spread to the masses of the society and this affects the poor. To pay dowry, poor people have to sell their property as a last resort, further impoverishing us.

Therefore, a social problem like dowry is one of the barriers that GB women borrowers are facing in their familial and community life.

10.3.1. GB women borrowers free movement in the community

Table 4. *Women Borrowers' Movement outside the Home*

Question	N	Yes	No	N/A
Does your family prevent you from going out?	61	8.2	91.8	-
Do you need consent to visit your parents' houses?	61	54.1	42.6	3.3

Table 4 shows that ninety-two percent of the GB women borrowers declared that their family members don't prevent them from going out, suggesting that they have the autonomy to visit their neighbors and participate in different community events. However, 54% of GB women borrowers still need consent from their male partners to visit their parents' house. This is because attending community events or visiting their neighbors is usually close by and takes place for a short period of time, whereas parents can live in far away villages and they would often need to stay there for more than one day. This finding reflects the strength of patriarchal norms in Bangladesh.

10.3.3. Are GB women borrowers able to transfer their center leadership skills to other public spaces?

The purpose of this question is to know the status of GB borrowers' leadership experience and to know whether borrowers are able to transfer their leadership skills outside of the GB. The GB centers follow GB by-laws to select group chairs and center chiefs every year.

10.4. Women's public space development through political engagement:

Table 6 shows that 44.3% percent of participants reported that their center leadership skills have enhanced their ability to contribute to their local community. Interestingly, 80.3% felt that they gained from being involved in civic activities.

Table 6: *Percentage of GB Women Borrowers' Public Space Development*

Questions	N	Yes	No
Are GB women borrowers able to transfer leadership skills to community activities?	61	44.3	55.7
Do you get together to solve neighbors' problems collectively?	61	91.8	8.1

Do women's interactions at regular center meetings facilitate group identity; promote cohesion and women's awareness among center borrowers?	61	100	-
Did you vote in the last union council election – the one that took place in 2009?	61	98.4	1.6
Do you gain from being involved in civic activities?	61	80.3	19.7

Some themes that emerge from the qualitative data regarding the transfer of leadership skills to community activities are:

- GB borrowers are participating in a variety of public space activities where they are transferring skills gained in the GB;
- Borrowers' leadership skills have prepared them to take a leadership role in community activities;
- Borrowers are able to speak in public, raising awareness of the needs of the community;
- As women gain confidence in centre activities, they become more active in familial and social activities.

Some excerpts from participants that support these points are:

> My courage has developed by joining GB. I am a group chairperson. I mix with my neighbors, chat with them, unite with tyhem and bring my grandchildren to school. My son is a musician and I attend his many concerts. My name is on different schools' committees, the immunization committee, and in the community forestry committee. I am a member of the Bastee Shikha. My speaking power has increased, which was absent before joining GB because I was only a housewife and had been doing domestic jobs only. (Nurjahan).

Few GB women borrowers become formal leaders in the local councils; however, many borrowers are informal leaders in the community. They resolve conflicts in the village and organize many social events in their neighborhood. One of the participants of the study says, "Many NGOs call me to talk in their public meetings" (Nasima).

> I am a member of Baste Sheka. I have 15 tenants. I manage to renovate my rented houses. I manage my tenants and I collect rent from them. Neighbors come to me for familial conflict resolutions, I completed grade 10 so I can read books, different magazines, and newspapers; moreover, I discuss reading materials with women's rights themes with my neighbors. I attend different NGOs and UP meetings and workshops and speak there. (Asma).

Table 6 also shows that 91.8% of women borrower respondents reported that they solve neighbors' problems collectively. This usually takes place through *Sallish, Bichar;* it is the informal community hearing meetings. These informal community hearing meetings are common in rural Bangladesh where inter-family conflict, conflict with neighbors, crimes like stealing, burglary, rape, and violence against women are usually resolved informally. Generally the *Morol* (community head), plays a major role in resolving the village disputes; sometimes Upzilla councilors become involved as well. If the village community hearing meetings (*Salish, Bichar*) fail to resolve problems, people then go to the local legal courts. Poor people, especially poor women, never get a chance to be informal arbitrators in the community. However, GB women borrowers have broken this tradition and have started to solve their neighbors' problems, as reported by one GB women borrower who is also a councilor of a Local Union Council:

> If some people cut down trees illegally or their cattle damage the crops of the neighbors, the victims come to me. As an elected member of the union council,

> I have some power to resolve these disputes. First, I myself try to resolve the problems, but if I fail to resolve problems, I call for a Gramm Salist (village hearing meeting). I announce this in the village. Other elite people join in the *Sallish*. The *Salish* elite's verdict is based on the hearing. We try to create a compromise between the two parties, but if they are unwilling to compromise, then we village hearing leaders impose certain sanctions such as a social boycott if money is not paid on time. Sometimes family members or his/her relatives take the responsibility to rectify the situation or pay fines. If we village elites fail to resolve issues of concern or complaints through the village hearing, we then refer the issue to the court. So far we have now resolved our community problems by our community elites and we do not need to refer cases to the formal courts. (Halima).

In addition to solving problems collectively, which creates solidarity among borrowers, the centre meetings are also a space where borrowers become informed about information pertaining to their development and human rights and interact with centre members, resulting in social solidarity and social cohesion. Table 6 indicates that all agree that borrowers' regular attendance at the centre meetings and interactions among them facilitate this collectivity. The following interview excerpts reinforce the benefits of the leadership roles in the GB:

> Feroza Begum says, "My children have grown up. I have received loan TK 200,000 [CDN$2832] and began a poultry farm and dairy firm with this loan in my home. My daughter-in-law and I both manage my poultry firm. I vaccinate chickens and look after my cattle. I live in my parent's village. I bought land and cultivate it. My intelligence and life skills

have increased because I deal with many business people, and attend different arbitration events and social events. Many neighbors come to me to receive ideas for their economic and social development. I tell them my life story and give them advice to assist them with their own economic and social empowerment. I bring people to the immunization center, veterinary clinic, health clinics, and the GB office. I discuss problems and solve problems collectively in the center meetings. I advise people and tell them 'times have changed, so you people also need to change.' I advise my female neighbors to not depend on males; rather they should earn money and fulfill their children's needs".

Another participant if the study says, "Our village roads are not good. I lobby the UP office for pavement improvement and sewer upgrading in our village. I also campaign against dowry and teenage marriages in our community. I give advice to neighbors about the negative consequences of violence against women, slapping children, teenage marriage, dowry marriages, and conflicts among kin, etc. I inform the police if anyone eve teases the girls, threatens girls and/or rapes girls." (Monowara).

Rawshanara, one of the respondents of the study says," I am against child marriage and dowry marriages. I am against robbery and corruption. I promote women's equal rights in different forums in our UPzilla. (Rawshanara is newly elected UPzilla Vice-Chair).

The presence of women in male space is generally considered to be both provocative and offensive (Abdullah & Zeidenstein, 1982). For example, Momela, one of the participants, reports: "My presence (as well as other women) with the majority male elites in community informal community tribunals, which were monopoly male space before, is challenging and persuasive." Halima, another participant, also comments that male elites don't like women's participation in council meetings or village hearing meetings. This study's participants mention these issues for various reasons, which are categorized under the following themes:

- Patriarchy and classism hinder women's public space development
- Patriarchy and ageism hinder women's empowerment
- Civic activities become a double burden to the women
- The competitive and complex social environment is a barrier for women borrowers' involvement in community leadership
- Women do not see a need to participate in other community activities aside from GB.

Some excerpts illustrate these themes:

> People do not value women; rather rich people criticize and feel jealous of us. Even my husband does not like me to go to public meetings or political party meetings; however, he accepts my attendance in GB meetings/workshops. (Safur).

> My husband dislikes my attendance in the community meetings and involvement in community activities. To run in a UP councilor election, there needs to be a huge campaign and money. I don't want to waste my money for an election campaign. I have no education, hence cannot read, which is essential to be a formal leader. (Hanufa).

> My male neighbors do not value women's public work and they do not count women's community activities. (Delawara).

Males do not give opportunities for women to be involved in social work. They criticize women's work and infer women are breaking purdah in the community. (Peara).

Table 6 indicates that 80.3% of GB women borrowers feel that they benefited from being involved in civic activities or as Halima says:

> My mind has opened, my intelligence, experience and ability to speak to different people has also increased through engaging in civic activities. I am satisfied with my public work that serves people. I distribute relief and senior's allowances to my neighbors. Moreover, I have developed my family decision-making skills. However, only a few women like me in my community have developed such skills.

As shown in Table 6, 19.7% of participants reported that they don't gain anything from their involvement in civic activities. The qualitative data indicates that this is because they have experienced eve teasing and criticism from males who call them names such as 'unreligious', 'women who break *purdah*', 'outgoing women', and 'outspoken women'. They also say that the men undermine them, do not respect them, and even do not listen to them when they want to speak in the community meetings. They are harassed by many people for participating in these activities, even by their own families.

Shilppi, a participant of GB women borrower, says, "The Matabbor [rural elites] do not like to sit down in the Council meetings with women and some Mullahs [religious leaders] criticize women if they are walking around the neighborhoods because I am a young women, the young boys on the street eve-tease me."

Nevertheless, this is the experience of a minority of the borrowers who participated; most participants reported positive experiences from community participation, as reflected in Saleha's comments:

> If I am not present in my community hearing committee, the union parishad member (Councilor) will wait until I arrive before making the decision. My community people have encouraged me several times to run in the union parishad elections, but I am not running because I get more honour without being a formal councilor in my community. I would personally dislike serving as a councilor because the male councilors are corrupt when it comes to the public budget and allocation of resources.

The study findings show that GB women borrowers' rate of participation in local elections and parliamentary elections is outstanding. Moreover, women borrowers' participation in informal community hearing meetings is satisfactory.

10.4.2. Borrowers' communication with their neighbors

Table 7 indicates the frequency of interaction between GB women borrowers and their neighbors, and the GB's role in encouraging these relationships. All of the respondents of the study communicated with their neighbors, but prior to joining GB, only 55.7% stated that they knew their neighbors. This striking change probably has come about through forming a group with other neighboring women and attending weekly center meetings, as this has allowed for frequent interactions and the development of friendships with the neighborhood women.

Table 7: *Communication with Neighbors*

Question	N	Yes	No
Do you communicate with your neighbors?	61	100	-
Did you know GB members before joining?	61	44.3	55.7

*Note a dash indicates that this response option was not chosen.

Communication with neighbors was explored further in Table 8 and in Table 9.

Table 8: *GB Women Borrowers' Frequency of Communication with their Neighbors*

Question	N	Rarely (once a year or less)	Occasionally (more than once a year, but less than once a month)	Leisure time (if possible)	Regularly (once a month)	Regularly (more than once a month)
How frequently do you communicate with your neighbors?	61	-	3.3	9.8	9.8	77.0

*Note a dash indicates that this response option was not chosen.

Table 8 indicates that 77.0% of the respondents communicate with their neighbors more than once a month. Women's interactions and movement in their neighborhoods makes it possible for them to discuss and share information and concerns. Moreover, I observed in the data collection process and in attending centre meetings that the borrowers' frequent communications with their neighbors increased their mental courage and reduced their shyness. Ultimately, this empowered them to make decisions in the family and in the community. The reasons for communicating with their neighbors are presented in Table 9 and Table 10.

Table 9: *Reasons for Communication with Neighbors (Multiple answers)*

Item	N	%
Chat	61	100
Share Business Information	58	95.1
Discuss Group Centre Discipline	52	85.2

Resolve Neighbors Conflict	48	78.7
Develop Community School	32	52.5
Discuss Children Education	53	86.9
Environmental Maintenance	44	72.1
Other Community Affairs	45	73.8

Table 10 indicates that all women chat with their neighbors and share business information, their personal life, family issues and different community issues. This communication with neighbors helps GB borrowers to broaden their perspective and participate more effectively in their community. Table 10 presents the 'other' reasons for communicating with neighbors. The range of issues in Table 10 is broad, and includes advising neighbors about how to improve the family, health issues, education and unemployment.

Table 10: Other Reasons for Communication with Neighbors

Reasons for Communication	N	%
Give advice, family advice, family planning, keep family small, improve family, community affairs, public events, live in harmony	12	19.7
Health discussion & health committee, Maternal health, immunization, children's health, hygiene	8	13.1
Unemployment, economic improvement, microenterprise, family prosperity, life insurance, earn money	8	13.1
Others (education loan, security, relief committee, puja committee, moral education)	8	13.1
Dowry-less marriage	4	6.6
Assist borrower installments, help each other	3	4.9
Fish culture, plantation	2	3.3

In GB group-based microcredit and other community development activities, Grameen Bank borrowers are encouraged to participate in the local governance system. The Bangladesh Union Counsel is a form of local governance. The study finds that many GB women borrowers participated in the Union Parishad (UP) Elections in 1997 and 2003. GB women borrowers' local council election participation shows that their election wins have increased from the 1997 election to 2009. Among GB members, there were 57 UP Chairpersons elected in 1997, and this figure increased to 81 in the 2003 UP election. For UP councilor's positions, 3,325 GB women members were elected in 1997 and 4,116 in 2003.

Moreover, by 2009, a strong presence of GB members and family members in the UP elections for chairperson and vice chairperson (female) could be seen. For the latter, in particular, 23.7%, nearly one quarter, were associated with the GB (Grameen Bank, 2009). The data indicates that GB women borrowers and their family members' are engaged in the local council elections, more of them are winning elections and that the trend is increasing. This data could be interpreted as meaning that the GB groups, center management and leadership development processes have empowered GB members to participate more actively in their communities.

10.5. GB women borrowers' participation in different community organizations

In Bangladesh, public spaces are like local union councils, village tribunals, village development committees, pavement committees, school committees, village irrigation committees, trade associations, rural electrification committees, sports and music clubs and religious festival committees are occupied by rural male elites like politicians, businessmen, male teachers, male village chiefs, quacks, sportsmen, marriage negotiators, male contractors, religious leaders, and philanthropists. Women's clubs are rare in the villages in Bangladesh.

Therefore, rural poor women have been excluded from the public decision-making processes and public resource sharing for long (Abdulah, 1982).

However, during the last three decades, the GB, NGOs and other micro finance organizations have been intensively working with poor women in the rural areas and have created awareness about their rights and responsibilities and exposed them to helpful public resources. As noted, the GB Sixteen Decisions contribute to this awareness. The data in Table 11 reflects the effectiveness of the GB in encouraging community participation among its borrowers. All participants responded that they are engaged in GB centers, but beyond that there wasn't any one type of community setting in which a high percentage participated. The highest were business associations, school committees, and village irrigation committees and farmer associations, and within the other category, the highest were participation in an NGO and various forms of healthcare organizations (Table 11). The organizations in which the women borrowers participate include NGOs like ASA, BRACK, Proskika, Nejera Kori, Destiny and Vocational Training Organization and civic organizations like Janatar Darbar, Widow/Seniors Allowance/Relief Committee.

Table 11: *Percentage of Borrowers' who participate in Different Community Organizations (Multiple responses)*

Question	N	%
GB Centers	61	100.0
Business Associations	8	13.1
School committees	10	16.4
Rural Electrification committee	2	3.3
Village irrigation committee/farmer association	8	13.1
Parent committee	5	8.2
Village development committee	3	4.9

Question	N	%
Sport and music club	3	4.9
Conflict resolution committee	2	3.3
Festival committee	2	3.3
Union council/Up Zilla Council	4	6.6
Other (Puja committee, Madrasa, polling agent, Women's Club, ASA. BRAC, PROSHIKA, Nejara Kori, Destiny, relief committee, National Bank, Islamic life insurance, vocational education, Janater Darber, post office, Immunization, widow/ seniors allowance committee)	41	67.2

10.5.1. Supports are needed for GB women borrowers to take part in decisions that pertain to family and community

The survey indicates that all participants know how to sign their name which is significant in Bangladesh where most rural women do not (Belal, 2008). Regarding borrowers' education, the data shows that the 33% who attended center schooling were illiterate before joining the GB. Briefly, the sample of 61 women borrowers are predominantly between the ages of 31-50, married and living with their husbands, and equally divided between nuclear and extended family living arrangements. The participants were very aware about dowry and teenage marriage issues, and have a strong voice in their family and for their children's education. For example, Safia Begum, a study participant says:

> Higher class people spend a lot of money on their daughters' weddings, giving gifts. This practice has spread to the masses of the society and this affects the poor. To pay dowry, poor people have to sell their

> property as a last resort, further impoverishing us in Bangladesh.

Rina Rani, a borrower participant, says her health was affected by her own teenage marriage. She says:

> My father was a poor man; he married me as a teenager to release his tension from his family. He thought I would be a burden as an adult unmarried girl for the family. Hence I was unable to study. My first baby came when I was 15 years old. This pregnancy terribly affected my body and heath because there was huge bleeding at the baby's birth. Moreover, the baby was very small. Therefore, I know the bad effects of child marriage. So I am not marrying my daughter as a teenager. Now I am earning by using the GB loan and receiving an educational loan for my daughter.

Therefore, social problems like teenage marriages are one of the barriers that GB women borrowers are facing in their familial and community life. The borrowers' reported that their male partners respected them. However, in the decision-making process male dominance over females is a major problem. For example, 25% of participants reported that their male partners made decisions without consulting them. However, 82% indicated that they manage the GB loans that they received. Helal Uddin, Grameen Bank branch manager and a participant of the study, mentions:

> Grameen Bank gives loans to its women borrowers. They do their businesses in collaborations with their husbands and with their family members. However, loan control by the women borrowers is still progressing.

The statistics and statements of the GB borrowers confirm that women borrowers are becoming empowered to control and use their loans, rather than their husbands. I am hopeful that loan control by the women borrowers will further increase.

Regarding their public space empowerment, the findings indicate that the vast majority of women are engaging in community organizations and do not face problems engaging in these activities. The survey also indicates that 96% communicate with their neighbors more than once a month and that 56% did not know their neighbors before joining GB. Eighty percent have already become GB group chairpersons and center chiefs at least once. Almost all know the Sixteen Decisions by themselves. 25% of participants reported that they have connections with other NGOs like Annesha, Life Insurance Company, Nutrition projects, Grameen Shikha, and We Do (Nejera Kori), BRAC, ASA and many others.

11.0 Dowry and teen marriage

As noted, dowry is one of the most strongly entrenched patriarchal traditions in Bangladesh. Dowry creates problems like physical violence, rape, murder, suicide and desertion. Dowry statistics (1997-2003) indicate that dowry-related violence is increasing day-by-day in Bangladesh (Ain O Salish Kendro, 2000). Therefore, dowry problems need to be addressed more rapidly so that the dowry predators can be punished for the violence against women. The Grameen Bank's 11th decision is about anti-dowry marriage and anti-teenage marriage. This research also looks at this issue to know the commitment GB borrowers have to protest against this social problem.

The GB's Sixteen Decisions do speak against dowry, but not forcefully enough. The GB maintains that gender development is an evolutionary process that takes place through women's economic development, as provided through the microcredit program. An important component of gender development is for men and women to learn how to make decisions together through consensual processes (Abendroth, 2007). Hence there needs to be greater emphasis on consensual decision-making between women and men, something that the GB could do by involving women borrowers and borrowers' family members in special meetings for both men and women. Table 12 shows that GB women borrowers are overwhelmingly opposed to dowry and teenage marriage. The data also show that only 3.3 percent would allow their children to enter into a teen marriage and 14.8 percent would support a dowry marriage for their children. These statistics indicate GB women borrowers are very aware of the evils of dowry and teenage marriage, which reflects the positive impact of the 11th decision of GB campaigns. The existing male-dominated marriage agreements benefit the groom and his family and reflect the common perception that the groom's income potential exceeds the bride's value.

Table 12: *Percentage of Respondents who like Dowry and like Teenage Marriage*

Question	**N**	**Yes**	**No**
Do you like dowry marriage?	61	1.6	98.4
Do you allow your children marry with dowry?	61	14.8	85.2
Do you like teenage marriage? marry as a teen	61	1.6	98.4
Do you allow your children to marry as a teen?	61	3.3	96.7

As mentioned earlier, the GB anti-dowry position can be found in the 11th of the Sixteen Decisions – "We shall not take any dowry at our sons' weddings, neither shall we give any dowry at our daughters' wedding. We shall keep our centre free from the curse of dowry." GB launched an anti-dowry campaign in 1984 because the practice of giving dowry as prerequisite to marriage was widespread in Bangladesh, particularly at the village level. This practice has resulted in violence committed by the husbands of women whose families failed to fulfill the dowry requirements. Dowry devalues women and contributes to their subordinate position; it carries an underlying assumption that women have limited or no productive capacity and therefore no ability to contribute to their family's affairs. Dowry can lead to family conflict and poverty, a point emphasized by Feroza, a study participant,

> Those people who look for dowry, they are greedy for other's wealth; they want money without working hard. Dowry marriages drain the savings of parents and impoverish them because parents need to spend money or give a dowry to the grooms. I gave a dowry and spent a huge amount of money on my daughter's wedding because they demanded a Honda motorcycle for a dowry. I spent all my savings and sold my properties to pay the dowry. Now the bridegroom bullies my daughter. My daughter blames me that her dowry marriage makes her unhappy. I became poor, but I again take loans from GB and start work to regain my economic strength (Feroza).

Similar viewpoints on dowry are presented by Monowara and Mina, other participants:

> My daughter becomes an object in her father-in-law's house. They bully her, blame her that she is not beautiful and say that is why they demand dowry from me. I gave a motorcycle to the bridegroom, but his parents said the motorcycle has less horsepower and is not beautiful; the bridegroom is not satisfied with the motorcycle or with my daughter, they asked for more money to replace the motorcycle. They tortured my daughter. (Monowara).

> Dowry is against the law; it creates illegal pressure on bride's parents for dowry. (Mina).

With respect to teen marriage, the Child Marriage Act in 1961 banned child marriage in Bangladesh (Mizan, 1994). Nevertheless, ten respondents reported they were married as teenagers. In addition to campaigning against dowry, the GB 11th Decision opposes child marriage – "We shall not practice child marriage." The participants in this study reflected this opposition in their views expressed in the interviews. The themes that emerged repeatedly were:

- Teenage marriage negatively affects women's health
- Teenage marriage leads to exposure to difficult life problems before the mother has developed the intelligence and maturity to deal with them
- Teenage marriage affects the couple's education
- Teenage marriages are banned in Bangladesh

Some of the interview excerpts speak to these themes:

> I was married at the age of 14 and I got pregnant within six months; I was sick during my pregnancy periods and postnatal stage. My son was also sick and he also suffered from malnutrition. Now I cannot work hard. My health has been damaged because of teenage marriage and pregnancy. As my body shape was destroyed, my husband married again another young girl. (Nasima).

> Teenage marriage is like letting a young girl die before her physical maturity. Moreover, teenage girls do not have the intelligence, they don't understand family life or conjugal life, and they become puzzled in the new environment of their father-in-law's house. (Aliha).

> My first daughter married when she was studying grade 5. She became pregnant immediately after marriage. Her education stopped. She was unable to get GB scholarships and educational loans for her higher education. Both my daughter and I lost economically and socially by her teenage marriage. (Feroza).

> Teenage girls have less intelligence, cognitive development and less experience about their life, so they are unable to adjust to the new environment. Moreover, they are physically immature. The kids suffer from malnutrition if teenage girls birth children. (Shilpi).

These responses to dowry and teenage marriages reflect the impact GB's campaigns against these issues and their emphasis within the Sixteen Decisions.

13.0. Discussions

This study demonstrates some gains for women in the private and public realms through participating in local elections, and village development committees. However, raising male awareness about women's civic participation in the communities is also crucial. It needs to be accelerated so that the process of women's empowerment can move at a faster pace. Although women are progressing, the system of patriarchy has been around for centuries. In that regard, if GB mounted a strong public campaign against dowry, dowry violence and teenage marriage, it would enhance the likelihood of eliminating these social ills. Such a strategy would follow from Gender Development theory (Mies, 1998; Miles 1996) that believes that gender inequality should be addressed directly rather than through the indirect approach that the GB uses.

A consciousness-raising process would need to investigate the interplay between the family and community spheres and identify cultural and customary obstacles to the full participation of women in decision-making. The results of studying such a process could provide a basis for overcoming these obstacles and facilitating the inclusion of women in decision-making. An important component of the GB program is the education of the second generation. The GB borrowers' children, the second generation, are pursuing higher education. The GB has encouraged the second generation or children of borrowers to develop their education by providing them with education loans. These youth have the skills to protest on the street, to lobby for their own rights, and are capable of taking action for the rights of marginalized women. Through collective actions, these women borrowers and their second generations could fill this gap.

Several microfinance impact studies show that microfinance and microenterprise development have had a positive impact on specific socioeconomic variables such as asset building, enhanced income-earning capacity, reduction in the severity of poverty, improvement in the quality of life, improvement in children's education, improved household nutrition, reduction in the extent of social exclusion and stimulated economic development for the disadvantaged in Canada. C.K Prahalad and Stuart Hart (2002) stated in their 'Bottom Pyramid' theory that "Investment at the bottom of the pyramid" means lifting billions of people out of poverty and desperation, averting social decay, political chaos, terrorisms, and environmental meltdown and minimizing the gap between rich and poor". Prahalad and Hart emphasized the synergy of microfinance with 'bottom of the pyramid' strategies as micro financing serves as an effective means of 'providing access to credit, and increasing the earring potential of the poor'.

Microfinance is an activity centered on the poor (Chu, Michael 2007). It is the friend of the local community. Microfinance has a clear record of social impact and has been shown to be a major tool for poverty reduction and gender empowerment (Aghion and Morduch 2005, p.

4). All microcredit literature agrees that enterprises with relatively little capital should be able to earn higher returns on their investments than enterprises with a great deal of capital (Aghion and Morduch 2005, Yunus 2008, Cofi Anan, 2005, Gibbons 2002, Harris 2006, Rhyne, 1997, Drake 1997, Chu 2007, Shrrage 1997, White and Campion2001, Rosengard 2000, Beck, Barr 2004). Microfinance movement has lifted the profile of NGOs (Morduch 1999). Micro lenders serve the poor and make profits. However, profitability has been elusive for most institutions (p.4), it must generate a revenue stream sufficient to cover all expenses and yield a surplus.

Grameen Bank (GB) micro financing not only addresses the issue of poverty, but also works for community development. Grameen Bank and its sister organizations in Bangladesh provide loans to farmers for organic production, agro forestry, the production of organic fertilizer, seed production and preservation, the purchase of agricultural machines, fisheries, livestock, aquaculture, integrated pest management, boats and rickshaws for rural transportation, bicycles, solar panels, biogas plants, and recycling waste businesses. Christen and Drake (2002) concluded that instead of helping to eradicate poverty, MFIs are involved in doing high profit businesses. Muhammad Yunus of Grameen Bank cautiously made an important point that the development finance community must continue to be innovative in the areas of targeting tools, products, service delivery and operations in order to reach the full range of low-income families. However, a focus on financial sustainability encourages MFIs to place a greater emphasis on making a profit rather than on the well-being of clients as this has a negative impact on borrowers' lives (Goetz & Sen Gupta, 1996; Morduch, 1999; Rahaman, 1999; Shrrage, 1997; and Awal, 1994).

Moreover, there are some problems with Grameen Bank. For example, Grameen Bank operates and provides loans to poor people at a 20% interest rate (currently reduce to 16%). Although there have been many success stories of women who have been emancipated through Grameen microcredit, Robin Isserles (2003) cautions that many women are still dominated by their husbands and they do not actually enjoy the benefits from their financial gains or loan investments. GB made a profit of $6.03 million dollars in 2005 (Gramen Bank's annual report 2005, p. 54). Although it claims to be a social benefit institution, it now operates on a for-profit basis – like a private bank. The Grameen Bank credit operation is totally different from that outlined above in Yunus' statement. Thus, GB follows the capitalism approach by charging interest and making profits from its investments (Awal, 1994).

However, the introduction of the profit motive into microcredit degrades MFIs organizations' commitment to the very poor. To reduce this dichotomy, GB has an intensive socio-economic program called the Sixteen (16) Decisions that helps women promote a group peer support lending system. This creates social collateral among GB borrowers. The Sixteen decisions provide women with a space to meet and discuss various social development issues such as health, education, environment, agriculture, and village events as well as installment payments. The Sixteen Decisions represent the social development agenda. However, Rahman (1999) interprets this collective social collateral as a way of enhancing social solidarity, and a strategy for ensuring high repayment rates.

Therefore, the question remains about GB's sustainable development accomplishments because it is working and maintaining the neoliberal capitalistic status quo without any fundamental changes to power relations within the society. It does not challenge the big businesses but rather allows small businesses to run parallel to big businesses; however, small businesses cannot compete with big businesses. Moreover, according to Rosengard, Jay (2000) some MFIs have poorly designed loan and savings products, and inappropriate organizational structure which are common reasons for MFI's failure. For example, Comparmatos, an MFI in Mexico failed because of inappropriate loan products, corruption and constant staff rotation. GB's success because of its high volume lending, loan repayment rate and high profit are well liked features among development practitioners.

Grameen Bank operates nationwide through 2,185 branches. The repayment rate has been highly satisfactory (99%) since 1979. The Bank serves a total of 8.6 million borrowers through 130,000 rural landless associations in 70,370 villages in Bangladesh. The total loan disbursement totalled $14.65 billion since its inception. Of this amount, $8 billion was repaid. Current savings to borrowers total $5.2 billion (Grameen Bank updates, July 2017). To date, its monthly loan disbursement is $58 million and 100% of the loans are financed from borrowers' deposits. However, Isserles (2002) challenges that the bank's high repayment rates do not indicate high efficiency; but he fails to point out the increase in the quality of women's lives.

The Alterna Savings Community Loan Fund (ASCLF) in Toronto has been operating since 2001. Alterna Savings had 37 new loans in 2006-2007 and 12 existing loans, which amounted to $127,000 in Ottawa. The Ottawa Community Loan Fund (OCLF) provides bigger loans to its clients than Alterna in Toronto. However, there needs to be caution around loan delinquency because the OCLF only started its program in June 2007.

According to White and Campion (2001), of the seven thousands NGOs providing microfinance services in the world, seven are transformed very big MFIs: Bank of Rakayat Indonesia (BRI), BancoSol, BRAC Bank, Grameen Bank, SEWA India, PRODEM in Bolivia, and ADEMI in the Dominican Republic. This transformation helps people access commercial capital, provides the ability to mobilize local savings, attracts savers, improves governance and accountability, improves customer service, and expands outreach and push to attain self-sustainability. However, regulated MFIs have regulatory frameworks that may not be suited to poor clients. A survey conducted in 1996 by Drake and Rhyne found that 78 percent MFIs banks responded that they are profitable and have stable financial sustainability. They use individual lending (p.56). This is a big challenge for MFIs; however, Grameen Bank, BRI, BancoSol, and BRAC Bank are operational champions because they have strong commitment to microcredit from high levels of the bank. Therefore, Drake and Rhyne (2002) said that without an internal champion, success is tough (P. 63).

The study also indicates that the majority of GB's borrowers are aware of dowry-less marriage, teenage marriage, and the related domestic abuse, which may not be applicable to upper class women and middle class urban women. A study conducted by the Japan Bank for International Cooperation (JBIC) has found that the practice of dowry is expanding across Bangladesh. Although the GB women borrowers are aware of these issues, it is embedded in the culture (JBIC, 2006). The Bangladesh government has enacted legislation against dowry-related violence called the *Dowry Prohibition Act, 1980*; however, this act needs to be enforced. The government, especially the Ministry of Women and Children's Affairs and the Women's Council, should be proactive in enforcing the dowry act at the grassroots level. The GB and other NGOs in Bangladesh could launch a massive campaign and lobby the government to enforce the act more quickly. Therefore, a separate activism strategy needs to be developed to address these issues. Although GB's Sixteen Decisions have included economic issues and other social issues, none directly discusses gender equality. Does this omission inhibit the family and community development of GB borrowers? Given the influence of the GB; therefore, perhaps a revision of the Sixteen Decisions is needed.

In relation to teenage marriage, the study results indicate it often takes place for economic reasons as it is easier for parents to find educated and well-to-do husbands for younger girls.

Moreover, young women are often the victims of eve-teasing and harassment. Parents fear their daughters would be sexually assaulted or kidnapped. Therefore, teenage marriage is viewed as protection for girls in rural Bangladesh.

11.0. Why Microfinance has succeeded in Bangladesh. Is it possible in North America?

In Bangladesh, the Grameen Bank's (GB) micro lending concept has become very successful. Although there are many delinquent payments changes by the GB top lebel management and inflation problems since its inception, it has tailored its microcredit program to the Bangladeshi culture. The bank researched Bangladeshi's local live culture and implemented a system that is suitable to the local community that helps poor people start their own small business in their neighborhoods even in the home, which was convenient and less risk for them, relief them from maid works and day labor jobs in elites house, and eventually reduce their poverty.

Grameen bank is using a lending policy that is different from commercial banks. GB adopted the local culture and developed a simple lending operation. However, how do we re-kindle (re-build) the entrepreneurial spirit within North American culture? It's difficult when global corporations want to sell everything to people. Their '*one stop shop*' principles are displacing small businesses by undercutting their prices until small businesses fail. The self-employment culture and MFIs programs are not popular in Canada largely due to the domination of big businesses. North American municipalities can initiate pilot projects focused on microenterprises self-sufficiency so that small businesses can offer an alternative to corporate globalization, but small enterprises need appropriate support from the government and other agencies.

Grameen America started in New York and is operating in Harlem, Brooklyn, Queens, and Jackson Height areas and other states of USA. It has nineteen branches in twelve cities across USA and these branches serve 92,290 American micro borrowers. It disbursed USD$ 307 million within nine years and the repayment rate is 100%. It has created 85, 155 jobs in America (Grameen America, August, 2017). These Grameen American branches have been providing microloans to American micro-entrepreneurs in America since November 2007. This microloan program is very popular in USA. It is moving fast to meet people's business capital needs and it has created many self-employment opportunities in New York. Grameen America provides "soft" loans to borrowers for six months with easy collateral-free loans to its clients. Clients have weekly mini savings opportunities in Grameen America and its clients get interest on their mini weekly savings. From the above mentioned Grameen Amerca loan statistics indicate group-baesed micro-credit program is working in North America. Similarly micro credit can work in Canada, but here community banking services need to be tailored and adapted to Canadian socio-economic and environmental context.

14. Conclusion

Although the Grameen Bank has been serving its micro-borrowers for their economic social development and leadership development, the bank is not engaged in promoting gender equality. If the GB experimented with a gender equality program, it would be useful to study its impact upon those who were part of it as compared to the more conventional GB program. Moreover, although the evidence of this study suggests that the GB's program has had an impact upon the family and community development of women borrowers', the study suggests that the impact could be enhanced through adapting the Sixteen Decisions to address gender development and patriarchal issues more directly. Moreover, it is necessary that GB women borrowers create strong ties among themselves and organize for collective action against dowry, teen marriages and against all forms of discrimination, violence and abuses. These findings are the indication of overall awareness of GB women borrowers. However, to shift these social ill norms, these women and their family members need institutional support where they could be closely associated to organize their voices and to protest against these social ill norms. Moreover, government law enforcements are necessary for accelerating their collective actions and to protest against dowry and teen age marriages.

The GB has been instrumental in providing income-generating opportunities to women and providing for their overall empowerment through the extension of collateral-free banking to rural poor women in Bangladesh (Ahamed & Hakim, 2008; Mahmud, 2004; Rouf, 2011; Todd, 1996). The study finds that women's dependency on male family members is being reduced and there is an emerging pattern of more equitable relationships in their households and in the society. The GB women borrowers are also emerging as a social force to fight prejudices and obstacles to economic and social progress in Bangladesh. The present survey shows that women's participation in the GB program results in their increased participation in their families and communities. However, there is still a need for improved gender equality, to ensure women's access to productive resources, to break down patriarchal dominance in the family and in the community, and to alter economic and institutional arrangements to promote more choices for women.

15. References

Abdullah, T. A., & Zeidenstein S. A. (1982). *Village women of Bangladesh: Prospects for change.* Oxford: Pergamon Press

Abendroth, H. G. (2007). Matriarchal society and the gift paradigm: Motherliness as an ethical principle. In Genevieve Vaughan (Ed.), *Women and the gift economy,* pp. 99-107, Toronto: Inanna Publications

Aghion, Beatriz and Morduch, Jonathan (2005). *The Economics of Microfinance.* Massachusetts: MIT press

Ahmed, S., & Hakim, M. (Eds.). (2004) *Attacking poverty with microcredit.* Dhaka: The University Press Limited and Palli Karma-Sahayak Foundation

Ahamed, M. (1997). The Third Sector: Its nature and Characteristics. *The Journal of Social Studies*

Ain O Salish, Kendro. (2000). *Human rights in Bangladesh: 1999.* Dhaka: Shahitya Prokash.

Allen, Tim, and Alan Thomas (eds., 2000). *Poverty and development into the 21st century.* Oxford, UK: Oxford University Press

Alterna Savings (2008). *Community Banking,* Retrieved from www.alterna.ca., retrieved dated 26/11/2008

Amin, R. Becker, S., & Bayes A. (1998). NGO promotes micro-credit programs and women's empowerment in rural Bangladesh: Quantitative and qualitative evidence, *The Journal of Developing Areas,* pp. 221-36

Atlantic Canada Opportunities Agency (2002). The Atlantic Microcredit socio-economic impact study final Report, Coady International Institute, St. Francis Xavier University, Antingonish, Nova Scotia

Bangladesh Demographics. (2010). *Demographics of Bangladesh.* Retrieved from http://en.wikipedia.org/wiki/Demographics_of_Bangladesh#Age

Belal, A. R. (2008). *Corporate social responsibility reporting in developing countries: A case of Bangladesh.* Farnham, U.K.: Ashgate Publishing Ltd.

Bailey, Alison (1998). Locating Traitors Identities: Toward a view of privilege-cognizant White Character. *Hypatia Summer,* p. 13 3

Barr, Michael (2004). Microfinance and Financial Development. *World Bank Policy Research Working Paper* #3341

Beck, Kunt and Levine (2005). SMEs, growth and Poverty: Cross-Country Evidence. *Journal of Economic Growth* #10

Belcourt, M. et.al. (1991). *The glass box: Women business owners in Canada.* Canadian Council on the Status to Women. Ottawa, Canada

Benjamin, Tal (2000). Self-Employment in Canada - trends and prospects. CIBC

Calmeadow Foundation (2005). *Annual Report 2005.* Toronto. Self-employment Development Initiatives

Canadian Advisory Council on the Status of Women (1998).*Women entrepreneurs: building a stronger Canadian economy.* Ottawa

Chambers, R. and Conway, G. (1992). Sustainable rural livelihoods: practical concepts for the 21st century. *IDS discussion paper* 296. Brighton, p. 7

Christen, R. & Drake, D. (2002). Commercialization: the new reality of microfinance in *the commercialization of microfinance: banking business and development*. Deborah Drake and Elisabeth Rhyne (eds.). Bloomfield, Connecticut: Kumarian Press

Chu, M. (2007). Commercial returns at the base of the pyramid: Innovations. In B. Aghion & J. Morduch (Eds.), *The economics of microfinance* (pp. 115-146). Cambridge: MIT Press

City of Toronto/United Way of Greater Toronto (2005). *Strong Neighborhoods: A Call to action 2005*. Toronto: United Way

Coady International Institute St. Frances Xavier University (2005). Retrieved from www.coady.stfx.ca dated June 7, 2008

Counts, A. (2008). *Small loans, big dreams*. New Jersey: Hoboken: John Wiley & Sons, Inc.

Daly, H. E. (2003). *Ecological economics: the concept of sale and its relation to allocation, distribution, and uneconomic growth*. Alberta: CANSEE, Jasper.

Drake, C. and Rhyne, E. eds., (2002). *The Commercialization of microfinance: balancing business and development*. Bloomfield, C.T. Kumarian Press, Inc.

Esbcobar, A. (1992). *Encountering development: the making and unmaking of the third world*. Princeton, NJ: Princeton University Press.

Frankiewicz, Cheryl (2001). *Calmeadow metro-fund: a Canadian experiment in sustainable microfinance*. Toronto: Calmeadow Foundation

Goetz, A. M. (2001). Women development workers: Implementing rural credit programs in Bangladesh. *World Development, 24* (1), pp. 45-63. Retrieved from http://180-scholarsportal:info.ezpnxy.library.yorku.ca/pdf, dated August 17, 2017

Gibbons, D.S. (1995). *Grameen Readers*. Dhaka: Grameen Bank

Goetz, Anne Maria (2001). *Women development workers: implementing rural credit programs in Bangladesh. World Development* Vol. 24(1), pp. 45-63

Gonzalez, A. (2007). *How long does it take to achieve sustainability*? Retrieved from http://www.microfinancegateway.org/content/article/detail/24108, date d 16, June 2008.

Grameen America (2017). Grameen America impact. Retrieved from http://www.grameenamerica.org/impact dated September 15, 2017

Grameen Bank. (2009). *Grameen Sixteen Decisions*. Retrieved from http://www.grameen-info.org

Grameen Bank Annual Report. (2009). *Grameen bank annual report*. Dhaka: Grameen Bank

Grameen Bank. (2010a). *Monthly statement*. Retrieved from http://www.ethicalmarkets.com/2010/08/15/grameen-bank-monthly-update-june-2010/

Grameen Bank. (2010b). *A t a glance*. Retrieved from http://www.grameen-info.org/index.php?option=com_content&task=view&id=26&Itemid=175

Grameen Bank (2008). *Grameen bank statistics*, http://www.grameen.org (June 16, 2008)

Grameen Dialogue (2005). *Grameen dialogue #60*. Dhaka: Grameen Trust

Habermas, J. (1991). What does socialism mean today? In Kapoor, I. (2002). *The devil's in the theory: a critical assessment of Robert chamber's work on participatory development. Third World Quarterly*, No. 1 Carfax Publishing

Hakim, A. and Salehiuddin A. (Eds.), *Attacking poverty with microcredit* (pp. 148-153). Dhaka: The University Press Limited.

Harris, D. S. (2006). *Pathways out of poverty*. Connecticut: Kumarian Press, Inc.

Helmore, K. and Singh, N. (2001). *Sustainable livelihoods: building on the wealth of the poor*: Bloomfield, Connecticut: Kumarian Press Inc

Henry, S. (2006). How MFI's and their clients can have a positive impact on the environment. Good practices in business development services: how do we enhance entrepreneurial skills in MFIs clients? Paper presented at the *Micro Credit Summit* Halifax held in November 2006. Toronto: Alterna Savings

Hick, S. (204). *Social Welfare in Canada*. Toronto: Thompson Educational Publishing, Inc.

Hopwood, B. and M Mellor, M., O'Brien, G. (2005). Sustainable development: mapping different approaches: *Sustainable Development*, Vol. 13. University of Nothhumbria, UK, pp. 38-52

Hossain, S. R. (2006). Women's Rights in *Hunan rights in Bangladesh* (Eds.) M. Hossain & S. Hossain (pp. 139-153). Dhaka: Ain-0- Salish Kendra (ASK)

Hulme, D. & Mosely, P. (1996). *Finance against poverty.* Vol. 2. London: Routledge.

Human Resource and Social Development http://www.hrsdc.gc.ca/eng/ei/types/special.shtml date December 16, 2008

Isserles, R. G. (2003). Microcredit: The rhetoric of empowerment, the reality of development as usual. *Women's Studies Quarterly,* Vol. 3(4), pp. 38-57.

Jahan, R. (1995). *The elusive agenda: Mainstreaming women in development.* Dhaka: The University Press Ltd.

Japan Bank for International Cooperation (JBIC). (2006). *Ex-post monitoring survey of the rural development credit* (Grameen Bank) project-summary report on preliminary findings. Dhaka: Japan Bank for International Cooperation

Johnson, S. (1998). Microfinance north and south: contrasting current debates. *Journal of the International Development,* Vol. 10 (6), pp. 799-810

Johnson, S. & Rogaly, B. (1997). *Microfinance and poverty reduction.* Oxford: Oxfam.

Koffi, Annan (2005). Grameen Dialogue (2005). *Grameen dialogue* #60. Dhaka: Grameen Trust

Korten, D. (2006). *The Great Turning from Empire to Earth Community.* Connecticut: Kumarian Press Inc.

Korten, D. (1995). *Economic growth-centered with people-centered development.* Connecticut: Kumarian Press Inc.

Khandker, S. R. (1998). Micro-credit program evaluation; A critical review. *IDS Bulletin,* Vol. 29(4), pp. 11-20

Kofi, A. (2005). Message from Kofi Annan. *Grameen dialogue* #60. Dhaka: Grameen Trust

Lang, Amanda (2015). *As U.S. moves to regulate payday loan industry, why not Canada?* CBC news, February 09, 2015

Lovins A. and et al. (1999). A road map for natural capitalism in *Harvard Business Review.* pp. 143-158

Mahmud, S. (2004). Microcredit and women's empowerment in Bangladesh. In S. Ahmed &

Morduch J. (1999). The Microfinance Promise. *Journal of Economic Literature.* Vol. 37 (4), pp. 1569-1614.

Morduch, J. (2000). The microfinance schism. *World Development,* Vol. 28(4), pp. 617-629

Mayoux, L. (2009). *Sustainable learning for women's empowerment: Ways forward in microfinance.* Herndon: Stylus Publishing.

Mies, M. (1998). *Patriarchy & accumulation on a world scale: Women in the international division of labor.* London: Zed Books Ltd.

Miles, A. (1996). *Integrative feminisms: Building global visions.* New York: Routledge

Moser, C. (1989). Gender planning in the third world: Meeting practical and strategic gender needs. *World Development,* Vol. 17(11), pp. 1799-1825

Moser, C. (1993). *Gender planning and development: Theory, practice and training.* New York: Routledge

Otero, M. & Rhyne, E. (1994). *The new world of micro enterprise finance: building healthy financial institutions for the poor.* West Hartford, Connecticut: Kumarian Press, Inc.

Polanyi, K. (1957). *The great transformation.* Boston: Beacon Press

United Way (2004). *Poverty by Postal Code.* United Way. Toronto

Prahalad, K and Hart, S. (2002). The fortune at the bottom of the pyramid. *Strategy + Business,* No. 26, pp. 2024.

Quadir, F. (2003). How is civil society? Authoritarian state partisan civil society and the struggle for democratic development in Bangladesh. *Canadian Journal of Development Studies,* Vol. 31 (3), pp. 425-438

Rahman. A. (1999). Micro-credit Initiatives for equal and sustainable development: Who pays? *World Development,* 27(1), pp. 67-82

Rouf, K. A. (2011). Grameen Bank women borrowers familial and community relationships development in patriarchal Bangladesh. *International Journal of Research Studies in Psychology.* Vol.1 (1), pp. 17-26. ISSN 2243-7681.

Rathgeber, E. (1990). WID, WAD, GAD: Trends in research and practice. *Journal of Developing Areas,* 24(4), pp. 489-502

Rouf, K. A. (2013). Islamic Sharia-based Group Micro lending Initiative and Implementation Trajectory Experience in Kandahar, Afghanistan. *Journal Research in Peace, Gender and Development (RJPGD)* Vol. 3(8), pp. 133-141

Rouf, K. A. (2008). *Green microcredit for environmental development.* Unpublished Master's Thesis. Toronto: York University.

SEDI (2007). Self-employment Development Initiative Policy. Toronto

Shragge, E. (1997). *Community economic development-in search of empowerment.* Montreal: Black Rose Books

Shuman, M. H. (2006). *The Small mart revolution.* San Francisco: Berreit-Koehler Publishers

Small Business Quarterly. Vol. 9(1) May 2007. Industry Canada

Srinivas, H. (2003). Environmental management practices for microcredit programs and different sectors of microenterprises actively. *Microfinance Gateway*

Srivastava, K.L. (2006). Social entrepreneurship for sustainable development: some insights and experiences from India. *University Network for Social Entrepreneurship,* Working paper

Todd, H., (1996). *Women at the centre: Grameen bank borrowers after one decade.* Bolder Colorado: Westview Press

White, Victoria and Campion, Anita (2001). Transformation; *Journey from NGOs to Regulated MFI.* Best Practices, Bethesda MD. Download at www.microlinks.org. CGAP

The Hunger Project (2010). Reducing Child Marriage and Domestic Violence: Bangladesh Retrieved from http://www.thp.org/where_we_work/south_asia/bangladesh/overview?gclid=COGRttL G_qUCFcbsKgodqUrLnw

The Ministry of Women and Child Affairs. (2007). *Gender equality in the NSAPR*. Dhaka: Policy Leadership and Advocacy for Gender Equality (PLAGE-11)

Todd, H. (1996). *Women at the center: Grameen Bank borrowers after one decade*. Dhaka: The University Press Limited.

United Nations. (2000a). *United Nations millennium declaration document* A/Res/55/2. New York

Wong, W. A. (2002). *The poor women: A critical analysis of Asian theology and contemporary Chinese fiction by women*. New York: Peter Lang

World Commission on Environment and Development (1987). *Our common future (The Brundtland Report)*. Oxford, Oxford University Press

Yunus, M. (1994). *Banking on the poor*. Dhaka: Mahatab Offset Printers

Yunus, M. (2008). *Creating a World without Poverty: Social business and the future of capitalism*. Dhaka: Subarna Publishers Ltd.

Yunus, M. (2002). *Grameen bank -II: designed to open new possibilities*. Dhaka: Grameen Bank

Yunus, M. (2010a). *Grameen dialogue 2010* #72: Bangladesh: Grameen Trust

Yunus, M. (2010b). *Building social business: A new kind of capitalism that serves humanity's most pressing needs*. New York: Public Affairs

Zeller, M. (2004). *Review of poverty assessment tools*. Report submitted to IRIS and USAID as part of the Developing Poverty Assessment Tools Project. Retrieved from http://www.povertytools.org

Zeller, M. and Meyer, R. (2002). The triangle of microfinance: financial sustainability, outreach, and impact. Washington, D.C.: Food Policy Research Institute, *Food policy Statement*, # 40.

Compare and Contrast Grameen Shikka (Education) and Bangladesh Rural Advancement Committee (BRAC) Education in Bangladesh

Abstract

Grameen Shikka child education services and BRAC education programs in Bangladesh are well known for NGOs managed community child education in the world. Their programs are targeted to poor children and they are inclusive to community partners in Bangladesh although their child education programs are in experimental stages. BRAC education program is widely circulated in the world and many agencies want to replicate its model to different countries. This research is author's personal what programs and strategies these two organizations are using that are different from Bangladesh publicly and privately managed children schools. This research attempted to know what are their programs, how they are working and managing child education, their cost-effectiveness of the programs in Bangladesh. The author reviewed literatures related to child inclusive education, uses secondary sources of information about these two organizations and their web texts. In addition, the author also uses his personal experience working in Bangladesh. The study indicates that BRAC-BEP program and GS child education services are inclusive to poor children in Bangladesh. Their programs are popular in their operating areas. Although public child education system is free in Bangladesh; however, these two agencies schools and their child learning centers have huge demand in Bangladesh. Throughout this study, the author realizes that it needs a nation-wide study to compare and contrast performances and the effectiveness of the systems of the publicly managed child education and NGOs managed child education, and privately managed child education in Bangladesh.

Key terms: BRAC; Grameen Center School; Grameen Shikka; and Non-formal education.

1. Introduction

Bangladesh has a high drop-out rate in both primary and high schools. Primary enrolment rate is 86%; so 14% children never attend school. About a half of the primary entrants drop out before completion of grade five. Nearly half of the primary graduates did not enroll in high school. Total Net Intake Rate (NIR) 91% (UNICEF, 2005). Total Youth Literacy Rate (15–24 years) is 64%, (1995-2004). Total Adult Literacy Rate (15 years and over, (1995-2004) is 47%. Adult male literacy rate is 54% and adult female literacy rate is 41% (Source: UNICEF Bangladesh, 2005). Grameen Shakti (GS) and BRACC-BEP attempted to fill up the gap of child illiteracy. GS tries to fill up deficiencies of youth vocational skills through its vocational training services to unemployed youths in Bangladesh.

2. Objectives of the Research

Grameen Shikka and BRAC are two national level NGOs in Bangladesh. The author intended to research on NGOs managed community child education in Bangladesh managed by Grammen Shikka education services and BRAC education program. This study could assist Grameen Shikka and BRAC–BEP and other educational agencies in Bangladesh to share their (GS and BRAC-BEP) services and implementation strategies that they are using. The research report could assist other NGOs too to get information and ideas about these two organizations.

3. Research Questions

3.1. What are the educational services provided by GS and BRAC? How are they operated in Bangladesh?
3.2. What are the benefits that children and youths get from GS and BRAC education program?
3.3. How many GS/BRAC total graduates graduated at different levels? How many of them get employment or get involved in business?
3.4. Do GS and BRAC graduated scholars encourage and coach neighboring poor children for schooling and studying;
3.5. What are the perceptions of GS and BRAC scholarship recipients regarding child marriage, dowry, and women's autonomy in the family?
3.6. Do GS and BRAC run their programs as revenue generating social enterprise? If so, how they generate revenues? How could they manage their programs if donations discontinue or reach self- sufficiency? What are their future expansion plans/services of GS and BRAC?

4. Methodology

This research collects and studies Bangladesh NGO's non-formal education program materials, particularly BRAC, BEP and GS. Analyze their texts. The researcher would like to talk with BEP and GS executives over Skype in order to understand their non-formal education systems, services, strategies and monitoring devices in Bangladesh.

5. Background of Grameen Shikka and BRAC Education Program

Grameen Shikka (Education) is a Grameen family organization and it was established in 1997. It formally started education programs in Bangladesh although Grameen Bank (GB) Center School informally first initiated by the author (Kazi Abdur Rouf) in 1981. Before Grameen Shikka (GS), Grameen Bank Center Schools were very popular in Bangladesh during 1981-1988.

Grameen Skikka spreads its education services to poor children and poor people in Bangladesh in order to create illiteracy-and-poverty-free society by providing educational services to poor children and financial support to poor meritorious students in the form of scholarships. GS is working for to promote mass education through formal and non-formal methods; to organize and facilitates pre-school child education and adolescents girls, boys and adult people; to promote new and appropriate educational technologies- satellite Internet, distance learning methods etc. as well as innovate ideas and methods for child education with a view to alleviating illiteracy; and to conduct research and undertake experiments in education. Its vision is to spread education to poor children and people in order to create illiteracy free society and poverty. On the other hand BRAC-BEP endeavor is to provide child educational services to poor children in Bangladesh. With this aim, BRAC-BEP organizes and facilitates non-formal primary level education for poor children in Bangladesh. It has agenda to improve access to education to poor children. Their (GS and BRAC-BEP) main objectives are to promote child education in outreach rural areas. However, GS has additional services to provide information technology support to poor students and unemployed youths, and conduct educational research in the field of education.

Grameen Shikka is registered with the office of the Registrar, Joint Stock Companies as well as with the NGO Affairs Bureau. Its main objectives are to promote mass education in rural areas, organize facilities for education and training, provide financial support in the form of loans and grants for the purpose of education, use information technology to bring an end to illiteracy, and development of education, promote new technologies and innovate ideas and methods for development of education, and conduct research and undertake experimentation in the field of education.

Grameen Shikka is an extension of Grameen Bank's efforts to address one of the basic needs of the rural poor-education to help them break away from the shackles of poverty. It is part of the Grameen Bank's multidimensional agenda, built around its core micro-credit program, to focus on poverty alleviation. Grameen Shikka, which literally means 'rural education', was established in 1997 to spread literacy as well as to create awareness on diverse issues like health, human rights, gender equity etc among the rural poor and their children through formal and informal methods.

Since 1997, Grameen Shikka has included *'Pre-school Program'*, *'Early Childhood Development Program'*, *'Non-formal Education for Slum Children'*, *'Vocational Training Program'* and *'Life Oriented Education Program'* in 64 districts of Bangladesh to educate and to create awareness on diverse issues like health, human rights, gender equality, etc. among rural poor children and youth through formal and informal education (Grameen Shikka, 2013). Moreover it has *Arsenic Mitigation Program* and *Vocational Training Program* in different districts of Bangladesh.

6. Author attachment to Grameen Center Schools and the background of Grameen Bank Center Schools (1981-1988)

The author first informally initiated the Grameen Bank Luhuria Center School in 1981, when he was working with Grameen Bank Narandia Tangil branch in Bangladesh in 1981. In collaboration with GB and other field staff, he causally started literacy and numeracy basic learning for children in Luhuria village after office hours. Parents encouraged children to come to this center school. There were 56 children in this center school. The center school provided education coaching services to poor children with love and care. Children did physical exercises, chorus songs, arts, and other fun activities. Children enjoyed those activities very much. This message spread to other neighboring centers. Other customers of the branch asked the bank manager to start a center school in their areas. In 1981, the Narandia Tangil branch informally assisted with my initiative to run 36 center schools in 1981-1983. The aim of GB center schools was to develop schooling behavior among marginalized children, make them ready for schooling stage, and coach poor children to learn literacy, numeracy and basic religious education. Center school activities had increasing impact on elementary school enrollments, class performances, and happiness among these children.

In 1982, author was posted to GB Dhaka head office and was assigned to manage the special programs of the bank, such as managing women workshops, exchanging visit and center school programs, child welfare programs, vegetables seeds distribution and fruits/ timber samplings distribution programs and ORS campains etc. With the help of UNICEF Bangladesh, the author collected 10,000 literacy books and 10,000 numeracy books. He distributed these books for free to five zones of GB branches in 1982. The GB center schools were very popular in the community. Each school contained on average 50 children of different grades – from preschool to grade 6. In 1984-1988, GB center schools numbers reached 400,000 across Bangladesh. All GB center schools were managed by the borrowers themselves.

GB management aware of child education demands. The Grammen Shikka (Grammen education), a separate sister organization incorporated as an NGO in Bangladesh in 1997 initiated by Muhammed Yunus. Grammen Shikka become an independent body deals with education programs like collecting funds for children education, managing funds, organizing GB schools, supply educational logistics to children, provide stipends, scholarships to students. Side by side GB introduced education loans to GB borrowers' children for continuing their higher education. GS initiated child education program near Dhaka and Tangail in a limited scale financed by Save the Children Fund USA. GS experiments some of child education ideas, but GB schools were not parallel like government elementary schools. The author was assigned to draft student higher education loans manual for GB borrowers' children in 1997. Then GB stated education loan to borrowers' children. GB student loans have been financing to second generation of GB borrowers since 1997.

7. Why GB Center School discontinue

Grameen Bank main program is micro-credit. As GB did not have a budget for center schools, GB could not supply logistics to the center schools. GB increased multiple loan products that loaded field staff with loan transactions. The GB center schools had ran and had managed by GB without funding from GB or other sources. Without resources, it was difficult for GB field offices to continue the GB schooling program. Hence GB center schools didn't incubate continuously because of constrained funding. However, GB field staff encouraged guardians to save money regularly and pay center schools' teachers and those who teach in schools. According to this model, many center schools were managed by GB borrowers themselves. However, child education slogans/ campaigns were continued by GB through GB sixteen decisions.

By September 15, 2011 Grameen Shikka (GS) has supported more than 3200 poor students with scholarships. GS has provided pre-school education to more than 100,000 children in Bangladesh. GS started its vocational training program in early 2008 (Grameen Shikka 2013). AS of January 2013, it provides 2000 youths with vocational training. Its vocational training courses are: training in tailoring and dressmaking to poor adolescent girls and women in Chilmari, solar installation technician training, industrial sewing, garment machine mechanics, electrical and electronic control, electronics and telecommunications, computer fundamentals and applications, mobile phone repairing, solar home system management etc. (Ibid, 2013). GS has satellite training centers across Bangladesh too. GS provides scholarships to poor trainees. These scholarships cover 50-80% of the total course fees, but those who are totally unable to pay fees, are provided by GS with full scholarships. Training fees range from ($7-$25) depending on the trade courses. GS set up a manpower company, called Grameen Employment Services Ltd. (GESL), to train employed young people interested to work abroad and assist them to find jobs overseas.

8. Literature Review

Young children's development does not occur in isolation; rather it takes place in a rich context of direct and indirect influences (Bronfenbrenner, 1979). The author believes that children and their education programs should be linked with comprehensive family services and community services especially to disadvantaged children although it is expensive and time consuming but it could be more effective. For example child education program need to be directly connected with child welfare, parenting services, nutrition and health services and other child poverty eradication programs.

Grameen Shikka has parenting care giving program. Under this program, GS assists parents/caregivers to increase their knowledge, skill and confidence for overall development of their children aged 0-3. Particular developmental needs of the target children include various motor, cognitive, languages, social and emotional needs. Grameen Shikka has so far provided parenting training to more than 135 thousand parents/caregivers in different districts of Bangladesh. This program assists caregivers to increase their knowledge, skills and confidence for overall development of children aged 0-3. Different motor, cognitive, linguistic, social and emotional development support that needs to the children.

Non-formal education for slum children: Grameen Shikka in conducting 20 non-formal slum schools (one-room school) in slum areas in Dhaka City. There are 600 students in these schools. Thirty students are in each school. These non-formal schools are providing education up to Grade- 5. Students receive lesions in local Bengali, simple English, and math, environment and social responsibilities etc. Government curriculum books are used in these schools. Non- formal Education for Slum Children is undertaken to provide basic education competencies to slum children. This program is financially supported by CISD.

Daniel J. Weigel & Sally S. Martin (2006) in their paper 'Identifying Key Early Literacy and School Readiness Issues: Exploring a Strategy for Assessing Community Needs ', mentions the above the perceived assets need to be available to address early literacy and school readiness issues in his diagram. This holistic mapping allowed us to target and involve a wide variety of professionals involved in early childhood issues from a broad geographic area, many of whom would not have been able to travel to a central location on a regular basis (Morrow, Leslie and Mandel, 1995). This process could ensured that everyone's voice and ideas included for the disadvantaged child justice education. This mapping also provides vital information to those designing and delivering child educational intervention programs. Such a technique allows for the potential agencies to better target programs than otherwise might have occurred had programs been implemented without such information. Children acquire skills and knowledge in a variety of formal and informal settings, including the home (Purcell-Gates, 1996; Strickland & Taylor, 1989), child care programs (Bryant et al., 1994; Dickinson & Smith, 1994), and other community settings (Kuby & Aldridge, 2004).

Despite the variety of programs that have been developed by GS and BRAC-BEP in Bangladesh, not all programs are available in each community. There are still many poor children and families who have not had access to programs that fit their needs. Before offering new or additional programs, educators and service providers would be best served by assessing the needs of their local community (Dickinson,

1994; Morrow, 1995; Daniel et al., 2006; and Murphy & Burns 2002). Needs assessment is the term used to describe efforts at collecting information to guide program and service delivery efforts, and it is the first step in Jacobs' (1988) comprehensive model of planning and evaluation of family service programs. Reviere, Berkowitz, Carter, and Ferguson (1996) define needs assessment as 'a systematic and ongoing process of providing usable and useful information about the needs of the target population—to those who can and will utilize it to make judgments about policy and programs' (p. 6).

9. Outputs and Outcome of the GS Education Program

9.1. Grameen Shikka Programs, Outputs and Outcome

Children, families, schools, and local communalities need to be ready for schooling their children and to accommodate the diverse needs and experiences of children and their families (Walker, et al., 1994). Schools teaching (outcomes) to children depend on children, their families attention and the community support services. Therefore, with these in mind although GS and BRAC-BEP has developed their program; however, it is not enough. However, these two NGOs are working with poor children. They have included some financial services to meritorious and needy students. An important component of Grameen Shikka's literacy program is the Scholarship Management Program. Under this programme financial support in the form of scholarship is provided to poor meritorious students to enable them to continue their studies. For example, GS scholarships are assisting 3,600 poor meritorious students to carry on their studies in 2009.

Although richly endowed with talents, these poor boys and girls endure extreme hardships to continue their education. Some live in squalid conditions crammed in small houses; they do not get three meals a day. Many cannot buy text books and stationery. Some houses do not have electricity; they cannot buy fuel for lamps. These unfortunate children finish their studies in day light. They cherish big dreams to become doctors, engineers, computer scientists etc but find themselves at odds end to fulfill these dreams.

In 2011, Secondary School Certificate (SSC) finals 121 students got A+, 115 got A, 58 got A-, and 34 got B. Many GS scholars, who started to receive scholarships when they were in high schools, are now studying business, engineering, medicine, literature and social sciences in colleges and universities. Many of them are certainly going to emerge as leaders in the near future. GS has been conducting a non-formal basic education program in 20 schools with a total of 600 students in slum areas of Dhaka City. There are 13, 000 children who are serving under physical and intellectual development program. GS has 500 child development centers with more than 7,000 students in 2010. Grameen Shikkha has provided parenting training to more than 135 thousand parents/ caregivers in Bangladesh (Grameen Shikka, 2013). This program assists caregivers to increase their knowledge, skills and confidence for overall development of children aged 0-3. In collaboration with UNICEF and Bangladesh Shishu Academy, GS has trained more than 2,500 Grameen Bank officials, local government leaders and officials, school teachers, religious leaders etc.; more than 4,000 Grameen Bank center leaders; and nearly 135,000 Grameen Bank borrowers on parenting skills (Grameen Shikka 2013). GS *Life Oriented Education Program (LOEP)* is an integrated non-formal functional education program for poor rural adolescent girls and women to improve their literacy and numeracy skills, life oriented skills related to health, legal matters, child development, civic consciousness, social services, income generation, business professional development, etc. It was closed in 2004 due to fund constraint.

Many international donors are funding to Grameen Shikka to run GS education programs. Funders are the Hunter Foundation UK, A. L. Jameel of Saudi Arabia, Vidar Jorgensen USA, the Green Children Corporation USA, Grameen Foundation USA, NOKIA, Rotary International District 2670, Japan, Her Majesty Queen Sofia, Spain, Citi Foundation, the Shirin Merali Foundation, USA.

Table 1: GS Vocational Training Graduates –as of September 2011

Descriptions	Boys	Girls	Total
Electrical & electronic control	100	0	100
Elec. House wiring/fan motor rewinding	47	0	47
Electronics	87	2	89
Industrial sewing	81	98	179
Dress making & tailoring	17	147	164
Solar	154	0	154
Mobile phone servicing	164	0	164
Garment machine mechanics	85	0	85
Computer applications & Internet	347	192	539
Computer hardware	7	0	7
Graphics	5	3	8
Total	**1,094**	**442**	**1,536**

Source: Grameen Shikka Annual Report 2012.

10. 2. Grameen Student Loan Program

Grameen Student Loan Program started in 1997. Author was assigned to draft the student loan manual for GB borrowers' children in 1997. As of February 2013, GB provided $ 34.27million of student loans to 51,814 students (male 39,817, female 11,997) for university education, medicine and engineering education and study abroad (Grameen Bank Annual Report 2012).

11. Bangladesh Rural Advancement Committee (BRAC)

The Bangladesh Rural Advancement Committee (BRAC) is a non-governmental development organization that was founded in early 1972. It initially focused on assisting refugees returning from India to their newly independent country at its earlier stage. Then from 1980s, BRAC has been involving rural and unban development activities in Bangladesh.

11.1. BRAC Education Program (BEP)

The Bangladesh Rural Advancement Committee (BRAC) is a non-governmental development organization that was founded in early 1972. It initially focused on assisting refugees returning from India to their newly independent country. BRAC main program is non-formal primary level education for poor children in Bangladesh in 1985 is well marketed all over the world although Grameen center school child non-formal education innovations had run 1980-1988 massively across Bangladesh. BRAC education program objectives are to provide quality primary education for children outside formal education institutions; to improve access to education, especially for girls and to enhance the success of formal primary education through pre-primary schools. BRAC education program has formally named in 2003 that carries out its program in five major areas: (1) Non-formal Primary Education for underprivileged children; (2) the Pre-primary Schools program; (3) The Adolescent Development Program (ADP); (4) The Multi-purpose Community Learning Centers with IT facilities; and (5) The Mainstream Secondary Schools Support program for building the capacities of rural secondary school teachers for improving classroom pedagogy. BRAC continued its education throughout years by receiving resources from abroad (BRAC, 2013).

BRAC initiated the BRAC Education Program-BEP an effort to address some of these challenges. In 2003 it was renamed as BRAC Education Program (BEP). School premises are rented from the community, but GB center schools run in GB center house in free. BRAC's educational activities started in 1985 with just 22 one-room schools. The activities covered three upazillas, served less than 700 children administered by five paid staff (BRAC-BEP-2013).

BRAC also has Adolescent Centres where adolescents are given a residential 'Training of Trainers' (TOT) which enables them to facilitate the adolescents courses themselves. Moreover, BRAC has *'Multi Purpose Community Learning Centres'*. BRAC Multi-Purpose

Community Learning Centres are mostly run by local women selected by the BRAC Program Organizers (POs). BRAC employs one facilitator per school/centre, except for multilingual schools, which have two facilitators. The average number of learners per facilitator ranges from 25 to 33 BRAC 2013).

11.2. BRAC Funding Sources

According to the 2007 Audit Report of BRAC, the annual cost (January to December) of the Education program of BRAC is BDT 3,322,331,606 (equivalent to USD 47,461,880 according to current conversion rates). The average cost per learner is USD 23 per year. BRAC- BEP program is donor-supported. BRAC funders to BRAC education program (BEP) are DFID, CIDA, Royal Netherlands Embassy, Royal Norwegian Embassy, Oxfam, NOVIB, UNICEF and Aus-Aid.

12. Primary comparison between BRAC and GS child education programs, and vocational education programs

BRAC education and Grameen Shikka education programs' target mainly: children aged 5+ who eligible for pre-primary schooling; out-of-school children (8-10 and 11-14 years), with a special focus on girls; youth (15-24 years); poor populations and the unemployed; and children with special needs (children from poor urban slums, remote rural/hard-to-reach areas, children with disabilities). They also provide family literacy; environmental education; and female gender preference with individual care and attention. The average number of learners per facilitator ranges 25 to 33. BRAC school premises were rented out by the community, but GB center schools were not rented. BEP has reached 470 of the 482 upzillas in all 64 districts of Bangladesh (BRAC, 2013). GS has vocational training program for unemployed youths that service is not available in BRAC-BEP program. According to BRAC (2013) almost 1.1 million children participate in BRAC schools each year. 3.8 million Children have graduated and 2.3 million children have successfully completed the pre-primary school (BRAC-BEP, 2013).

13. Conclusion

Both Grameen Shikka and BRAC-BEP organizations deal with basic literacy skills, basic numeracy skills and life skills. Both have strategies for community and parental involvement in the schools. They have the School Management Committee (SMC) for each school management. Both agencies believe community active participations are important for effectiveness of the education programs. However, effective monitoring and evaluation processes are crucial for the ongoing enhancement of the program. BRAC-BEP education focuses on social issues: child rights, child marriage, gender, dowries, sexual abuse, substance abuse, child trafficking, domestic violence, acid throwing, divorce, terrorism, etc.; health issues: reproductive health, STIs, HIV/AIDS, family planning, personal hygiene, etc. and life skills: decision-making, negotiations, effective communication, problem-solving, critical and creative thinking, etc. GS could include these tips in its lesson planning and learning. GS has started trade courses, technical skills training for the rural unemployed youths that are very effective to get employment in Bangladesh. BRAC could include trade courses and technical skills trainings to rural unemployed youths in Bangladesh.

Now it is an age of information technology (IT), but it is expensive for disadvantaged people in Bangladesh. The IT knowledge and facilities available to them could help them searching for job markets, access to information on e-businesses and e-markets, e-health, e-nutrition and many other e-news. Moreover, these marginalized people could engage in virtual networking with other people through web networking. Hence availabilities of IT resources, access to Internet facilities and availability of computer training for them can benefit them to learn and to develop their skills on how to use information technology like use computers, repairs computers and use Internets etc. Hence Grameen Shikka and BRAC could provide IT facilities and provide training to disadvantaged people in rural Bangladesh so that they could develop and apply IT knowledge and skills in their life. Therefore, these community organizations could built-in IT training programs and IT resources available to them so that these people could get benefit from IT resources and IT trainings across Bangladesh.

Although GB field staffs encourage child education, campaign for education and motivate borrowers running center schools by themselves, but GB field workers were overloaded with GB loan services. However, GS staff and GB staff could collaborates each other to promote and implement massive child literacy program in Bangladesh. Although BRAC education program objectives are to provide quality primary education for children outside formal education institutions; to improve access to education, especially for girls and to enhance the success of formal primary education through pre-primary schools; however, it could also focus on child poverty and parental literacy issues. Moreover, they could include parent workshops or home-visitor programs in their programs. This could help NGOs know more about the children and their family issues (Kuby et al., 2004). The researcher is personally gain valuable experience from the study that might assist him to develop his future professional career in NGOs managed education programs.

14. References

BRAC. (2013). *BRAC pre-primary School.* Retrieved August 13, 2013 from 2017 http://education.brac.net/pre-primary-schools

BRAC. (2013). *BRAC Home.* Retrieved August 13, 2013, from http://education.brac.net/

BRAC (2013). *BRAC Inclusive Education.* Retrieved August 13, 2013, from http://education.brac.net/inclusive-education

BRAC. *(2013). Support to Formal Schooling: Cooperation with Government.* Retrieved August 13, 2013 from http://education.brac.net/support-to-formal-schooling-cooperation-with-government

BRAC. (2013). *Multi-purpose Community Learning Centres (Gonokendros).* Retrieved August 13, 2013, from http://education.brac.net/multi-purpose-community-learning-centres

Bronfenbrenner, U. (1979). *The ecology of human development: Experiments by nature and design.* Cambridge, MA: Harvard University Press

Bryant, D. M., Burchinal, M., Lau, L. B., & Sparling, J. J. (1994). Family and classroom correlates of Head Start children's developmental outcomes. *Early Childhood Research Quarterly, Vol.* 9 (3-4), pp. 289-309

Country Profile Bangladesh (2013). *BRAC Education Program.* Retrieved August 14, 2013, from http://www.unesco.org/uil/litbase/?menu=4&programme=28

Education Watch Interenational (2017). *In defence of the 'no dreadlocks' school.* Retrieved from http://edwatch.blogspot.ca/ dated September27, 2017

Education Watch Report 2016 Full (2017). *Literacy, Skills, Lifelong Learning,* retrieved from http://www.campebd.org/page/Generic/0/6/18, dated Septem 27, 2017

Dewey, John, (1938). Experience and Education, Nework: Kappa Detla Pi

Dickinson, D. K. (Ed.). (1994). *Bridges to literacy: Children, families, and schools.* Cambridge, MA: Blackwell

Dickinson, D. K., & Smith, M. W. (1994). Long-term effects of preschool teachers' book readings on low-income children's vocabulary and story comprehension. *Reading Research Quarterly, Vol.* 29(2), pp. 104-122

Grameen Bank Annual Report (2012). *Grameen Scholarship Program.* Grameen Bank. Packages Corporation: Dhaka, Bangladesh

Grameen Shikka (2013). *Grameen Shikka Introduces Industrial Electrical Wiring Training.* Retrieved dated August 12, 2013, from http://www.grameenshikkha.com/

Grameen Shikka (2013). *Grameen Shikka Scholars Perform Excellent in 2013.* RetrievedAugust12,2013,fromhttp://www.grameenshikkha.com/index.php?option=com_content&task=view&id=64&Itemid=94

Grameen Shikka (2013). Programs. Retrieved August 10, 2013, http://www.grameenshikkha.com/index.php?option=com_content&task=blogsection&id=4&Itemid=59

Grameen Shikka (2013). *Projects*. Retrieved August 13, 2013, from http://www.grameenshikkha.com/index.php?option=com_content&task=blogsection&id=6&Itemid=91

Morrow, L. M. (1995). *Family literacy: Connections in schools and communities*. Newark, DE: International Reading Association

Murphey, D. A., & Burns, C. E. (2002). Development of a comprehensive community assessment of school readiness. *Early Childhood Research & Practice*, *4*(2), Retrieved February 6, 2006, from http://ecrp.uiuc.edu/v4n2/murphey.html

Kuby, P., and Aldridge, J. (2004). The impact of environmental print instruction on early reading ability. *Journal of Instructional Psychology*, Vol. 31(2), pp. 106-114

Reviere, R., Berkowitz, S., Carter, C. C., & Ferguson, C. G. (1996). *Needs assessment: A creative and practical guide for social scientists*. Washington, DC: Taylor & Francis.

Rouf, K. A. (2014). Community Green Economic Development by leasing and utilizing Government Jurisdiction Ponds by Grameen Fisheries and Livestock Foundation in Bangladesh. *International Journal of Research Studies in Management*. Vol. 3(2), pp. 1-16

Rouf K. A. (2013). Compare and Contrast Grameen Shikka (Education) and Bangladesh Rural Advancement Committee (BRAC) Education in Bangladesh. *Journal of Research in Management*, Vol. 1(*1*), pp., 1-9

UNICEF Bangladesh (2005*). Bangladesh Profile*. UNICEF Bangladesh. Dhaka

Walker, D., Greenwood, C., Hart, B., & Carta, J. (1994). Prediction of school outcomes based on early language production and socioeconomic factors. *Child Development*, Vol. 65(2), pp. 606-621

Weigel, D. J. & Martin, S. (2006). Identifying Key Early Literacy and School Readiness Issues: Exploring a Strategy for Assessing Community Needs. *Early Childhood Research and Practice (ECRP)*, Vol. 8(2)

Renewable Energy Context, Scope, Application and Green Business of Grameen Shakti in Bangladesh

Abstract

Energy from fossil fuel (coals, diesel, kerosene, wood etc.) generates carbon, carbon dioxide emissions, green house emissions that pollute air, pollute water and destroy environment resulted global warming that's harmful to living beings, threat to living beings and nature. Hence energy scientists are looking for alternative energy resource uses that are environmentally friendly and good for human being. They are provoking for renewable energy (solar radiation energy, bio gas energy, wind energy, water wave energy, CNG energy and hydropower energy) use because PV technologies produce very small amount of CO_2 compared to the emissions from conventional existing fossil fuel energy technologies. This paper talks about fossil fuel energy and renewable energy use and their consequence and impact respectively in the nature and society. In the paper, the author incorporates his working experience with Grameen Shakti (GS) and statistical data from different renewable energy (RE) implementing organizations in Bangladesh during his visit to Bangladesh in 2014-2015.

The paper identifies different RE resources and different RE projects undertaken in the world particularly Bangladesh. The study explores RE resource utilization different business models, programs, and their benefits in Bangladesh. The study discovers Grameen Shakti, a sister organization of Grameen Bank, is the largest RE implementing organization not only in Bangladesh, but also in the world. GS has developed a micro-utility RE financial model that has disseminated to the IDCOL partnered RE implementing agencies in Bangladesh. The RE technologies need further improvement for to not only more handy at the micro level, but also valuable at the economic scale.

Key terms: Bio-gas; climate change; fossil fuel energy; Grameen Shakti; green house gas emission; global warming; renewable energy; and solar panel.

1.0. Introduction

It has been alarming the global warming is increasing because of fossil fuel CO_2 emission and other greenhouse gases consequences climate change. Now carbon emission, green house emissions are serious issues for environment pollution and climate change that have been forefront to the global community. Today's development in the advanced countries has resulted in global climate change and massive environmental damage. Many programs have already been initiated throughout the world in order to reduce GHG emission. However, Bangladesh has huge renewable energy (Solar, biogas, and wind pump etc.) potentials because of its geophysical condition in Bangladesh. Rural people of Bangladesh depend on biomass, crop residues, plant debris, animal dung and wood for fuel creating deforestation, flood, soil erosion and health hazards etc. affects human and other to living beings. Women and children, on whom the burden of collecting fuel falls, suffer the most. They are the worst victims of indoor air pollution such as smokes in the kitchens.

Many NGOs, private agencies and public institutions are involved in renewable energy green businesses and earn income by selling renewable energy products to people in Bangladesh. The paper studies the context of renewable energy in Bangladesh, its scope and applications there. The research also discerns renewable energy business models that exit in Bangladesh. In the paper, the author incorporates his working experience with Grameen Shakti (GS) and the collected data from different RE implementing organizations in Bangladesh during his visit to Bangladesh in September 2014-April 2015.

2.0. Environmental Issue

Green house gases (CO_2 Ch_4, and N_2O) emitted in burning of different types of fuel lead to air pollution, environmental pollution and global warming. GHG emissions factors are mostly due to CO_2 are shown below.

Table 1: GHG emission factor

Items	GHG emission factor
Kerosene	2.5 ton CO_2/ton
Wood/straw	1.7 ton CO_2/ton
Diesel genets	1.3 ton CO_2 /MWh
Diesel	0.897 ton CO_2/MWh
Bangladesh grid (natural gas 90%)	0.452 ton CO_2/MWh
Natural gas	0.452 ton CO_2/MWh
Hydro, Solar, Wind	0

Source: Solar and Wind Energy Resources Assessment (SWERA, 2007

The gradual increase of global temperature and its consequences affect Bangladesh, risen the sea level of Bay of Bengal. It is because of climate change and because of radiant energy leaving the planet is naturally retained in the atmosphere. The concentration of the atmospheric gases slowly increases and helps to rise temperature. This issue is being termed as 'global warming', which accelerates the earth's climate change.

The anthropogenic activities include mainly the production and consumption of fossil fuels, as well as the intensification of agricultural activity and changes in land use and land cover. Energy production and use, the largest sole source of CO_2 emissions and a large contributor of CH_4 and N_2O emissions, accounted for 81.7 percent of emissions in industrialized countries in 1998 (united nations Framework Convention on Climate change, UNFCCC, 2000). Another estimate shows that the earth's atmosphere receives around 27,000 million tons of CO_2 in the recent years. As a country the USA is the largest CO_2 emitter in the world, which releases 5,729 million tons of CO_2 every year with 19.7 million tons of per capita emission, and the nearest contributor is China which releases 3,719 million tons with 2.9 million tons of per capita emission. Carbon dioxide, the greenhouse gas largely blamed for global warming, has already reached a record-high level in the atmosphere (Hanley, 2004). It has increased by 30% in the last 200 years as a result of industrial emissions, automobiles, and rapid forecast burning, especially in the tropics. Much of these have taken place since 1960. From 1973 to 2006, the emission of CO_2 has increased at a rate of 79.05%. Other pollutants (e.g. SO_2) are also released at high level from the combustion of coal.

3.0. World Energy situation

Many developed countries including some developing countries are adopting large scale investment in renewable energy technologies (RETs) since the global reserve of non-renewable sources like petroleum, gas, coal etc. gets reduced. Global renewable energy (wind power, solar hot water, geothermal heating, and off-grid solar photovoltaic (PV) capacity) increased at a rate of 15-30 percent annually during the period 2002-2006. Mass production of electricity using RE has recently been familiar throughout the world. UN predicts that 50% of the world's population now lives in cities and this figure will be 60% in 2030. Over 75% of energy consumption is directly related to cities and per capita energy consumption is increasing fast in many cities especially in the developing countries (The World Watch Institute, 2007). The fasted growing energy technology in the world is grid-connected solar PV (growing capacity by 60% per year from 2000-2004), to cover more than 400,000 rooftops in Japan, Germany, and the United States (Kabir & Endlicher, 2012). The average annual growth of PV market over the last 15 years is 30 percent. Table-2 shows World Energy generation, supply, consumption and CO_2 increasing trend from 1973 to 2006 (Ibid, 2012).

Table 2: GHG Emission Factor

Fuel mixed grid electricity production contains huge CO_2, CH_4, N_{2O} emission.

Fuel Type	Fuel Mix	CO_2 emission	CH_4 emission	N_2O emission	Fuel conversion efficiency	GHG emission factor
	%	Kg/GJ	Kg/GJ	Kg/GJ	%	(tco2/MWh)
Small hydro	4.9%	0.0	0.0000	0.0000	100.0%	0.000
Natural gas	90%	56.1	0.0030	0.0010	45.0%	0.452
Diesel (#2 oil)	5.1%	74.1	0.0020	0.0020	30.0%	0.897
Electricity mix	100%		-	-	-	-452

Note: Global warming Potential of GHG

1 ton CH_4= 21 tons CO_2

1 ton N_2O= 310 tons CO_2

The GHG emission from electricity production of 20062 MKwh in 2004 is 9 million tons. The emission is increasing with the years.

Source: RETScreen analysis in SWERA report 2007.

With availability of effective bright roof areas, satisfactory global irradiation and sunshine duration, the environmental concerns are very practical and pragmatic consideration for the installation of the photovoltaic systems. As a result, countries with capacity of technological innovation and strong economy have emphasized on harnessing energy from the renewable resources. The Kyoto Protocol prescribed that countries largely contributing to GHG emission could take part in emission trading, clean development mechanism and joint implementation to reduce their shares of GHG emission. Germany, Japan, Netherland etc. are some of the industrialized countries, which have been shown their obedience to the protocol since it was adopted.

4.0. Significance of the study

4.1. Bangladesh energy concerns

Before 2006, only 40% people of the country 9Bangladesh) are connected to grid electricity and the rest depend mostly on biomass energy, kerosene and diesel powered electricity. Remote villagers and coastal energy users are suffering from energy use. Most of the households do not have access to electricity as there is no power distribution network in the coastal areas. Kerosene is the most common fuel used by the households for illumination purposes. Price of kerosene is often subject to fluctuations with price going up in the event of scarcity of supply. The quality of light from kerosene lamps is poor and not adequate enough for all purposes. Besides, it pollutes the household environment through emission of smokes and is also hazardous. The households have to use dry cell for running different appliances like radio, emergency lighting. The price of dry cell is relatively high. This causes extra financial burden to the household budget. Biomass fuel is scarcity for cooking. The scarcity takes serious in the rainy season in Bangladesh because biomasses are under water.

Small-scale private generators are in operation in some village markets to provide electricity to the shops for limited hours, usually after the evening. The commercial shops in the non-electrified market places use kerosene lamps, candles, etc. which are not found suitable for their activities. The electrified shops face problems of load shedding, irregular supply of electricity and poor service by the utility agencies.

Most of the industrial units and irrigation pumps located in the coastal areas have no access to the grid-based supply of electricity. They are run by diesel. The diesel engines are facing many mechanical problems. The electrified industrial units suffer due to load shedding, non-cooperative attitude of the utility agencies and their poor service quality. Load shedding and frequent interruption in the supply of electricity affect the industrial units adversely causing a cut in production and revenue.

Bangladesh is also not a big contributor to global greenhouse gas emission. But the imminent consequences of climate change in the country are likely to be higher due to sea-level rise and frequently occurring catastrophes. Meanwhile the country has experienced massive destruction due to severe cyclones in the south and frequent flood events, which are reported to be the result of global climate change. It is evident that due to the accelerated industrial growth of the developed countries, relatively low-lying countries (e.g., Bangladesh, Maldives) are getting more vulnerable to climate change. Therefore, use renewable energy technology, environmentally friendly clean energy, and use of renewable energy education is essential to reach out to mass people in Bangladesh

4.2. Dhaka Mega City energy problem

The population of Dhaka City rose to 6.15 million in 1991. The number of inhabitants in the Dhaka Mega City rose to 14 million in 2008 now (2015) it is 17.9 million. Unofficially the number would be higher than formal statistics. With the dramatic growth of the size of the city population, the demand for energy consumption has also been increased manifold. However, the power situation is not satisfactory at all. The whole system of electricity distribution is poorly managed and continues with more than 30 percent system loss mainly through illegal connections (Alam et al. 2004). Power supply is quite inadequate compared to its peak demand in summer. Dhaka Megacity is supplied around 1, 000-1,200 MW of electricity against the peak demand of nearly 2,000 MW. The country as a whole continues to have 1,500 MW of deficit, while Dhaka City lacks more than 500 MW. Electricity crisis can immediately solve by nuclear power plant. But the problem would be with the disposal of highly radioactive wastes, nuclear power would be increasingly important source of the world`s electricity mix (Doman, 2004).

5.0. Why need Renewable Energy

Reduction of global greenhouse gas emission to seize global warming requires minimizing the use of fossil fuels. To achieve this, a large scale use of renewable energies must be made over the globe for production of electrical and thermal energy. World resources of oil, gas, and coal are limited and there is a global concern about this but for Bangladesh the situation appears to be extremely unhappy as per capita reserve of fossil fuels is only 1/50th to 12/100th of world per capita.

According to a recent study by the World Health Organization, around 46,000 people die every year in Bangladesh from exposure to indoor air pollution caused by inefficient traditional cook stoves, with 70% of the victims being children under age of five years. Around 90% of the households in Bangladesh uses biomass fuels and low efficiency stoves for cooking resulting incomplete combustion and corresponding Indoor Air Pollution (IAP) through emissions of greenhouse pollutants and particular materials. It causes severely adverse health impacts which are particularly acute for women and children who are the most exposed groups to indoor air pollution.

5.1 CO2 Emissions in Bangladesh

SWERA (2007) finds GHG (Green House Gas) emission from electricity grid (20,062 MKWh) is 9 million tons. By 2020 electricity demand should be doubled and CO_2 emission would be around 18 million tons.

Table-3: CO_2 Emission Energy Production in Bangladesh:

Description	Quantity of emission
Energy-related Carbon Dioxide Emissions	32.9 million tons
Per capita energy consumption	4.0 million Btu
Per capita carbon dioxide emissions	0.23 tons

Source: International Atomic Energy Agency (IAEA), 2003

At least 89% of air emissions associated with electricity generation could be prevented if electricity from photovoltaic displaces electricity from the grid (Fthenakis et al. 2008). Scheer, 2002) reported that the impending damage to the earth by fossil fuels can only be protected with a solar-based economy. Renewable energy emission of CO_2 is very low. Technologies on wind power generation have been reported as the lowest CO_2 emitter. Hydro and solar PV systems also have low emissions, with average reported values at less than 100g/kWh CO_2 (Evans et al. 2008).

5.2. Large electricity deficit in Bangladesh

The country had an initial installed capacity of 5,202 MW (current rerated capacity is 4,000 MW mainly due to ageing of infrastructures), while average electricity generation at present is around 3,700-3,800 MW against the present demand of over 5,000 MW (BPDB, 2009; World Bank and GTZ, 2009). Alongside, the country's electricity demand is increasing over 500MW each year (Stromsta, 2009).

Therefore, Bangladesh has been suffering from energy crisis. Huge load shading, lack of sufficient energy for agricultural irrigation is because of energy crisis. Heavy industries in Bangladesh cannot be developed because of energy crisis. Before 2000s, rural people use biomass fuel for cooking. 50% energy obtained from biomass energy in the rural areas. Indigenous gas (available within the field), oil (petroleum and coal (few from Bangladeshi coal mines and imported) are the major source of primary commercial energy in Bangladesh. Hydroelectric energy sources are managing by the public sector which is very limited and inefficient. The country's power is being mostly generated with conventional fuel (82% indigenous natural gas, 9% imported oil, 5% coal) and renewable sources (4% hydropower and solar). According to Bangladesh Bureau of Statistics (BBS, 2006), around 32% people of the country had electricity connection, and around 4% have natural gas supply. Currently around 40% people are connected with electricity grid. But still 60% people throughout country are still remaining without electricity (Kabir & Endlicher, 2012). However, the annual GDP growth of electricity is gradually rising (BBS, 2006). The electricity connection statistics show more disparity between urban and rural areas. In the urban areas, 70.32% households are connected with electricity, while only 29.68% of the rural households are having electricity connection (BBS, 2006).

Bangladesh is one of the most disaster prone countries in the world, and is vulnerable to various devastating disasters like cyclone, flood, tidal surge, sea level rise etc. The imminent consequences of global warming due to increase of GHG emissions will certainly affect the deltaic Bangladesh. The country has experienced with massive coastal cyclones and saline intrusion. It is predicted that in the near future, more severe impacts are likely to happen if immediate measures are not undertaken. This tremendous power shortfall and air pollution drives for alternative energy (solar home systems) exploitations in Bangladesh. Solar home systems (SHSs) has covered more than 2.2 million households providing at least some lighting (February, IDCOL, 2015).

6.0. Energy status in Bangladesh

About 90% of the population in vast rural areas was practically without electricity before 1980s. For the benefit of this vast rural people, REB (Rural Electrification Board) was established in 1977. It provides electricity to consumers in a selected area by forming a Rural Electric Co-operative called Pally Bidyut Samity (PBS). Activities of rural electrification co-operative are given below:

Table 4: PBS (Palli Bidyut Samity activities in Bangladesh

Description	Achievement
Area coverage/PBS	2000 sq. Kms
No. Of PBS	67
Number of villages energized	41,125
Number of 33/11 KV sub-station constructed	328
Length of power distribution lines	1,73, 125 Km
Number of population in programme area Category wise connection	9,25,13,296
Domestic	45,42,099
Commercial	6,06,666
Irrigation	1,38,869
Industry	95, 0559
Others	12,043
Total	53,94,736

Source: SWERA, 2007.

Table 5: Production and consumption of Natural Gas in Bangladesh

Category	2000-01	2001-02	2002-03	2003-04	2004-05
Gas Production Gas (109cft	372.16	391.53	421.16	454.59	486.75
Consumption (109cft)					
Electricity	175.27	190.03	190.54	199.40	211.02
Captive	0	0	0	32.03	37.87
Fertilizer	88.43	78.78	95.89	92.80	93.97
Industrial	47.99	53.56	63.76	46.49	51.68
Tea-garden	0.65	0.72	0.74	0.82	0.80

Brick field	0.44	0.53	0.52	0.12	0
Commercial	4.06	4.25	4.56	4.83	4.85
Domestic	31.85	36.74	44.80	49.22	52.49
CNG	0	0	0.23	1.94	3.62
Total Consumption	348.69	364.61	401.04	427.65	456.30

Source: BBS (2006)

6.1. Imported Fossil Fuels

Bangladesh transport system depends almost totally on imported liquid fuels, but good news is after 2008, CNG fuel is using from national source. Kerosene is used widely for lighting in villages while diesel generators are getting unavoidable. The amount of crude oil and petroleum products imported in Bangladeshh is shown below in Table 6.

Table 6: Import of Petroleum Products and Crude Oil

Year	Crude Oil		Petroleum Products	
	Qty (Thousands Tons)	Value (Million US$)	Qty (Thousands tons)	Value (Million US$
2001-02	1225	220	2072	2536
2002-03	1331	289	2214	3319
2003-04	1252	314	2262	4015
2004-05	1063	364	2692	7214

Source: British Petroleum, (2005)

The cost imported petroleum products is huge. Now Bangladesh is using less polluting local CNG fuel in vehicles and it is popular here. However, natural gas reserves in Bangladesh are likely to be depleted before 2020 and electricity production from gas may stop. Therefore, more energy supplies using RETs must be developed and utilized.

6.2. Electrical Energy

During financial year 2005-06, per capita consumption was 136kWh in Bangladesh whereas per capita electricity generation was reported to be 167kWh (SEWERA, RERC, 2007). At present, the electricity situation little better.

The availability of the most useful form of energy, electricity, is again extremely small as shown below:

Table-7: Electricity Generation and Consumption in Bangladesh, 2005-2006.

Items	Quantity
Installation Capacity	5,275MW
Average demand	4,300-4,500MW
Average generation	3,200-3,300MW
Per capita generation	167 kWh
Per capita consumption	136 kWh

Figure below presents the fossil fuel supply for electricity generation which shows that natural gas is the major energy source.

Fig. 1. Generation pattern FY2004

Natural gas	89%
Oil	7%
Hydro	4%

The shortfall in electricity generation continues till today mainly due to old inefficient generators requiring heavy maintenance.

7.0. Renewable Energy application in Bangladesh until 1990s

Solar energy owns a share of more than 99.9% of all the energy converted on earth (Kaltschmitt & Wiese, 2007). The amount of energy sent to the earth from the sun each year is equivalent to almost 15,000 times of the world's commercial energy consumption and more than 100 times the world's proven oil, gas, and coal reserves (Islam, 2005). The continuous supply of the solar energy to the earth's surface is equivalent to a power of about of 100,000 TW (Kuhne & Aulich, 1992). Solar energy is inexhaustible and available throughout the year all over the world.

Despite the availability of enormous potential of renewable energy, there has not been any significant progress in the promotion and development of RETs by public sector and other sectors until 2010. It is because highly expensive installation devices, high maintenance costs and lack of strong political commitment. Till to date, the large part of the energy demand of the country is fulfilled by traditional biomass, which is predominating particularly in the rural areas. Biomass is the source of energy supply to the rural villagers, but it is unhealthy. Hence there is immense potential in solar energy utilization across Bangladesh because Bangladesh is rich is sunshine whole year. Wind and tidal energy generation potentials exist in the coastal areas. Now huge solar home system is installing across Bangladesh rural areas by NGOs, Private sector even public sector promote sloaar home stystem (SHS) in Bangladesh. Present Government of Bangladesh gives more importance and supports to solar home system installation in rural areas of Bangladesh.

8.0. Bangladesh Renewable Energy sources and technology practices

Bangladesh through a small country has numerous potential sources of renewable energy, for instance, biomass, solar energy, hydropower, wind and tidal energy. Rural people use energy from traditional biomass-cow dung, domestic wastes, jute stick, rice straws, twigs, etc. Hydropower generates around 5% of the total consumption in Bangladesh. So solar and wind energy is find a great potential source of energy in Bangladesh.

Table-8: Renewable Energy Prospects in Bangladesh

RES Type	Capacity (up to December'08)	Theoretical Potential
Wind	1 M	2,000 MW
Hydro	230 MW	672 MW
Solar PV	15 MW approx	50,436 MW
Solar Thermal	3,000 m3	20<>106 m2
Biogas	.3 million m3	3,675 <>106 m3

Source: Based on Alam et al. (2003).

In Bangladesh, although very few biomass gasification plants have been installed, many biogas projects undertaken in Bangladesh. For example, over 24,000 biogas plants have been installed all over Bangladesh (Energy & Power, 2007). Biogas plants in the rural areas are run mainly with animal dung and domestic wastes. The urban solid wastes include wastes from households, industries, hospitals are used in biogas production, but urban biogas production is very limited.

8.1. Solar Energy technologies

Generation of solar electricity from solar radiation is basically made with solar cell, which is mainly a silicon–made solid device. A solar cell is defined as a device that directly converts sun-light into electrical energy through the process of PV systems. In order to generate electricity from solar radiation, an off-grid stand-alone or island system generally needs several devices, such as, solar panel, battery, inverter, charge-controller and necessary cables and tools. Energy is generated by the solar panels as direct current (DC), and converted to alternating current (AC) by the inverter. The battery is needed for the off-grid PV systems to store power, and the charge controller maintains the battery at the highest possible state of charge (Grameen Shakti, 2015; SWERA, 2010). Solar cells are electrically connected and placed between glass and tedlar plate, and framed by an aluminum frame. Number of solar-modules and other components (batteries, charge regulators, inverters) can form large photovoltaic systems.

Basic considerations of Solar PV Applications

The geophysical features of Bangladesh favour installations of solar home systems everywhere in Bangladesh (Alam et al., 2004; Eusuf, 2005; SWERA, 2010). It is appropriate areas with more than 25° Celsius in most all time round the year. Solar panels can be installed in the wall of the buildings so that enough wind to keep temperature close to 25^{Oc} Celsius. Solar tracking system can be effectively used between 23^{Oc} and 550 latitudes of both hemispheres (Kabir & Endlicher, 2012). Moreover, site selection is very important for the installation of large-scale solar PV plants. Mounting of panels is essential to capture optimum level of electricity. The locations having more provision of having sun occurrence are likely to be most suitable areas.

8.2. Solar Energy

Solar PV generated lighting program in Bangladesh primarily includes on rural houses, small businesses, and income generation activities in the remote rural areas which is being implementing by Grameen Shakti, and other NGOs in Bangladesh. Many SPV aimed at providing income generating opportunities through running motors, permitting longer working hours and facilitating longer selling hours by rural traders.

In Bangladesh, the private sector, commercial as well as non-profit organizations have chosen at least an important renewable energy source for the economic realization. In the initial promotion of SPV, Rahimafrooz, a private battery manufacturing company in Bangladesh played an important role despite having it an unprofitable business due to high tariffs and duties. Rahimafrooz continued to emphasize manufacturing solar grade deep cycle batteries to go with the imported systems. Other private companies like Microelectronics, First

Bangladesh Technology and Bangladesh Energy Advanced Studies have also looked for a market share for producing solar panels in Bangladesh.

The government sponsored organization infrastructure Development Company Limited (IDCOL) in Bangladesh has been involved to a large extent in the promotion of SPV systems and has already installed around 450,000 solar home systems all over Bangladesh through the partner NGOs (Haque, 2008; IDCOL, 2009).

8.4. Roof-top grid connected PV System

A 1.5 KW roof-top grid connected PV system has been developed and installed on the roof of Renewable Energy Research Center (RERC) in Bangladesh with the support of the Ministry of Science and Technology. It has carried out R & D activities on solar cookers, solar water heaters, solar dryers, SHSs, etc. (IDCOL, 2014; SWERA, 2010).

8.5. Roof Mounted Solar PV System

Compared to the solar tracking systems, roof-tied PV system is a cheaper option for the households. Grid connected roof-mounted system appears to be very profitable and secured, although the initial investment is high.

8.10. Wind Energy

Wind energy utilization in Bangladesh is still in the early stage of in the coastal areas, there is a very good potential of generating 20,000 MW of electricity (SEWRA/RERC, 2007). In 2008, 50 wind turbines having capacity of 20 KWh each has been installed in Kutubdia, a detached off-shore island of Cox's Bazar District with the self-funding of the BPDB (Kabir & Endlicher, 2012; The Daily Ettefaq, 2008). This wind-battery hybrid system has rarely helped in solving the electricity crisis in the island.

9.0. Institutional Arrangement for Renewable Energy (RE) exploitations in Bangladesh

The public agencies like Bangladesh Power Development Board (BPWB) and the Rural Electricity Board (REB) both have been carrying out projects to promote renewable energy activities. Many NGOs are involved in renewable energy business in Bangladesh. World Bank and Government Bangladesh supported Apex organization IDCOL is supporting them.

10.0. Scope of Renewable Energy use in Bangladesh

Bangladesh has an enormous potential in solar energy, and therefore, the installations of small and large-scale PV systems can help to reduce its current share of GHG emission. One family using a typical solar home system can save yearly 290 litres of kerosene per family by using solar lighting technology and can prevent the emission of 0.76 ton CO_2 per year (SWERA, 2007).

In Bangladesh, 60% of the total population still depends on biomass based energy. Agricultural residues (rice straws, jute sticks, rice husks etc.), cow dung, twigs etc. have been being used as fuel for cooking by the rural households since time immemorial. But the inefficient use of traditional fuel sources produces immense indoor air pollution causing massive health hazards particularly to women and children. At the same time, there has been a decline in the supply of biomass mainly due to the high population pressure on agricultural production (Grameen Shakti, 2015).

The major attention of the RE technology is still concentrated into the rural areas although the urban areas generate enormous solid wastes which can be used for power generation and to produce compost. By 2010, the renewable energy sources (especially hydropower) contribute only 4% of the total power generation (4,000 MW) (Hussain & Badr, 2005).

The country has potential in wind power generation particularly in the coastal areas, although there is still lack of reliable wind speed data. Bangladesh being an agrarian country produces enormous biomass energy which can be used to generate biogas for clean fuel for cooking and electricity for lighting in the rural areas. In spite of enormous potential biogas technology has not been well accepted due to initial expenditure of bio-gas plants.

In Dhaka Megacity, the application of solar PV systems on the bright roof-tops can generate more than 1,000 MW of electricity preferably through grid connected PV systems.

10.1. Favourable Geophysical Situations in Bangladesh

The geographical location of Bangladesh on the globe, space availability (land availability, available bright roof surface etc.), global horizontal irradiance (GHI), sunshine hours etc. have been identified as the geophysical situation. The receipt of solar radiation depends on the latitude of the area. The geographical location of Bangladesh (between 20034' and 26038' north latitude and between 88001' and 92041' east latitudes) lies in one of the best locations, which is well-supportive to capturing enough solar radiation for electricity generation (Islam, 2005; Hossain & Badr, 2005). Bangladesh is grouped as the first category with best location for PV systems. However, due to lack of financial and technological support, political commitment, it fails to exploit the abundant solar energy at the optimum level.

11.0. Renewable Energy Service Promotions and Supports by IDCOL in Bangladesh

Bangladesh government promotes and supports renewable energy; saving energy and GH emission reduction have been the goals. The legal framework for the support of the renewable energy sources of the country is Infrastructure Development Company Limited (IDCOL), a project of the World Bank Bangladesh. IDCOL is providing financial support, technological support to implement the RE projects in Bangladesh. GS, BRAC, Rahimaforz etc. get solar panel installation support from IDCOl Bangladesh.

Until 2010, IDCOL has installed nearly 450,000 home systems (mostly off-grid systems) through the partner organizations having a total installed capacity of nearly 25MW (IDCOL, 2014). Grameen Shakti leads the installation process providing more than 60% of the systems alone in Bangladesh. Solar home system normally used by the rural households consist of 4 florescent bulbs of 7 W each, 1 black-white TV of 15 W and a radio of 5W. One family using this small system can save yearly 290 litters of kerosene by using solar lighting technology and can prevent the emission of 0.76 ton CO_2 per year (SWERA/RERC, 32007). By installing 450,000 solar home systems all over Bangladesh can save 130 million litters of kerosene and 342,000 tons of CO_2 each year. It has been identified that there is a large power deficit in Bangladesh, but there is a large untapped solar energy potential (favourable geographical situation and geographical location on the globe, incidence of global horizontal irradiation, sunshine duration and day length, temperature, available bright roof tops) and the rising concerns of climate change (e.g. CO_2 emission reduction through clean energy, obligation to the UNFCCC and Kyoto Protocol).

Wide scale used RETs in Bangladesh are shown in the following Table 9

Table 9: Wide scale use of RETs (renewable Energy Technologies)

Technologies	Number of Units (by 2007)
Solar Home System	Above 1000,000
Improved biomass cooker	3000,000
Biogas plants	25,000
Biomass bracketing machines	100

Source: SWERA, 2010.

RETS technologies demonstrated in Bangladesh are solar water heaters, solar dryers, solar cookers, water lifting wind turbine, wind electricity generators, hybrid generators-solar wind/diesel, grid connected wind turbine, micro-hydro generator and LED lamps. IDCOL has invited proposals for developing a 1-2 MW solar panel assembly plant in Bangladesh.

12.0. Barriers to greater utilization of renewable energy technologies in Bangladesh

There are plenty of barriers hindering (as of 2007) widespread development of potential RETs in Bangladesh. The main barriers are lack of information among the public and policy makers about the renewable energy resources, technical/economic information about RETs; assembly of renewable energy technology components and equipment are currently limited and the high upfront cost at the end user level for renewable energy is a major barrier

The following results for CO_2 reduction have been found for various proposed applications of RETs.

Table 10: Potential for electricity generation from solar and Wind energy technologies and the scope of CO_2 mitigation by 2020

RET	Indicative Potential	In place of conventional generation using Grid	CO_2 reduction potential ($MtCO_2$/year)
Hydro electricity (existing (230 MW)	300 MW	Grid1.4	
Solar Home system	50 W, 2 million	Kerosene & Grid	1.5

Solar lights for the poor	10 w, 2 million	Kerosene	0.6
Wind Diesel hybrid micro grids	100 kW.300	Diesel genset	0.1
PV Diesel hybrid micro grids	100 kW. 300	Diesel	0.1
Wind electricity generation (minimum)	200 MW	Diesel genset	2.1
Grid connected PV (if grid is stable)	200MW	Grid	0.8
Total			6.6

Source: SEWRA, 2007

13.0. IDCOL's financing to various Renewable Energy Programmes in Bangladesh

SHS is a convenient mode of supply power for small electrical loads such as lights, radio, and black & white TV. The supply has proved to be reliable and the systems can be managed in rural areas with little training. The main components of an SHS are a solar panel, a battery, and a charge controller.

IDCOL starts its solar program in January 2003 with the support from International Development Association (IDA) and Global Environmental Facility (GEF) to fulfill basic electricity requirements in the rural areas of Bangladesh. IDCOL provides both grant and refinancing for 50,000 SHS over a period of five and –half years (January 2003-June 2008). The target was achieved in August 2006, three years ahead of the project completion period and US$2.0 million below estimated project cost of US$20 million. Therefore, the target was revised to finance a total of 200,000 SHSs by the year 2009 with additional support from the World Bank, GTZ and KFW (IDCOL, 2014).

Table 11: Progress with SHS's installation up to January 2007 PO wise installation of SHSs

Participating organization	Number of SHSs Installed
Grameen Shakti	61,309 *GS start its SHS distribution in 1997, before IDCOL support to GS. It is also supplying SHSs to people with its own resources.
BRAC foundation	22,115
Srizony Bangladesh	3,387
COAST Trust	1,270
TMSS	994
Centre for Mass Education and Science	1,263
Integrated Development Foundation	1,255
Shubashati	1,077
UBOMUS	1,620
BRIDGE	698
PMUK	61
RSF	1,600
PDBF	121
HF	139
Mukti Cox's Bazar	76
Other	77
Total	97,062

Source: SWERA 2007.

Many job opportunities created through SHS program. For example, through GS, 7,000 people have employed in Bangladesh.

Table-12: IDCOL Program Benefits (2014)

Program achievement:	3 million SHS
Number of beneficiaries:	13.5 million people

Power generation:	150 MW
Fossil fuel saving:	216,000 ton/yr
CO_2 reduction:	503,000 ton/yr
Job creation:	60,000
IDCOL investment:	USD$ 500 million

Source: IDCOL, 2014.

Solar powered irrigation system is an innovative, economic and environmentally friendly solution for the agro-based economy of Bangladesh. IDCOL has financed 38 NGOs and approved financing of additional 76 solar PV based submersible water pump in different locations of the country. IDCOL has a target to finance 1,550 pumps by 2016. IDCOL provides subsidy, soft loan and technical support to ensure effective implementation of the program. IDCOL also financed to NGOs for biomass gasification based power plants in Bangladesh.

IDCOL claims that through IDCOL more than 70,000 direct jobs created in Bangladesh. Due to SHSs, students now benefit from extended hours of studies at night in better lighting condition, small businesses enjoy extended operating hours and women feel more secured at night. The existing SHSs installed under the program reduces approximately 528,000 ton of CO_2 annually (IDCOL, 2014).

14.0. Grameen Shakti

Grameen Shakti is a non-profit organization established in 1996 to promote, develop and popularize renewable energy technologies in remote rural areas of Bangladesh. Currently, GS is one of the largest and fastest growing rural based renewable energy companies in the world. GS is also promoting Small Solar Home System to reach low income rural households. It enlighten houses by solar power, cook comfortably by bio-gas.

Table-13: Grameen Shakti Programs at a Glance as of February, 2015

Description	This Month	This Year	Since Inception
No. of Solar Home System	16,594	33,184	1,583,319
No. of Biogas Plants installed	279	556	30,847
No. of Improved Cooking Stoves	9,767	19,299	910,204
No. of Branches	0	0	1,245
No. of Persons trained	124	238	44,252

Grameen Shakti is providing loans to SHS receivers both GB borrowers and to the non-GB members. Till February 2015, GS has alone installed 1,583,319 solar home systems covering 64 districts in Bangladesh. It is working at the grass roots village level and selling SHS to villagers with credit who pay their SHS prices at an instalment basis over three years. For the solar PV installation, GS selects areas where there is no availability of conventional grid electricity or areas with low coverage by Rural Electrification Board (REB) or areas with almost no possibility of the extension of rural electrification within 5-10 years period.

Grameen Shakti is working not as a charity rather follows social business model. It has successfully blended technology with social market forces to develop a market- based approach to reach the rural people. It does not provide direct subsidies to RE users. It has developed an innovative micro-credit service model to RE users to reduce costs and to reach economy scale in Bangladesh.

14.1. Installations of SPV Systems by Grameen Shakti

Within a period of one and an half decade, it has been able to develop a large number (2500) trained technicians, (mostly women) and altogether 7,000 employees for preparing, installing and taking care of the home systems. It has targeted to empower 7.5 million people all over the country through renewable energy technologies (Grameen Shakti, 2009). It continues to provide solar home systems at a rate of

10,000 systems per month. The price of the SHS is still expensive for the rural poor (Hackett, 2009). The application of solar PV systems by GS until now includes mostly stand-alone PV systems, SHSs to run CFL lights, black and white television, mobile chargers, refrigerators for vaccine preservation etc.

Grameen Shakti SHSs is also used to light up homes, shops, fishing boats etc. Moreover, people also used to charge cellular phones, run televisions, radios and cassette players. People also use for operating TVs cassettes, audios, VCPs etc., operate small fans and amplifiers, running computers and cellular phones, and running DC motor driven equipments such as drill machines, soldering irons etc.

Fig. 2

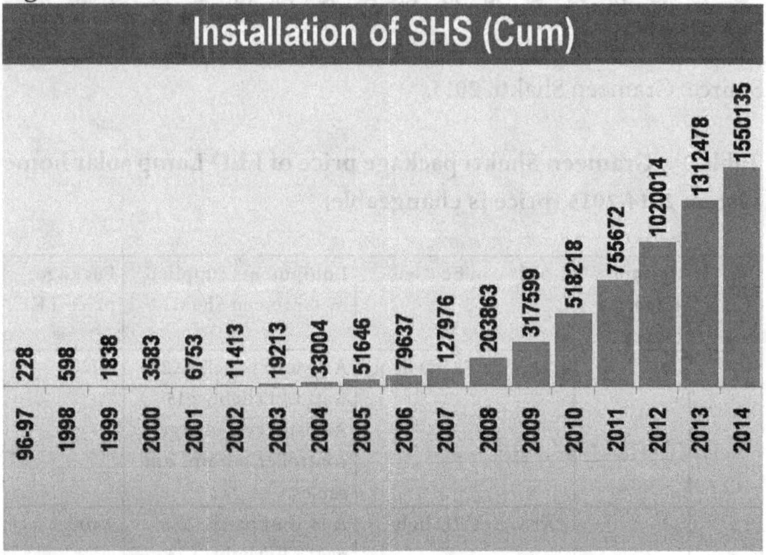

Source: Grameen Shakti, 2015.

Grameen Shakti SHSs users become the owner of an electric power generating and supply system. They do not need to pay monthly electricity bill in every month. SHSs life span is more than 20 years. There is no load shedding with SHSs. Moreover, this technology is clean, safe and is environmental friendly & health hazards free.

Fig-3

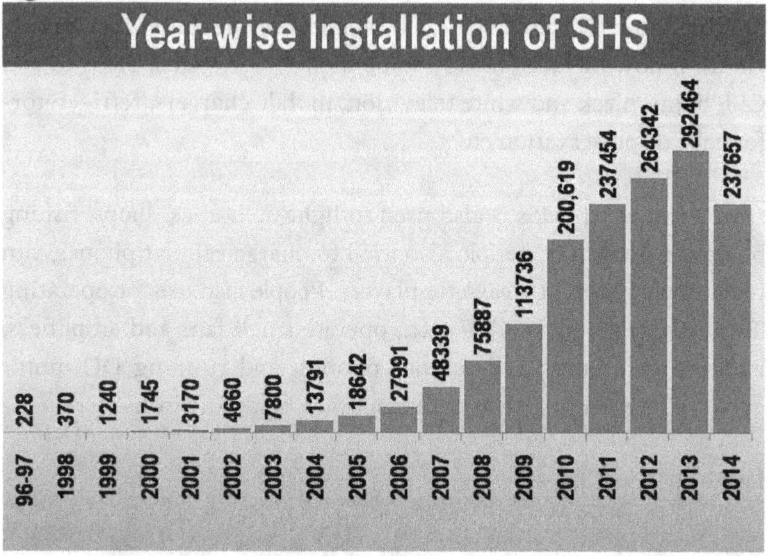

Source: Grameen Shakti, 2015.

Table-14: Grameen Shakti package price of LED Lamp solar home system 2014-2015 (price is changeable)

SL.	System Capacity (Watt)	Loads can be used	Equipments supplied by Grameen Shakti	Package price TK.
1	10	2X2.5 watt LED light	A 10 watt panel, 2X2.5 watt LED light, a 15 AH battery, a charge controller, a frame and cables	8,100
2	15	2X3 watt LED light	A 15 watt panel, 2X3 watt LED light, a 15 AH battery, a charge controller, a frame and cables	9,400
3	20	3X3 watt LED light	A 10 watt panel, 3X3 watt LED light, a 20/23 AH battery, a charge controller, a frame and cables	12,000

4	20	3X3 watt LED light	A 20 watt panel, 3X3 watt LED light, a 15 AH battery, a charge controller, a frame and cables	13,000
5	30	2x3 watt LD light and a 15" LCD/LED TV	A 10 watt panel, 2X2.5 watt LED light, a 30 AH battery, a charge controller, a frame and cables	15,500
6	40/42	3X3 watt LED light and a 15" LCD/ LED TV	A 10 watt panel, 2X2.5 watt LED light, a 40/45 AH battery, a charge controller, a frame and cables	22,000
7	50	4X3 watt LED light and a 15" LCD/ LED TV	A 50 watt panel, 4X3 watt LED light, a 55/60 AH battery, a charge controller, a frame and cables	27,100
8	60	5x3 watt LED light and a 15" LCD/ LED TV	A 60 watt panel, 5X3 watt LED light, a 60 AH battery, a charge controller, a frame and cables	30,600
9	63/65	5x3 watt LED light and a 15" LCD/ LED TV	A 63/65 watt panel, 5X3 watt LED light, a 70/80 AH battery, a charge controller, a frame and cables	31,600
10	75	6x3 watt LED light and a 12 watt fan and 15" LCD/LED TV	A 75 watt panel, 6X3 watt LED light, a 80 AH battery, a charge controller, a frame and cables	34,100
11	80	7x3 watt LED light, a 12 watt fan and a 15" LCD/LED TV	A 80 watt panel, 7X3 watt LED light, a 880 AH battery, a charge controller, a frame and cables	36,600

12	83/85	7x3 watt LED light, a 12 watt fan and a 15" LCD/LED TV	A 83/85 watt panel, 7X3 watt LED light, a 100 AH battery, a charge controller, a frame and cables	37,600
13	100	9x3 watt LED light, a 12 watt fan and a 15" LCD/LED TV and a 15" LCD/LED TV	A 100 watt panel, 9X3 watt LED light, a 100 AH battery, a charge controller, a frame and cables	41,600
14	130/135	7x3 watt LED light, two 12 watt fans and a 15" LCD/LED TV and a 15" LCD/ LED TV	A 130/135 watt panel, 7X3 watt LED light, a 130 AH battery, a charge controller, a frame and cables	46,100
Warranty for different parts off LED Solar Home system Solar Panel: 20 years LED Lamp; 3 years 15 AH Battery: 3 years Change Controller: 3 years				

Source: Grameen Shakti, 2015.

From the above list of Grameen Shakti's SHSs packages, the most popular demand are serial number 3, 4, and 5 items in Bangladesh.

GS has been successful in promoting and constructing both domestic and larger sizes biogas plants to rural villagers. GS Bio-gas Program has a unique financial mechanism based on credit, which makes bio-gas plants affordable to the villagers. People use cow dung in their bio-gas plants. Bio-gas technology can be also used with the home wastes. Grameen Shakti provides free services after sales including monthly visits by GS engineers for two to three years. People use slurry of bio-gas plant for organic fertilizer.

Bio-gas protects women and children from in-door air pollution and related diseases such as coughs, asthmas etc. It helps keep the environment clean and stops the spread of diseases by transforming pollutants into clean energy. It saves fire woods resulted stops deforestation.

Fig-3

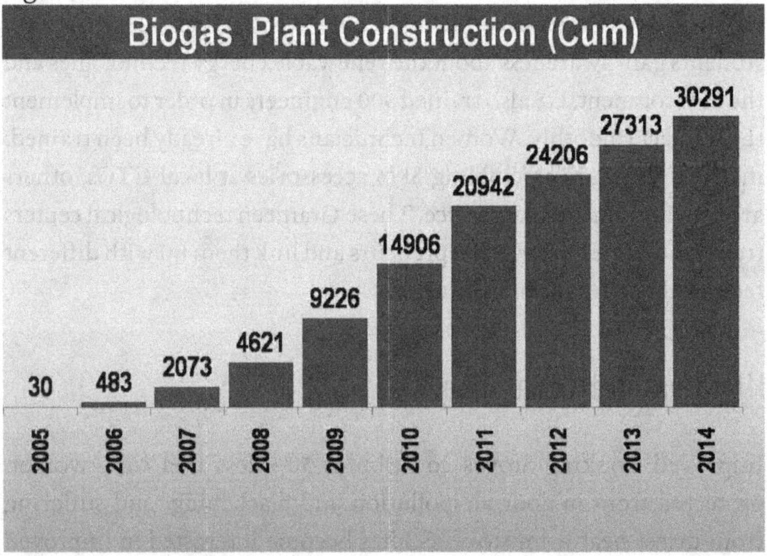

Source: Grameen Shakti, 2015

14.2. GS Wind Energy Program

GS is also working in the field of solar thermal project, but it is still in pilot stage. GS installed 4 hybrid power stations (combination of wind turbine and diesel generator) in four cyclone shelters of Grameen Bank in the coastal areas in Bangladesh (Grameen Shakti, 2015). The power generated from the wind turbines is connected to the four cyclone shelters located in the southern coastal belt of Bangladesh. Appliances powered with this system are light, fan, water pump etc.

14.3. Grameen Technology Centers

GS has set up 45 Grameen Technology Centers (GTCs) across Bangladesh. These GTCs are producing SHS accessories by manufacturing these locally. GTCs are also contributing to women empowerment by developing Solar Technicians in the villages.

Women members of 5000 SHSs user families are also trained on proper repair and maintenance of their systems. Besides these, 20,000 school students gain awareness about the renewable energy technologies and the environment. GS also trained 300 engineers in order to implement this project smoothly. Women technicians have already been trained, many of them are assembling SHS accessories at local GTCs, others are providing after sales service. These Grameen technological centers train renewable energy entrepreneurs and link them up with different technical and financial institutions.

14.6. GS Improved Cooking Stoves GS

Improved Cooking Stoves contributes 50% less fuel cost, women protected from in-door air pollution and blackening, and suffering from direct heat from stove. GS has become interested in improved cooking stoves (ICS) because it helps women and makes their lives easier. GS sees a potential market of at least 2 million ICSs in the first three years of the program.

Fig-4

Source: Grameen Shakti, 2015

14.7. Bio-fuels

India established the first biodiesel produce from Jatropha plant in Hyderabad of Andra Pradesh (GTZ, 2008). It is expected that at least 2.5 m. tons of biodiesel can be supplemented to the total demand of around 50 m. tons for Indian vehicles. Jatropha plant in the dry-arid part of the Indian State has promoted the local's income generation. Grameen Shakti has started to cultivate Jatropha on a plot basis in Dhaka in 2010, but it is yet not cultivate at mass scale.

14.8. Social Business and Nabin Udoykta Program of Grameen Shakti-

Social Business and Nabin Udoykta Program of Grameen Shakti is a new dimension in Bangladesh. All the activities of Grameen Shakti execute are fully related to social business perspective. It is a new category of cause-driven business. The social businrss concept is the company must cover all costs and make profit, at the same time achieve the social objective. In a social business, the investors/ owners can gradually recoup the money invested, but cannot take any dividend (profit) beyond that point. Grameen Shakti follows all seven principles of social business that Muhammadd Yunus has identified.

Grameen Shakti has been attached to 'Nobin Udyokta Program' of Yunus Center haka, a very promising project to bring new young entrepreneurs in the light. The children (2nd generation) of Grameen Bank Borrowers are included in the Grameen Shakti Nobeen Udyokta Prpogram. This project is piloting in Birulia, Ahshulia and Dhamshona Union of Savar Upazilla of Dhaka district. Till now (2014), six Nobin Udyokta projects have been presented at the Grameen Executive Design Lab Dhaka for approval of investing of Tk. 1.4 million. Four Nobin Udyokta have received Nine Hundred Thousand Taka till 2014. These projects include tailoring, textile business, telecom service, grocery shop, dairy farm etc. Rest of two projects is now in the process to be invested as early as possible. Moreover, more than 10 promising project are in pipe line to be presented in the Grameen Executive

Design Lab in near future. There is a plan to invest 50 million Taka among 250 Nobin Udyoktas across Bangladesh by 2015 (Grameen Shakti, April, 2015).

Table-26: Grameen Shakti Programs at a Glance February, 2015

Total Office	**1528**
Branch Office	1245
Grameen Technology Centre	34
ICS Production Center	67
D-Ionized Water Plant	1
Number of districts covered	Covered all districts
Number of Upazilas covered	508 Upazila
Number of villages covered	50,000 villages
Total beneficiaries	Around 17.67 million people
Total employees	11,230
Total installation of SHS	1,583,319
Total Number of Improved Cook Stove (ICS)	910,204
Total biogas plant constructed	30,847
Total installed power capacity	63.33 MWp
Daily power generation capacity	171.00 MW-hr
Installation rate	Over 20,000 SHSs/ month
Installation of micro utility systems	Over 9,605 system
Number of trained technicians (Mostly woman technicians)	22,822 technicians
Number of trained customers (Mostly woman)	839,725 users
Full Paid customer (ownership)	604,694 customers
User under maintenance agreement (After 3 Years)	44,759 customers
Future plan- total installation of SHS by 2015	2 million

Future plan- biogas plant construction by 2015	100,000
Future plan- Improved Cooking Stove construction by 2015	2 million
Green Jobs Creation by 2015	100,000

Source: Grameen Shakti, February, 2015

15.0. National Energy Policy

The first National Policy (NEP) of Bangladesh completed and gazetted in 1996 was adopted mainly with the aim of achieving sustainable economic growth and developing sufficient energy for different sectors (Islam & et al. 2006; Islam, 2005). The guidelines of the renewable energy were mentioned in the NEP. Later, the government adopted Private Power Generation Policy in order to promote private sector participation in power generation. In 1996, import duty and value added tax from solar PV and wind turbines were withdrawn by the government. In April 2004, Bangladesh Energy Regulatory Commission (BERC) was established and started functioning. The major objectives of the renewable energy policy mentioned in the NEP 2004 are targeted to provide energy for sustainable economic growth to meet the energy needs of different zones of the country, ensure environmentally sound sustainable energy development programmes causing minimum damage to environment, encourage public and private sector participation in the development and management of the energy sector, to bring entire country under electrification by the year 2020. Moreover this program ensures reliable supply of energy to the people at reasonable and affordable price and too develops a regional energy market for rational exchange of commercial energy to ensure energy security (MPEMR, 2004).

The Renewable Energy Program in Bangladesh has emphasized on the exploitation of solar, wind, biomass gasification, biogas and hydro energy. The major objectives of the renewable energy policy aim to exploit potential RES and disseminate RETs in the rural, semi-urban and urban areas; to inspire private sector investment in RE; to promote clear energy for CDM etc. The policy has targeted to develop RES to meet 5% of the total power demand by 2015 and 10% by the year 2020 (MPEMR, 2008).

16.0. Limitations of the study

The report contains secondary sources of statistical data collected from various organizations and web pages. For biogas plant installation, village cooperatives can be created to promote the technology among the villagers. Funds for renewable energy projects have to make available along with additional resources for innovative activities of RETs. However, the report does not discuss how renewable energy villages' cooperatives are working in Bangladesh. As the study conducted by the author with his own resources that was very limited, hence the primary data collection on renewable energy was not possible.

Many problems are suffering by the coastal energy users. Therefore, the community institutions could be engaged and financed for developing Wind Pump Energy infrastructure facilities around the coastal areas in Bangladesh. However, this study does not have detailed research on coastal areas renewable energy services in Bangladesh.

17. 0. Recommendations

RETs along with technologies for energy conservation and energy efficiency can help overcome energy shortages and lead the country to progress provided necessary steps are taken now without delays. Solar radiation is excellent for all locations of Bangladesh. Large scale utilization of solar and wind energy should help energy security in the face of impending energy crisis from dearth of conventional energy supply. Renewable energy public education could be included in the formal and non-formal adult education in Bangladesh. Ongoing SHS program should be strengthen to enable installation of 500,000 units by 2020.

The program for biogas project and biomass cooking improve stove can solve rural firewood cooking problems so these two technologies can be promoted through public extension agencies, and green NGOs in Bangladesh. The government sponsored Infrastructure Development Company (IDCOL) has to initiate financing (micro-credit) for solar home systems in the urban slums (like off-grid remote areas). In order to promote sustainable wind power generation, an efficient management system and strong coordination among the respective authorities have to be ensured in Bangladesh.

19.0. References

Alam, M.S., Kabir, E., Rahman, M. and Chowdhury, M.A.K. (2004). Power sector reform in Bangladesh: Electricity distribution system, *Energy*, Vol. 29, pp. 1773-1783

BBS (2006). *Bangladesh Statistical Year Book*, Bangladesh Bureau of Statistics, Planning Division, Ministry of Planning, Government of the People's Republic of Bangladesh, Dhaka

BPDB (2009). *Annual Report*, Bangladesh Power Development Board (BPDB), Dhaka

British Petroleum (2005). *BP Petroleum Review of World Energy*, BP, Plc.

Doman . E. (2004). Global Energy Use: Status and Trends, *Encyclopaedia of Energy*, pp. 11-21

Energy and Power (2009). Fiver Coal Fired Power Plants Planned, *Energy and Power*, a Fortnightly Magazine, Vol. 6 (24), July, Dhaka

Eusuf, M. (ed.) (2005). *Solar Photovoltaic Systems in Bangladesh: Experiences and Opportunities*, Dhaka: University Press Limited

Evans, A., Strezov, V. And Evan, T.J. (2008). Assessment of sustainability Indicators for Renewable Energy Technologies, *Renewable and Sustainable Energy Reviews*

SEWEA (2010). *Wind in Power: 2009 European Statistics*, The European Wind Energy Association (RWEA), Brussels, February.

Fadai, D. (2007).Utilization of Renewable Energy Sources for Power Generation in Iran, *Renewable and Sustainable Energy Reviews,* Vol. 11, pp. 173-181

Fathenakis, V. And Kim, H. C. (2009). Land use and electricity generation: a life-cycle analysis, *Renewable and Sustainable Energy Reviews,* Vol. 13 (6-7), pp. 1465-1474

Hackett, M. (2009). *Grameen Shakti Internship Report,* 5 November to 18 January, Submitted the University of Adelaide, South Australia

Haque, M. E. (2008). Achievement of DCL in promoting renewable energy technology in Bangladesh, Paper submitted at the *National Seminar on Renewable Energy* (Focus on Climate Change and Mitigation: Role of Renewable), Organized by the Renewable Energy Research Centre, University of Dhaka, 24-25 March

Hussain, A. and Badr, O. (2005). Prospects of Renewable Energy Utilization for electricity Generation in Bangladesh, *Renewable and Sustainable Energy Reviews,* Vol. 11 (8), pp. 1617-1649

IDCOL (2015). *IDCOl Updates.* Dhaka: IDCOL, February, 2015

IDCOl (2014). *IDCOL Annual Report 2013-2014.* Dhaka

IDCOL (2013). *IDCOL Newsletter.* Dhaka: Infrastructure Development Company Limited.

IDCOL and SNV (2006). *National Domestic Biogas and Manure Programme in Bangladesh: Implementation Plan,* Infrastructure Development Company Limited (IDCOL) and Netherlands Development Organization (SNV), Dhaka

IEA (2008). *Key World Energy Statistics, Communication and Information Office,* International Energy Agency, Paris, France

Islam A. K. M. S. and Islam, M. (2005). Status of Renewable Energy Technologies in Bangladesh, *ISESCO Science and Technology Review,* Vol. 1, pp. 21-60

Islam, K. (2005). Photovoltaic market potential in Bangladesh-Constraints, future potential diversification, in M. Eusuf (edited), *Solar Photovoltaic Systems in Bangladesh Experiences and Opportunities,* Dhaka; University Press Limited, pp. 75-84

Islam, N. (2005). Renewable Energy and government Policy in M. Eusuf (edited), *Solar Photovoltaic Systems in Bangladesh Experiences and opportunities,* Dhaka; University Press Limited, pp. 153-170

Grameen Shakti (2015). *Grameen Shakti update programs.* Dhaka: Grameen Shakti.

Kabir, . H. (2011). *Renewable energy as a perspective for power supply and greenhouse gas emission reduction in Bangladesh*, Department of Geography, Humboldt Universitat zu Berlin

Kabir, M. H., and Endlicher, W. (2010). *Analysis of the determining factors of solar PV applications in Dhaka Megacity, Bangladesh*, in Proceedings of the International Conference on Renewable Energy, June 26-July 2, 2010, Pacifico Yokohama, Japan

Kaltschmitt, M. and Wiese, A. (2007). Basics of Renewable Energy supply, in M. Kaltscmitt, W. Streicher and A. Wiese (edited). *Renewable Energy: Technology, Economics and Environment*: Springer, Berlin, pp. 23-29

Kabir, Humayun and Endlichrer, Wilfried (2012). *Exploitation of Renewable Energy in Bangladesh: Power supply and climate change protection perspective*, Dhaka: A.H. Development Publishing House

Kuhne, H. M. and Aulich, H. (1992). *Solar Energy System; Assessment of present and Future Potential*, Renewable Series, Butterworth-Heinemann Ltd.

MPEMR (2004). *National Energy Policy*, Ministry of power, energy and Mineral Resources, Government of the People's Republic in Bangladesh, Dhaka

MPEMR (2007). Renewable *Energy Policy of Bangladesh*, Power Division, Ministry of power, energy and Mineral Resources, Government of the People's Republic in Bangladesh, Dhaka

Power & Energy (2007). Renewable: Asian biogas technology: Steps towards Success, *Power and Energy*, a fortnightly magazine, Vol. 4(17), February 16-28

REN21 (2009). *Renewables Global Status Report: 2009 Update* (Paris: Renewable Energy Network for 21st Century Secretariat)

Rouf, K. A. (2015). Renewable energy context, scope, application and Green business of Grameen Shakti in Bangladesh, *Global Journal of Human-Social Science Research*, Vol. 5(3), Version 1.0, pp. 1-27

Schhaeffer, J. (2008). *Solar Living Source Book, 30th Anniversary* Special Edition, New Society Publishers, Canada

Sorensen, B. (2005). *Renewable energy: Its physical engineering, use,, environmental impacts, economy and planning aspects*, 3rd Edition, Elsevier Academic Press.

Stromsta, K. E. (2009). Bangladesh financing world Bank Loans Big Money to Small-scale Renewable Projects, *Recharge*, August 7,

Sufian, M. A. and Bala, B. K. (2006). Modeling of electricity energy recovery from urban solid waste system: The case of Dhaka City, *Renewable Energy*, Vol. 31, pp. 1573-1580

SWERA/UNEP (2010). *Analysis Tools: SWERA renewable energy explorer*, Retrieved May2010, Available at http://na.upep.net/swera-ims/masp2/

SWERA (2007). *Solar and wind energy resources assessment (SWERA)-Bangladesh final report 2007.* Dhaka: Renewable Energy Research Centre (RERC).

The Daily Ittefaq (2009). Government's new thoughts to mitigate water and electricity crisis, *The Daily Ittefaq*, 20 April, Dhaka

The Daily Star (2010). Kutubdia wind power plant under threat, *The Daily Star*, July 19, Dhaka

UNFCCC (2000*). National communications from parties included in Annex 1 to the convention: Greenhouse gas inventory data from 1990 to 1998.* FCCC/BI/2000/11, 5 September 2000, United Nations Framework Convention on Climate Change

Weiss, I., Sprau, P., Helm, P. (19980. The German PV market-an assessment and analysis of the German PV power systems market, presented at the *Second World Conference and Exhibition on PV solar energy conversion, Vienna*, July 1998.

Wengenmasyr, R. (2008). Hydroelectric power plants: Flowing energy in R. Wegenmayr and T. Buhrke (edited). *Renewable Energy: Sustainable Energy Concepts for the Future*, Weinheim, Germany: Wiley-VCH Verlag GmbH Co., pp. 22-25

World Watch Institute (2007). *State of the World 2007-Our Urban Future*, Washington DC.

Grameen Nabeen Uddugta (NU), new entrepreneur, social business education and service in Bangladesh

Abstract

I conducted a post-doc research on the Grameen Bank Nabben Uddugta (NU,) new entrepreneur, social business equity funding (NUSBEF) project, and its impact on second-generation of GB borrowers in Bangladesh in 2014-2015; and I write this preliminary report on the Grameen NUSBEF program attached with the Faculty of Environment, York University and with York Center for Asian Research, Canada.

The purpose of this empirical policy research is to explore the policies, procedures, and strategies of this new social business equity funding project of the Grameen sister organizations, and to identify challenges facing second-generation of GB borrowers in running their small social businesses in Bangladesh. The study examines whether second-generation of GB borrowers participate in family and community green enterprises in a more egalitarian way than their parents; examine whether they are involved in recycling/repairing green businesses as an alternative to consumer credit; are they advocate for the Sixteen Decisions of GB (a holistic socioeconomic and environmental messages) for alleviating rural unemployment and social injustice, and for other social issues. The study also intends to look at whether these borrowers encourage their neighbouring unemployed young to be involved in small business in order to address these social issues in Bangladesh.

The research findings would help the Yunus Center social business design lab and the social business equity funding implementing agencies Grameen Bank and Grameen sister organizations to improve the social business funding program for better services to second-generation borrowers of Grameen Bank in Bangladesh. The research generates a new knowledge of social and green financing, and social and green-enterprise development that could be used by social and community green-financing organizations elsewhere in the world. The findings of the research has shared with Grameen Bank, the later being the Grameen sister organizations' executive.

Key words: Grameen Bank; equity funding; new entrepreneur, social business.

1. Introduction

Grameen Bank (GB) has been implementing group-based micro-credit service in Bangladesh since 1976; however, it introduced micro-enterprise loans (Nabeen Udduk (NU) Reen (loan)) for fast-moving borrowers of Grameen Bank as well as second-generation of GB borrowers in Bangladesh in 1999. Grameen Bank Nabben Uddugta social business funding program initiated in 2008. During Kazi Rouf's PhD research data collection in Grameen Bank (GB) in 2010, he found that 12% of GB borrowers had received micro-enterprise loans (loans larger than the GB micro-credit) from GB. This GB micro-enterprise loan size ranges from USD $400 to USD $8000. With micro-enterprise loans, fast-moving GB borrowers and their children get involved in micro-enterprise businesses in Bangladesh. This loan is also attracting them to engage in medium-size businesses in Bangladesh. After completing their higher education, many second-generation children of GB borrowers start businesses. Some of them take over their parents' businesses.

The NU social business loan/funding project is designed by the Yunus Center Social Business Design Lab and this project is implementing by the Grameen sister organizations in Bangladesh. Now the grameen NU social business equity funding project has been piloting in Bangladesh by Yunus Center since 2013.

Muhammed Yunus resigned from Grameen Bank in 2010, but he carries the idea of the Nabeen Uddugta social business loan with him, and he has been piloting the Nabeen Uddugta social business equity funding (NUSBEF) program through the Yunus Center and the Grameen sister organizations, the later of which are a little different from GB. Muhammed Yunus is piloting this new social business equity funding investment project through Grameen sister organizations. The Yunus Center and the Grameen sister organizations that oversee the NUSBEF investing program are: Grameen Shakti Samajic Babsah, Grameen Telecom Trust, Grameen Kallyan, and Grameen Trust. These Grameen sister organizations are implementing the NU social business equity funding program in Bangladesh in addition to performing their own jobs. NUSBEF is a partnership equity funding programs between the investing Grameen sister organizations and the Nabeen Uddugta (NU), new entrepreneur, receiving the investment funds. They are using the Yunus Center Social Business Design Lab guidelines and formats in implementing the NU social business equity financing program in Bangladesh.

Yunus Centre has been organizing monthly social business workshops/seminars and giving NU social business funds to NUs through the Grameen sister organizations in Bangladesh. Table-1 contains information on social business equity investment funding to NUs by Grameen sister organizations, apart from Grameen Bank, in Bangladesh.

Table 1: Grameen sister organizations providing investment funding to NUs

Investing Grameen sister organizations	Male NUs receiving NUSBEF	Female NUs receiving NUSBEF	Total	%
Grameen Trust	521	11	532	26
Grameen Kallyan	128	10	138	7
Grameen Telecom Trust	591	11	602	29
Grameen Shakti Samajik Babsha	756	40	796	38
Total	1996	72	2068	100

2. Objectives of the Study

1. To know the policies and strategies of GB micro-enterprise loans and incentives provided to second-generation clients of GB by this new loan product
2. To explore differences among GB micro-credit, micro-enterprise loans and social business loans.
3. To examine the business performance status of second-generation borrowers compared to first-generation GB borrowers and to know their motives in encouraging and coaching neighbouring poor children for schooling.
4. To discover challenges faced by second-generation borrowers in managing/running their businesses.

2.1 Specific Objectives

2.1.1 To discern motivations of second-generation clients of GB to be involved in micro-enterprises

2.1.2 To see if these new entrepreneurs are aware of and work for community issues like the practice of dowries, teenage marriage, school drop-out in child education, and concerns for public security, water pollution, rural sewage, dying rural artisan products, marketing problems, and helping neighbouring disaster victims.

3. Research Questions

1. What are the policies, strategies, terms and conditions of GB micro-enterprise and social business equity funding that is applicable for the recipients?
2. What incentive is GB providing to second-generation clients?
3. How are second-generation clients of GB motivated to pursue social business loans and to get involved in micro-enterprises and in social business?
4. How do second-generation businesses perform compared to first-generation GB-borrowing businesses?
5. Do GB graduated borrowers and the children of GB borrowers encourage and coach neighbouring poor children for schooling; get involved in public well-being programs/services; develop local community-living economic values?
6. What are the challenges he/she faces in running his/her business in Bangladesh?

4. Significance of the Study

Working-age youth constitute 24% of the labour force in Bangladesh. However, unemployment rates among Bangladeshi youth (age 15-24) are 9.3% for females, 8.6% for males, and 8.9% overall (Asia Pacific Youth Employment Network, 2012). Therefore the Grameen young new-entrepreneur social business equity funding program is a very important one and essential for addressing the issue of unemployment in Bangladesh. Many young unemployed are receiving Grameen NU social business equity financing without mortgages from Grameen sister organizations very easily and becoming self-employed. Moreover, NUs are hiring their neighbourhood unemployed youth to work in their businesses. Although the Yunus Center social business equity investment program for unemployed youth entrepreneurs has started recently (2013) as a pilot scheme in Bangladesh, this program has huge scope in Bangladesh. Thousands of unemployed youth have benefited and self-employed through this program. The success of the NU social business investment program would be a model for youth entrepreneurship development in Bangladesh and in other parts of the world.

By the end of 2015, 2068 second-generation Grameen Bank new entrepreneurs received social business equity funding financed by Yunus Cente social business design lab, Dhaka. These new entrepreneurs have pursued social business by receiving social business equity funding averaging USD$470 from Grameen sister organizations that mentioned above. In addition, Yunus Center organized social business development seminars and workshops for the new prospective entrepreneur and on-going entrepreneurs who have able to expose about grameen social business equity funding services. Moreover, Yunus Center social business design lab also providing information to NUs about prospective businesses in their areas. The whole process assesses NU's capability and capacity to run business, find out local business initiatives, build confidence of the NUs, assist entrepreneurs to get new business ideas and develop a business plan. The workshop and seminar instil awareness of market information and the business safety net, strengthen NUs' management skills, and link them with other similar business initiators to identify business and financial challenges and learn how to minimize business and financial risk and recover from attendant losses. NU also receive post–loan services like post-business counseling srvices, business mentoring and business management training etc. from Yunus Center social business design lab (Yunus Center, 2015).

This research attempted to explore policies and strategies of the GB equity fiunding loan program (NU social business equity loan program), identify problems/challenges that NUs are facing and discover their needs. The study explores status of their businesses in Bangladesh as well as discerns whether Grameen micro-entrepreneurs need further support services to improve their social businesses in Bangladesh. Studying this Grameen NU social equity funding loan program could assist NU, GB, grameen sister organizations and the Yunus social business design lab to improve these two programs and their strategies. The study would assist micro-enterprise loan receivers of GB borrowers and the social business equity loan receivers of the second-generation borrowers of GB to get better support service to run and expand their business. This research could provide lessons helpful to other micro-credit institutions (MFI) in Bangladesh and elsewhere. This work also helps the academicians' future research in equity financing project development.

Although many studies have been conducted on the impact of Grameen Bank general loans in Bangladesh, there is no study on GB micro-enterprise loans and the Grameen NU social business equity funding program. The study identified problems for the first time. The social business equity funding agencies of Grameen sister organizations can be benefitted from the study. They (implementing agencies) could think about the problems and challenges that are facing by NUs.

5. Methodological approach of the study

I developed a questionnaire to collect data using a survey method. A questionnaire containing open-ended and structured questions designed to collect data from randomly selected beneficiaries through face-to- face interviews in Bangladesh. Then beneficiaries (respondents) randomly selected from each selected grameen sister organizations-Grameen Kallayan, Grameen Shakti Samajik Babsha, Grameen Telecom Trust, Grameen Trust and Yunus Center. Moreover, I used participatory observation, literature review, institutional ethnography (organizational manuals, policies, and text analysis) methods for this study. I visited Grameen Bank, Grameen sister organizations and Yunus Center to collect relevant data from second-generation

GB micro-entrepreneurs and NU social business equity investment partners. I also attended five workshops of the Yunus Center social business design lab in Bangladesh and gathered six clients' stories and collected information on grameen sister organizations' institutional legal structures, operational context, their funding models, operational strategies, procedures, and the challenges they are facing. Moreover, I maintained a diary when I was collecting primary information from the participants and take field notes to record interviewees' main ideas and find secondary data from Grameen web pages and Grameen annual reports.

5.1 Time table and duration

I began this research in July 2014 supoorted by Professor Ellie Perkins, Faculty of Environment Studies, York University. The data collection and data processing completed in December 2015. Then process data, analyse data, write this paper with my own resources and share research findings with grameen executives and Faculty of Environmental Studies, York University. This research has accepted to present the findings at the Comparative International Educational Society (CIES) Conference held in Vancouver in 2016. I presented this research at the York Center for Asian Research (YCAR), and Social Economic Center, University of Toronto.

6. Screening process to deliver Grameen social business funds to NUs in Bangladesh

The field workers of the Grameen sister organization visits young rural unemployed and finds potential new entrepreneurs (NUs). The field workers discuss the Grameen social business equity investment partnership opportunity with the NUs. They share Yunus Center Social Business Design Lab guidelines and procedures of the grameen equity investment partnership program with NUs. The field workers discuss this information with the local potential NU through one-on-one counselling as well as workshops and seminars in the village. They evaluate the potential NUs' business potentials following the Yunus Center Design Lab screening process. The potential NUs also share their business ideas with the Grameen field workers.

The field workers prepare a list of the potential NUs and their rough business ideas, and sends the list to the Dhaka head office of the respective Grameen sister organization. Then the business analyst of the sister organization calls each potential NUs to refine their business proposals and present their business plans at the Dhaka Yunus Center Design Lab Workshop. The business analyst and potential NUs together develop the business equity partnership investment plan and write all the information in the prescribed form. The screened business proposals are submitted to the Yunus Center Social Business Design Lab Workshop for review and approval.

6.1 Yunus Center Social business design lab workshop participants

Grameen social business for Nabeen Uddugta (NU) is a new concept and its practice is also new style equity funding which just recently beginning in Bangladesh designed by Yunus Center Social Business Design Lab. Prospective NU is the second generation of GB borrower's unemployed rural youth in Bangladesh. Prospective NU participants for the Yunus social business design lab workshops are: business people, social business practitioners, potential investors/ entrepreneurs, the donor community, academics, innovators, social workers, NGO personnel, philanthropists and young entrepreneurs although the workshops are mainly for NUs.

6.2 Yunus Center social business design lab workshop and procedures for the disbursement of social business funds to young new entrepreneurs

The Yunus Center social business design lab is structured to enable brainstorming, and to train and involve its participants in social business. In this process, many new ideas are generated in the workshops, and they assist attending participants in using these ideas in their businesses. People from different backgrounds also join in this program to learn about social business and brainstorm on potential social business ideas. This workshop brainstorms to develop social business ideas into real-world companies, generates awareness and provides training about social business, creates linkages between investors and entrepreneurs of social business and allows informative exchanges about successful social business projects. As of 21 December 2015, one hundred and sixty-five participants from national and international organizations with diverse background attended the Yunus Center social business executive workshop program, including a large number of international participants (Yunus Center, 2015).

The Yunus Center Social Business Design Lab is a meeting-place for people of diverse backgrounds having the same goal: developing social business for the betterment of society. It is a half-day-long program for people who are interested in social business. The prospective NUs present their business proposals at the Yunus Center Social Business Design Lab Workshops held in Dhaka.

6.3 Grameen social business workshops/seminars are using the popular education learning method

Yunus Center social business design lab workshops and seminars follow popular education learning styles. The workshops and seminars use power points, videos, popular songs/music, jocks/ funs and films. Moreover, workshop facilitators facilitate group discussions that enhance two ways interactions of communications among workshop participants. Grameen social business design lab workshops/seminars encourage discussion that follows democratic way of discussion among the attended workshop participants. Facilitators of the workshops focus on NUs business issues they are facing and struggling with; they respect NUs' voices and choices, values and their local business cultures. Grameen social business equity funding scheme beliefs and prefers NUs short-term and long-term goals and visions. Each Grameen social business workshop has an agenda that is prepared according to need of the NUs need. NUs show their business products and their handicraft products in the workshop and in the Annual Social Business Day in Dhaka. NUs social businesses promote local handicrafts, local living economy, solidarity economics, agricultural businesses, and neighbourhood community economy in rural Bangladesh. Moreover, NUs discuss their family members' lending contribution to the business. They also report in the workshops how their family members informally share their time to run their businesses and how many employees will work in their social businesses.

As mentioned earlier, the Yunus Center Social Business education follows adult learning strategies and use popular education tools. Here family members are informally voluntarily working together to run NUs businesses; they (family members) distribute their time and labour where all family members share their effort to success the business. It is like diverse economic practice where family members of NUs contribute their time for their businesses. It is like household gift economy sharing unpaid work. The family members contribute their time for free, but ultimately they receive the benefits (food, housing, clothing etc.) of the businesses.

Popular education is an education of, for and by the people. It is an education as a practice (or praxis) of freedom. Grameen social business education program is following the popular education approach where NUs and workshop participants engage each other and the educator as co-learners to critically reflect on the issues in their community and then take action to change them. Popular education is understood to be popular, as distinct from merely populist, in the sense that: it is rooted in the real interests and struggles of disadvantaged people. It is overtly political and critical of the status quo. Grameen social business education program is committed to progressive social and political change because Grameen social business popular education program is based on a clear analysis of the nature of present profit making business inequality, exploitation and oppression and is informed by an equally clear political purpose. This has everything to do with the struggle for a more just and egalitarian social order among disadanataged NUs. The process of popular education has the following general characteristics:

- Its curriculum comes out of the concrete experience and material interests of people in communities of resistance and struggle
- Its pedagogy is collective, focused primarily on group as distinct from individual learning and development
- It attempts, wherever possible, to forge a direct link between education and social action.

According to Paulo Freire (1994) popular education is an educational approach that collectively and critically examines everyday experiences and raises consciousness for organizing and movement building, acting on injustices with a political vision in the interests of the most marginalized. Popular education requires the 'learners' to define what they need in order to learn. Lessons are not dictated by a teacher or leader based on what they know or what they think is important (Nadeau, 1996). Grameen social business workshops are popular adult education learning tool that is non-hierarchical between NUs and other workshop business reviwers. The boundaries between NUs' learners and workshop trainers are intentionally blurred, with each teaching the other according to their personal skills, knowledge, and lived realities in order to develop business skills. Grameen social business popular education also defined as a technique designed to raise the consciousness of its participants and to allow them to become more aware of how personal experiences are connected to small business problems and larger societal problems. It has the potential to empower NUs to collectively organize to change business issues affecting their lives. The key components to Grameen social business popular education are:

- Understanding that learning starts with what is important in the lives of the participants;
- Understanding that social business learning is a process that names and addresses small business power imbalances in the business world and empower NUs to be in the collective business group for changing the profit maximizing business ethos; and
- Understanding that the main goal of Grameen social business education is to create a positive business environment for NUs in order for social change.

The term popular education conveys what each body of literature has in common: a concern for an education that serves the interests of 'ordinary' people, as perceived by 'ordinary' people. There is an assumption of a conflict between the interests of big business groups as a ruling dominant class in one hand and the interests of small business ordinary people and grassroots community groups on the other hand. The notion of 'popular' refers less to the idea of education for the people interested in education for the people and more to the idea of education by the people and with the people. It did not foster learning that questioned the status quo. Grameen social business workshops, seminars and training services are following the popular education learning style and its different features/components of coaching by the Yunus Center social business learning program.

According to Denise Nadeau (1996), popular education refers to the marginalized and exploited people's education for improving the conditions of the poor and oppressed. It is a democratic and participatory leaning. Some scholars regarded it project-based learning for uplift the bottom people. It is a community work that prefers local values placed on facilitating learning through skilled conversation. Grameen social business adult education using popular education methods identify social business problems/challenges and work for solving social business problems that exist in the community. Grammen social business equity funding is a program that has designed for the disadvantaged poor entrepreneurs in Bangladesh. The Grameen social business entrepreneurs' workshops are not only orient those (NUs) about business management and business plan, but also exposed them, orient them on to how marginalised NUs could overcome their family business struggle, small business economic struggle, sweet equity funding struggle for starting or running business following the popular education model. Because Grameen social popular business education is an approach that critically examines and learns from the lessons of NUs past business struggles and from concrete everyday business situations in the present. It is a deeply democratic process; equipping NUs' communities to themselves name and create the vision of the alternatives they are struggling for. Grameen social business equity funding workshop and training program respect NUs' knowledge and values. Moreover, the facilitators respect NUs business experiences and expertise. They (workshop facilitators) also pay attention and listen to their challenges that NUs are suffering from. It equips NUs to define their own struggles and to make their voices heard. It involves a process whereby the NUs could collectively pursue their problems and build networking among them although they do business individually. Moreover, they could collectively (family members) solve their business problems including identifying the resources, and skills they need. Grameen social business popular learning process develops within the process the consciousness of and commitment to the interests of the marginalised NUs as part of their struggle.

However Grameen social business scheme believes that women and men at the community and grassroots level are the primary agents for social change. John Dewey, a famous American education scholar, highlighted popular education is an education that the challenge of education for a better 'life'. He says, "To prepare him for future life means to give him command of himself: ... so that he will have the full and ready use of all his capacities (Dewey 1966, p. 27). Grameen Social Business Design Lab beliefs that NUs have sufficient knowledge/skills on their own that they can work out the solutions to their business problems. So M. yunus believs NUs no need formal business training diploma for receiving Grameen social business NU equity funding. However, I do not agree with this Grameen social business design lab notion of NUs have pre-business enough business management knowledge like proper business record keepings and business networking among them because many NUs reported during my data collection that they need business financial management skills and trade skills for running their businesses well. Anyway Grameen social business brings rural new entrepreneurs ongoing consciousness-raising about the necessity of unemployed NUs to initiate social business in rural areas in Bangladesh.

Grameen social business project intends to promote social purpose community beneficial business that address the issue of youth unemployment, lack of business capital and lack connections/networks among marginalised youth entrepreneurs in Bangladesh. Yunus Center Social Business Design Lab facilitates business network among the grameen new entrepreneurs. Because the motive of the Grameen social business equity funding program is to empower poor unemployed youth to be successful in their business by their own efforts as well as interactions and exchange of business ideas among them; and they become to be a role model entrepreneurs in their locality that ultimately could impacted their economic uplift and social change for the marginalized business people in Bangladesh.

6.4. System of approval of the Grameen social business equity funding to NU

Business analysts and executives of Grameen sister organizations attend the Yunus Center social business design lab workshop in order to organize and facilitate the workshop for NUs. They (grameen sister organizations' business analysts and executives) review the NUs submitted business proposals in the workshops. After reviewing the business proposals in the workshops, the business equity financings are approved in the workshop right away. The NUs receive business funding immediately after approval of the business proposals. If any business plan does not satisfy the review team, the NU could resubmit his/her revised business proposal at the next workshop.

Table 4: Year- wise Grameen Bank and Grameen social business design lab funding to NUs

Year	NUL distribution agency names	Funds to NUs	%
2008-2012	Grameen Bank (GB)*	2500	49%
2013	Yunus Center and Grameen sister organizations	66	1%
2014	Yunus Center and Grameen sister organizations	462	9%
2015	Yunus Center and Grameen sister organizations	2068	41%
Total	Grameen Bank, Yunus Center and Grameen sister organizations	5096	100%

*Grameen Bank is disbursing NU micro-enterprise loans with its own channel which is different than the Yunus center social business design lab and Grameen sister organizations social business equity funding implementation strategy.

7.0. Meaning of social business and Nabben Uddugta (NU) social business

According to Muhammed Yunus, a social business is a non-dividend company dedicated entirely to achieving a social goal. In social business, the investor gets his/her investment money back over time, but never receives dividends beyond that amount. The sole purpose of the business is to solve a predetermined social problem in a sustainable way. A social business operates in a free market like a profit-making business, but the goal of a social business, rather than for profit maximization, is to overcome poverty and attain financial and economic sustainability, and while the investor gets back his or her investment amount, no dividend is given beyond the investment money. The workforce gets a market wage with better working conditions and the investee does business with joy. Many academicians use the term social enterprise which is similar to social business. Social entrepreneurs are influencing the regulatory and investment environments to hold businesses more accountable to their social and environmental performance and to support social enterprises. They reflect enlightened human values (Jack, Mook, & Armastrong 2009; and Yunus, 2015).

Entrepreneurs are special people, they don't talk about starting a business, rather they do it (Cook, 1986). Deepak Chopra said that there are moments in life when the door opens and lets the future in. Tim Moore (2005) mentions his lessons learned from his businesses are: Early failure can be overcome, accept help from others when it is offered, once he discovers that he was good at something, he works hard to develop those talents. Sometimes he has to go with his 'gut' instincts when making decisions. More advises business people learn to motivate him and others. Im Moore mentions in his book that when starting out a business; price the product or service below that of the neighbouring competition. Moreover he mentions, "Find a marketing hook to distinguish business person from the competition; provide top notch customer service, invest some of the money in a secondary area and know when it is time to change direction and do not bleed the company coffers dry" (Moore, 2005, p. 25).

Entrepreneur need to be prepared to accept the consequences of his actions. There is always a solution, even to what seems like an insurmountable problem. Personal attributions are important of a successful entrepreneur. The essential attributes are: Self confidence, optimism, positive attitude and enthusiasm, determination/tendency and toughness, passion, self-reliance, a strong work ethic, assertiveness and an ability to motivate others, integrity to business, respect to others, humility, and imagination. Tim Moore asserts the following professional attributes could assist entrepreneur to be a successful entrepreneur:

- A willingness to take risks;
- A sense of urgency;
- Good communication skills; and
- Have a vision and excellent aptitude.

Tim Moore (2005) advises to entrepreneurs from his long day business experience that an entrepreneur must remain steadfast. Moreover, he finds in his experience that being able to remain positive and confident during the difficult times is the difference between success and failure. According to him if anyone wants to be a successful entrepreneur, he must looks, sounds, and acts in a confident manner at all times.

An entrepreneur should be capable of analyzing himself or herself. He or she must know his or her strengths and weaknesses and then build upon the strengths and closely monitor or avoid the weaknesses. He must be able to cope with stress, meet payrolls, satisfy customers and creditors, and generally make things happen. An entrepreneur must have a strong desire to succeed, to work hard and smart, overcome obstacle, and make money. The advantages of self-employment are limitless. It is an opportunity to be freedom, and to be creative. It is about doing one's own thing. Of course, there are constraints and restraints in the business, but less so than those which exist for an employee. At some point, income from self-employment can easily exceed that of a very senior employee.

Social enterprises are revenue-generating businesses with twist- social and economic objectives following capitalism.A social enterprise has two goals: (1) to achieve social, cultural, community economic and environmental outcomes; and (2) to earn revenue. Social enterprises are businesses whose primary purpose is the common good. The social entrepreneurs use methods and disciplines and the power of the marketplace to advance their social, environmental and human justice agendas. Yunus's social business promotes the same objective that is in line with community-beneficial businesses in USA and the Community Investment Corporations (CIC) that is UK based. The social business accelerates the process of poverty eradication to an unthinkable pace using the same market mechanism which accelerated global prosperity for the rich in the first place (Yunus, 2015).

7.1. Is Grameen social business equity funding following sweat equity system?

The answer is yes. A NU puts his/her labour and time in the business and his effort that also contributes to his business consider as business equity. Grameen social business equity considers NU's experience as an asset of his business. NU business equity usually his pre-existing business products, current shop and business assets like machines, fridge, electricity facilities value, car, van, truck etc. that are used in the business.

Sweat equity is a party's contribution to a project in the form of effort and toil, as opposed to financial equity such as paying others to perform the task. Sweat equity has also an application in social business, for example, the owner of social business put his effort and toil to build his business. An auto owner puts his own efforts and toils in his auto-mobile business to increase the value of the vehicle in a sweat equity auto business. Moreover, the term sweat equity explains the fact that value added to someone's own house by unpaid work results in measurable market rate value increase in house price. The more labour applied to the home, and the greater the resultant increase in value; the more sweat equity has been used. Sweat equity usually used in the real estate business or house ownership business where house owner work himself in the constriction of the house for the real estate business company. The real estate counts his/her labour wage as an equity value of the house value. Moreover, sweat equity is used to describe the non-financial investment that people contribute to the development of a project such as a start-up business. For example, sweat equity is counted from the founders of the company, as well as advisors and board members. In many situations where some members of a partnership are contributing their money and others are spending time; here partnership composed of cash and non-cash sweat equity. Sweat equity is rewarded the same as cash equity through a distribution of stock or other forms of equity in a start-up business. Sweat equity is important to the successful start-up of a new social business, especially when cash is in short supply. However, it is essential to value sweat equity vigilantly.

Moreover, it needs to be careful and aware that in early stages of a business, it is easy to overvalue it, offering stock in exchange for effort. However, over time, such business could become very expensive and erode the equity available to follow-on investors. Sweat equity should be measured in terms of the long term value of the effort, the long term commitment of the entrepreneurs, and the value-added by the social business entrepreneurs to the overall goals of the social business. Sweat equity can also be considered factual and truthful. For example, a homeowner may spend time fixing, repairing, and renovating their home. The value of their efforts is considered sweat equity and adds to the value of the home.

Recently sweat equity has been used to describe a party's contribution to a project in the form of effort- as opposed to financial equity, which is a contribution in the form of capital. In a partnership, some partners may contribute to the firm only capital and others only as sweat equity. Sweat equity can be called 'stock for services' and sometimes 'equity compensation'. This type of equity for service programs involving patent lawyers and securities lawyers who specialize in start-up companies as clients.

Grameen sister organizations do not add their service cost in a monetary value in the NU social business equity partnership funding rather they charge five percent investment service charge for covering the grameen portion equity funding cost. The five percent service charge is popular to NUs. However, this five percent investment service charge by the grameen equity investing agencies is not covering their service costs. It may be a token charge at the pilot phase of the grameen social business equity funding. However, the NUs are very happy for grameen five percent service charge fee for maximum five years because it is very cheap for them in Bangladesh.

7.0. Uniqueness of the micro-enterprise and social business equity partnership loan (literature review)

The micro-enterprise program/service of GB is a people-centered development program that has multiplier effects among marginalized people (Anan, 2005; Bornstein & Davis, 2010; Dees, 2003; Gibbons, 1995; Goetz, 2001; Henry, 2006; Harris, 2002; Khandlker, 2005; Mahamud, 2004; and Yunus, 2010b; 2008). The second-generation of GB borrower gets involved in micro-enterprise business by using the Grameen social business equity funding (SBEF). The children of GB borrowers have taken up the opportunities offered by the Grameen micro-enterprise loan service and the Grameen social business equity partnership funding program, helping the marginalised GB second generation to become economic and social actors in their communities in Bangladesh (Yunus, 2010b). Now social scientists, leaders, philanthropists, academicians and researchers think capitalism has created poverty by focusing exclusively on profit for business. Capitalism creates a selfish civilization, instead of a human-valued civilization. Therefore, business should be dedicated to operating responsibly so that it could make a people's economy in society (Yunus, 2014). Such a type of social business program could be developed in North America to engage marginalised people in social businesses by providing business capital to entrepreneurs by financing institutions in North America and elsewhere.

Social business entrepreneurs are high achievers, highly motivated, leaders not followers and posses a lot of initiative, drive and energy. They do not have to set alarm clocks to wake up in the morning; they are usually so turned-on, so self-motivated, that they would wake up before the alarm anyway (cook, 1986). Entrepreneurs are true wealth creators in the society. They are people who are richly rewarded by providing new products or services that are wanted or needed by the customers (Cook, 1987). Entrepreneurs are those persons (business owners) who seek to generate value through the creation or expansion of economic activity by identifying value through the creation or expansion of economic activity by identifying and exploiting new products, processes or markets. Social entrepreneurship is a process that starts with a perceived social opportunity, translates it into enterprise concepts, ascertains, and acquires the resources necessary to execute the enterprise, launches and grows the enterprise and harvests the future upon attainment of the enterprise's goals. Social entrepreneurship can take many forms, begening from starting a business to expanding an organization, to pertaining with another firm.

Social entrepreneurship addresses social problems or needs that are unmet by private markets or governments. Social entrepreneurship creates innovative solutions to immediate social problems and mobilizes the ideas, capacities, resources and social arrangements required for sustainable social transformations (Smith, 2005). Social entrepreneurs are people who realize where there is an opportunity to satisfy some unmet need that the welfare state will not or cannot meet. Social enterprises are private organizations dedicated to solving social problems, serving the disadvantaged people, and providing socially important goods that were not, in their judgement, adequately provided by public agencies or private markets (Thompson et al., 2000). Social entrepreneurship is motivated primarily by social benefit. It is a multidimensional construct involving the expression of entrepreneuring virtuous behaviour to achieve a social mission.

Social entrepreneurial activity is enterprising human action in pursuit of the generation of value through the creation of expansion of social and economic activity by identifying and exploiting new products, processes or markets. Entrepreneurial capabilities, entrepreneurial culture and market conditions are certainly directly relevant to those actively engaged in business start-up. Research indicates that entrepreneurial individuals experience have many benefits including:

- Being three to four times more likely to start a business;
- Gaining valuable entrepreneurial skills such as business planning, networking and sales; which are valued by employers;
- Improving their chance of landing their dream businesses;
- Gaining knowledge to supplement their income;
- Social entrepreneurs have unlimited earnings potential; and
- Entrepreneurs are often motivated by the possibility of earning a higher income than the one they would traditionally earn as an employee.

Many society's problems today require entrepreneurial solutions. In fact, charity workers, nurses and social workers often need to think entrepreneurially in order to solve socio-economic problems of community. Therefore these people are sometimes referred to as social entrepreneurs.

Essentially, social entrepreneurs are:

- Ambitious people who are tackling major social issues;
- Mission-driven, because wealth creation is not as important to them as solving a problem;
- Strategic, because they act on opportunities others may not have seen;
- Resourceful, because they often have limited access to capital;
- Driven to produce results; and
- They seem to thrive on the enjoyment of being in business for them.

Entrepreneurship offers people the chance to be their own boss, make meaningful decision and answer to no one but themselves. Its independence also leads to flexibility in creating work schedules and goals. However, entrepreneurship is considered much riskier than traditional employment. Business owners often experience a high degree of anxiety and stress. They create a new enterprise out of nothing. They pioneer ventures where risk is high. According to George Gilder, a successful enterprise drives entrepreneurs to upward mobility. They have faith in business success, faith in future good and faith in the rising return of investment etc. These all are necessary to sustain the spirit of work and enterprise. These qualities only evolve after years of experience. Grameen´NUs are the opportunity seekers and winners (Yunus, 2016). These NUs think their needs are everybody`s needs. Grameen new entrepreneurs are innovative, breakthroughers, inventionists and their social products are thought to be the special talent of a few lucky individuals. NUs are successful entrepreneurs who can easily identify the market gap of their business products. Moreover, they discover of new or better products that fill up the local community market gap through their business in Banngladesh.

I worked in Grameen Bank and its other sister organizations in Bangladesh for three decades and I found that the different programs of Grameen Bank contributed to reducing poverty and promoting small entrepreneurship, coperativism and environmentalism in Bangladesh that admitted by David Bornstein and Susan Davis (2010). Yet, even though the Grameen micro-enterprise program and NU social business equity partnership investment program have been working since 2013 (for a few years), there is no research being conducted on these programs. During my study I find many poor entrepreneurs are still seeking micro-enterprise business capital and self-employment support services for their businesses. Grameen social business equity partnership capital to NUs is very essential in Bangladesh for their business start-up and social business expansion.

8.0. Findings

Grameen Bank micro-credit has been widely published in news media, electronic media, and social media. Many journals and books published on Grameen Bank activities. However, below this paper is talking about Grameen NU social business equity funding service survey findings that was conducted in Bangladesh in 2014-2015. Here below the Diagram-1 talks about differences among Grameen group-based micro-credit, Grameen micro-enterprise loans program and Grameen social business equity investment funding program.

Diagram-1: Differences among Grameen group-based micro-credit, Grameen micro-enterprise loans program and Grameen social business equity investment funding

Grameen group-based micro-credit and grameen micro-enterprise loan program	Yunus Center Grameen social business funding program

Grameen micro-credit is providing micro loan, but Grameen micro-enterprise loan (GMEL) is a bigger size loan than micro-credit. GMEL can be received by the fast moving Grameen Bank borrowers for manufacturing businesses, poultry/dairy farming, and for medium size business.	Children of GB borrower and rural unemployed youth (outside GB borrower) can receive Grameen social business funding on equity basis. Here social business fund receiver is an individual investment partner of the Grameen investing agency.
GB loans are for six months with 20% interest rate. Here there is no equity partnership between borrower of GB and GB. It is a group-based micro-financing program.	NU (new entrepreneur) receives business equity funding with five percent fixed interest rate for a period of maximum five years. NU and Grameen investing agency are joint partners of the businesses on equity basis.
A diminishing method uses for calculating interest rate- interest is calculated on the outstanding loan amount.	Five percent interest is not on annual basis; rather five percent interest is on the disbursed loan for five years
Borrower of GB needs to repay his/her loan at the weekly center meeting every week.	NU repays his/her instalments of the loan every three months or agreed terms and conditions. He/she does not need to attend weekly meeting for repaying his/her loan
Grameen borrower can receive housing loan, student loan for his/her children's higher education	NU receives equity funding for business purpose only. NU can become the owner of the business property after repaying his portion of loan and interest.
Here loan proposal is done informal way	NU need formally submit and present his/her business equity proposal to Yunus center social business design lab
No mortgage required	NU must enter into business equity partnership
No need to sign loan documents in the non-judicial stamp by GB micro-borrower.	NU must sign memorandam of understating (MOU) of the business equity partnership document in the non-judicial stamp
Grameen micro-credit and GB micro enterprise loan have been available in Bangladesh for more than three decades. It is a regular national program in Bangladesh.	Grameen NU social business equity funding is a pilot project initiated by Yunus Center and implemented by Grameen sister organizations in Bangladesh for only three years to date.

Grameen new entrepreneurs are involved in diversified businesses in Bangladesh. They are involved in setup IT centers, community information centers, sports/music/theatre clubs, web-page designing and multimedia studios businesses. Even they engage in businesses like poultry and livestock farming, poultry feed manufacturing and selling, fisheries, equipment leasing, garments manufacturing and marketing, and the manufacturing of leather and ceramic products. Second-generation of GB borrowers run businesses that have promoted much public good, local living economics and social business in villages in Bangladesh. This progressive Grameen equity financial program keeps youth in rural social businesses, reducing the tendency of losing them to urban migration.

Below Table-2 shows types of business owned by the new entrepreneurs (NUs), and the second-generation of GB borrowers' who are the receivers of grameen social business equity funding services in Bangladesh. Table-2 indicates they are involve in businesses like establishing Kindergarten schools, coaching centers, child care centers, community information centers, and community clubs. Thirty two percentage of new entrepreneurs have retailing/grocery businesses, only few (13%) of them have manufacturing businesses.

Table 2: Types of business owned by NUs of Grameen Bank (GB)

NU businesses	Number	%
Manufacturing	8	13%
Agribusiness/livestock/fisheries	7	12%
Retailing/Grocery	19	32%
Kindergarten/coaching center	5	8%
IT/Electronics	4	7%
Repairing/recycling	3	5%
Processing	5	8%
IT/repairing/recycling	2	3%
Construction	2	3%

Wholesales	4	7%
Others	1	2%
Total	**60**	**100%**

Although Bangladesh is an agricultural country, 12% NUs businesses are in agricultural/livestock/fisheries farmings and businesses. I asked NUs about their income turnover status in agricultural production, raising livestock and fish cultivation. They mentioned the incomes from these businesses are not on daily basis. Therefore, it is challenging for them to continue such businesses without regular daily income and repay monthly loan instalments regularly.

Now-a-days business is very competitive. Table-3 data shows NUs are facing different problems and challenges in their businesses. Here 33% respondents are suffering from competitions in their businesses; 31% respondents mention they do not have customer service skills, trade skills, IT skills and financial management skills. The strike, occupied movement and political turmoil; and natural disasters in Bangladesh disturb NUs business too. For example, 22% of NUs reported that they feel business insecurity and physical insecurity because of recent political turmoil and frequent natural disasters in Bangladesh.

Table 3: NUs' facing problems/challenges in their businesses (multiple responses)

NUs' facing problems/challenges in their businesses	Frequency	%
Competition	20	33%
Buying raw materials from distance place	8	13%
Lack of business and physical security	13	22%
Lack of customer-service skills	2	3%
Lack of trade skills/IT skills	6	10%
Lack of trade skills	5	8%
Lack of financial management skills	6	10%

Business irregular turnover	8	13%
Others (Get big loan from GB, repaying instalment amount is high, fisheries turnover after one year, less capital, carry & collect hide from different places, more interest, strike and occupied movement disturb businesses, more kinds sale (less cash sale), employees problem, political turmoil, poultry birds death risk and virus problem, heavy rain, cyclone and storm, repay TK. 13,400 in every months, daily business income information send SMS message to GB head office every day, not experienced in business, customers not paying upfront, guardians give less tuition fees etc.)	31	52%
Total respondents	**60**	**100%**

The study thinks Grameen micro-enterprise loan borrowers and grameen social business equity loan receivers can run their businesses more competitively and efficiently if they have financial literacy knowledge, business literacy training and other support services.

9.0. Discussion

9.1. Direct benefits of the study

This advanced-level post-doctoral social business research study directly beneficial to Grameen Bank, to Grameen sister organizations, to the Yunus Center social business design lab, and to GB micro-enterprise loan receivers and the second-generation of GB borrower social business equity funding receivers (new entrepreneurs) in Bangladesh. This study gives social entrepreneurs a space to discuss the Grameen micro-enterprise financing experience, grameen social business equity investment partnership experience connect them to university social business research and social enterprise organizations to provide them with the GB micro-enterprise research data.

The unemployed people involve business and engage in constructive public wellbeing different social environmental and civic activities instead looking for paid employment andf or involve in subversive activities in Bangladesh. The paper suggests initiate community economic activities for the youth; develop social businesses education programs/services for them so that they could involve in income generating activities in their communities and use their potentiality engaging in social businesses. The Grameen new entrepreneur social business equity funding education and services assist youths divert their minds from extremism and trauma resulting from politics of war to devote themselves to social businesses like set up kindergarten school, child care center, computer training center, distributing winter clothing to vulnerable poor people, repairing and recycling green social businesses etc. in Bangladesh.

Moreover, this post-doc GB micro-enterprise financing and grameen Nabeen Uddagta (NU) social business equity partnership investment research broadens and improves the researcher's knowledge about GB social businesses, familiar with the Yunus center social business financing model and their implications in communities in Bangladesh and elsewhere.

9.2. Outputs, outcomes, and potential usefulness of the research

This post-doctoral research touched on the work of the Grameen Bank (GB) micro-enterprise development program, and Grameen social business equity funding (investment partnership with NU) program in Bangladesh. This research can be useful to micro-finance institutions (MFIs) and other social financing agencies in Bangladesh, North American, Asian, African and Latin America. This report can be learning lession to Grameen sister organizations those are involving in grameen social business equity funding services in Bangladesh. By reading this article these grameen sister organizations would know about their strengths, weaknesses, opportunities of their legal structures, funding models, products and services, operational strategies, policies, and monitoring and accounting systems. Moreover, European, North American and South Asian social enterprise organizations, educationalists, social economy researchers, policy makers, and business students can be benefited from this paper too.

9.3. Benefits of the Grameen NU social business investing program

Yunus Center reports that there are many benefits of Grameen Nabeen Uddagta Social Business Equity Funding Service in Bangladesh. The benefits are Grameen NU social business equity funding service is an anti-colonial localization process that empowers marginalised poor people in Bangladesh. It is a sustainable business development model in Bangladesh. I observe during my data collection that second-generation micro-entrepreneurs of GB and new entrepreneurs (NUs) of grameen social business equity funding receivers are involved in businesses like community information centers, sports/music/theatre clubs, web-page designing, multimedia studios, poultry and livestock farming, poultry feed manufacturing and selling, fisheries, equipment leasing, garments manufacturing and marketing, and the manufacturing of leather and ceramic products. These local social businesses are well liked by community people and beneficial to community people.

10.0. Policy Implications

As mentioned earlier Grameen Bank and Grameen sister organizations in Bangladesh have been popular instrumental in providing income-generating opportunities to poor people (particularly for empowering women through the extension of collateral-free banking) in Bangladesh for last more than three decades. This policy empirical research examined whether the second-generation of Grameen Bank

(GB) borrowers could adequately enhance the developmental status of GB women borrowers and emancipate them from the dominance of their rich business mate in their community life. It further explored the GB micro-enterprise loan program and the Grameen Nabeen Uddugta (New Entrepreneurs) social business loan policy, strategy, the barrier GB Nabeen Uddugta borrowers face, and the leadership of these borrowers and their ability to transfer their leadership skills to other public spaces, especially in social enterprise development in their community.

Moreover, the research explored whether the Grameen social business loan products and their policies have resulted in increased social business participation by the household of the second-generation of GB borrower, and in the increased tendency of the community toward social development. Using the case of Bangladesh, this policy research brief recommended that GB and grameen sister organizations should include gender equality in its social business loan product to address the role of women in the family and in the community. The report also asked question is the second-generation borrower of GB able to remove obstacles to economic and social progress and higher education in their life, and are they able to break down patriarchal dominance in society, to alter gender bias economics and institutional arrangements, and to promote more choices for women's participation in social business in Bangladesh?

The findings of this policy empirical research assists me to write this paper and write a book on the GB micro-enterprise loan, the Grameen Nabeen Uddugta (New Entrepreneur) social loan policy and strategy, and the barriers/challenges the second generation of Grameen NU borrowers face in implementing their social businesses in Bangladesh. It is anticipated that the report would incorporate the support that is needed for the GB micro-enterprise loan borrower and the second generation of Grameen NUs to take part in decisions that pertain to family and community issues in order to promote their development in the family sphere, social enterprise sphere and for their leadership development in the public sphere in their community in Bangladesh. Moreover, this policy empirical research report generates new knowledge in the field of social enterprise management and development. The paper might help the Government of Bangladesh, other Bangladeshi micro-finance institutions, and the governments and non-governmental organizations (NGOs) of many other countries get ideas about the policies and strategies of the Grameen NU social business loan program in Bangladesh. This research can be a lesson for both developed and developing countries, and for NGOs, on the Grameen Bank social business product and service, and grow interest in initiating a new-entrepreneur social business equity funding/loan project for the marginalized people in their own country.

11.0. Conclusion

Grameen Bank has been influential in providing income-generating opportunities to poor people particularly for empowering woman through the extension of collateral-free banking in Bangladesh since 1976. However, Grameen NUs social business education is for learning and preparing NUs business proposals. The Yunus Center Social Business equity financing system and its different steps assist NUs to go for their business actions. It is a bottom up, negotiated and inclusive learning process for solving business problems and education for social capital. Here entrepreneurs are learning business by running and managing business. Grameen social business design lab is coaching the entrepreneurs to strengthen the capacity of grassroots new entrepreneurs and empowering the powerless bottom business people. The workshops are brainstorming the NUs for their good and to support them for their self-help business initiatives. Yunus Center Social Business Design Lab is motivating entrepreneurs for community social business development and build up networking among them. The field workers are trying for commitment for overcoming the challenges that NUs would face in their journey of business. Grameen NUs' social business education is also asssist NUs in exploring and understanding their local marketing context of their social businesses.

This policy empirical research also provides information on the second generation of Grameen Bank borrower, new entrepreneurs' social business equity funding services and their social entrepreneurship developmental status in Bangladesh. The study indicates there is a huge market for social business equity financing in Bangladesh. Therefore, it is better to implement the Grameen social business equity funding program fully assigned to an organization. Moreover, the study suggests expanding the NU social business equity funding program to both inside and outside Grameen Bank borrowers' families in Bangladesh. The study also proposes for organizing social business open house meetings, seminars, symposiums and workshops in different districts/Upzillas across Bangladesh throughout the year in addition to conducting workshop and seminars in Dhaka.

Yunus Center Social business Design Lab could print one page flyer on Nabin Uddugktta social business concept, partnership pattern, design of business proposal and contact information. The flyer can contain 'Grameen Social Business' partner agencies' names, address, phone numbers and emails, investment methods and repayment system, and business ownership system etc. These flyers could be distributed to Grameen Bank branches, Grameen Shakti offices and other field offices of Gramen's sister organizations in Bangladesh.

Yunus Center Social Business Design Lab could setup a telephone hotline social business service for young entrepreneurs in Bangladesh. This hotline service could serve to answer the queries of young new entrepreneurs of Bangladesh. At the initial stage, the piloting of social business implementation services might continue under present system for a while. However, as social business program has huge market in Bangladesh and this project has gotten popular, a separate implementing agency with an energetic middle age innovative chief executive is essential for regularly implementing this program in Bangladesh.

Moreover, as GB has a huge network across Bangladesh and there is a huge demand for social business equity funding loans among fast-moving borrowers of GB, Grameen Bank could continue social business funding services to its fast-moving borrowers too although surprisingly Grameen bank has squeezed its NU social business funding services after 2012. As mentioned earlier this policy empirical research report generated a new knowledge in the field of social enterprise management in the field of entrepreneurship development in Bangladesh and elsewhere in the world. Detail information with findings about the study is included in my book that published in June 2017.

12.0. References

Asia Pacific Youth Employment Network (2012). *The situation of youth employment in Bangladesh*. Retrieved from http://apyouthnet.ilo.org/stats/youth-employment-statistics-in-bangladesh, dated January 08, 2015

Bornstein, D. and Davis, S. (2010). *Social entrepreneurship: what everyone needs to know?* New York, Oxford University Press

Brookfield, S. (1987). *Understanding adult education and training.* San Francisco: Jossey Bass

Dees, J. G. (1998). Enterprising nonprofits. *Harvard Business Review* (January-February) pp. 55-67

Dewey, J. (1966, first published 1897) My Pedagogic Creed, in F. W. Garforth (Ed.) John Dewey, *Selected Educational Writings*. London: Heinemann

Freire, Paulo (1994). *Pedagigy og hope: Revisiting pedagogy of the opprssed.* NY. Continum, Graveline, Fyre Jean

Henry, S. (2006). *How MFIs' and their cliennts can have a positive impact on the environment. Good practices in business development services: How do we enhance entreprenuerial skills in MFIs clients of Alterna Savings*

Toronto? Paper presented at the Micro Creditt Summit, HaliFax held in November 2006

Gibbons, D. (1995). *The Grameen Reader.* Dhaka: Packages Corporation Ltd.

Goetz, A. M. (2001). Women development workers: implementing rural credit programs in Bangladesh. *World Development* 24(1), pp. 45-63

Gibbons, D. & Meehan, J. (2002). Financing Microfinance for poverty reduction. In Daley-Harris, S. & Awimbo, A. (Eds.). *More Pathways out of Poverty.* Connecticut: Kumarian Press

Grameen Bank Annual Report (2012). *Grameen Scholarship Program.* Grameen Bank. Packages Corporation: Dhaka, Bangladesh

Khusru, A. (2015). *Grameen NUs' social businesses.* Paper presented at the Social Business Summit, Berlin, Germany, November 5-6, 2015

Khandlker, S. (2005). *Microfinance and Poverty: Evidence Using Panel Data from Bangladesh.* World Bank Economic Review

Kofi, A. (2005). Message from Kofi Annan. *Grameen dialogue* #60. Dhaka: Grameen Trust

Mahamud, S. (2004). Micro credit and women's empowerment in Bangladesh. In Saleuddin Ahamed & Muhammad Hakim (Eds.), *Attacking poverty with Micro Credit (pp.153-188).* Dhaka University Press Limited and Palli Karma-Sahyak Foundation

Martin, I. and Rahman, H. (2001). The politics of really useful literacy: six lessons from Bangladesh, in J. Crowther, M. Hamilton and L. Tett (Eds.) *Powerful literacies*. Leicester: NIACE

Nadeau, Denise (1996). *A training guide on popular education and organizing.* Toronto: Doris Marshall Institute

Jack, Q. Mook, L. & Armastrong, A. (2009). Understanding the Social Economy-A Canadian Perspective. Toronto: University of Toronto Press

Rouf, K. A. (2017). *Green and social business strategies,* Dhaka: Subarna

Rouf, K. A. (2017). *Green and social entrepreneurial basics*, Dhaka: A. H. Development Publishing

Rouf, K. A. (2017). Grameen Nabeen Uddugta (NU), new entrepreneur, social business funding education and service in Bangladesh. *International Journal of Research Studies in Management,*

HYPERLINK "http://www.consortiacademia.org/index.php/ijrsm/issue/view/118" \t "_parent"Vol. 6 (1)

Yunus, M. (2015). *Social business.* Speech at the Social business Summit, Berlin, Germany, 5-6 November, 2015

Yunus, M. (2010b). *Building social business: A new kind of capitalism that serves humanity's most pressing needs,* New York: Public Affairs

Yunus, M. (2008). *Creating a World without Poverty.* Dhaka: Subarna Publications Ltd.

Yunus Center (2015). *Yunus Center Social Business Design Lab.* Retrieved from http://muhammadyunus.org, dated December 28, 2015

Yunus, M. (2015). *What is social business?* Retrieved from http://muhammadyunus.org, dated December 28, 2015

Revenue-Generating Social and Economic Mission-Entwined Organizations

Abstract

Researchers, academicians, social scientists, policy makers, executives, and state leaders realize that classical economics, profit-maximizing corporations and traditional businesses are unwilling or unable to altruistically strive for public wellbeing in fulfilling the needs of society. Profit-maximizing capitalism destroys humanity and the harmony of society. Corporations are harmful to the environment; it has created poverty, unemployment, malnutrition, inequality, injustice and abnormality in the community. Hence many economists, policy makers, executives, academicians and state leaders comprehend that business policies should be adapted to enhance public wellbeing. They think that the sociology of economics and sociology of business as well as political economy are missing in profit-maximizing business capitalism. Therefore, many thinkers believe it is necessary to include social objectives alongside profit-maximization to establish more altruistic businesses with practices that promote rather than hinder public wellbeing. Such kind of social business organizations exist in many countries in different forms. For example, However, Grameen Bank is a social business institution claimed by Muhammad Yunus that serves millions of poor in Bangladesh for their economic emancipation and social empowerment.

In order to establish people-centered social enterprises/social businesses, different scholars suggest different types of business models that blend both social and economic missions to address social, economic and environmental problems that originate from profit-maximizing businesses. They suggest and develop different types of financial and legal models for different types of socio-economically entwined business organizations. Grameen bank is serving the poor for their economic development, social emancipation and poverty eradication. The author has worked in Grameen bank and many other SME organizations, and visited many revenue-generating socio-economically entwined business organizations as well as reviewed and evaluated different social economy organizations in different countries in the world. This paper is a nutshell description of different social enterprises in order to catch the readership of various kinds of social entrepreneurism around the world. Moreover, this manuscript explores different legal and financial models of different socio-economically entwined business organizations and tries to find out their gaps. The study finds that different revenue-generating social businesses have different names and that these different social enterprises/ businesses have been crafted and implemented differently in different countries/societies. Grameen Bank, BRAC, ASA, PROSHIKA, Nijara Kori, PKSF and many other MFIs, NGOs are also examples of social business in Bangladesh because they have been serving disadvantaged people both economically and socially for long. However, it still remains challenging for these business organizations to work independently as separate legal social business entities because these social entrepreneurial organizations are not registered under a separate Legal Act in different countries, rather they are registered under either a Private Business Act or Charity Act. However, it is urgent and essential for these social entrepreneurial businesses to be registered under separate Acts in order to get the status of independent social entrepreneurship entities around the world.

Key Terms: Community Economic Development; Grameen Social Business Design Lab; Nabin Udyokta; Social Business; Social Entrepreneurship; Social Enterprise; Social Economy and Social Investment.

1.0. Why needs revenue generated socioeconomic blended business organizations (Rationality of Social Enterprise)

The profit-maximizing capitalism can never deliver equitable distribution of income in the society. Today's world, 85 individuals own more wealth than all those in the bottom half. Top half population of the world own 99% the wealth of the world, leaving only 1% for the bottom half. Out of 7.6 billion world population, the numbers of young population are around 1.8 billion who are job seekers (Grameen Dialogue 93, 2014, pp. 3). It may get worse in future because technology will remain under the control of the people at the top. In capitalism, maximizing personal profit is the core of economic rationality. Therefore, government and the non-profit sector are necessary, but insufficient to address society's greatest challenges. Hrence the social economic missions blend businesses are necessary to address the private sector monopoly profit maximizing exploitative market oppressions. As the public sector funding is limited and this sector is inefficient to serve the community, hence social economy activities and services are crucial for public wellbeing services. Hence Muhammad Yunus (2013) provokes for social business that must create value for society, not just shareholders. Now the world needs, for example, systemic challenges for facing systemic solutions and the beneficial corporation (B Corp) movement, CIC, Grameen Social Business, Community Economic Development agencies that offer a concrete market-based social business and scalable solution. The emergence of social enterprises, and the range of goods and services social entrepreneurial businesses produce, has evolved against the backdrop of capitalist states reforms towards a mixed economy of private, public and third sector provider.

Social entrepreneurs are influencing the regulatory and investment environments to hold businesses more accountable to their social and environmental performance and to support social enterprises. They reflect enlightened human values (Jack, Mook, & Armastrong 2009; and Yunus, 2014). Social entrepreneurs have launched enterprises to provide many necessities like blindness, solar power, biomass, fuel, low-energy cooking stoves, educating bottom poor kids and adults, healthcare services to disadvantaged people. For example, the Canadian National Institute for Blinds (CNIB) and Balance Toronto provide health products like reading glasses, hearing aids to visually impaired people. In Bangladesh, BASF Grameen manufactures malaria nets is working to address the issue of mosquito bites and protect people from malaria disease. Grameen DANONE Yogurt is selling to rural people with affordable prices in Bangladesh.

In the revenue generated socioeconomic twisted business framework, social enterprises have emerged as an effective tool to deliver policy objectives in two key areas of social and economic policy: service delivery and social inclusion. Hence, many scholars think social enterprises pioneer in leading to social cohesion and social inclusion. Its dominant feature is civil society development. Social enterprises can support the financial and regulatory sustainability of civil society initiatives aimed at supporting disadvantaged groups and develop partnerships for social innovation. A social enterprise has two goals: (1) to achieve social, cultural, community economic and environmental outcomes; and (2) to earn revenue. Social enterprises are businesses whose primary purpose is the common good. The social entrepreneurs use methods and disciplines and the power of the marketplace to advance their social, environmental and human justice agendas. However, social enterprises are revenue-generating businesses with twist- social and economic objectives following capitalism.

2.0. Different names of the Revenue Generated Social and Economy Missions twisted Businesses

Social enterprises, social businesses, social economy, social entrepreneurships, social capital partners, social clubs, social financing, social housing, social investment organizations, and social purpose businesses are revenue generated social entrepreneurial businesses. The Community Investment Corporations (CIC) UK based, L3C-USA based, Beneficial Corporations (B-Corporation) social entrepreneurships, social capital partners, venture philanthropy, farmers cooperatives, commercial cooperatives and financial cooperatives (credit unions) are latest models social economic organizations. Other forms of social entrepreneurial organizations are members based organizations (workers cooperatives, trade unions), non-profit mutual associations, professional associations, business association, housing cooperatives, networking organizations and revenue earned cultural associations.

Moreover, the Chamber of Commerce, mutual insurance, not for profit organizations, non-governmental organizations, community enterprises, community economic development projects, micro-finance institutions (MFIs), commercial non-profits are also termed social enterprises. The civil society organizations, community foundations, enterprising non-profit programs, not-for profit, non-profit organizations (NPOs), self-help groups, solidarity economy belongs to social economy agencies too. Because all theses social enterprises perform social and economic objectives under different framework, different strategies and different funding models.

3.0. Entrepreneurship

The word 'entrepreneur' originates from the French entreprendre and the German unternehmen, both of which mean literally 'to undertake', as in accepting a challenging task. They refer to the groundbreaking development of the concept by Cantillon (1680-1734) and Say (1767-1832) (see, e.g., Dees, 1998: 2f). An entrepreneur is a risk taker person driven by the burning desire to put his business idea into action. He is ready to tackle difficulties, to experiment boldly, to work long hours, and to experience personal setbacks and disappointments without becoming discoursed. He is not satisfied until his project is implemented successfully, producing the desired results-either financial reward or social improvement. Entrepreneurship is an integral part of human nature. Social business offers a new and exciting way of expressing it. Social business also provides an outlet for the creativity that millions of people harbour within themselves. Grameen equity funding is an example social business that has stated recently in Bangladesh.

4.0. Social Entrepreneurship

'Social entrepreneurship' describes an initiative of social consequences created by an entrepreneur with a social vision because it is exercised by individuals. Entrepreneurship is best thought of as an extended activity which may well be carried out by a team or a group of people (Stewart, 1989). To be an entrepreneur may therefore mean being an individual, a member of a group, or an organization who/which carries out the work of identifying and creatively pursuing a social goal. In fact, some scholars even refer to organizations that pursue both commercial and social objectives as hybrids (Davis, 1997). In a sense, these hybrids pursue two bottom lines, one of which deals with profit while the other deals with social value.

According to Bornstein and Davis (2010) social entrepreneurs is a process, a way to organize problem-solving efforts. Social entrepreneurs carry risks. They have relationship between the individual and society. Social entrepreneurship to be understood with appropriate flexibility-its aims at creating social value, either exclusively or at least in some prominent way; (2) it shows a capacity to recognize and take advantage of opportunities to create that value 'envision'; (3) it employ(s) innovation in creating and/or distributing social value; (4) it is/are willing to accept an above-average degree of risk in creating and disseminating social value. According to A. M. Peredo and M. MacLean (2006) the social entrepreneurship allows the entrepreneur to balance the interests of many people and remain true to the mission in the face of moral intricacy. Social entrepreneurs excel at recognizing and taking advantage of opportunities to deliver the social value they aim to provide. Social entrepreneurs show risk-tolerance, innovativeness, and pro-activeness showed by commercial entrepreneurs. Social entrepreneurs have 'social value' i.e. contribute well being in a given human community. However, this definition dos not allows wealth creation.

In contrast with social entrepreneurs, social business is a very specific type of business- a non-loss, Non-dividend Company with a social objective. A social business may pursue goals similar to those sought by some social entrepreneurs, but the specific business structure of social business makes it distinctive and unique. Hence social entrepreneurship and social business are similar concepts. Social business is not a non-profit organization. The foundation, for example, would get its money back and be able to use it for some other worthy purpose. However, it is not possible in the traditional NGOs who could own a social business. By contrast, a social business is designed to be sustainable. This allows its owners to focus not on asking for donations, but for investment. However, it would need to be separated from the NGOs for legal, tax and accounting purposes.

Social entrepreneurship has many benefits like systematically identify people with innovative ideas and practical models for achieving major societal impact and to develop support systems to help them achieve significant social impact. Social entrepreneurship shifted to organizational excellence. It is contagious (Bouchard, Ferraton, & Michaud (2006); Quarter, Mook, & Armstrong (2010); Bornstein & Davis (2010); Putnam (1996); McFarlan (1999); Mort, Weerawardena & Carnegie (2003); Mintzberg (1991); Mendall & Neamtan (2010), Peredo & McLean (2005); Amin & Hausner (1997); Belal (2008); D'Amours (2007); Rothschild & Russell (1986); Shrage & Fontan (2000); Salamon & Anheier (1997); Owen & et al. (2000); MacLeod (1997); Hall (2009); and Peredo & McLean (2006). For example, social economy organizations like micro-credit institutions all over the world are doing well that become a social economy model for the world. In Bangladesh, Canada and many other countries various other social economic business models invented and functioning that better serve the disadvantaged community people in economic way and democratic way. These organizations created huge employment opportunities in the world. It is efficiently meeting the social and economic needs of the marginalized people (Lasby, & et al. (2010); Quarter, Mook, & Armstring, 2009; Schugurensky & Mccollum (2010); and Yunus 2010).

Below the paper describes different concepts of social entrepreneurial organizations, their different financial and legal models, and their contributions to different societies.

5.0. Social Economy

According to Quarter et al. (2009) the social economy is a bridging concept for organizations that have social objectives central to their missions and their practice, and either has explicit economic objectives or generates some economic value through the services they provide and purchases that they undertake. The majority social organizations are charities in Canada (Lasby, Hall, & et al. (2010); and Salamon (1999) termed it a form of mobilizing economic resources towards the satisfaction of human needs. The SEOs have democratic principles of one member/one vote with very high participation rates. It is serving the public as well as mutual associations, cooperatives making connection to people and the communities (Quarter et al., 2009).

In Canada and many other countries various other social economic business models invented and functioning that better serve the disadvantaged community people in economic way, democratic way (Quarter et al. 2009); Bornstein & Davis (2010); Schugurensky & Mccollum (2010); and Lasby et al. (2010). These organizations created huge employment opportunities in Bangladesh and Canada. Social entrepreneurship has many societal impacts MacMartin (2007); Mendall & Neamtan (2010), Amin & Hausner (1997), Belal (2008), D'Amours (2007), Rothschild & Russell (1986); Salamon & Anheier (1997); Owen, et al. (2000); MacLeod (1997); Hall (2009); and Peredo & McLean (2006).

Not-for-profits/NGOs, civil societies, non-profit organizations (NPOs), Self-help Groups, Solidarity Economy etc. organizations are belong to social economy because they are performing social and economic objectives under different framework, different strategies and different funding models (Quarter et al., 2009). These social economic organizations are very important because they are working in opposite to multinational corporations and private sectors who are monopoly in profit maximizing exploitative market (Bornstein & Davis, 2010; Quarter et al. 2010; Schugurensky & Mccollum, 2010; and Yunus 2010). Social economy organizations encompass the full range of human needs and interests (Lasby et al., 2010; and Yunus 2010). They provide opportunities for economic development and solidarity in the community.

Social economy renaming 'Third Sector' that organizations set up for social purpose can generate economic value-they may produce and market services, employ people and own valuable assets (Quarter et al., 2009). At the Economic and Employment Summit in Quebec in 1996 define social economy objectives are serves to members and community. Here SEOs managements are independent (Chantier de l'economic sociale, 2005). The Human Resources and Social Development Canada (HRSDC, 2005) defined the social economy is a grass roots entrepreneurial, not-for-profit sector, based on democratic values that seek to enhance the social, economic conditions of communities and focus on their disadvantaged members. The Walton Council, Belgium, termed it 'social market economy'. These social entrepreneurships have 'double bottom line' means placing equal emphasis on profit and social benefit. However, there are challenges found in CBEs like maintaining a balance between individual and collective needs, and among economic and social, goods.

Jack Quarter et al. (2009) included social economy organizations that are incorporate or non-incorporate cooperatives, social enterprises, community development initiatives, public sector nonprofits, non-profit member associations and civil society organizations. Non-profit and non-governmental organizations refers them to social, social purpose and citizen-sector organizations and social entrepreneur refers to founders of organizations even it is not legally structured as a profit seeking entity (Bornstein & Davis, 2010).

According to A. Mendell and M. Neamtam (2010) social economy is a process of re-engaging government in new ways and working across boundaries to participate in new policy design. The figure below diagrammatically describes the intersection between the private sector, public sector and social-economic organizations three areas. The common characteristics of the social economy organizations include social and economic missions, social ownership, volunteer/ social participation, and civic engagement.

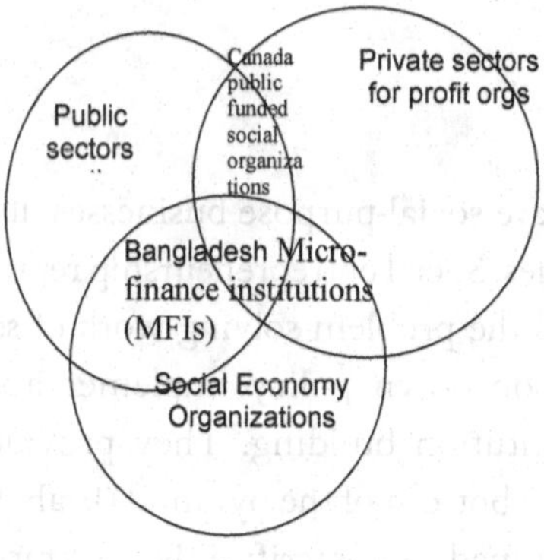

These social economic missions blend organizations are very important to address multinational corporations, private sectors monopoly profit maximizing exploitative market and limited public sector funding and public sector inefficiency to serve the community social economy. They are working for the well-being of the disadvantaged people in the society. These organizations created huge employment in the different countries.

Daniel Schugurensky and E. Mccollum (2010) mention that in Canada and internationally, the social economy makes a significant contribution to the social, economic, cultural and environmental well-being of communities. The Human Resources and Social Development (HRSD) in Canada (2005) acknowledges that 'the Government of Canada is just beginning to understand the power and potential of social economy enterprises and organizations.' In Bangladesh, MFIs are intensively working for the poor and they are popular to them; on other hand, Canadian Charitable organizations, civil society organizations, credit unions are providing service, meet needs of the citizens. However, there are fewer interactions among public sectors and social economic organizations. Many social organizations, community economic programs gets funding from public sectors in Canada, which are less in Bangladesh. Currently many private sectors opened their foundations and funds to work with social and economic missions.

6.0. Social Business

Social businesses are social-purpose businesses. It has blended social and economic values. Social entrepreneurship represents fundamental reorganizations of the problem solving work of society-a shift from control-oriented top down policy implementation to responsive, decentralized institution building. They provide services and do businesses with the bottom of the pyramid (Prahalad 2003). They are do-gooders, many made self-sacrifice. For example, the Bangladesh Ashraon Housing Project has funded by public sector and this project is intensively monitored the gross root workers. This project is funded by Government of Bangladesh for the rural landless and rural vulnerable women in Bangladesh.

According to Muhammad Yunus (2013) a social business is a Non-loss, Non-dividend Company designed to address a socioeconomic objectives. These organizations' profits are used to expand the company and to improve the product/service. This model has grown from the work of Grameen sister organizations and others following social principles. Social business is a cause-driven business. In a social business, the investors/owners can gradually recoup the money invested, but cannot take any dividend beyond that point. Purpose of the investment is purely to achieve one or more social objectives through the operation of the company, there is no personal gain is desired by the investors. The organization must cover all costs and make revenue, at the samc time achieve the social objective, such as, healthcare for the poor, housing for the poor, financial services for the poor, nutrition for malnourished children, providing safe drinking water, introducing renewable energy, etc. in a business way. The impact of the social business on people or environment is worthy, rather than maximizing profit solely. The objective of the social business organization is to achieve social and economic goals.

It is not for maximizing profit but for maximizing social benefit. It is not a charity. It is not part of corporate social responsibility. It does not fall within the category of NGO or cooperatives. It is distinct from private entrepreneurship in strict sense of the term. It is a sustainable business proposition but it is a market-based solution for poverty reduction. It is about combining business principles with social objectives. It is not social objectives versus profit objectives rather it has combination of the two. It is designed and operated as business enterprise with products, services, customers, markets expenses and revenues, but with the profit maximizing principle replaced by social benefit principles.

7.0. Features and Goals of Social Business

A social business is needed to generate enough surpluses to pay back the invested capital to the investors as early as possible. Moreover, it needed to generate surplus for expanding the business, for improving the quality of business, to increase efficiency of the business through introducing new technology, to innovative marketing to reach the deeper layers of low-income people and disadvantaged communities. There are eleven features of Social Business Organizations (SBOs).

- They are innovative;
- The SBO rejects the traditional methodology of the conventional banking;
- SBO provides banking services at the doorstep of the poor it serves;
- SBO provides physical and non-human inputs (e.g., microcredit, machines, tools, training) to poor people;
- It empowers borrowers through positive reinforcement;
- SBO promotes the unity, conscience, and social cohesion among group members through social solidarity;
- SBO applies logical appeal to increase integration among group members;
- Commodity fetishism: the SBO applies social relationships to increase social capital;
- The SBO provides organizational support to create income-generating self-employment;
- Collective consciousness: the SBO uses moral force to create two-dimensional social entrepreneurs; and
- SBO help to create a world without poverty, illiteracy, diseases, and slum dwellers.

8.0. Community Economic Development (CED)

Community economic development (CED) is action by people within a specific geographic community or group of communities to create local economic opportunities and improve quality of life (Salamon & Anheier (1997). In Canada, Community Economic Development (CED) organizations are social enterprises serving people with disabilities, Aboriginal People from the crown body Community Futures Development Corporations Canada, and Canada Institute for Health Information. In Bangladesh, CED organizations are micro-credit institutions (MFIs) and Bangladesh Rural Development Board (BRDB), Bangladesh Asrayan Prokalpa and Nijerra Kori etc. CED recognizes that local challenges and opportunities are as varied as the individual communities themselves. By using knowledge and resources resident in the community, CED identifies and capitalizes on local opportunities to stimulate economic growth and employment. This can include developing entirely new businesses or industries, adding value to existing sectors, strengthening capacity, and improving local infrastructure to help communities achieve their full economic potential. Communities have increased economic opportunities and capacity to respond to challenges, as well as the necessary investments in public infrastructure. CED projects are in regions that have below average standard of living or involve groups who experience extraordinary challenges. Hence special arrangements are created by government, foundations or some other parenting organizations to support the initiative (Jack & et al., 2009).

In Canada, Western Economic Diversification Canada (WEDC) contributes to community economic development in urban centres and rural areas through initiatives that capitalize on opportunities for growth and development, and enable communities to adjust to challenges that hinder competitiveness and quality of life. A significant proportion of WEDC's community economic development funding stems from the western agent for national programs such as government infrastructure development programs offered by the Federal Government of Canada. WEDC supports to community economic development include:

- Encouraging regional approaches to economic development through partnerships with communities and non-profit organizations,
- Helping rural communities identify and capitalize on new sources of economic growth and employment,
- Increasing the capacity of rural communities to undertake value-added processing and encourage new opportunities for skilled employment,
- Enhancing Aboriginal participation in the economy,
- Designing and delivering regional and community development programs to help western Canadian communities make a successful transition into the 21st century economy,

- Revitalizing urban communities by supporting initiatives that undertake inner city and
- Renewal and build community capacity, enhance knowledge and skills, and foster economic development.

However, MFIs are prominent in running CED activities in Bangladesh. BRDB supports local copeeratives. BRAC Arong supports local handmade embrodary products of female village organizations (VOs).

9.0. CED Funding Sources

Investing in infrastructure to sustain rural and urban communities, CED funding sources in Canaada are:

- The Community Infrastructure Improvement Fund is a two-year national program that invests over $46 million in the Western Canada for the rehabilitation and improvement of existing community infrastructure that is non-commercial and accessible to the public. There are also many CED organizations like PKSF, Grameen Bank, BRAC etc. are working for improving rural community infrastructures in Bangladesh.
- Western Diversification Program is the main program through which WEDC invests in projects that support strategic outcomes related to innovation, business development and entrepreneurship, community economic development and policy, advocacy and coordination. Women Entrepreneurship Development Bangladesh and SME Foundation Bangladesh are CED organizations working for entrepreneurship development in Bangladesh.
- Western Canada Business Service Network is a group of several independent organizations that receive funding from WEDC to provide a range of services to help create and build small businesses across the West. One of the Network partners, Community Futures Development Corporations, also undertakes broad-based community economic

development initiatives in rural western communities. PKSF is an apex organization, funding too many socio-economic organizations in Bangladesh for community social and economic development in Bangladesh.

- The CED invests $3.2 million in the West over five years to support business and to encourage sustainable growth in Western Canada's Francophone communities. PKSF also provides more than $2 billion funds to MFIs in Bangladesh. Grameen Bank microenterprise loans to micro-entrepreneurs in Bangladesh that promotes SME development in Bangladesh. Similarly Bangladesh Rural Development Board (BRDB) is also working for social enterprise development there.

PKSF is an apex CED organization that delivers refinancing funds (wholesale microloan financing) to MFIs and support MFIs training programs in Bangladesh. It has 274 partnering organizations; it provides loans to 8547214 micro-borrowrs through its partnering organizations and offered training 3 million people in Bangladesh. It provides TK. 216562 million ($2707 million) wholesale micro-financing to MFIs Bangladesh for MFIs loan funds (PKSF Annual Report, 2015). PKSF Bangladesh vision is to implement policies and action programmes involving multiple dimensions of human living and human poverty; pursue a life-cycle approach to human progress, catering to the appropriate needs at all stages of life. The policy planning and action programming will centre on human beings and focus on socio-economic development and environmental protection. The support and services provided relate to education, workforce development, health and nutrition, infrastructure, inclusive and appropriate financing for planned economic activities, social issues and social capital, response to climate change impacts, gender issues, cultural dimensions, sports and social advocacy etc.

10.0. Community Based Enterprises (CBEs)

Community Based Enterprises (CBEs) often constitute a culturally appropriate way of addressing problems such as poverty-alleviation.

According to A. M. Peredo, and J. Chrisman (2006) the community based enterprises are typically rooted in community culture; natural capital and social capital is integral and inseparable from economic considerations, transforming the community into an entrepreneur and an enterprise. The CBEs are important when public sectors and private sectors development efforts have been largely unsuccessful. In such situation social economy scientists encourage the creation of small businesses owned by the community. The CBEs are alternative socioeconomic model where the community acts as an entrepreneur when its members acting as owners, managers and employees, create or identify a market opportunity and organize themselves in order to respond to it. CBEs are managed, governed by the people, rather than by the government. CBEs structures are designed to be participatory, not only representative. Here community may come together to solve its problems. However, CBEs success depends on Social Capital: there people depend on social relations to fulfill their needs.

Bourdieu (1997) and R. Putnam (1973) say that community networks allow resources to be pooled, actions to be coordinated, and safety nets to be created that reduce risks for individual community members. They are based on available community skills, multiplicity of goals-economic, social and environmental benefit and will be directed by profits, but dependent on community participation (Peredo & Chrisman, 2006). However, there are challenges found in CBEs like maintaining a balance between individual and collective needs and among economic, social, environmental and cultural goods.

11.0. Civil Society Organizations

Civil Society Organizations are primarily associations and organizations representing the mutual needs of a membership in the society. They work for professional interests, labour rights, recreation, sports, religion and environment. For example, Bangladesh Medical Association, Bangladesh Agriculturalist Association etc. are associations lobbying for medical doctors and agriculturalists interest. In Canada,

Farmers Cooperatives organized for to lobby for their products, rights and to link their products to the local and the international markets. The Canadian Chamber of Commerce and the Dhaka Chamber of Commerce in Bangladesh work for promoting trade and commerce of the respective countries although performance is different of each of them. Desjardins, a credit union in Canada, is successful financial credit unions are working across Canada. Alterna Community Banking program provides loans to Alterna Credit Union disadvantaged people in Toronto and in Ottawa. Such model is absent in Bangladesh. Milk producers' cooperatives are smoothly functioning in Bangladesh. These organizations have social objectives, social ownership, the assets belong to members, social participation and have civic engagement.

12.0. Difference between Social Entrepreneurs and Business Entrepreneurs

Social entrepreneurs, the bottom line is to maximize some form of social impact, usually by addressing an urgent need that is being mishandled, over looked or ignored by other institutions. For business entrepreneurs, the bottom line is to maximize profits or shareholders wealth, or to build an ongoing, respected entity that provides value to customers and meaningful work to employees. Social entrepreneurs earn profit through social enterprises and business people are concerned about social responsibility. Social entrepreneurs involve elements of newness and dynamisms. They are clean-tech, green-tech (Dees, 2002). According to Greg Dees (2001) social entrepreneurs are one species in the genus entrepreneur (meaning social entrepreneurs are a subgroup of entrepreneurs). A. M. Peredo and M. McLean (2006) mention 'social business methods' are social economic entrepreneurs approach applying principles from for-profit business without neglecting the core mission. However, the private sectors are maximising profit making, tax evasion, loan defaults and share scandals indicates poor ethical performance of private businesses. They provide sub-standard poor quality goods to market that create health hazards to people.

To better understand social entrepreneurship, Austin et al. (2006) distinguished between two types of entrepreneurship. In their framework, commercial entrepreneurship represents the identification, evaluation, and exploitation of opportunities that result in profit. In contrast, social entrepreneurship refers to the identification, evaluation, and exploitation of opportunities that resulting social value. These social organizations can also pursue commercial entrepreneurship, social entrepreneurship, or some combination of both.

13.0. What's a social enterprise?

According to OECD social enterprises have developed from and within the social economy sector, which lies between the market and the state and is often associated with concepts such as 'third sector' and 'non-profit sector'. The social enterprise concept does not seek to replace concepts of the non-profit sector or social economy. Rather, it is intended to bridge these two concepts, by focusing on new entrepreneurial dynamics of civic initiatives that pursue social aims. Social enterprises produce these benefits while reducing the draw on public and philanthropic funds. They earned income or replace grants and donations to produce a dramatically higher ROI. For example, a non-profit that earns 50% of its budget through its social enterprise is effectively matching every dollar of 'public income' with a dollar of 'marketplace income', doubling the social return on investment (ROI) of those public dollars. Canadian government sometimes offers such benefits to community economic development programs. However, such funding model to social enterprise is rare in Bangladesh.

Social enterprise is emerging as sector between the traditional worlds of government, nonprofits and business. It addresses social concerns. However, it is more efficient than government to solve every social problem (Hall, 1998). As social needs continue to spike in light of shrinking government budgets, employment rolls, and social safety nets, social enterprise is emerging as a self-sustaining, market-based, business-like and highly effective method of meeting social needs.

Social enterprise, also known as social entrepreneurship, broadly encompasses ventures of nonprofits, civic-minded individuals, and for-profit businesses that can yield both financial and social returns. According to Social Enterprise Canada *"Social enterprises are businesses owned by non-profit organizations, that are directly involved in the production and/or selling of goods and services for the blended purpose of generating income and achieving social, cultural, and/or environmental aims. Social enterprises are one more tool for non-profits to use to meet their missions to contribute to healthy communities"* (Social Enterprise Council of Canada, 2015). From the above discussion it is found that social enterprise should have a clear social and/or environmental missions set out in their governing documents. It generates the majority of their income through trade and reinvests the majority of their profits. It is to be autonomous of state and it has interests of the social mission.

Social enterprises are also emerging in the provision of community services, including in the educational, cultural and environmental fields. The key economic and social elements are as follows:

Economic Criteria

1. Unlike traditional non-profit organisations, social enterprises are directly engaged in the production and/or sale of goods and services
2. The financial viability of social enterprises depends on the efforts of their members, who are responsible for ensuring adequate financial resources, unlike most public institutions
3. Activities carried out by social enterprises require a minimum number of paid workers, even if they may combine voluntary and paid workers.

Social criteria

4. Social enterprises are the result of an initiative by citizens involving people belonging to a community or to a group that shares a certain need or aim

5. Decision making rights are shared by stakeholders, generally through the principle of 'one member, one vote'. Although capital owners in social enterprises play an important role, decision-making power is not based on capital ownership
6. Social enterprises are participatory in nature in the management of activities
7. Social enterprises include organisations that totally prohibit the distribution of profits and organisations such as co-operatives, which may distribute their profit only to a limited degree. Social enterprises therefore avoid profit maximising behaviour, as they involve a limited distribution of profit
8. Social enterprises pursue and promote social responsibility at local level.

Grameen bank and its sister organizations (Grameen Health, Grameen Shakti, Grameen Education, Grameen Agricultural Foundation, Grameen Shamogree, Grameen Trust, Grammen Telecom etc.) are social enterprises or social businesses that serving social (education, health care, nutrition services), economic (income generating services), environmental services (installation of solar energy home system, bio-gas, providing training to rural women for manufacturing improved cooking) and promoting green and social businesses in Bangladesh. These are social responsibility program at the rural local level. Village people manage the group micro credit operation at the village level. These programs are not for profit maximizing rather provides rural people social services for their wellbeing in Bangladesh.

14.0. Social Enterprise Leverage (Power/Weight)

Social enterprises produce higher social returns on investment than other models. A classic employment-focused social enterprise, for example, might serve at least four public aims: fiscal responsibility-it reduces the myriad costs of public supports by providing a pathway to economic self-sufficiency; it provides public safety-by disrupting cycles of poverty, crime, incarceration, chemical dependency and homelessness. Moreover, social enterprises generate economic opportunity and create jobs in communities and ensure social justice--it gives a chance to those most in need.

Social economic organizations could address the above mentioned issues in an accountable and transparent manner because here philanthropic mission is the first place in addition to revenue generation commitment. However, in Canada cooperatives and nonprofits have millions of members and manage millions of dollars every day (Schugurrensky & McCollum, 2010). Therefore Yunus (2013), Quarter, et al. (2009), Hall (2000), Polanyand Putnam (1996) idea of social business is not a utopian dreams but viable alternatives to organizing economic enterprises. According to M. Yunus (2013) social business will not replace traditional business rather it coexist with traditional business and expand social businesses in the world.

There are three characteristics distinguish a social enterprise from other types of businesses, nonprofits and government agencies:

- It directly addresses an intractable social need and serves the common good, either through its products and services or through the number of disadvantaged people it employs.

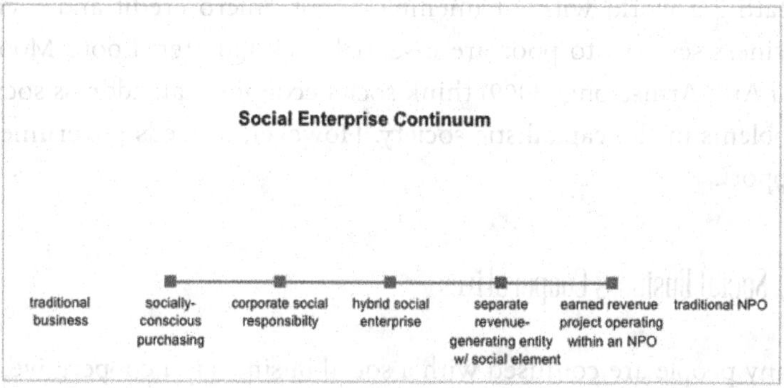

Source: BC **Centre for Social Enterprise** Newsletter April 2015.

- Its commercial activity is a strong revenue driver, whether a significant earned income stream within a non-profit's mixed revenue portfolio, or a for profit enterprise.
- The common good is its primary purpose.

The top five missions of social enterprises are workforce development, housing, community and economic development, education, and heath. Social enterprise business models are equally diverse, including: retailing business service and manufacturing businesses; contracted providers of social and human services; fee-based consulting and research services; community development and financing operations; food service and catering operations; arts organizations; and even technology enterprises.

15.0. Benefits of Social Business

Social businesses have many advantages. It is lasting. It does not only create employment opportunities but also create an enabling environment for unleashing the creative capacity and entrepreneurial skill of the youth. However, the financial institutions are designed for the rich in the capitalist society. Institutions designed for the rich will not do any good to the poor. Yunus (2014) hopes if people want creating a world without unemployment, micro credit and social business services to poor are essential. Jack Qurater, Loore Mook, and Ann Armstrong (2009) think social economy can address social problems in the capitalistic society. However, it needs government support.

16.0. Social Business Cooperatives

Many people are confused with a social business is a cooperative. A cooperative is owned by its members. It is run for profit to benefit the member-shareholders. Robert Owen (2000) had made clear cooperative social objectives: to empower the poor, to encourage self-sufficiency, and to promote economic development. Today, some co-ops still create social benefits. For example, there are housing co-ops that make affordable homes available to working-class people and to disadvantaged people, food co-ops that bring healthy nutrition within the reach of city dwellers, and banking co-ops that provide financial services to consumers who might otherwise be underserved.

In Canada Farmers Cooperatives organized for to lobby for their products, rights and to link their products to the local and the international markets. They co-operate each other. However, in Bangladesh farmers are not well organised and they have not strong cooperatives. Therefore they are not unite and suffering more to fulfill their needs and rights.

Mondragon is Spain's largest workers cooperative with a number of integrated functions including manufacturing, banking, and education. It is interesting to note that the evolution of Mondragon includes the formation of an educational institution, which is closely linked to the human resources needs of both manufacturing and service cooperatives within Mondragon (McLeod, 2012). In Bangladesh there are no workers cooperatives where they could own theshares of the company and they deprived and exploited more by the employers. However Grameen Bank clients are the share holders of Grameen Bank meaning they own Grameen bank. They have 93% share with Grameen Bank (Grameen Bank Annual Report, 1996).

Cooperatives are organizations that are owned by the members who use their services or purchase their products (Lasby et al., 2010). They are working in different sectors in Canada like in housing, childcare centers, financial services (credit Unions and insurance) renewable energy, social services, arts, and culture, retail sales and in agricultural goods and services. There were 5,753 non-financial co-operatives, with 5.6 million members, 85,073 employees, $27.5 billion revenues and $ 17.5 billion assets (Canada Cooperative Secretariat, 2007). 12 million Canadians are associated with cooperatives; there are 1,140 credit unions with 3,400 service locations, 10.5 million members, 64,600 employees and 248.8 billion in assets. Financial co-operatives transact 12.7% of the Canadian financial GDP for the financial sector (Mook, Quarter & Ryan, 2010). The co-operatives have tremendous contribution to the well-being and economic growth of Quebec. Desjardins, a credit union in Canada is successful financial credit unions are working across Canada, which is absent in Bangladesh.

However, Comilla Cooperatives in Bangladesh were famous in the world in 1960s. Its model replicated rapidly in Bangladesh in 1970s and early 1980s by the government become mission drift. In Bangladesh, there are no private daycare centers, private sports centers, or private shelters. However, Grameen Shamogree, Arang, Karu Palli, Nari Prabatana Shops collect embroidery products, handmade toys, souvenirs from the rural poor women that create some employment in the rural poor. Many of these businesses (except Grameen Shamogree) are running under the shadow of BRAC and BRDB and Nari Pakka respectively, but they are earning money selling their products in a market place.

Co-op by definition is a socially beneficial activity. An example is the Self-Employed omen Organization's (SEWA), a trade union that helps self-employed Indian women pursue the goals of 'full employment': Work security, income security, food security, health care, child care and shelter. SEWA has now over 900,000 members throughout India. These women select their own leaders, and effectively run the organization for the benefit of the rank-and-file.

17.0. Grameen Social Businesses

Grameen social business has clear focus on eradicating extreme poverty combined with the condition of economic sustainability has created numerous models with incredible growth potential (Yunus, 2014). The framework of a social business is based on 7 principles.

Grameen Social Businesses have seven principles are as follows:

1. Business objective will be to overcome poverty, or one or more problems (such as education, health, technology access, and environment) which threaten people and society; not profit maximization.
2. Financial and economic sustainability.
3. Investors get back their investment amount only. No dividend is given beyond investment money.
4. When investment amount is paid back, company profit stays with the company for expansion and improvement.
5. Environmentally conscious.
6. Workforce gets market wage with better working conditions.
7. ...do it with joy.

The Yunus Center Social Business Design Lab (YCSBDL) is promoting and supporting grameen social businesses. It facilitated many workshops on Grameen type social businesses. Currently Nabin Uddug social business projects are operated and invested through Grameen sister organizations-Grameen Shakti Samajik Babsha, Grameen Trust, Gramen Telecom Trust, Grameen Shikka, Grameen Kallayan, Gramen Motsha Foundation and Gramee Krishi Foundation. I have visited many Nabin Uddug social businesses in Bangladesh and I have received many feedbacks from the Nabin Uddugktta entrepreneurs, local young entrepreneurs and university/college students. The Nabin Uddug social business campaigns by Muhammed Yunus have revolutionized in Bangladesh.

Grameen social business targets business opportunities neglected by traditional profit maximizing companies in Bangladesh. The present economic system is not designed to have any moral responsibility. Discussion on moral responsibilities is an after-thought. According to M. Yunus (2014) moral issues were never included in the present economic system. He said that social business is a new kind of business which is based on selflessness, replacing selfishness, of human being.

Conventional business is personal-profit seeking business (Grameen Dialogue 93, 2014). The social business is a non-dividend company to solve human problems. Here owner can take back his investment money, but nothing beyond that. After getting the investment money back all profit is ploughed back into the business to make it better and bigger. It stands between charity and conventional business and carried out with the methodology of business, but delinked from personal profit-taking.

Grameen Bank is inspiring the second generation of Grameen Bank borrowers' families to believe that they are not job seekers, they are job givers. Poor can be a business person by using loans. According to M. Yunus, there are two types of business (1) Traditional business- profit making and dividend distribute to business owners/shareholders; (2) Social business – everything for the benefit of others and nothing is for the owners-except the pleasure of serving humanity. The second kind of business built on the selfless part of human nature.

The social business might be described as a 'non-loss, non-dividend company' dedicated entirely to achieving a social goal. According to Muhammad Yunus (2014) a social business is a selfless business whose purpose is to bring an end to a social problem. In this kind of business, the company makes a profit-but no one takes the profit.

18.0. Types of Grameen Social Businesses

Muhammad Yunus classified Grameen social business into two types. (1) One is a non-loss; Non-dividend Company devoted to solving a social problem and it is owned by investors who reinvest all profits in expanding and improving the business. The Grameen social businesses include Grameen Danone, Grameen Veolia Water, BASF, Grameen Telecom Trust and Grameen Intel has been of this type-1 social businesses. First Grameen Social Businesses is Grameen Danone, a joint venture yogurt company is created in Bangladesh that produces, markets and distributes its products much the same as any for-pro yogurt company. Yogurt container is biodegradable-no plastic is allowed. Grameen Veolia, another joint venture type-1 Grameen social business, water treats surface water for contaminants and then pipes it to where it is needed. The examples mentioned above fit into this category. Muhammad Yunus calls all these businesses as 'Type-1' social businesses.

The second kind is a profit-making company owned by poor people, either directly or through a trust that is dedicated to a predefined social cause. A social business owned by the poor benefits the poor by generating income for them directly. Yunus call it Type-11 social business. Grameen Bank, which is owned by the poor people who are depositors and customers, is an example of this kind of social business. The Otto Grameen textile factory owned by Otto Trust use the proceeds to benefit the people of the community where the factory is located. Unlike a non-profit organization, a social business has investors and owners. Moreover, in a Type- 1 social business, the investors and owners don't earn a profit, a dividend or any other form of financial benefit. The investors in a social business can take back their original investment amount over a period of time they define. Personal financial benefit has no place in social business. They serve as a touchstone that is at the heart of social business idea.

Muhammad Yunus (2013) uses the term 'Impact investing', means for an investment strategy whereby an investor proactively seeks to place capital in businesses that can generate financial returns as well as an intentional social and/or environmental goal. This concept of combined financial and other benefits is known as triple bottom line or blended value. Impact investing is differentiated from socially responsible investing in that an investor will proactively seek investments that generate both financial as well as specific social and/ or environmental returns. Grameen social business aims to create economic opportunities for the Children of Grameen Bank's members through the Nabin Udyokta (NU) program. Grameen Byabosa Bikash (GBB), Grameen Telecom Trust, Grammeen Kallyan etc. are key partners of implementing Grameen social businesses in Bangladesh. GBB established in 2001, provides technical assistance and training support along with monetary support to the new entrepreneurs in Bangladesh. GBB is working towards poverty eradication by creating new entrepreneurs there. GBB has started implementing social business such as nursery, fishing farm, duck farm, nursery, toy factory; bamboo mat works etc. in Bangladesh since 2001. Similarly, other Grameen sister pertners are working for poverty eradication, develop rural social businesses and income generation in the Bangladesh.

19.0. Corporate Social Responsibility (CSR)

The concept of Corporate Social Responsibility (CSR) was an earlier and still quite prevalent approach to generating societal benefits through business. CSR arose when companies began to notice that an increasing number of customers cared about more than just price and quality; they cared about a company's demonstrated commitment to social and environmental issues as well.

Companies became more involved in charitable activities and started reporting on their efforts to improve conditions for their employees and other stakeholders. The idea of sustainable business practices broadened this concept with a stronger focus on environmental impact and specific metrics, such as an organization's carbon footprint. However, the suspicion persisted that there were some companies who treated CSR and sustainability primarily as a marketing tool that was not well integrated with the operations of the company. This often resulted in accusations of *'green washing'* and impacts on society were questioned. At the same time, executives in many companies struggled to justify investments in CSR and sustainability when the link to increased profits was difficult to establish. Grameen bank and its sister organizations are not investing for CSR, but they distribute colt, clothing, rags wood beds to poor people in the winter every year. These organizations withholds their instalments collection during disasters periods even right off death clients' interest and provides some grants for desist funerals.

20.0. Community Interest Corporation (CIC)

One of the alternative legal structures now emerging is the community interest company (CIC) in UK. This is a new legal vehicle for business available since 2005; the British government refers to as 'social enterprise'. According to UK authorities, 'CIC' will be organizations pursuing social objectives, such as environmental improvement, community transport, fair trade etc. Social enterprises are playing an increasing role in empowering local communities and delivering new and innovative services at local level.

A CIC is a new type of company introduced by the Umited Kingdom Government in 2005 under the Commpanies (Audit, nvrstigations and Community Enterprise) Act 2004, designed for social enterprises that want to use their profits and assets for the public good. CICs are working for the benefit of the community. The CICs businesses surpluses are principally reinvested for that purpose in the business or in the community, rather than being driven by the need to maximise profit for shareholders and owners. CICs tackle a wide range of social and environmental issues and operate in all parts of the economy. By using business solutions to achieve public good, it is believed that social enterprises have a distinct and valuable role to play in helping create a strong, sustainable and socially inclusive economy. CICs are diverse. They include community enterprises, social firms, mutual organisations such as co-operatives, and large-scale organisations operating locally, regionally, nationally or internationally.

21.0. Legal Forms and Social objectives of CIC

CICs must be limited companies of one form or another. A CIC cannot be a charity, an Internal Private Service or an unincorporated organisation. A charity can convert to a CIC with the consent of the Charity Commission. In so doing it will lose its charitable status including tax advantages. A charity may own a CIC, in which case the CIC would be permitted to pass assets to the charity. CICs are more lightly regulated than charities but do not have the benefit of charitable status, even if their objects are entirely charitable in nature.

Those who may want to set up a CIC are expected to be philanthropic entrepreneurs who want to do well in a form other than charity. This may be because CICs are specifically identified with social enterprise. They are looking to work for community benefit with the relative freedom of the non-charitable company form to identify and adapt to circumstances, but with a clear assurance of not-for-profit distribution status. The definition of community interest that applies to CICs is wider than the public interest test for charity.

A Government regulator is responsible for examining each proposed CIC to make sure it passes what's called the Community Interest Test (CIT). This means satisfying the regular that the purposes of the CIC 'could be regarded by a reasonable person as being in the community or wider public interest.' The community interest test (CIT) that a CIC must pass is less strict than the rules a charity must meet in the UK. However, the CIC also does not enjoy the tax benefits that a charity gets. A CIC pays taxes on its revenues in much the same way as any ordinary business gets. A CIC pays taxes on its revenues in much the same way as any ordinary business. Also, the assets held or generated by the CIC, including any surplus of revenues over expenses, are subject to what is called an asset lock. This is a legal requirement that the assets of the CIC be used solely for community benefits. Like a profit-maximizing company, a CIC has one or more owners. A charity can own a CIC; so an individual, a group, or another company. However, a political party is not permitted to own a CIC in UK.

A CIC can solicit funds from investors and it can even issue shares of stock, just like a traditional corporation. In this respect, a CIC is similar to Yunus concept of a social business. Grameen Danone and Grameen Veolia Water, for example, are both owned jointly by the Grameen companies and their parent corporations-Danone and Velia Water, respectively. However, unlike a social business, a CIC may pay dividends to shareholders (this is the exception to the asset lock rule), through these dividends are limited by law. Currently, the maximum dividend per share is 5 percent above the Bank of England base lending rate, and the total dividend declared in any given year is limited to 35 percent of the company profits. The CIC is a restricted profit company, but it does not qualify to be the kind of social business that Yunus has been promoting. However, a CIC could become a social business; CIC owners and shareholders explicitly and clearly renounced the acceptance of dividends or any other form of profit distribution beyond the amount of investment. As of end of 2009, there were over 3000 CICs registered in the UK. Some have become quite successful and well-known; for example, Firely Solar, which uses sustainable technologies in producing events for organizations ranging from the Glastonbury Music Festival to Greenpeace etc. There is also considerable discuss about creating a similar legal structure in Canada. Paul Martin, ex-Prime Minister described the potential for good of businesses organized for social purposes. However, social business separate legal structure still is not in a charter.

22.0. Low-Profit Limited Liability Company (L3C)

L3C is another type of social enterprise concept developed in USA. The first law establishing the L3C structure was enacted by the state of Vermont in 2008. As of end of 2009, the concept had also been recognized by Michigan, Utah, Wyoming, and Illinois, and considered in North Carolina, Georgia Oregon, South Dakota, Tennessee, and Montana. The crow Indian Nation and Oglala Sioux Tribe also recognize the L3C structure. CIC has been enacted in eight other states—Illinois, Michigan, North Carolina, Maine, Utah, Wyoming, Louisiana, Rhode Island—and two Native American nations—the Crow and the Oglala Sioux since 2009 (Americans for Community Development 2011).

An L3C is a business entity formed to finance socially minded projects and organizations, and may include funds from non-profit or for-profit entities (Witkin 2009). Its purpose is to attract a range of investment sources for socially beneficial, limited-profit ventures, and thereby improve the viability of such ventures. As L3C structures are very new, there are no known examples of an L3C structure to support the financing of a renewable entergy (RE) project.

The L3C is a variant form of the limited liability Company (LLC), but specifically enables a divergent mix of corporations, individuals, non-profits, and government agencies to organize under one 'umbrella' for a charitable or socially beneficial purpose. Like all LLCs, the L3C is essentially a partnership with corporate protection. An L3C can include for-profit or non-profit entities, but has no definitive structure or required participation of any entity type. The L3C can also serve to attract the right foundation with a compatible mission to become a member and use this investment vehicle alternative.

The L3C is a for-profit venture that, under its state charter, must have a primary goal of furthering an exempt purpose. It fits within the definitions in the federal regulations for PRIs (Program Related Investments). Project investments made under an L3C can be used to lower the risk profile or reduce the cost of capital for a particular project. The model essentially turns the venture capital model on its head. L3Cs can develop social and economic purpose missions, making it easier for socially motivated investors to locate the branded L3C that satisfies their needs and investment objectives.

23.0. The L3C and Alternative Energy Funding

As per internal revenue service (IRS) regulations, foundations are required to spend 5% of their net assets on charitable giving every year (Lakamp et al 2010). The strategy, using primary rate interfaces (PRIs), allows private foundations to make equity investments in for-profit entities. The renewable energy projects rely heavily on various tax benefits to improve the cost of the associated power and induce investment. However, renewable energy projects and the developers utilize the tax benefits to their full value. Accordingly, a separate "tax equity investor" is sought to invest in the project. Because non-profits have no use for tax credits or depreciation, they cannot take direct advantage of the tax benefits. With the L3C structure in place, the tax benefits can be concentrated and absorbed by a tax equity investor that has the "tax appetite" from other businesses to utilize. The ideal project will be able to take advantage of both tax benefits and the low cost of capital provided by the foundation participation. The L3C allows the tax benefits to be fully utilized and thus lowering the cost of energy to the end user by accessing a wider base through foundations and non-profits (Ibid, 2010).

The L3C like the CIC is fundamentally a for-profit company that pursues a social business. Like other business, an L3C has one or more owners, which can include individuals, charities, or for-profit companies. And like a CIC, an L3C can pay dividends on any financial surplus it generates. However, there are no written guidelines limiting the size of profits and no public regulator is designed to pass judgement on whether a particular L3C is paying profits that are 'excessive'.

Like other limited liability companies, the L3C has a pass-through status in regard to U.S. federal income taxes. That is, the corporation itself pays no income tax. Instead, all items of income, expense, gain, and losses are 'passed through' to the members (owners) of the L3C in proportion to their ownership shares. However, the Internal Revenue Service (IRS) rules defining 'program-related investment' (PRIs) are complicated and difficult to follow (Yunus, 2013).

The legal and financial structure of the L3C makes it possible for an organization like a foundation to invest money in a business with social purposes and recover its initial investment. However, the difference between the L3C and the social business is the same as with the CIC-the creation of profits to benefit owners and the payment of dividends from those profits are part of the agenda of the L3C, while they are deliberately excluded from the concept of the social business.

L3Cs have been established for a wide array of economic sectors including (Capriccioso et al, 2010): Farming and agriculture, real estate/housing, socially responsible consulting, environmental services, education, healthcare, low-income assistance, construction services, journalism and publishing, financial and legal services and entertainment industry. The L3C structure allows the L3C Missouri Mission Center to provide a wide range of services and incentivize employees to reduce costs. The Mission Center L3C serves a wide range of non-profit and L3C customers. The services offered include accounting and human resources. The Mission Center started with a loan from wealthy supporters and is doing business while securing equity from foundations and individuals.

The 'L3C' is a legal form intended to bridge the gap between for-profit and non-profit functions..., [it] combines the financial advantages and governance flexibility of the traditional limited liability company with the social advantages of a non-profit entity. The primary focus of the L3C is not on earning revenue or capital appreciation, but on achieving socially beneficial goals and objectives, with profit as a secondary goal (Capriccioso et al, 2010, p. 33).

B Corporation

There is another new concept in structuring a social business is the so-called *B Corporation.*

In the United States, a benefit corporation or B-corporation is a type of for-profit corporate entity, legislated in 28 U.S. states, that includes positive impact on society and the environment in addition to profit as its legally defined goals. B corps differs from traditional corporations in purpose, accountability, and transparency, but not in taxation.

The purpose of a benefit corporation includes creating general public benefit, which is defined as a material positive impact on society and the environment. A benefit corporation's directors and officers operate the business with the same authority as in a traditional corporation but are required to consider the impact of their decisions not only on shareholders but also on society and the environment. In a traditional corporation shareholders judge the company's financial performance; however, with a B-corporation shareholders judge performance based on how a corporation's goals benefit society and the environment. However, shareholders determine whether the corporation has made a material positive impact. Transparency provisions require benefit corporations to publish annual benefit reports of their social and environmental performance using a comprehensive, credible, independent, and transparent third-party standard. In some states the corporation must also submit the reports to the Secretary of State, although the Secretary of State has no governance over the report's content. Shareholders have a private right of action, called a benefit enforcement proceeding, to enforce the company's mission when the business has failed to pursue or create general public benefit. Disputes about the material positive impact are decided by the courts.

There are around 12 third-party standards that meet the requirements of the legislation. Benefit corporations need not be certified or audited by the third-party standard. Instead, they use third-party standards similarly to how the Generally cepted accounting Principles (GAAP) are applied during financial reporting, solely as a rubric a company uses to measure its own performance. In April 2010, Maryland became the first U.S. state to pass benefit corporation legislation. As of October 2014, 28 states have passed legislation allowing for the creation of benefit corporations.

24.0. Differences of Social Business from Traditional Corporations

Historically, Bangladesh even United States corporate law has not been structured or tailored to address the situation of not-for-profit companies who wish to pursue a social or environmental mission. While corporations generally have the ability to pursue a broad range of activities, corporate decision-making is usually justified in terms of creating long-term shareholder value. A commitment to pursuing a goal other than profit as an end for itself may be viewed in many states as inconsistent with the traditional perspective that a corporation's purpose is to maximize profits for the benefit of its shareholders.

The idea that a corporation has its purpose to maximize financial gain for its shareholders was first articulated in Dodge vs. Ford Motor Company in 1919. Over time, through both law and custom, the concept of 'shareholder primacy' has come to be widely accepted. This point was recently reaffirmed by the case eBay Domestic Holdings, Inc. v. Newmark, Walton, Bangladesh, and Samsung Bangladesh. In US, the Delaware Chancery Court stated that a non-financial mission that 'seeks not to maximize the economic value of a for-profit Delaware corporation for the benefit of its stockholders' is inconsistent with directors' fiduciary duties.

In the ordinary course of business, decisions made by a corporation's directors are generally protected by the business judgment rule, under which courts are reluctant to second-guess operating decisions made by directors. In a takeover or change of control situation; however, courts give less deference to directors' decisions and require that directors obtain the highest price in order to maximize shareholder value in the transaction. Thus a corporation may be unable to maintain its focus on social and environmental factors in a change of control situation because of the pressure to maximize shareholder value. Of course, if a company does change ownership and the result is no longer in adherence to its initially described benefit goals, the sale could be challenged in court. However, social business mission and vision always remain for both economic and social well-being of the people.

Mission-driven businesses, impact investors, and social entrepreneurs are constrained by this (traditional business values) legal framework, which is not equipped to accommodate for-profit entities whose mission is central to their existence.

Even in states that have passed 'constituency' statutes, which permit directors and officers of ordinary corporations to consider non-financial interests when making decisions, legal uncertainties make it difficult for mission-driven businesses to know when they are allowed to consider additional interests. Without clear case law, directors may still fear civil claims if they stray from their fiduciary duties to the owners of the business to maximize profit.

By contrast, benefit corporations expand the fiduciary duty of directors to require them to consider non-financial stakeholders as well as the financial interests of shareholders (Lane, 2014). This gives directors and officers of mission-driven businesses the legal protection to pursue an additional mission and consider additional stakeholders besides profit (Lane, 2012, 2013). The enacting state's benefit corporation statutes are placed within existing state corporation codes so that it applies to benefit corporations in every respect except those explicit provisions unique to the benefit corporation form. Although there are many social business organizations like Grameen Bank, BRAC, ASA, POSHIA, PKSF, Nijera Kori, etc. are contributing to Bangladesh economy and public wellbeing; however, there is no Act for social business organizations in Bangladesh.

Similarly, in reality, 'B Corporation' carries no special legal status in USA, there is no law defining the B Corporation or specifying any special regulations that apply to it. The idea of the B Corporation was created by an organization called B- Lab, which was founded in June 2006 by a young social entrepreneur named Cohen Gilbert. However, the B Corporation has no real legal status. Gilbert and his associates at B lab are trying to carve out a place in the economic system for a company that dictates all or part of its profits to social causes. The idea is to formally acknowledge the company's responsibilities to society alongside its economic responsibility to make a profit for investors that benefit society while possibly diminishing profits. Moreover, B-Lab offers a rating system that allows companies to measure their own environmental and social performance by answering a series of survey questions. The results yield a point score, and only companies that achieve a 'passing' score (currently set at 80 out of a possible 200) are eligible to be designed as B Corporations (CSRWire USA, 2010). Unfortunately, California doesn't have laws explicitly addressing that.

Despite this uncertainty, some entrepreneurs have embraced the B corporation idea. As of the end of 2009, there were over two hundred B corporations formed in the United States. However, a B corporation is not the same as a social business because each B Corporation makes its own decisions about the role of profit. So a B corporation is free to pay dividends to shareholders and to claim a share of the company profits for themselves. It seems this weaken the power of the B corporation concept-perhaps fatally (Yunus, 2013).

The existence of the new, alternative forms of business structure -the CIC, the L3C and the B Corporation-reflects the same global situation that social enterprises/social economy organizations are trying to solve humanitarian problems. These new alternative have been devised indicates that many people around the world desire to solve these humanitarian social problems. However, a new regulatory structure essential that could be tailored to the needs of social business should be created-sooner the batter.

In response to the negative impacts of traditional corporations, a new type of corporation with a formalized purpose that includes generating positive impact for society in its core was needed. The corresponding legislation; however, takes time to develop and to be adopted. Independent of the legislative process, a new business certification system was introduced to recognize impact-driven companies: "B Corporations" ("B Corps"). In 2007, a non-profit organization called B Lab was founded to establish and manage the B Corporation certification system which has helped to build a constituency of businesses that is attracting lawmakers' attention. It is a new form of corporations is mobilizing companies toward a sustainable future. Under the banner of 'profitable sustainability' these pioneering companies are actually recovering the 'corporate charter' as a social invention which was originally conceived to bring together the power of private enterprise with the public good" (Karl Ostrom, PhD, Co-Executive Director of NBIS, 2016).

25.0. B Lab

B Lab is a non-profit organization with the mission of using the power of business to address the world's most pressing socio-economic challenges. In its goal of using business as a force for good, B Lab focuses on three initiatives: Building a community of Certified B Corporations so one can tell the difference between 'good companies' and just good marketing; accelerating the growth of the impact investing asset through use of B Lab's global impact investing rating system (GIIRS) Ratings & Analytics by institutional investors; and promoting legislation creating a new corporate form that meets higher standards of purpose, accountability and transparency.

B Lab certifies companies in a similar way that Fair Trade USA certifies Fair Trade Coffee or the U.S Green Building Council certifies leadership in energy and environmental design (LEED) buildings. In this role, B Lab established a standard for responsible and impact-driven business. In addition, B Lab attempts to solve the issue with existing corporate law where shareholder value maximization is the sole fiduciary responsibility of the corporation. Two independent Standards Advisory Councils oversee B Lab's certification standards, including the global impact investing rating system (GIIRS) for impact investors. B Lab is backed by a diverse set of funders, including the Rockefeller Foundation, USAID, and a variety of corporations, private foundations and individuals. There are currently about 20 employees across four different locations in the US. B Lab's website is www.bcorporation.net.

26.0. Grameen Social Business Initiatives

Muhammed Yunus considered Grameen as the seed of social business in Bangladesh that established in 1970s. Grameen bank and its other sister organizations are following the principles of social business for solving the problems of employment and income, hunger, malnutrition, healthcare, agriculture, housing, hygiene, education, environment, energy, communication, transportation etc. Grameen sister organizations are running as social businesses in Bangladesh (Yunus, 2014).

Grameen social business plays a very important role in solving the financial crisis, the food crisis, and the environment crisis. Furthermore, it can provide the most effective institutional mechanism for resolving poverty, homelessness, hunger and ill health (Grameen Dialogue 2014). Social business can address all the problems left behind by the profit-making businesses and at the same time it can reduce the excesses of the profit-making businesses. Muhammad Yunus (2013) asserts that social business must be an essential part of the growth formula because it benefits the mass of people who would otherwise be disengaged. And when people are energized, so is the well-being economy. Through access to credit, improved health services, better nutrition, high-quality education, and modern information technology, poor people will become more productive. They will earn more, send more, and save more- to the benefit of everyone, rich and poor alike.

27.0. Grameen Youth Entrepreneur Loan

Grameen Bank has introduced entrepreneurial loan for those who have got higher education loan, and who are enterprising, industrious, enthusiastic and hardworking. It was introduced in Grameen Bank in 2008. This is an opportunity created for the children of GB families who want to be self-employed for income earning. This is to encourage them to deviate from the conventional way of seeking job after completion of higher education but going for creating job for themselves as well as for others. Those who chose this path and took loans from Grameen Bank for business were called Nobin Udokta (NU) or New Entrepreneurs. However, currently B is slow to provide loans to micro-enterprise loans to new youth entrepreneurs. However, Yunus Center carry this concept and implement the concept through Grameen sister organizations in Bangladesh.

28.0. Nobin Udyokta (New Entrepreneur)

For educated second generation of GB borrowers and for other young people, GB sister organizations have started campaigning to redirect their mind from traditional path to hunting for jobs to creating jobs for themselves and others, through entrepreneurship. GB called those who chose that path and took loans from Grameen Bank or Grameen sister organizations as Nobin Udokta (NU) or 'New Entrepreneurs'. It is targeted to the youth in Bangladesh who wants to use their creative power to become entrepreneur not only to generate their own employment but also to create employment opportunities for others. The social business idea started getting root in Bangladesh by Yunus Center.

By Mid October 2014, 380 NU projects have already been approved by the participating organizations for equity investment of TK. 8, 45, 57000 (US$1, 09 million). Among the NUs about 7% are female and 93% are male entrepreneurs. Their age varies from 18-35 years with most of them coming from 20-30 years of age (Latifee, 2014, Grameen Dialogue 93, pp. 6). By December 2016, number of NUs business project presentation increased to 14,000. This program is very popular among young entrepreneurs in Bangladesh. The NUs are engaged in different kinds of business activities including telecom, IT, repairing and recycling electronic products, manufacturing engineering, handicrafts, Livestock, Live Stock feed production, drug store, fish and agro-farming, trading, nursery, whole sale and retail business. Their (NUs) business insight, continuous thinking, information gathering, networking, skill development, keeping commitments and risk taking attitude are all important for them to become successful entrepreneurs. There are funds available for social business from Yunus Social Business Fund (YSBF) in Haiti, Colombia, Albania, Tunisia, Uganda, India, Mexico, Brazil and Grameen Credit Agrocole Social Business Fund in France.

29.0. Grameen Social Business Design Lab (GSBDL)

Grameen Social Business Design Lab is a daylong program organized by the Yunus Centre Bangladesh for the people who are interested in social business since 2013. This design lab is structured in a way to train, brainstorm, and involve its participants in social business as well as develop new ideas. People from different backgrounds join in this program to learn about Social Business and brainstorm on potential social business ideas. Prospective participants of Design Lab are business persons, social business practitioners, potential investors/ entrepreneurs/donor communities, academics, innovators, social workers, NGO personnel, philanthropist, young entrepreneurs and others (Grameen Dialogue, 89, pp. 7). Project proposals including the business plan are presented in GSBDL for consideration. Grameen Social Business Design Lab has developed well designed forms and formats for preparing and presenting NUs' business project proposals and guidelines on how to do it for NUs.

Muhammad Yunus mobilizes Grameen sister organizations to be involved in implementing Nobin Udoktas Loans. Grameen Social Business Design Lab is a platform for Nabin Udyokta and Grameen sister organizations could bring the entrepreneurs to present their social business designs in front of a group of experienced business executives and social activists, to seek their advice. This platform encourage people to two things: it encourages people to come up with social business ideas, and develop this platform as a sounding panel for getting the concept of social business more business-ready through its application in concrete situation. Yunus Centre organized the first

Design Lab in January, 2013. Now Grameen Design Lab conduct workshop in every month. Nobin Udyoktas present their business plans at the Grameen Design Lab Workshop with the help of Grameen sister organizations who are the social business angel investors. Nobin Udyoktas receive loans from Grameen sister organizations after approval the loan in the Grameen Design Lab workshop.

Now implementation structure of Grameen social business lab has built, the speed of expansion spread quickly across Bangladesh. For example, by the end of May, 2017, 16000 NUs presented their business plans in the design labs and 512 loans were disbursed. Many internees from across the world, social business academicians, researchers, executives, philanthropies are attending the Design lab workshops. The author attended many Grameen Design Lab workshops in 2014-2015 and in 2017, and he has learned about the practical process of the preparing Nabin Udyoktas loan proposals, business proposals, review of the business proposals, and approval of the business proposals and loan disbursements. In the business proposal, NUs need to address the following social objective questions:

- What is my social objective e: Whom do I expect to help with my social business?
- What social benefits do I intend to provide?
- How will the intended beneficiaries of my business participate in planning and shaping the business?
- How will the impact of my social business be measured?
- What social goals do hope to achieve in my six months? In my first year? In my first three years?
- If my social business is successful, how can it be replicated or expanded?
- Are there additional social benefits that can be added to the package of offerings I will create?

30.0. From Grammen Micro-credit to Grameen Equity Funding

Grameen sister organization investors provided equity investment with the Nabin Udokta individually. Nabin Udokta receives percentage of business investment equity from Grameen with 5 percent business transfer fee through the years of the agreed agreement. Grameen communication monitors the business and collects the investment equity instalment. Grameen Investors do not take any profit from their investment, except for getting their investment money back. The NU is responsible for paying back whatever money they received as equity within an agreed period. Grameen offers an exciting opportunity for any entrepreneur in Bangladesh. The entrepreneur may have some or no capital in his business. He can be the managing partner or a paid manager of the business he owned.

Grameen Social Business concept uses some terminologies that are different from Grameen classical loan program.

GB uses Terms	GB Social Business uses Terms
Loans, borrowers,	Investment, /business innovator/ entrepreneur/job provider, owner of the business/manager of the business
Loan, loan interest	Equity, Investment fee, transfer ownership fee,
Loan provider	Investor, equity provider (1005, or 40%-60% equity provider/sharer
Borrowers no age limit	Age limit < 14 - 35 age,
GB loan size <$500-$1000	Entrepreneur needs any amount of % of money as share for his business
Fully repaid the loan	Transfer ownership of the business
20% interest fee per year with diminishing method	20% fixed investment fee for the whole period of investment

Target group poor women and group based	Second generation of GB borrowers, unemployed young entrepreneurs and individual investment
Self employment	Slogan is 'Not job seekers, Job providers

Grameen investors shall be monitoring the performance of the managers/managing partners, but Grameen investors shall not get involved in the actual running of the business. As the business makes profit, the Grameen investors receive their dividend. When Grammen investors have received enough dividends to equal to the amount of equity Grammen investors have invested, Grameen investors stop taking further dividend. It is time for investors to move to on to the next investment with the money they got back. But grameen investors' objectives shall not be achieved until Grameen establishes the entrepreneurs as the owner, because their intentions were to transform a job-seeker into a job-giver (Yunus, 2013).

Grameen social business items in Bangladesh are setup dental clinic, nursing center, community information center, compost/worm production, door mate produce from garment wastage, fruits plant nursery, setup KG school and community school, community adult learning center, irrigation project, fish culture, poultry and dairy farming, mini garments industries, fashion design and tailoring, bee keeping culture, installing solar home system, biogas plant, buying rice husking machine, IT center, computer training center, manufacturing paper products from recycling papers, pottery business, hide and leather business, old clothing business, winter clothing business, electronics business, repairing shoes, electronic products TV, Cell Phone, Radio, Computer, IPod, repairing auto mobile engines, house repairing, manufacturing bamboo products, toys, makings mosquito nets, oil processing plant, cottage industries, handmade bags, manufacturing pads, carom board, poultry feed, Ayubade medicine, milk processing plant, cult making, rings making, restaurant, etc.

According to social business guidelines, investor can sell his shares at the market value, but he has to reinvest the additional money he receives beyond the face value, into another social business, or in the same social business. Investor can not enjoy additional value created by his investment (Yunus, 2013). In the NU programme, Grameen made an easy rule. In selling the shares of a NU business, the investor will take an amount equivalent to the original fixed sum of 5% over it. Grameen call this additional amount "share transfer fee". Fixed amount of 5% is only a small fee for covering all these services over a period of several years.

By September, 2013, Yunus Center developed basic methodology, reporting formats, identification and assessment procedures, etc. Grameen sister organizations brought the NU projects to the Design Lab for getting critical assessment from a group of experienced professionals. Now more Grameen companies (Grameen Telecom Trust, Grameen Bybosha Bikash, Grameen Shakti, and Grameen Kalayan) have initiated their own NU programs. Common facilities, like computerized MIS, and accounting software, common training facilities, are being developed by Yunus Center. Innovations are added by each Grameen company to make the programme more effective. A rigorous implementation structure is emerging to make sure NUs get thorough orientation, training in business management, accounting, reporting and have access to support services.

31.0. Grameen Screening Process of Selecting NUs in Bangladesh

Grameen sister organizations have field staff to work with the Nabin Udyoktas (new entrepreneurs), is responsible for identification, screenings of the potential entrepreneurs to help them develop their business plans, and prepare the NUs to make presentation of their plans to the participants of the Grameen Design Lab. The whole process starts with the home visit of the potential entrepreneur and getting to know him and his family in all details, captures his dreams and fears, and tries to build confidence in him.

Social Entrepreneurship formal discussion in small groups of 4 or 5 takes place to let them get to know each other. Once a sizable number (say 30-50) of young men or women have been contacted the village staff will organize an orientation and identification camp in a village (Yunus, 2014). Experienced field officials and leaders will attend the workshop to carry out the identification and confidence building process. Participants learn the rules and procedures of NU programme, ask questions to get a clear picture of the programme. They assess each other's business proposals and strength of their business will. At the end of an intensive 'get-to know-your-entrepreneur exercise', field officials make a short list of the participants who have impressed them as entrepreneurs likely.

Entrepreneurs selected are invited to Dhaka where they'll give final shape to their business proposals and give them a professional appearance with the help of trained staff of the investors. Project summaries are prepared in English for a five minute presentations at the Grameen Design Lab Dhaka where the entrepreneurs have to defend their business projects. Participants give some good advice and flag some issues to help better implementation. In rare cases an entrepreneur is asked to modify his proposal to make further improvement and present it to the next Lab. Once the project is approved, handholding process for implementation begins. Investor and the entrepreneur now go through a process of bonding together for a successful journey ahead. All regulatory issues are threshed out, necessary documentation is completed. Once monitoring and accounting training are completed, disbursement day (D-day) funds are released and business starts running. Grameen Communication, a Grameen software company, has developed an accounting and a monitoring software (advised by M. Yunus) to collect MIS and accounting information from each NU business on a daily, weekly and monthly basis. Daily figures are sent by the NUs via text messages to Grameen Communication. All information accumulates at the central server, which produces reports for each investor on daily, weekly, monthly basis or for any other period as the investor would like to have.

32.0. Urgently need Legal Structures of Social Business

Legal and regulatory systems do not currently provide a place for social business. Profit-maximizing companies and traditional non-profit organizations (foundations, charities, and NGOs) are recognized institutions covered by specific rules regarding organizational structure, governance and decision making principles, tax treatment, information disclosure and transparency, and so on. However, social business is not yet a recognized separate business organization category. This needs to change. The sooner there is a defined legal and regulatory structure for social business-preferably one with consistent rules in countries around the world-the easier it will be for entrepreneurs and corporations to create a multitude of social businesses to tackle the human problems that are plaguing society. Yunus thinks (2013) the best option today is to organize one's social business under the traditional structure of a for-profit business. The for-profit legal framework/structure was used for all of Grameen's social business. The legal system gives the for-profit company great freedom and flexibility to experiment with its business model. Thus, a social business organized as a for-profit company must be just as financially efficient as any other for-profit company, since it doesn't benefit from any tax breaks.

In the future, governments can and should create a separate law for social business, defining it adequately for regulatory purposes, and indicating the responsibilities and obligations of the stakeholders. The law should lay down the rules and procedures that a social business must follow in order to switch to a profit-maximizing company. At the same time, Lawyers should amend the existing company law to include the rules and procedures under which a profit-maximizing company can switch to a social business company. Under US law, foundations can invest in for-profit companies only if the investment qualifies as a 'program-related investment' (PRI). Unfortunately, the rules defining PRIs are complicated, and violating them can lead to serious tax problems for the foundation. As a result many foundations shy away from such investments (Rouf, 2012).

There are serious limitations to using the non-profit structure for social business. Perhaps the most significant is the strict legal and regulatory scrutiny that non-profits often experience. Robert A. Wexler (2009 in Yunus 2013), an American attorney in his article 'Effective Social-Enterprise-A menu of Legal Structures' comments about the difficulty of winning tax-exempt, non-profit status for such organizations in the United States. However, Yunus definition of social business, there's no good fit with the non-profit structure. The most important reason for not using the non-profit legal structure for creating a social business is that a non-profit organization is not owned by anyone; so it can't issue shares. Owever, a social business has one or more owners who can issue shares, and can buy and sell shares, just like any for-profit company.

For all these reasons, the concept of social business that Yunus has in mind does not match into a not-for-profit legal format at all. The non-profit linked to a for-profit company. It's not unusual for non-profit organizations to create for-profit subsidiaries that sell goods and services, and thereby produce income that goes to support the works of the non-profit organization. A charity hospital that owns and operates a shopping mall might be an example of this kind of relationship.

However, it's important to create social business funds to provide credit and equity to social business.

Yunus (2013) alerts people that social business might be misused and perverted. A few powerful people will look for ways to distort the concept and twist it for their own benefit-just as some misguided people have applied the term 'microcredit' to describe companies that are really just loan sharks in disguise. Therefore, well-intentioned people need to be guard against those who would abuse the good name of social business.

Rouf, K. A. (2012) and Yunus, M. (2013) suggest that social business could be set up in such a way as to encourage entrepreneurship. The social business investors could create a center in which entrepreneurs are brought together with other people who have the knowledge, skills, experience, or technology needed to start successful social business. Investors could set up an investment fund, a training program, or a marketing agency. The agency (investing organization) could create a mentorship program for aspiring entrepreneurs or sponsor contest to select and promote the best new business concepts. Like Grameen Social Business Design Lab, Canada could open-up and encourage dialogue and collaboration among social economy organizations, but they have to adopt flexible governance (Amin & Hausner, 1997). However, I think all over the world, governments need new mechanisms to seed and grow social innovations that has agreed by Mendell & Neamtan, (2010).

33.0. References

Amin, A., & Hausner, J. 1997). *Beyond market and hierarchy: Interactive governance and social complexity.* Cheltenhham: Edward Elgar

Austin, J., Stevenson, H., & Wei-Skillern, J. (2006). Social and commercial entrepreneurship: Same, different, or both? *Entrepreneurship Theory and Practice*, Vol. 30(1), pp. 1-22

Belal, A. R. (2008). *Corporate Social Responsibility Reporting in Developing Countries-A case of Bangladesh.* England: Ashgate Publishing limited

Bornstein, D. (2004). *How to change the world: Social entrepreneurs and the power of new ideas.* Oxford, UK: Oxford University Press

Bornstein, David and Davis, Susan (2010). *Social Entrepreneurship: What everyone needs to know*: New York, Oxford University Press

Boschee, J. (1995) Social Entrepreneurship. *Across the Board*, Vol. 32(3), pp. 20-23

Bouchard, M.J., Ferraton, C., and Michaud, V. (2006). *Database on Social Economy Organizations: The Qualification Criteria*. Chaire de recherche du Canada en économie sociale, collection recherche no R-2006-3, Université of Montréal

Chantier (Leo de I'economic sociale. (2005). *Social economy and community economic development in Canada: Next steps for public policy*. Montreal: Author

Cooperative Secretariat. (2007). *Cooperatives in Canada (2004)*

Capriccioso (2010). *Who is the L3C Entrepreneur? The Pioneers of Social Enterprise's Revolutionary New Suffix, inter Sector Partners*, L3C, May 2010

Cnaan, Ram, Femida Handy & Margaret Wadsworth (1996). Defining who is a volunteer: Conceptual and empirical considerations. *Nonprofit and Voluntary Sector Quarter* 25 (3), pp. 364-383

Cone, C. L., Feldman, M. A. and DaSilva, A. T. (2003b) Causes and Effects, *Harvard Business Review*, Vol. 81(7), pp. 95-103

CSRWire USA (2010). *Maryland First State in Union to Pass Benefit Corporation Legislation*. CSRWire USA

D'Amours, M. (2007). *L' e'conomic sociale au Que'bec: Cadre the'orique, histoire, re'aliti'es et defis*. Anjou: Editions Saint Martin

Dart, R. (2004). Being Business-Like in a Nonprofit Organization: A Grounded and Inductive Typology. *Nonprofit and Voluntary Sector Quarterly*, Vol. 33 (2), pp. 290-310

Davis, T. (1997). *The NGO Business Hybrid: Is the Private Sector the Answer?* Baltimore, MD: Johns Hopkins University

Dees, J. G. (2001). *The meaning of social entrepreneurship revisited*. Working Paper

Stanford: Stanford University Graduate School of Business. Available at: http://www.fuqua.duke.edu/centers/case/documents/dees_SE.pdf

Dees, J. G. (2003). *Social entrepreneurship is about innovation and impact, not income*. Skoll Foundation. Available at: http://www.fuqua.duke.edu/centers/case/articles/1004/corner.htm

Dees, J. G. (1998). *The Meaning of "Social Entrepreneurship.* Stanford University: Draft Report for the Kauffman Center for Entrepreneurial Leadership

Dees, J. G., Emerson, J. and Economy, P., Eds. (2002). *Strategic Tools for Social Entrepreneurs: Enhancing the Performance of Your Enterprising Non-profit.* New York: John Wiley & Sons, Inc.

Elson, Peter, Andres Gouldsborough & Robert Jones (2009). *Building Capital, Building Community: A Comparative Analysis of Access to Capital for Social Enterprises and Nonprofits in Ontario and Quebec.* Toronto: Social Economy Centre

Favreau, L. (2006). Social Economy and Public Policy: The Quebec Experience. *Horizons Vol.* 8(2): pp. 7-15

Fowler, A. (2000) NGOs as a moment in history: beyond aid to social entrepreneurship or civic innovation? *Third World Quarterly*, Vol. 21(4), pp. 37-654

Gartner, W. B. (1988). Who is an entrepreneur? Is the wrong question. *American Journal of Small Business*, Vol. 12(4), pp. 11-32

Grameen Communications (1998, 1 January 2004). *Grameen: Banking for the Poor.* Retrieved 19 January, 2004, from http://www.grameen-info.org/

Grameen Dialogue (2014). *Grameen Dialogue -93.* Dhaka: Grameeen Trust. October 2014

Grameen Dialogue (2014). *Grameen Dialogue -91-92.* Dhaka: Grameeen Trust. July 2014

Grameen Dialogue (2014). *Grameen Dialogue -90.* Dhaka: Grameeen Trust. January 2014

Grameen Dialogue (2014). *Grameen Dialogue -89.* Dhaka: Grameeen Trust. October 2013

Halseth, G., and Ryser, L. (2006). *Innovative Services and Voluntary Organizations.* Prince George: University of Northern British Columbia

Hall, John. (1998). Genealogies of Civility. In Hefner (Ed.), *Democratic civility.* (pp. 53-78). New Brunswick, NJ: Transaction

Hall, Michael et al. (2005). *The Canadian Nonprofit Sector and Voluntary Sector in Comparative Perspective.* Toronto; Imagine Canada

Herbst, K. (2003). Business-social ventures: Reaching for major impact. *Ashoka Journal.*

Hebb, T., Wortsman, A., Mendell, M., Neamtam, N., and Rouzier, R. (2006). *Financing Social Economy Enterprises.* Ottawa: Carleton University

Hines, Ruth (1988). Financial accounting: In communicating reality, we construct reality. *Accounting, Organizations and Society* Vol. 13 (3), pp. 251-261

Human Resource and Skills Development Canada (HRSDC). (2005). *What is the social economy?*

Ilana DeBare (2008). *B Corporation Plan Helps Philanthropic Firms.* San Francisco Chronicle.

Johnson, S. (2000). *Literature Review on Social Entrepreneurship: Canadian Centre for Social Entrepreneurship*, p. 16

Lane, Marc (2014b). *Social Enterprises: A New Business Form Driving Social Change.* The Young Lawyer. Retrieved 18 November 2014

Lane, Marc (2014a). *Emerging Legal Forms Allow Social Entrepreneurs to Blend Mission And Profit".* Triple Pundit

Lane, Marc (2012). *Representing Corporate Officers and Directors.* Aspen Publishers: Wolters Kluwer Law & Business. Retrieved 8 August 2012

Lang, Marc (2011). *Phone conversations with Robert Lang*, January-August 2011

Lasby, D.M., Halll, M.H., & Ventry, R.M et al. (2010). A Portrait of the Ontario Social Economy. In (eds.) *Researching the Social Economy.* Toronto: University of Toronto Press Incorporated

Leadbetter, C. (1997). *The Rise of the Social Entrepreneur.* London: Demos

MacLeod, G. (1997). *From Mondragon to America : Experiments in community economic* Pateman, C. (1970). *Participation and democratic theory.* Cambridge [Eng.]: University Press. *development.* Sydney, N.S.: University College of Cape Breton Press

McFarlan, F. Warren (1999). Working on Nonprofit Boards: Don't Assume the Shoe Fits, *Harvard Business Review, Vol.* 77(6), November-December, pp. 2-11

Mook, Laurie & Jennifer Sumner (2010). Social accounting for sustainability in the social economy. In J.J. McMurtry (Ed.), *Living Economics.* Toronto: Edmond Montgomery

Mook, Quarter and Ryan (2010). What's in a Name in (eds.) Laurie Mook, Jack Quarter and Sherida Ryan (2010). *Researching the Social Economy.* Toronto: University of Toronto Press Incorporated

McMartin, A. (2007). *Cooperatives in Canada (2004 data).* Ottawa: Co-operatives Secretary.

Mendall, M. & Neamtan, N. (2010). The Social economy in Quebec: Towards a New Political Economy. Social economy organizations are more in Quebec in Canada and are operating for long time. *Anseraj*, Vol. 1(1), pp. 8-22

Mintzberg, H. (1991). The Effective Organisation: Forces and Forms. *Sloan Management Journal*, Vol. 32(2), pp. 54-67

Mort, G. S., Weerawardena, J. and Carnegie, K. (2003). Social entrepreneurship: Towards conceptualisation. *International Journal of Non-profit and Voluntary Sector Marketing,* Vol. 8(1), pp. 76-89

Nelson, G., Janzen, R., Trainor, J., & Ochocka, J. (2008). Putting Values into Practice: Public Policy and the Future of Mental Health Consumer-run Organizations. *American Journal of Community Psychology,* Vol. 42, pp. 192–201

Network for Business Innovations and Sustainability (NBIS, 2012). *B Corporations, Benefit Corporations and Social Purpose Corporations: Launching a New Era of Impact-Driven Companies.* A white paper presented by NBIS. (www.NBIS.org)

Newman's Own (2005). *The Common Good.* Retrieved 4 June 2005, from http://www.newmansown.com/5_good.html

Owen, D. L., Swift, T. A., Humphrey, C. and Bowerman, M. (2000). The new social audits: accountability, managerial capture or the agenda of social champions? *European Accounting Review,* Vol. 9 (1), pp. 81-90

Pally Karma Shauhauk Foundation (2015). *Annual Report 2015.* Retrieved from http://pksf-bd.org/portal/web/wp-content/

uploads/2016/03/Annual%20Report%202015.pdf dated September 30, 2017

Peredo, A.M., and MacLean, M. (2006). Social Entrepreneurship: A Critical Review of the Concept. *Journal of World Business Vol.* 41, pp. 56–65

Peredo, A. M. & McLean, M. (2006). Social entrepreneurship: A critical review of the concept. *Journal of World Business* Vol. 41, pp. 56–65, retrieved from www.socscinet.com/bam/jwb Dated January 09, 2011

Peredo, A. and McLean M. (2005). Social entrepreneurship: A critical review of the Americans for Community Development, *What is the L3C?* available at http:// www.americansforcommunity development.org/downloads/What%20is%20the%20 L3C%20 080711-1.pdf

Peredo, A.M., and Chrisman, J. (2006). Toward a Theory of Community-Based Enterprise. *Academy of Management Review,* Vol. 31 (2), pp. 309-28

Pomerantz, M. (2003). The business of social entrepreneurship in a "down economy". In *Business,* Vol. 25(3), pp. 25-30

Polany, K. (1957). The economy as instituted process. In K. Polany, C. Arensberg, and H. Pearson (Eds.), *Trade and Market in the Early Empires,* pp. 243-70. New York: Free Press.

Prashad, S. (2007). *Good green goals.* Toronto Star A12

Putnam, R. (1996). *The Decline of Civil Society: How Come? So What?* Ottawa: John L. Manion Lecture

Quarter, J. (2000). Beyond the Bottom Line: Socially Innovative Business Owners. Westport: *Greenwood/Quorum,* pp. 1-13; 15-31

Jack, Q. Mook, L. & Armastrong, A. (2009). *Understanding the Social Economy-A Canadian Perspective.* Toronto: University of Toronto Press

Quarter, J., Mook, L., & Hann, J. (2011), forthcoming). Non-financial Co-operatives in Canada: 1955 to 2005. In L. Mook, J. Quarter, & S. Ryan (Eds.), *Businesses with a difference: Balancing the social and economic.* Under review, pp. 1-15

Reis, T. (1999). *Unleashing the New Resources and Entrepreneurship for the Common Good: a Scan, Synthesis and Scenario for Action.* Battle Creek, MI: W. K. Kellogg Foundation, p.27.

Rothschild, J. & Russell, R. (1986). *Alternatives to bureaucracy: Democratic participation in the economy,* pp. 307-328

Rouf, K. A. (2013). Incorporation Act Issues for Revenue Generating Green Social Enterprises and NGOs Transforming into Green Social Enterprise Microfinance Institutions (MFIs) in Ontario, Canada. *Journal of Business Administration and Education, Infinity Press.* Vol. 2(1), pp. 1-20

Salamon, L. (1999). *Partners in Public Service: Government –Nonprofit Relations in the Modern Welfare State.* Baltimore: John Hopkins University Press

Salamon, L., and Anheier, H. K. (1997). *Defining the Nonprofit Sector: A Cross National Analysis.* Manchester: Manchester University Press

Schugurrensky, D. & McCollum, E. (2010). Notes in the Margins: The Social Economy in Economics and Business Textbooks. in (eds) Laurie Mook, Jack Quarter and Sherida Ryan (2010). *Researching the Social Economy.* Toronto: University of Toronto Press Incorporated

Shrage, E., & Fontan, J. M. (2000). Introduction. In E. Shrage & J. M. Fontan (Eds.*). Social Economy: International Debates and perspectives* (pp 1-21). Montreal: Black Rose

Scott, K. (2003). Funding Matters: The Impact of Canada's New Funding Regime on Nonprofit and Voluntary Organizations. Ottawa: Canadian Council on Social Development

Spear, R. (2006). Social Entrepreneurship: A Different Model? *International Journal of Social Economics,* Vol. 33 (5/6), pp. 399-410

Social Enterprise Council of Canada (2015). *Definition of social enterprise.* Retrieved from http://www.socialenterprisecanada.ca/learn/nav/whatisasocialenterprise.html#sthash.ULBeqi01.dpuf dated April 12, 2015

Social Enterprise Typology (2015). *Virtue Ventures,* retrieved from – www.virtueventures.com dated April 15, 2015

Stephens, A. (2003). *Ice Cream with a Mission.* New Statesman, pp. 132:17-18

Stevenson, H. H. andJarillo, C. J. (1990) A Paradigm ofEntrepreneurship: Entrepreneurial Management. *Strategic Management Journal*, Vol. 11(Special Summer Issue), pp.17-28.

Stevenson, H. H., Roberts, M. J. and Grousbeck, H. I. (1989). *New business ventures and the entrepreneur.* Homewood, IL: Irwin

Stevenson, H. H., Roberts, M. J. and Grousbeck, H. I. (1989). *New business ventures and the entrepreneur.* Homewood, IL: Irwin

Stewart, A. (1989). *Team entrepreneurship.* Newbury Park: Sage Publications

Students for Informed Career Decisions. (2000, 21 July 2000). *Ben and Jerry's.* Retrieved 3 February, 2004, from http://www.stanford.edu/group/SICD/BenJerry/be njerry.html

Taylor, N., Hobbs, R., Nilsson, F., et. al. (2000). *The Rise of the Term Social Entrepreneurship in Print Publications.* Frontiers of Entrepreneurship Research

The Northland Institute. (2001). *What is Social Enterprise.* Retrieved 19 January, 2004, from http://northlandinst.org/SocialEnt.cfm

The Social Enterprise Program News. (2003). *Mission Branding: Hirschberg on Using Business to Change the World.* Retrieved 3 March, 2004, retrived from http://www 1.gsb.columbia.edu/social enterprise/news/031112_hirshberg.html dated September 28, 2017

Wexler, Robert, A. (2009). Effective Social Enterprise-A menu of Legal Structures,' Exempt *Organization Tax Review*, Vol. 63(6), pp. 565-576

Witkin (2009). *The L3C: A More Creative Capitalism*, San Francisco: Triple Pundit,

Yunus. M. (2013). *Building Social Business.* Dhaka: The University Press Limited.

Yunus, Muhammad (2003). *Commonwealth Lecture*, retrieved frpom http://www.grameen-info.org/index.php?option=com_content&task=view&id=220&Itemid=172 dated September 28, 2017

Yunus, Muhammad (2013). Social Business Entrepreneurs are the Solution. http://www.grameen-info.org/index.php?option=com_content&task=view&id=217&Itemid=172&limit=1&limitstart=0.

Index

C

H

T

U

V

W

Y

Printed in the United States
By Bookmasters